BEHIND
THE LODGE DOOR

BEHIND
THE LODGE DOOR

CHURCH, STATE AND FREEMASONRY
IN AMERICA

by
Paul A. Fisher

TAN BOOKS AND PUBLISHERS, INC.
Rockford, Illinois 61105

Reprinted by TAN Books and Publishers, Inc. in September, 1991.

Originally published in March, 1988, hardbound, by Shield Publishing Co., Bowie, MD. Second Shield edition, hardbound, October, 1989. Shield paperbound edition, December, 1989.

Library of Congress Catalog Card No.: 91-66415

ISBN: 0-89555-450-X

Printed and bound in the United States of America.

TAN BOOKS AND PUBLISHERS, INC.
P.O. Box 424
Rockford, Illinois 61105

1991

To Ruth and our children
Maureen Elizabeth
Kathleen Ruth
Sean Paul
Ann Regina
Margaret Veronica
Megan Marie
Matthew O'Mara
Patricia Siobhan
Terrence Jerome

CONTENTS

World War I • Communism And Freemasonry • The Craft And
Spanish Communism • Communist China And Masonry • Masonry,
Communism And The Catholic Church • Masonry's Political
Orientation Confirmed • Masonry Wins Again • Masonry In Japan

PART IV: TARGETING MEN FOR THE FRATERNITY

The Lure • Targeting The Candidates • The Binding Oaths
• Symbolism • Masonry And The Media • Masonry And
Politics • The Fraternity's Disguised Power • The Military And
Masonry

AMAZING DISCOVERY

AMAZING DISCOVERY

Prejudice by Supreme Court Justices is not a thought which comes readily to mind when thinking of the American system of justice.

Yet, for at least three decades (beginning in the 1940s) the opinions of a significant number of Justices were influenced by an anti-Christian and anti-Catholic philosophy when rulings were fashioned on the religion clause of the First Amendment to the U.S. Constitution.

Moreover, because of *stare decisis,*—the legal doctrine which holds that a principle of law established by one judicial decision is accepted as an authoritative precedent for resolving similar legal conflicts—the religion clause opinions rendered by the Court during that 30-year epoch have formed the basis for virtually all subsequent decisions on the clause since that time.

Although many people have been outraged by the Court's decisions regarding the place of religion under the Constitution, most citizens are convinced the American judicial system is eminently fair and just.

The latter view prevails largely because of a perception that Court nominees are carefully scrutinized to assure representation on the bench of a broad spectrum of the nation's varied groups. For example, it is generally thought that certain segments of the population have a non-defined "right" to a seat on the Court. When selections for a vacancy on the bench are under consideration, careful thought is given to a "Black seat," a "Jewish seat," a "Catholic seat," and a "woman's seat," not to mention choosing jurists who are sympathetic to labor, industry, and the medical and academic fraternities.

Strangely, however, mention is never made of two other groups in society which apparently have been successful in making silent claims to seats on the Court. Those two groups are Unitarians and Freemasons. Masons dominated the high bench from 1941 to 1971. That was an era when traditional Judeo-Christian values were removed from the curricula of public schools—and from public life generally.

That amazing (and rarely discussed) facet of American jurisprudence was discovered completely by accident when the author was conducting research on the religion clause of the First Amendment to the Constitution.

Court's Dramatic Reversal On Traditional Religion

The research focused on trying to find a rationale for the Court's dramatic reversal of the role of Judeo-Christian religious values in public life, beginning in the 1940s.

Careful study showed that the Court's *Everson* decision [1] was the keystone opinion upon which almost all subsequent religion clause cases have been based. However, close scrutiny of the clause and the history of its conception and adoption, failed to uncover convincing evidence to support the Court's view that the Constitution erected a "wall" which separates things religious from things civil in our society.

For example, neither Constitutional history nor legal precedent prior to *Everson* support the following words frequently quoted from the majority opinion in that decision: "The 'establishment of religion' clause of the First Amendment means at least this: . . . No tax in any amount, large or small, can be levied to support any religious activities or institutions, whatever they may be called, or whatever form they may adopt to teach or practice religion . . . In the words of Jefferson, the clause against establishment of religion by law was intended to erect 'a wall of separation between church and State' *Reynolds v. United States, supra* at 164." [2]

Following *Everson,* the Court repeatedly leaned on the "wall" to impose its will, and prohibited public financial assistance to children attending schools teaching traditional religious values.

As a consequence, the high bench: outlawed released time for children to attend religious classes within public school buildings [3]; declared atheism and secular humanism to be religions protected by the First Amendment [4]; prohibited recitation of prayer in public schools, even though the prayer in question was approved by leaders of the three major faiths in the United States [5]; and banned recitation of the "Our Father" and oral Bible reading as religious exercises in public schools [6].

Related cases denied State funds to religious-oriented schools for teaching aids, periodicals, maps, etc.; banned singing of Christmas carols in public schools; prohibited public school teachers from teaching in religious schools; and held that a law permitting employees to observe the Sabbath as a day of rest impermissibly advanced a particular religious practice, and thus violated the religion clause.

Those decisions by the Court seemed to demonstrate a bias in favor of a totally secularist society, and my research could uncover no convincing evidence that the First Amendment ever was intended to quarantine religion from public life, a proposition being advanced suddenly by the Court in the 1940s.

The Court's curious tilt stirred nagging questions:

Why did the high bench suddenly take up an interminable series of religion-clause-cases in the middle of the 20th Century?

Why did the high bench in these latter years seem to ignore the legislative history of the religion clause in the Constitutional Conventions, and when it was crafted by the First Congress and sent to the people for ratification?

Why was a figure of speech—"a wall of separation between church and State" enshrined as a rule of law?

Legal briefs submitted by attorneys in the various religion-clause-cases provided no answers; nor did the Court's numerous opinions on the subject illuminate the dilemma.

Bias On The Bench

And then, by accident, the obvious answer suddenly suggested itself in mid-summer, 1975: There was bias on the bench.

That insight into the puzzle was partially provided by a 1975 article in *The Washington Post*, titled, "The World of Felix Frankfurter," which basically consisted of excerpts from a book by Joseph P. Lash, based on diaries of the late Justice Felix Frankfurter.

The article quoted Frankfurter's colleague, Justice Louis D. Brandeis, commenting on Justice Hugo L. Black, author of the majority opinion in the seminal *Everson* decision. Brandeis said:

> "Black hasn't the faintest notion of what tolerance means, and while he talks a lot about democracy, he is totally devoid of its underlying demand which is tolerance of his own behavior. . . ."
> [7]

That excerpt prompted me to visit the Manuscript Division of the Library of Congress to read portions of Frankfurter's diaries and papers, as well as available papers of the other Justices who participated in the *Everson* decision.

A box of Frankfurter's papers, titled, "Photocopies of Missing Manuscripts," contained a record of a conversation between Frankfurter and Brandeis, dated July 1, (no year, although internal evidence suggests 1922), in which the latter is quoted as saying he "never realized until [he] came to the Supreme Court how much [judges] are diverted by passion and prejudice and how closed the mind can be. . . ." [8]

In a conversation with Chief Justice William Howard Taft, Brandeis said the "lines of cleavage on the Court" are not political differences between Democrats and Republicans, but "on progressiveness, so called—views as to property" [9]

Conversing with Frankfurter on July 2, 1924, Brandeis said there is a great deal of "lobbying" on the Court, and results are achieved "not by legal reasoning, but by finesse and subtlety." [10]

Further, memoranda in Frankfurter's files (and in the files of other Justices) make clear that the minority opinions in the *Everson* decision reflected strong disapproval of the opinions and tactics of Justice William O. Douglas and Black, particularly because Black's majority opinion (joined in by Douglas) conceded that the State of New Jersey, if it chose to do so, could pay transportation costs for children to attend Catholic elementary schools. The minority were adamantly opposed to such a concession to the free exercise of religion.

In an April 30, 1952 memo to Frankfurter following the *Zorach v. Clauson* decision (343 U.S. 306), Justice Robert H. Jackson stated that the "battle for separation of Church and School is lost."

He added: "The doctrine of separation never had a chance against pressure groups, except that this Court should unswervingly apply it as an absolute. . . .

"The wavering came," he went on, "in *Everson*. Black, in all good faith, believed that strong words about separation of Church and State would be acceptable to its enemies if it were seasoned with bus fare refunds. What he overlooked was that the enemies of separation were at once given an incentive to further aggression and the dialectics to support it . . ." [11]

In a March 9, 1948 diary entry, Frankfurter wrote that Justice Harold O. Burton "hasn't the remotest idea how malignant men like Black and Douglas not only can be, but are."

Noting that Black's majority opinion in *Everson* contained "noble sentiments," Frankfurter said Burton did not realize "it is characteristic of Black to utter noble sentiments and depart from them in practice—a tactic of which the *Everson* opinion is a beautiful illustration." [12]

Frankfurter also apparently felt it historically useful to retain in his files a letter, dated April 12, 1945, from a correspondent at the University of Texas Law School which thanked the Justice "for your refusal to attend" a dinner given in Black's honor.

The correspondent added: "The perfume of public praise from people who ought to know better cannot eliminate the odor of the skunk. Official utterances may fool the public, but there is still no substitute for character . . ."

The writer was referring to Black. [13]

Justice Frankfurter's Religious Biases

That initial peek into papers of Justice Frankfurter revealed that interpretation of the Constitution frequently is subject to the personal prejudices of the Justices more often than is suspected.

Furthermore, as I perused Justice Frankfurter's papers, it became evident that he, like most people, had his own personal biases. His opinions in a number of religion-clause-cases suggest that his personal views entered into the judicial opinions he rendered.

For example, he admitted to being "a reverent agnostic" who did not believe in "spiritual Messiahs," [14] and that he was "rather leery of explicit ethical instruction." [15]

To a colleague on the bench (Wiley B. Rutledge) he said he did "not yield acceptance" to two earlier Supreme Court decisions that long had been viewed—particularly by many parents—as the judicial bedrock upon which rested the Constitutional right of fathers, mothers and legal guardians to educate their children in schools compatible with their religious beliefs. Those cases are: *Pierce v. Society of Sisters* and *Meyer v. Nebraska.* [16]

In *Pierce,* the Court held: "The fundamental theory of liberty upon which this Union reposes excludes any general power of the State to standardize its children by forcing them to accept instruction from public teachers only . . ." [17]

In *Meyer,* the Court said that the legislature of Nebraska attempted to "interfere with . . . the power of the parents to control the education of their young." But, said the high bench, no legislature "could impose such restrictions upon the people of a State without doing great violence to both the letter and spirit of the Constitution." [18]

The position taken by Frankfurter with his colleague, Rutledge, differed dramatically from the view he held some years earlier when he was a professor at Harvard University.

His papers show that he wrote a letter to the editor of *The New York Times* in 1925 expressing support for that newspaper's editorial comment favoring the Court's *Pierce* decision. [19] The letter in the *Times* prompted John H. Cowles, Grand Commander of Scottish Rite Freemasonry of the Southern Jurisdiction, to write the Harvard professor a note expressing opposition to the future Supreme Court Justice's opinion regarding *Pierce*. [20]

Frankfurter replied to Cowles: "I share your devotion to the public school, and am eager as you are that no divisive influence, due to difference of race or religion, should assert themselves in the common bond that makes a nation.

"But," he continued, "I do not want devotions coerced . . . coerced convictions are not truly convictions and are the most doubtful of foundations upon which to build." [21]

Those remarks by Frankfurter strongly indicated that his position favoring a "wall of separation" between Church and State in the *Everson* case was influenced more by personal bias than by the spirit, intention and legislative history of the religion clause of the First Amendment.

But there was more about Justice Frankfurter that raised questions as to his judicial objectivity regarding the First Right of the Bill of Rights.

His papers show he was a close personal friend and admirer of many views held by Justice Oliver Wendell Holmes and Harold J. Laski, two men who seemed to share anti-Catholic views. In that regard, Frankfurter wrote a foreword to a book titled, *The Holmes-Laski Letters, The Correspondence Of Mr. Justice Holmes And Harold J. Laski, 1916-1935.* [22]

In the foreword, he extolled the correspondence book, and said the *Letters* "surpass all others from the pen . . . high themes canvassed with enormous learning . . . expressing convictions unmarred by intolerance . . ." [23]

Although Justice Frankfurter viewed the letters as "unmarred by intolerance," there are passages in the volume which can be considered anti-Catholic. For example, a flippant remark is made about the

Immaculate Conception of the Virgin Mary. [24] And Laski wrote that education which is not secular and compulsory "is not education." [25] The Catholic Church, the latter said, should be "confined to Limbo . . . [and], above all, Saint Augustine. . . ." [26]

In one letter to Holmes, the British Socialist commented that "no one can read Catholic books and still believe in God—the thing is too utterly puerile to fit a big world like this." [27]

Laski also wrote of the "incapacity of the Roman Church to tell the truth," [28] and declared that he had certain profound convictions, among which is the following: "It is impossible to make peace with the Roman Catholic Church. It is one of the permanent enemies of all that is decent in the human spirit." [29]

Granted, those are statements by Laski, not by Frankfurter. But, it was the jurist himself who asserted in a foreword to the book that the communications between Laski and Holmes were "unmarred by intolerance." Since the above passages clearly demonstrate an "intolerance" toward the Catholic Church, there is at least a suggestion that the jurist shared his friend's viewpoint toward those aspects of Catholicism mentioned in the *Letters*.

The same can be said for Frankfurter's silence regarding the views set forth by Holmes in a letter to Laski concerning a book intended for use by Catholic schoolchildren which depicted Hell.

"It led me to wonder," wrote Holmes, "whether the world would not be better off if we never had invented the notion of sin . . . It makes me sick at heart, when one thinks what automatic dolls we are, to hear poor little devils told that what they thought were good actions were bad, because they had a thought of reward or punishment and did not do it simply for Christ—and the next minute to hear a puke in an apron [i.e., a Catholic nun] trying to scare them stiff with a picture of hell they are likely to be sent to. . . . As I was saying the other day, I don't believe men who took an active part in ordinary life could or at any rate would have invented such mean and dirty spiritual tortures. . . ." [30]

Frankfurter apparently sent his friend Dean Acheson, the former U.S. Secretary of State, an autographed copy of the *Letters*, and received the following response:

"Dear Felix:
The Holmes-Laski letters are a great joy and delight. Your inscription moves me much. I think the letters will raise hell in several quarters. The Catholics who have been taking pot shots

at O.W.H. will get juicy ammunition, as well as fury. 'The puke in an apron' will be hard to take. . .

Dean" [31]

Obviously, Mr. Acheson detected an anti-Catholic tone in Justice Holmes' remarks, even though Frankfurter, in his foreword, indicates he does not view such anti-Catholic remarks as "intolerance."

In passing, it is worthy of note that Laski was keenly aware that the judiciary is of inestimable value in shaping societies, such as ours, which are governed by three co-equal branches of government. [32]

My perception of Justice Frankfurter's impartiality was further eroded when I read a letter he wrote to Professor Eugene V. Rostow on August 9, 1957, in which he said: "After all, it isn't for nothing that for years I was one of the counsel of the American Civil Liberties Union . . ." [33]

That statement raised serious ethical questions when it is recalled that ACLU attorneys appeared regularly before the high bench in numerous religion-clause-cases at a time when Frankfurter was a sitting Justice.

For example, in the *Everson* and *McCollum* cases, the ACLU filed "friend of the court" briefs supporting the appellants. In *Zorach,* Leo Pfeffer, a member of the ACLU and one of its cooperating attorneys, represented the appellant and opposed release of public school students to attend religion classes off public school property. Also, in *Torcaso,* Lawrence Speiser, executive director of the ACLU's Washington, D.C. office, was joined by Pfeffer in representing the appellant, Mr. Torcaso. The ACLU attorneys argued that a belief in God could not be constitutionally imposed as a criterion for holding public office at State level.

In all of those cases, Justice Frankfurter voted to support the position argued by the ACLU. [34] Moreover, it seems that the positions argued by the ACLU attorneys were compatible with views we have noted Frankfurter expressed with regard to belief in God, "spiritual Messiahs," "explicit ethical instruction," and parental rights in education.

In that regard, attention is invited to note 34, *supra,* where it is shown that Canon number 3 of the American Bar Association's Canons on Judicial Ethics stipulates: "A judge . . . should not suffer his conduct to justify the impression that any person can improperly influence or unduly enjoy his favor, or that he is affected by kinship, rank, position or influence of any party or other person."

The more I read the papers of the members of the Court, the more impressed I was that the scale of justice in religion-clause-cases was tilted by a finger of bias.

We have seen that the ACLU attorneys convinced the Court that the beliefs of atheists should be protected; and it is abundantly evident that the "reverent" agnosticism of Justice Frankfurter has not been proscribed in the public forum. With that in mind, it has become increasingly difficult to comprehend how the Court can deny equal protection to students who believe in Judeo-Christian values.

Time after time, the Justices have ruled that the State can in virtually no way provide them benefits (except for the purposes of safety). Simultaneously, the high bench has repeatedly emphasized that the beliefs of atheists and agnostics should not be infringed in the nation's public educational system. No Court decision has limited the fora where the philosophy and values of the latter two groups may be propagated.

Unitarian Influence

This double standard was further emphasized by Justice Harold Burton's attitude toward the religion clause.

His papers reflect that he was an eminent member of All Soul's Unitarian Church in Washington, D.C. In April, 1947, his pastor A. Powell Davies, invited the Justice to attend a commemorative service at the Jefferson Memorial in the nation's capital. The letter of invitation made clear that Thomas Jefferson was an ardent Unitarian, and Pastor Davies expressed the hope that the occasion "will contribute substantially to exalting the spiritual and moral faith held by Jefferson . . ." [35] Rev. Davies also made clear that "Jefferson's Bible" would be read at the service.

"Jefferson's Bible" is a relatively little known work by the nation's third President. It essentially was composed to "extricate the gospel of Jesus from the maze of amazing and unbelievable dogmas and superstitions in which he believed it had been almost lost." [36]

After the ceremony, Burton wrote a letter to Davies congratulating him on the event "in honor of the free religious faith of Thomas Jefferson." [37]

Burton's participation in the event, and his comment on it, were strikingly contradictory to the position he took just two months earlier in the *Everson* case. In the dissenting opinion which he joined (written by Justice Rutledge, also a Unitarian, who was buried from Pastor

Davies church) [38], it was stated: The religion clause "broadly forbids State support, financial or other, of religion in any guise, form or degree. It outlaws all use of public funds for religious purposes." [39]

Despite that sweeping restriction on State support of religion "in any guise, form or degree," we find Justice Burton attending a religious service, in a building constructed and maintained with tax funds, for the precise purpose of giving the dignity and prestige of his august position as a Justice in the highest court in the land to join in "exalting the spiritual and moral faith held by Jefferson."

Justice Rutledge, in the dissent concurred in by Burton, also advanced the following strange concept of liberty which is found nowhere in the Constitution nor in the history of the origin and development of that fundamental charter of liberties:

> "Like St. Paul's freedom, religious liberty with a great price must be bought. And for those who exercise it most fully, by insisting upon religious education for their children mixed with secular, by terms of our Constitution the price is greater than for others." [40]

That is a stunning statement and a novel interpretation of the First Amendment. It is at odds with the Declaration of Independence which insists "that *all* men are created *equal, that they are endowed by their Creator* with certain *unalienable rights,* that among these are life, *liberty, and the pursuit of happiness.*" [Emphasis added].

It is a statement totally contrary to Section 1 of the Fourteenth amendment which echoes the "Declaration."

In reality, the Constitution nowhere demands a price greater for the religious liberty of Catholics and others who choose to integrate their religious values into education mandated by the State.

Rutledge, who had close ties to Unitarianism, must have known that the founder of Unitarianism, Michael Servitus, "with a great price," spoke against the reality of the Holy Trinity. He was seized in Geneva by order of John Calvin and was burned at the stake on October 27, 1553. [41] But our Constitution gives his followers no greater freedom than is accorded to those Christians and Jews who conscientiously insist on education which recognizes that "a knowledge of God is the beginning of wisdom."

So, if such restrictions on members of certain religious groups in our country do not exist in the Constitution, perhaps other influences helped to shape the Supreme Court's *Everson* decision. Could that influence have been Unitarian philosophy?

It has been noted that Justices Burton and Rutledge were attached to Unitarian beliefs. Moreover, the two of them, along with Justices Black and Douglas, were close friends of Pastor Davies.

Justice Douglas edited a book of commentary by Davies, published in 1959, in which he said that Justice and Mrs. Black "were choice friends" of the Unitarian Pastor. [42] Douglas also observed that his colleague, Justice Rutledge, "was drawn to Dr. Davies by a close spiritual kinship." [43]

The papers of Justice Black contain a copy of one of Pastor Davies sermons in which the minister said there is no "devil," no "diabolical powers or satanic elements in life." [44]

Following the death of his first wife, Justice Black was remarried in 1956 by Davies. [45]

In 1957, Black wrote a note of condolence to Mrs. Davies when her husband died, and told her he turned to the Pastor for help "in time of sorrow and in time of joy." [46]

In 1959, Black wrote to Mr. Russell B. Adams, chairman of the Davies Memorial Committee, to express his interest in "advancing liberal religion." [47]

In 1963, Justice Black attended services at All Souls Unitarian Church and listened to an entire sermon extolling the U.S. Supreme Court's many liberal decisions. [48] His records also show he contributed $325 to that church between 1959-1963 [49]

According to a Religious News Service dispatch in 1976, the distinctive value system of Unitarian Universalists "is least like that of Christians and most like that of nonbelievers."

That identifying characteristic of Unitarian beliefs was set forth in a study by Dr. Robert L'H. Miller, a Unitarian Universalist minister and associate professor of religion at Tufts University, the RNS press report said. [50]

Miller said that Unitarians hold Salvation "comes close to being a disvalue," as does Forgiveness. He characterized Unitarianism as being "[e]go oriented," and said Unitarian "values focus on competence rather than on morals." [51]

Pastor Davies insisted: "The religions of the creeds are obsolescent . . . the basis of their claims expired with yesterday." [52]

Liberalism, said Davies, causes "us to put our trust in the free exertions of our own minds instead of in the dogmas of the long-established churches. . . . Yes, it was liberalism which forswore the supernatural and forsook the ancient revelation." [53]

He also stated: "There is a religion that says Freedom! Freedom from ignorance and false belief. Freedom from spurious claims and

bitter prejudices. Freedom . . . with minds unimpaired by cramping
dogmas and spirits uncrippled by abject dependence." [54]

"Nostalgia," said Pastor Davies, "can go back to the old time religion . . . It can go back to the wish for supernatural intervention, or
salvationism. It can make a mother image of the Virgin Mary—which
is what the ancients used to do with their earth-goddesses, who were
also always virgins and always mothers—or it can do something similar with Jesus of Nazareth. It can turn God into a deified image of
human sentimentalism."

Referring to the traditional Christian beliefs which he ridiculed in
the passage immediately above, the Unitarian intimate of the Justices
said those holding traditional Christian beliefs make no effort to
achieve a fully human level, but rather adhere to a realm of "fantasy"
which, if sustained, "will surely bring us to disaster." [55]

Speaking of "this ancient God of miracles and interventions," Davies says He is "really dead," and there is "no longer any kindness in
letting anyone cling to such a fantasy. For if that is where we put our
faith, our dependence, or reliance, we shall be wiped off the face of
the earth." [56]

Justice Douglas, in his foreward to Davies' book, said the Unitarian
pastor once wrote a friend [Douglas?]:

"I do not think that morality depends upon any particular
system of religious doctrine. The ecclesiastical imperialism
which claims that there cannot be a universal good society until
Christian doctrine is accepted is both mischievous and gro-
tesque. What is needed is the identification of the spiritual and
moral values in all the great provinces of religious culture (and
outside them), so that the world may have a common basis for its
united life." [57]

Douglas said Davies "pleaded for the removal of the supernatural
from religion." In that connection, he quoted his Unitarian friend as
saying:

"There is no God in the sky. God is in the heart that loves the
sky's blueness. There is no army of angels, no hosts of sera-
phim, and no celestial hierarchy. All this is man's
imagining. . . ." [58]

Davies also declared: "Very little that entered into Christianity
came from Jesus." [59]

Clearly, Christians have reason to question the objectivity of Justice Burton in deciding religion-clause-cases when it is known that he was active in advancing "the free religious faith of Thomas Jefferson," a man who denied the Divinity of Christ, and opposed Trinitarian Christianity.

Further, Justice Rutledge's "close spiritual kinship" with a pastor who denigrated traditional Christian beliefs and declared that the "ancient God of miracles is dead," also raises doubts as to his sense of fairness in deciding such cases.

And certainly Justice Black's expressed commitment for "advancing liberal religion" chills those who looked for balance when the U.S. Supreme Court decided cases involving "the establishment of religion or the free exercise thereof."

More Cause For Concern: Freemasonry

But there was even more cause for concern by the average citizen. Justice Burton's papers led to the most surprising revelation of all: the influential role played by Freemasonry in shaping U.S. Supreme Court decisions involving the position of conventional religion in American life and, in all likelihood, numerous other decisions which collectively changed the social fabric of the nation between 1941–1971.

On October 13, 1949, McIlyar H. Lichliter, sent a a letter to Burton, addressing him as a 33rd degree Freemason. Lichliter, a 33rd degree Mason and Grand Prior of the Supreme Council, Scottish Rite, of the Northern Jurisdiction, Boston, Massachusetts, was responding to Burton's letter of October 8, 1949.

The Grand Prior wrote of a visit to the ancient Abbey of St. Marie, Longues-Sur-Mer, Calvados, France, which was owned and occupied by former Congressman Charles S. Dewey. The Abbey is the site of the tomb of Jacques DeMolay, the one-time Master of the Knights Templar before his execution in the 14th Century following a lengthy trial by both the Catholic Church and Philip IV (also known as "Philip the Fair"), King of France.

Lichliter wrote: "As you know, Pope Clement V and Phillip the Fair did a thorough job on May 11, 1314 when Jacques DeMolay was burned at the stake in Paris. They destroyed the records of the Templars or—as many believe—buried them in the Archives of the Vatican. . . ."

At that point, the word "quote" is handwritten in pencil, apparently to emphasize that particular passage for future citation.

Lichliter also observed that Justice Jackson had been nominated to receive the 33rd degree of Freemasonry. [60]

The letter's emphasis on Freemasonry, the Templars, a Pope and the Vatican stimulated curiosity. Also arousing interest was the fact two Supreme Court Justices were identified as Masons; and one of those men had retained in his files a letter from a fellow high-ranking Mason which indicated the Catholic Church had been responsible for executing a person esteemed by the Masons.

The recurring references to Freemasonry, and membership in that organization by members of the Court, suggested that a check of the historic record was in order to determine whether Masonic membership was a common characteristic of Justices over the years.

The record shows that from the inception of the Supreme Court in 1789 through 1940, there never were more than three Masonic Justices during any term, except on two occasions. During the period 1882-1887, four Masonically-identified Justices sat on a nine-man bench, and a similar situation prevailed during the 1921-1922 term.

However, suddenly, beginning with appointments to the Court by President Franklin D. Roosevelt—himself an ardent Mason—and continuing through the first three years of President Richard M. Nixon's first term [President Nixon is not known to be a Mason], members of the international secret society dominated the high bench in ratios ranging from five to four (beginning in 1941) to seven to two (beginning in 1946).

During the 1949-1956 terms, seven members of the Craft served on the Court with a former Mason, Justice Sherman Minton, who resigned from the Fraternity in 1946. [61]

A complete foot-noted listing of Masonic membership on the Court, beginning in 1789 and continuing through 1984, is set forth in Appendix A.

Additionally, beginning with the appointment of Justice Felix Frankfurter to the high tribunal in 1939, Justices who are not known to have been Masons but whose philosophy, it will be found, paralleled the thinking of Masonry, shared the bench with Masonic Justices.

Besides Frankfurter, those Justices were: Frank Murphy (1940-1949); William J. Brennan (1956-) [62]; Arthur J. Goldberg (1962-1965); and Abe Fortas (1965-1970). [63]

The dominance of Masons appointed to the Court by President

Franklin D. Roosevelt raises a suspicion that FDR's highly controversial "court-packing-plan" of 1937 may have been a deliberate effort to bring a preponderance of Masonic philosophy to the high bench.

In that regard, it is interesting to note that four Masons, who subsequently were appointed to the Court by Roosevelt, or President Harry S. Truman (also an ardent Mason), made statements supporting the "court-packing-plan. Those men were: Hugo L. Black; James F. Byrnes; Sherman Minton; and Robert Jackson. [64]

During that period of Masonic dominance of the high bench, the attention of the Court suddenly seemed to focus on religion-clause-cases. Moreover, the verdicts in those cases, one after another, placed increasing restrictions on the propagation of traditional religious values in the public arena. Indeed, those decisions by the Court reflected an unabashed bias favorable to the philosophies of Masonry and Unitarianism.

Those years also marked an epoch of revolutionary liberalism. This was evidenced, not only by the Court's obvious determination to move the nation away from an emphasis on Judeo-Christian values in public life, but also by a series of decisions, the cumulative effect of which encouraged the sale and distribution of lewd, obscene, and immoral matter. [65]

Further, it was a time when the Court dramatically reversed its long-held perception that there is no Constitutional right to advocate overthrow of the government by force and violence. [66]

With specific reference to the religion clause, the record shows that Masonic Justices voted with remarkable consistency.

Common agreement by the Court's Masonic contingent in a number of religion-clause-cases is evidenced by the following decisions which show a striking accord among such Justices in relation to their number on the bench: *Everson,* 7 of 7 [although the decision was 5 to 4, there was no indication in the opinions that Masonic Justices disagreed as to the importance of the "wall of separation" theory, nor on the importance of Virginia in crafting the religion clause] *McCollum,* 6 of 7; *Torcaso,* 6 of 6; *Engel,* 6 of 6; *Abington,* 5 of 6; and *Lemon,* 4 of 5.

Discovering Masonry's Secrets

When it was discovered that Freemasons dominated the Supreme Court, my knowledge of the Craft was minimal. However, in a general way, the Fraternity left a favorable impression, primarily because a

Shriner's parade in Washington, D.C. in the mid-1960s brought much pleasure to my wife and our very young children.

After noting that so many Justices were members of the Craft, it seemed highly important to learn the philosophy and teachings of the organization. The problem was finding such knowledge when the Fraternity is known to operate in secrecy.

However, it is commonly known that the Intelligence community collects most of its information by carefully culling open sources.

Because so many of the Justices and other high government officials, including President Roosevelt, were known to be members of the Scottish Rite of the Southern Jurisdiction, it seemed appropriate to search for the journal used by that organization to communicate with its membership on a regular basis. That publication is the *New Age* magazine, a monthly periodical.

In one issue of that journal, a member of the Rite said the *New Age* is "generally recognized as the most influential and widely read Masonic publication in the world." [67]

Accordingly, much time was consumed by reading every page of each monthly issue of that journal covering the years 1921 through 1981. The wisdom of that approach was confirmed in a report by the Craft itself, which stated:

> "The monthly issues of the *New Age,* if combined, would present a fine summary of Scottish Rite philosophy in action. . . ." [68]

They surely do. And when augmented by wide-ranging reading from a number of works related to the Craft (most of which were suggested by *New Age* articles or editorial commentary), it is evident that international Freemasonry historically has been a revolutionary world-wide movement organized to advance Kabbalistic Gnosticism; to undermine and, if possible, to destroy Christianity; to infuse Masonic philosophy into key government structures; and to subvert any government which does not comport with Masonic principles.

All evidence points to the fact that most members of the Masonic Fraternity are largely ignorant of its sinister designs.

It also must be stated emphatically that there is no evidence available which suggests any member of the Court ever subscribed to Masonry's revolutionary and subversive activities. That is not to say many of them have not shared the Craft's strong opposition both to the

Roman Catholic Church, and to encouraging or advancing traditional Judeo-Christian religious beliefs and values.

The facts available indicate that most men are lured into Masonry by the appeal of its deceptive facade which promises brotherhood, charitable and benevolent endeavors, and, not insignificantly, an opportunity for personal advancement in employment or in public life. However, once behind the lodge door, the nascent Mason learns quickly that charity begins at home, and that he is bound to the Fraternity by solemn oaths and threats of gruesome bodily harm and death if he should disclose Masonry's secrets.

Research makes clear that a vast amount of information exposing the clandestine and revolutionary activities of international Freemasonry has been known for years. However, the power and influence of the Craft is so awesomely effective that any effort to engage in a rational discussion of the Fraternity causes eyes to glaze over, and the issue, almost always, is automatically dismissed as a subject for discussion.

Such a conditioned reflex manifests a curious and arbitrary limitation on the age-old hallmark of the American concept of civil discourse known as the free exchange of ideas.

In fact, that uniquely American appreciation of open debate regarding important issues would seem to make secret societies an anachronism in this country. Yet, the fact is, membership in Freemasonry is larger in the United States than in any other country in the world.

It is now time to lift the veil to expose Masonry's underlying philosophy and its nefarious activities both abroad and in America.

PART I

UNDERSTANDING THE CONFLICT

1/ LIFTING THE VEIL

Although Freemasonry operates secretly, there is a surprising amount of information available about its influence on society.

For example, an article in the *New Age,* in 1946, called attention to the following remark by former French premier Andre Tardieu, who died the previous year:

> "Freemasonry does not explain everything; yet, if we leave it out of account, the history of our times is unintelligible." [1]

Masonic author and commentator Arthur E. Waite, writing about the 33rd degree of Freemasonry, said:

> "It must be confessed that the whole scheme has a certain aspect of conspiracy continually presenting itself and as frequently eluding the mental grasp." [2]

In 1976, a book by Fred Zeller, former Grand Master of the Grand Orient of France, titled, *Trois Points, C'est Tout* (Three Points, That's All), revealed that between 1912 and 1971, all of the Third and much of the Fourth Republic of France was dominated by Freemasons, who fought two major anti-clerical reforms in a battle against Church influence. [3]

And, in 1981, the world learned of the machinations of Grand Master Licio Gelli's Masonic Lodge known as *Propaganda Due,* or P-2, which precipitated the fall of the Italian Government that same year.

Despite that known background of Masonic intrigue, there continues to be a reluctance by the media and social commentators to expose Masonry's long history of working to subvert Church and State.

It is true the press did inform the public that Gelli's lodge included three Cabinet ministers, two under-secretaries, 30 members of Parliament, 70 top military officers, and a number of magistrates, civil servants, industrialists, university professors, policemen and journalists, among whom was the editor and publisher of one of the nation's most prestigious daily newspapers, *Corriere della Sera.*

The press also disclosed the financial machinations and tragedies surrounding bankers Roberto Calvi and Michele Sindona, including the former's strange death at Blackfriar's Bridge in London, and the involvement of the Vatican Bank with those two Masonic bankers. [4]

However, the press gave virtually no attention to the larger picture, that is, the philosophy and activities of the Freemason Fraternity itself, of which P-2 was a progeny.

Yet, it must be noted that Rupert Cornwell, Rome correspondent for the London *Financial Times,* does say in his book, *God's Banker,* which reports on the issue: "As early as 1738 Pope Clement XII described freemasonry as 'Satan's synagogue'."

And, the British journalist added, the Pope's fears "were well grounded." [5]

The *Financial Times* correspondent characterized P-2 as a "a state within a state," and "little short of a parallel state." [6] He also observed that Italy's late Fascist dictator, Benito Mussolini, had outlawed secret Masonic lodges. [7]

Still, despite the mind-boggling reality of what this one Roman Masonic lodge had done by gaining allegiance of so many key government officials, industrialists, members of the academic community and others, it seems curious that background information concerning P-2's parent entity, the Masonic Fraternity itself, was ignored by the media. It seems curious, because Freemasonry, over the centuries, is known to have played a secret and extraordinary role in attempting to mold societies according to its tenets.

What Mussolini Found

However, Cornwell's references to Pope Clement XII and Mussolini do provide a clue as to what the world-wide Masonic Fraternity is all about.

In that regard, the *New Age,* in one of a series of articles in 1949, commented on Mussolini's closing of the lodges prior to World War II.

(The series was written, incidentally, upon the recommendation of Justice Robert H. Jackson, who at that time was a 32nd degree Mason, and had recently returned to the United States after having taken leave from the Supreme Court to serve as Chief Prosecutor at the Nuremberg War Crimes Trials).

The article said the Italian dictator was prompted to investigate Masonic lodges after he noticed many Socialist deputies and government employees "obeyed the orders of Freemasonry in preference to the orders of the Socialist Party." [8]

It should be noted that the Masonic cult "adhered to Fascism at the beginning," and "officially was never hostile" to it until *Il Duce* prepared legislation against secret societies. [9]

As a result of observing what he perceived as disloyalty among the Masons, Mussolini approved the appointment of a 15-member commission comprised "mostly of Senators and university professors," who "unanimously advised the suppression" of the lodges—because:

- Italian Freemasonry was "dominated by an anti-national state of mind."
- The Craft obliged its members to "deny they are Masons," thus contributing to "corrupt the character of Italians."
- Freemasonry used its hold upon the machinery of Government in favor of purely private interests and ambitions.

The report, in many ways, so strikingly similar to the Italian Government's findings in 1981, further stated:

"Freemasonry has penetrated into the most delicate organs of the national life, using as its lever the chief banking institutions . . . Its chief weapon is secrecy, which debases men's conscience, making them prone to intrigue and obliging them to submit to discipline against which they cannot rebel without breaking their vows: [this] forces them to maintain an internal solidarity which annuls or overcomes every other duty of loyalty or justice, and . . . insures immunity to any one who profits by it.

"When one thinks of the characteristics of Freemasonry which have been set down above, and especially its ties with similar organizations abroad, one realizes that the existence of Freemasonry is a phenomenon of such gravity that it seems unbelievable that the State has permitted it hitherto." [10]

At that point, the article refers to a 1947 statement made by John Cowles, Grand Commander of the Scottish Rite of the Southern Jurisdiction, for the purpose of emphasizing the preeminent role played by Raoul V. Palermi, the former Grand Commander of Masonry in Italy who renounced the Fraternity and became friendly with Mussolini.

Cowles said:

> "In Italy, the regular Freemasonry stems as follows: Garibaldi, Ballori, Fera, Ricciardi, Burgess (Acting), and Palermi. The last named was head of both the Grand Lodge and the Supreme Council. He betrayed them both, proving a traitor, was expelled from Freemasonry, and later given a position under Mussolini . . ."

Cowles then referred to the situation facing Masonry in Italy immediately following World War II, long after Mussolini had been murdered. The post-War government, he noted, adopted a new constitution which included a provision (Article 14) prohibiting the existence of secret societies. [11]

The fact that the Grand Commander of Italian Freemasonry was "given a position under Mussolini," strongly indicates that Mussolini and his Commission had first hand evidence about the activities of Freemasonry.

Further, the fact that the new post-War government felt compelled to place a provision in the constitution banning secret societies gives credence to the findings of Mussolini's 15-member commission, and its fears about what such organizations can do to subvert a State.

However, Cowles noted that the new post-war Prime Minister, Alcide de Gasperi, a Christian Democrat, insisted that he did not view Freemasonry as a secret society, and would not war against it. [12]

In retrospect, it appears that de Gasperi's *naivete* regarding the Masonic Fraternity in 1947 contributed to the P-2 scandal of 1981.

Church Exposes Masonry In 1738

Freemasonry, as we generally know it today, entered history when the Grand Lodge of England was established in 1717.

In 1723, Rev. James Anderson, an English divine, wrote his "New Constitutions" for the Craft, many parts of which were "lifted" from the works of Jan Amos Komensky (also known as Jan Amos Comenius), a 17th Century bishop of the Moravian Church. Anderson's

"Constitutions" changed English Masonry from a more or less Christian orientation to "a universal creed based upon the Fatherhood of God and the Brotherhood of Man." This fundamental ideology of Komensky appealed at once "to freethinkers, to rationalists, and to lovers of magic and esoteric rites—to the love of mystery in myths, symbols and ceremonies." [13]

Fifteen years later, in 1738, Pope Clement XII, as Rupert Cornwell observed, issued his Pontifical Constitution, *In Eminenti*. The Pontiff declared:

> "We have resolved and decreed to condemn and forbid such [secret] societies, assemblies, reunions, conventions, aggregations or meetings, called either Freemasonic or known under some other denomination. We condemn and forbid them by this, our present constitution, which is to be considered valid forever.
>
> "We commend to the faithful to abstain from intercourse with those societies . . . in order to avoid excommunication, which will be the penalty imposed upon all those contravening to this, our order, none except at the point of death, could be absolved of this sin, except by us or the then existing Roman Pontiff."

That, indeed, was a very severe indictment of blossoming Masonry, to have the Pope caution his international flock that membership in this new secret society was considered a "reserved sin," absolution for which, except at the point of death, was reserved to the Holy Father personally. However, just thirteen years later, Pope Benedict XIV, in his Pontifical Constitution, *Providas,* reaffirmed Clement's censure of Masonry and similar secret societies. Moreover, since that time "more than 200" documents issued by the Vatican have condemned Masonry, [14] although the "reserved sin" status was dispensed with by Pope Paul VI, and the Church began a rapprochement with the secret society in the 1940s. That aspect of Masonic-Catholic Church relationships will be discussed later.

Barruel And Robison's Revelations

The general public's first true insight into Freemasonry did not come until 81 years after the Fraternity's founding, when two books lifted the veil which so decorously had concealed the Craft's activities, except as had been exposed earlier by the Vatican and, occasionally, by heads of State.

One book was written by John Robison, a highly regarded professor of philosophy and a member of the Royal Society of Edinburg. The Scottish professor said he found Masonry on the Continent much different than he knew it in the Lodges of England. Continental Masonry, he wrote, exhibited "a strange mixture of mysticism, theosophy, cabalistic whim, real science, fanaticism and freethinking, both in religion and politics." He found, too, that although everything was expressed decently, "atheism, materialism, and discontent with civil subordination pervade the whole." [15]

A more detailed expose of the Craft was set forth in a four-volume work by the Abbé Augusten de Barruel, a refugee from Revolutionary France, whose third volume was going to press just as Robison's book was being published. [16]

Barruel charged that many years prior to the French Revolution, men who called themselves "philosophers," conspired against God of the Gospel, against Christianity, without distinction of worship. The grand object of the "conspiracy," the Abbé asserted, was to overturn every altar where Christ was adored. [17]

These philosophers, the Abbé asserted, formed the sophisters of rebellion, who joined with Freemasons—a group he characterized as having a "long history" of hatred for Christ and kings. Continuing, the French-born cleric said that from this coalition came the "Sophisters of Impiety and Anarchy," who conspired "against every religion, every government, against all civil society, and even against all property . . ." This latter crowd became known as the Illuminati, from which sprang the Jacobins. [18]

Although this philosophy was believed to have been gestated in England, in reality, said the Abbé, it is "the error of every man who judges everything by the standard of his own reason, and rejects in all religious matters every authority that is not derived from the light of nature. It is the error of denying every possibility of any mystery beyond the limits of man's reason, and the discard of Revelation." [19]

The leading "philosophers" of whom Barruel spoke were the major Encyclopedists: Voltaire, Frederick II, King of Prussia, Denis Diderot and Jean D'Alembert. These men, he asserted, "acted in concert" to destroy Christianity and, he declared, the proofs of the conspiracy are drawn from their writings. [20]

The Abbé quoted Voltaire as saying: "I am weary of hearing people repeat that twelve men have been sufficient to establish Christianity, and I will prove that one man may suffice to overthrow it." [21]

The French historian noted that the principal Encyclopedists had a secret language and, in that connection, he cited a letter from Voltaire to D'Alembert in which it is stated: "the vine of truth is well cultivated. Translated, the statement means: "We make amazing progress against religion." [22]

Masonic sources, it should be noted, frequently have pointed out that most of the major actors among the Encyclopedists were Masons. [23]

[In that regard, Robison and Barruel are cited rather extensively in the following paragraphs, in order to establish that what was attested to of Masonry in Europe in the 18th Century has been confirmed by Masonic sources as a substantially accurate representation of Freemasonry in America and Europe in the 20th Century.]

Barruel said he was invited to become a member of the lower grades of Masonry, and consented to take the first two degrees which were given to him outright and in a humorous vein.

However, the third degree ritual demanded unswerving obedience to the orders of the Grand Master, even though those orders might be contrary to the King, or any other sovereign. Despite not agreeing to so bind himself, Barruel received the degree of Master Mason [24]

Those admitted to the first three degrees of Masonry, he explained, learn that Masonic and Christian eras do not coincide. For the Mason, the Year of Light begins at Creation, thus ante-dating Moses, the Prophets and Jesus Christ [25]

He noted that many beliefs of Masonry are quite similar to the beliefs and practices of the Manachees, such as the "follies" of the Kabbalah and magic; indifference to all religion; the same terrible oaths; and symbols of sun, moon and stars used inside the lodges. [26]

The French cleric described his own initiation and its attendant ceremonies and oaths. His account confirms that the Craft's degree and initiatory ceremonies of 1798 are almost identical to the Fraternity's practices today. [27]

He said his own initiation gave him sufficient credibility to converse with those whom he know to be more advanced in Masonry, "and in many of these interviews it happened, that, notwithstanding all their secrecy, some unguarded expressions escaped the most zealous adepts, which threw light on the subject." Other Masons, he continued, lent him their books, "presuming that their obscureness and the want of essential words, or the method of discovering them, would baffle all my attempts to understand them." [28]

With such understanding, he was able to learn the degree of Knight of the *Rose Crucis,* "or the Rosicrucians." The ornaments of the Lodge in that degree recall to the candidate "the solemn Mystery of Mount Calvary."

The Lodge room was draped in black with an altar prominently displayed, above which were three crosses. The middle one bore the inscription: "I.N.R.I."

"The brethren in sacerdotal vestments are seated on the ground in the most profound silence, resting their heads on their arms to represent their grief," Barruel wrote.

But, he said, it was "not the death of the Son of God, who died victim of our sins, that was the cause of their affliction." Rather, it was Christ's Crucifixion and the establishment of Christianity which moved the brethren to mourn loss of "the *word,* that is [their] pretended natural Religion . . .," which dates from that sacred Day.

This was evidenced in the ceremony, the Abbé said, by the response of the Senior Warden when he is asked the time of day by the Master of the Lodge. The Warden replied:

> "It is the first hour of the day, the time when the veil of the temple was rent asunder, when darkness and consternation was spread over the earth, when the light was darkened, when the *implements of Masonry were broken,* when the flaming star disappeared, when the cubic stone was broken, *when the word was lost.*" [29]

Those revelations about the philosophy and activities of Freemasonry were no less sensational than were the disclosures of Barruel and Robison regarding the Bavarian Order of Illuminati. The Order was a secret society founded by Professor Adam Weishaupt of Ingolstadt, Germany, and records show it was closely intwined with Masonry. Members of the Order, Barruel found, were the secret Masters of Masonry. [30]

Knowledge of the Order became public during search of a house occupied by one of the leaders, as well as by communications discovered at the Castle of Sandersdorf, a meeting place of the group. Other information was made known by an unidentified spy within the Order, and by depositions given by four professors of the Marianen Academy in Bavaria, who were members of the organization.

Weishaupt held views which, in later years, were echoed by the founding philosophers and adepts of international Communism, as well as others. Weishaupt proclaimed:

"Liberty and Equality are the essential rights that man in his original and primitive perfection received from nature. *Property* struck the first blow at Equality; political society or Governments were the first dispossessors of *Liberty:* the supporters of Governments and Property are the religious and civil laws; therefore, to reinstate man in his primitive rights of Equality and Liberty, we must begin by destroying all Religion, all civil society and finish by the destruction of all Property." [31]

According to Barruel, the doctrines of Illuminism came to Europe from Egypt through a Jutland merchant. [32]

Although Weishaupt hated religion, above all the Catholic Church, he greatly admired the effectiveness of her religious orders—particularly the Jesuits—in spreading the Gospel throughout the world. "What these men have done for the altar and throne, why should I not do in opposition to the altar and throne," the Bavarian professor remarked. [33]

Robison, referring to testimony of the four Marianen Academy professors, said the Order of Illuminati abjured Christianity; promoted sensual pleasures; considered suicide justifiable; viewed patriotism and loyalty to country as narrow-minded prejudices incompatible with universal benevolence; held private property a hindrance to happiness; and insisted that the goals of the Order were superior to all else. [34]

Also, he observed, members of the Order could be found only in the Lodges of Masonry. [35]

The Edinburg scholar said members of the group "insinuated themselves into all public offices, and particularly into the courts of justice." [36]

Weishaupt told his followers: "We must win the common people in every corner. This will be obtained chiefly by means of the schools, and by open, hearty behavior. Show condescension, popularity, and toleration of their prejudices, which we at leisure shall root out and dispel." [37]

Continuing in the same vein, he said: "If a writer publishes anything that attracts notice, and is in itself just but does not accord with our plan, we must endeavor to win him over—or decry him." [38]

The strength of the Order of Illuminati, he said, lies in its concealment; let it never appear in any place in its own name, but always covered by another name and another occupation. None is fitter than the three lower degrees of Freemasonry. . . . [39]

In addition to Masonry as a cover for Illuminati activities,

Weishaupt recommended that members of the Order find concealment in "a learned or literary society" which "may be a powerful engine in our hands." [40]

He taught his followers to try to obtain influence in all offices which have any effect in "forming or in managing, or even in directing the mind of man. . . ." [41]

All members of the Order, he said, "must be assisted . . . [and] preferred to all persons otherwise of equal merit." [42]

The organization believed that Jesus established no new religion, but only "set religion and reason in their ancient rights." [43]

Using the arcane language of Illuminism to explain his views on social conditions and the remedy for shaping society in the Order's mold, Weishaupt, in a letter to a colleague, referred to a "rough, split, and polished stone." The differences were explained by characterizing the rough and split stones as man's condition under civil government: "rough by ever fretting inequality of condition; and split since we are no longer one family, and are further divided by differences of government, rank, property and religion." However, when these differences are eliminated, and peoples of the world are "reunited in one family, we are represented by the polished stone." [44]

"Examine, read, think," Weishaupt admonished his devotees as he urged them to understand symbols and symbolic language used by the Order. Explaining, he instructed his followers: "There are many things which one cannot find out without a guide, nor ever learn without instructions . . . Your Superiors . . . know the true path—but will not point it out. Enough if they assist you in every approach to it." [45] Thus, the need for the membership at large to "examine, read, think."

The new Illuminee was "particularly recommended to study the doctrine of the ancient Gnostics and Manichaens, which may lead him to many important discoveries on the real Masonry." [46]

The Illuminati, Robision said, hoped to use women by hinting of their "emancipation from the tyranny of public opinion." [47]

The great aim of the Order, said the Scotch scholar, "is to make men happy," by "making them good." This was to be accomplished by "enlightening the mind, and freeing it from the dominion of superstition and prejudice." [48]

Robison also observed that Weishaupt was firm in the conviction that the Ancient Mysteries "were useful to mankind, containing rational doctrines of natural religion." [49]

Professor Renner, one of the Marianen Academy scholars who gave a written deposition about his knowledge of the Illuminati, said the Order bound adepts by subduing their minds "with the most magnificent promises, and assure . . . the protection of great personages ready to do everything for the advancement of its members at the recommendation of the Order." [50]

The Order enticed into its lodges only those who could be useful: "Statesmen, . . . counsellors, secretaries . . . professors, abbes, preceptors, physicians, and apothecaries are always welcome candidates to the Order." [51]

According to a joint deposition signed by Professor Renner and his three colleagues, the object of the first degrees of Illuminism was to train the adepts in the system of espionage. Once the member had so committed himself to such nefarious acts of espionage, treason, or other treacherous enterprises, he remained in a state of perpetual dread, fearing his superiors might at some time reveal the criminal activity, the four academicians testified. [52]

The revelations of Robison and Barruel caused a sensation, not only in Europe, but in America, and were synopsized in newspapers and recommended for reading.

On December 4, 1794, *The Herald* of New York editorialized on the history of the French Revolution, and said that history was the history of "the Popular Societies, the principal moving springs of action during the whole revolution." The editorial urged owners of newspapers in the new nation to make the history of those societies known, and recommended the works of Barruel and Robison. [53]

Further evidence of the popularity of the works of Barruel and Robison in America was indicated when a Protestant minister, G.W. Snyder of Frederick, Maryland, sent to President George Washington a copy of Robison's book, with a covering letter,. He said the President should be familiar with many of the points made by the Scottish scholar, since Mr. Washington was himself a Mason.

The President responded by noting that he never had presided over any Masonic Lodge, and had visited such establishments very seldom. Further, he observed, he did not believe the Lodges in the United States were "contaminated" with the principles of Illuminism. [54]

In a follow-up letter to Rev. Snyder, the President elaborated on his position and conceded that the doctrines of the Illuminati and Jacobins had indeed spread to the United States. No one, Mr. Washington said, "is more truly satisfied of this fact than I am."

Continuing, he said: ". . . I did not believe that the Lodges of Freemasons in *this* country had, *as societies,* endeavored to propagate the diabolical tenets of the first [the Illuminati], or the pernicious principles of the latter [Jacobins] (if they are susceptible of separation). That individuals of them [Masonic Lodges] may have done it, or that the founder or instrument employed to found the Democratic Societies in the United States, may have had these objects; and actually had a separation of the *People* from their *Government* in view, is too evident to be questioned." [55]

Freemasonry In Early America

The first Lodge of Freemasonry in America was established at Philadelphia in 1730, and claimed Benjamin Franklin as a member. Indeed, many leaders of the American Revolution, including Washington, were members of the Craft. [56] That is not surprising, since many of them also were Deists, the forerunner to modern day Unitarianism.

Historian Paul Hazard observed that Deists believed there "must be no form of constraint." They found no need for priests, ministers, nor rabbis. No more sacraments, rites, nor ceremonies; no more fasting, mortifying the flesh; no more going to church or synagogue. The Bible, to Deists, was a book just like any other. [57]

Deism, said Hazard, became devoted to the law of nature and free thinking; and upon the heels of Deism and Natural Religion, came Freemasonry. [58]

Actually, Masons were most active in bringing about the Revolutionary War in America, according to the *New Age*. A 1940 editorial in that publication declared: "It was the Masons who brought on the war, and it was Masonic generals who carried it through to a successful conclusion. In fact, the famous Boston Tea Party, which precipitated the war, was actually a recessed meeting of a Masonic Lodge." [59]

French historian Bernard Fay, writing of the Boston Tea Party, said the incident emanated from a tavern known as the "Green Dragon or the Arms of Freemasonry." A shabby band of "Redskins" were seen to leave the tavern on the afternoon of December 16, 1773, although no such persons had been seen to enter the building.

The group, reported Fay, rushed to the docks, jumped onto the ships anchored there, and threw tea into the harbor. The "Redskins" returned to the Green Dragon, but were never seen to leave. [60]

Fay also said Benjamin Franklin established a "network of Masonic newspapers" in all the English colonies, one of the most prominent of which was Peter Zenger's *Journal* in New York. [61]

Franklin, Fay wrote, utilized French Freemasons to aid the American Revolution. The American Revolutionary activist ingratiated himself to the widow of Claude Adrien Helvetius, the wealthy Encyclopedist, banker and atheist, who helped found the Lodge of Nine Muses—the intellectual center of French Freemasonry.

Through Madame Helvetius, Franklin was admitted to the Nine Muses and became Master of the Lodge. There he devoted himself to a propaganda campaign which swung French public opinion in favor of the American Masonic cause. Franklin's "admirable work," said Fay, was the most carefully planned and most efficiently organized propaganda ever accomplished, and "made possible the military intervention of France on the side of the Americans." [62]

Moreover, he asserted, Franklin's work also had "a great intellectual influence throughout Europe, spreading the idea, or what might be called the myth, of virtuous revolution." Up until that time, the French historian said, revolutions had been viewed "as crimes against society." Subsequently, revolutions "were accepted as a step in progress of the world," a step and a perception which "originated with the American Revolution and grew out of Franklin's propaganda." [63]

Legislatures Investigate U.S. Masonry

Despite the fact that Masonry was active in America since 1730, it was not until disclosures in "The Morgan Affair," almost 100 years later, that the American people became acutely aware of the Fraternity's "secret work."

When the public heard that one William Morgan, a Mason of Batavia, New York, allegedly had been murdered by members of the Craft for disclosing its secrets, the outcry was so vehement and widespread that thousands of the brethren resigned from the Fraternity. Legislatures of the States of New York, Massachusetts and Pennsylvania initiated investigations into the secret operations of Freemasonry, and developed testimony which was both amazing and frightening. The purported benevolent Fraternity was revealed to be a state within a state and bound its adherents with the most gruesome and terrifying oaths. In the national elections of 1830, the anti-Masonic political party mustered 130,000 votes.

The report of the New York State Senate Committee said of Free-masonry:

"It comprises men of rank, wealth, office and talents in power—and that almost in every place where power is of any importance—it comprises, among the other classes of the community, to the lowest, in large numbers, and capable of being directed by the efforts of others so as to to have the force of concert through the civilized world!

"They are distributed too, with the means of knowing each other, and the means of keeping secret, and the means of co-operating, in the desk, in the legislative hall, on the bench, in every gathering of men of business, in every party of pleasure, in every enterprise of government, in every domestic circle, in peace and in war, among its enemies and friends, in one place as well as another. So powerful, indeed, is it at this time, that it fears nothing from violence, either public or private, for it has every means to learn it in season, to counteract, defeat and punish it. . . ." [64]

The report noted that there were approximately 30,000 Freemasons in the State of New York—about one-fourth of the eligible voting population—"yet they have held for forty years, three-fourths" of all public offices in the State. [65]

Commenting on a situation which has perdured through the years, the report addressed the attitude of the press, as follows:

"The public press, that mighty engine for good or for evil, has been, with a few honorable exceptions, silent as the grave. This self-proclaimed sentinel of freedom, has felt the force of masonic influence, or has been smitten with the rod of its power." [66]

The New York legislators said Masonic witnesses on the stand "have sworn to facts, which in the opinion of bystanders, were not credited by a single one of the hundreds of persons who were present." Moreover, grand juries, "a majority of whom were masons," omitted to find bills of indictment "when there was proof before them of outrages not surpassed in grossness and indecency by any committed in the country since the first settlement." [67]

The committee also disclosed some of the oaths taken by Freemasons testified to by former Masons who recently had resigned from the Fraternity. Those providing such testimony were "personally known to a majority of the committee" as "men of standing in the community, whose characters for veracity are beyond reach of calumny." [68]

Penalties accepted by Masons in the first three degrees were:

Entered Apprentice: "To have his throat cut across, his tongue taken out by the roots, and his body buried in the ocean."

Fellow Craft: "To have his left breast torn open, his heart and vitals taken from thence, and thrown over his left shoulder, and carried to the Valley of Jehosaphat, there to become a prey to the wild beasts of the field and the vultures of the air."

Master Mason: "To have his body severed in two in the midst and divided to the north and south, his bowels burnt to ashes in the center, and the ashes scattered to the four winds of heaven."

Royal Arch: "To have his skull struck off, and his brains exposed to the scorching rays of a meridian sun." [69]

Much of the same information uncovered by the New York Senate in 1829, also was found five years later to be common in the State of Massachusetts, when a Joint Committee of the legislature of the latter State investigated the Craft.

Masons invited to appear before the Joint Committee refused to do so, and though the Massachusetts House approved subpoena power for the committee, the State Senate refused to do so. [70]

The committee found Freemasonry was "a distinct Independent Government within our own Government, and beyond the control of the laws of the land by means of its secrecy, and the oaths and regulations which its subjects are bound to obey, under penalties of death." The committee added: "in no Masonic oath presented to the committee, is there any reservation made of the Constitution and the laws of the land. [71]

The Joint Committee found Freemasonry to be a "moral evil," a "pecuniary evil," and a "political evil." [72]

In 1836, a committee of the House of Representatives of the State of Pennsylvania was provided additional testimony which largely confirmed what the legislatures of the two other States had learned about Freemasonry.

The Pennsylvania panel was informed that a Master Mason, promises under oath to protect the secrets of a brother Master Mason, "murder and treason only excepted, and those at my own option." [73]

In all, nineteen witnesses refused to provide sworn testimony to the committee. Other witnesses informed the legislators that Masons influence judicial decisions and consider Masonic oaths superior to all other oaths. [74]

Other Early Activities Of U.S. Masonry

But the State legislative committees never learned of numerous other activities of Masonry which remained virtually unknown to the public at large.

For example, members of the Craft overthrew the Spanish government of Baton Rouge, Louisiana in 1810 and ran up their own flag, a lone silver star on a field of blue, to establish their "newly created Republic of West Florida." The star represented the "five points of fellowship" under which the ringleaders of the rebellion held their meetings. [75]

The Grand Lodge of Louisiana and its federated lodges plotted revolution in Mexico, and the Scottish lodges entered Mexico in 1813 for the express purpose of introducing the Constitution of Cadiz, a revolutionary statement of governing principles which contained numerous anti-ecclesiastical provisions. [76]

Moreover, public officials in the United States were active in pressing Masonry upon the Mexican people. New York Governor Dewitt Clinton, in a letter, dated December 10, 1825, acting in his Masonic role as General Grand High Priest of the Royal Arch Masons in the United States, approved the request of Joel Poinsett to establish a chapter of the Royal Arch in Mexico. The letter further authorized Poinsett to establish other chapters of that discipline in South America. Poinsett, at that time, was the U.S. minister plenipotentiary to that country. [77]

In 1835, Stephen Austin met in New Orleans "with 35 prominent members of the local Lodge of Freemasons, and planned the campaign which liberated Texas from Mexican rule." [78]

Also, the Grand Lodges of Louisiana and Pennsylvania were busy chartering Masonic lodges in Mexico, and Poinsett used his considerable influence to have the Grand Lodge of New York charter the Grand Lodge of Mexico. The Mexican lodges virtually became the ruling political party of Mexico in the early 19th century. [79]

But it is a strange irony of history that, despite the growing national awareness of Freemasonry's grave threat to Judeo-Christian beliefs and values—and to government itself—the American people allowed their attention to be diverted suddenly by a deceptive concern for what was perceived as a greater and more immediate menace: the Roman Catholic Church.

Before exploring that aspect of American history, it is important to understand the underlying philosophy of the Masonic Fraternity and the actions which flow from such belief.

2/ THE MIND OF MASONRY

Earlier in this century, Father Hermann Gruber, S.J., a recognized authority on Freemasonry, carefully scrutinized the Masonic Fraternity on the basis of its numerous publications and reports. He found:

- The Masonic program coincides to an astonishing degree with the program of the French Revolution of 1789. [1]

- The Craft fosters in its members, and through them in society at large, the spirit of innovation. It furnishes in critical times a shelter for conspiracy. [2]

- Freemasonry propagates principles which, logically developed, are essentially revolutionary and serve as a basis for all kinds of revolutionary movements. [3]

- The Scottish Rite system, which is propagated throughout the world, "may be considered as the revolutionary type of French Templar Masonry, fighting for the natural rights of man against religious and political despotism symbolized by the papal tiara and the royal crown." [4]

- Treason and rebellion against civil authority are deemed only political crimes which do not affect the good standing of a Mason, nor do they result in the imposition of Masonic punishment. [5]

- Symbolic formulae and symbols are used so the work of Masonry may not be hindered. The symbol of the Great Architect of the Universe and of the Bible are of the utmost importance to Masonry, since symbols are explained and accepted by each Mason according to his own understanding. The official organ of Italian Masonry emphasized that the Grand Architect may represent the revolutionary God of Mazzini, the Satan of Carducci, God as the fountain of love, or Satan the genius of the

good, not of the bad. In reality, Italian Masonry, in these interpretations, adores the principle of Revolution. [6]

The ultimate aim of the Craft, Fr. Gruber said, is the overthrow of
all spiritual and political "tyranny" and class privileges, so that there
will be established a universal social republic in which will reign the
greatest possible individual liberty and social and economic equality.
[7]

To accomplish their goal, Masons believe the following is necessary:

1. The destruction of all social influence by the Church and
religion generally, either by open persecution or by so-called
separation of Church and State.
2. To laicize or secularize all public and private life and,
above all, popular education.
3. To systematically develop freedom of thought and conscience in school children, and protect them, so far as possible,
against all disturbing influences of the Church, and even their
own parents—by compulsion if necessary. [8]

Fr. Gruber's study was written in 1913, but it is curiously evident
that much of the Masonic program he outlined became manifest to the
general public during the three decades Freemasons dominated the
U.S. Supreme Court.

Certainly, the high bench has been militant in insisting that the
First Amendment mandates a scrupulous "separation of Church and
State." In that connection, the Court has said repeatedly that governmental funds can be provided only for education and related activities
which are completely sectarian.

Surely, the Justices' approval for dispensing contraceptives to children without parental consent, and authorizing them to have abortions
without the same consent, parallels Fr. Gruber's third point immediately above.

Of course, some may wish to dismiss the Jesuit's catalogue of Masonic chicanery as the views of an obedient priest written to affirm
earlier findings of Popes, historians, and legislative investigating committees influenced by Christian values.

But the priest's analysis of the Craft cannot be cavalierly ignored,
particularly in view of the unexpected tribute paid him by a prominent
Masonic historian, Ossian Lang, in a report to the Grand Lodge of

New York. Lang said: "A fine example of how the analytic mind of a scholarly non-Mason may discern the truth, may be found in the excellent article on Freemasonry contained in *The Catholic Encyclopedia*. The author of that article comes nearer to interpreting the history correctly of Freemasonry . . . than any Masonic writer whose publications have appeared in the English language. . . ." [8-A]

The View From The Lodge

Actually, Fr. Gruber's study, as well as the findings of Popes, historians and legislative committees, have been largely confirmed by members of the Craft itself. The fact is, a perusal of sixty years of writings in the authoritative *New Age* magazine leaves no doubt that Fr. Gruber and others of unimpeachable veracity have clearly explained the reality of the Masonic conspiracy to destroy Christian civilization.

A review of nearly two-thirds of a century of the official monthly journal of the Scottish Rite of Freemasonry of the Southern Jurisdiction—the rite to which so many Presidents of the United States, Justices of the Supreme Court and Members of Congress adhered—leaves one impressed by the consistent emphasis writers have given over the years to Albert Pike's *Morals and Dogma,* a book written in 1871 as a series of lectures, "specially intended to be read and studied by the Brethren of that obedience in connection with the Rituals and of the Degrees. . . ." [9]

Pike's 861-page tome is described as "the basis for Masonic philosophy," [10] and is given to each initiate into the Fourth Degree. [11] Moreover, the book has been viewed by the Brethren as "a secret book . . . not for publication. In case a mason dies or otherwise leaves the Council, the book should be returned to the Supreme Council or else destroyed." [12]

Certainly, such statements serve to convince the reader that Pike's book is a document of the highest importance to Scottish Rite Freemasonry. Indeed, it appears to be the very mind of Masonry.

The Introduction to the work, says the author was "about equally author and compiler; since he has extracted quite half its contents" from others. Moreover, it is explained that Pike changed and remolded sentences of others, and added his own words and phrases to the statements of writers in order to "use them as if they were his own. . . ." [13]

The official historian of the Scottish Rite of the Southern Jurisdiction, Charles Lobinger, said Pike's book "swarms with citations from Eliphas Levi," author of *Dogme et Rituel,* and that *Morals and Dogma* "is shown to be literal and verbatim extractions from those of the French Magus." [14]

Arthur Waite, a Masonic authority on, and translator of, Levi's works, has written:

"No person who is acquainted with *Morals and Dogma* can fail to trace the hand of the occultist therein and it is to be especially observed that, passing from grade to grade in the direction of the highest, this institution [Freemasonry] becomes more and more Kabbalistic." [15]

Another Masonic writer insisted that reading Pike's work makes one feel "he is contacting one of the greatest minds," and that some day Pike will be recognized "as one of the greatest religious teachers and reformers of history. . . ." [16]

Another author, writing in the same publication, recognized Pike's book to be "tedious reading and even difficult to understand." He suggested that the volume be read slowly over a three-year period.

Continuing, the latter writer said the book is "a summation of those philosophic and religious truths which are presented so graphically in the [degree] work," and he urged the study of Gnosticism and the Kabbalah as collateral reading. [17]

So it is made clear that Freemasonry is not fundamentally a fraternal insurance organization. It is an occult religion of Kabbalistic Gnosticsm, and Pike's book is the basic source document for brainwashing men in all degrees of Scottish Rite Masonry.

Pike's *Morals and Dogma*

Scottish Rite Masonry's Grand Philosopher and former Grand Commander wrote that the people, as a mass, are a "blind force," which must be "economized and managed" in order to attack "superstitions, despotism and prejudice." [18] And once the people are organized and guided by "a brain and a law," and motivated by Truth and Love, "the great revolution prepared for by the ages will begin to march." [19]

He said the force of the people becomes exhausted by prolonging "things long since dead; in governing mankind by embalming old, dead tyrannies of Faith; restoring dilapidaded dogmas; re-gilding faded, worm-eaten shrines; whitening and rouging ancient and barren superstitions . . . perpetuating superannuated institutions; enforcing the worship of symbols as the actual means of salvation; and tying the dead corpse of the Past . . . with the living present." [20]

Pike compared the unorganized mass of people to a "Rough Ashlar" [building stone], and the organized and direct masses as a Perfect Ashlar." It is a concept that had been first enunciated by Adam Weishaupt to guide his Bavarian Illuminati, as was noted earlier in the preceding pages of the book the reader is now pursuing. [21]

The Masonic leader identified Masonry with the Ancient Mysteries and star worship. The sun, moon and Master of the Lodge, he said, are the three sublime lights of Masonry. He characterized the Sun as the ancient symbol of the life-giving and generative power of the Deity. The Moon symbolizes the passive capacity of nature to produce (that is, the female of the species). The Master of Life *"was"* [emphasis added] the Supreme Deity, above both and manifested through both.

The Sun represents actual light, pours its fecunding rays upon the Moon, and both shed their light upon their offspring, the Blazing Star of Horus. The three form a great equilateral triangle in the center of which is the monific letter of the Kabbalah, by which creation is said to have been affected. [22]

In addition to exciting interest among neophyte Masons in pagan religions (which had been almost abandoned with the triumph of Christianity in the Fourth Century, A.D.), Pike's book also presents Masonry as an organization which thrives on tension, conflict and revolution—a struggle apparently directed toward what Pike called "the great revolution prepared for by the ages," which would usher in the "universal social republic," mentioned by Fr. Gruber. [23]

Lectures based on Pike's philosophy should immediately impress perceptive Masons that the tension, conflict and revolution referred to is the age-old pagan conflict with Christianity—particularly the Roman Catholic Church. The alternating black and white squares on the Lodge floor, Pike noted, serve to remind all Masons of that constant conflict. Those alternating blocks symbolize, he said, the "warfare of Michael and Satan; between light and darkness; freedom and despotism; religious liberty and the arbitrary dogmas of a Church that thinks for its votaries, and whose Pontiff claims to be infallible, and the decretals of its Councils to constitute gospel." Freemasonry, Pike said, owes its "success to opposition." [24]

Pike made it abundantly evident that Masonry has nothing to do with Old and New Testament religious values. The Craft, he insisted, is the successor of the Ancient Mysteries, and teaches and preserves the cardinal tenets of the old primitive faith. [25] All old religions "have died away and old faiths faded into oblivion;" but Masonry survives "teaching the same old truths as the Essenes taught and as John the Baptist preached in the desert," [26]

Masonry's "same old truths," were gathered "from the *Zend-Avesta* and the *Vedas,* from Plato and Pythagoras, from India, Persia, Phonecia, Greece, Egypt and the Holy Books of the Jews . . . These doctrines are the religion and philosophy of Masonry." [27] Obviously, Masonic philosophy makes no room for Christian truths, ethics and values.

Elaborating on Masonic philosophy, Pike said that while Christian Masons may believe the Divine Word became Man, others believe the same thing happened long before to Mithra and Osiris. Therefore, Christians should not object if others see in the Word of St. John what actually is the Logos of Plato or the Unuttered Thought of the first emanation of light or the Perfect Reason. "We do not admit that the Messiah was born in Bethlehem." [28]

The "truths" propagated by Masonry, Pike wrote, are based upon Jewish mystical lore known as Kabbalistic Gnosticism, which was passed to Masonry through the Knights Templar.

Explaining, Pike said there existed at the time of the Templars a sect of "Johannite Christians, who claimed to be the only true initiates into the real mysteries" of the religion of Christ. Adopting in part the Jewish traditions and tales of the Talmud, they said facts recounted in the Gospels "are but allegories." [29]

The Knights Templar, he continued, were from the very beginning "devoted to . . . opposition to the tiara of Rome and the crown of its Chiefs. . . ." [30]

The object of the Templars, he said, was to acquire influence and wealth, then to "intrigue and at need fight to establish the Johannite or Gnostic and Kabbalistic dogma. . . ." [31]

Again identifying Freemasonry with the Knights Templar, Pike declared: "The Papacy and rival monarchies . . . are sold and bought in these days, become corrupt, and to-morrow, perhaps, will destroy each other. All that will become the heritage of the Temple: the World will soon come to us for its Sovereigns and Pontiffs. We shall constitute the equilibrium of the universe, and be rulers over the masters of the world." [32]

He said the Templars, like other secret societies, had two doctrines: One was concealed and reserved for the Masters, which was Johannism; the other, publicly practiced, was Roman Catholic. Thus, Freemasonry, he said, "vulgarly imagined to have begun with the Dionysian Architects or German Stone-workers, adopted St. John the Evangelist as one of its patrons, associating with him in order not to arouse the suspicion of Rome . . . [and] thus covertly proclaiming itself the child of the Kabbalah and Essenism together." [33]

The Johannism of the Adepts, he added, "was the Kabbalah of the earlier Gnostics." [34]

Referring to the trial of the Templars, (which lasted from 1307 to 1314, and involved charges that Templars denied Christ was God, abjured other basic Catholic beliefs, including the Sacraments, spat and urinated upon the Crucifix, and regularly engaged in homosexuality and other obscene acts) [35]), Pike said: Pope Clement V and Philip the Fair [of France] could not fully explain to the people at large "the conspiracy of the Templars against the Thrones and the Tiara. To do so would propagate the religion of Isis." [36]

Jacques De Molay, Grand Master of the Knights Templar was executed in 1314. However, before he died, according to Pike, he instituted what came to be called the occult Hermetic or Scottish Masonry, the Lodges of which were established in four metropolitan areas, Naples, Edinburg, Stockholm, and Paris. These Lodges, Pike asserted, were the initial Lodges of modern Freemasonry. [37]

The former Grand Commander of the Scottish Rite also asserted that the secret movers of the French Revolution had sworn upon the tomb of De Molay to overthrow Throne and Altar. Then, when King Louis XVI of France was executed [1793], "half the work was done; thenceforward, the Army of the Temple was to direct all its efforts against the Pope." [38]

The Church and Christianity are clearly the major enemies of Pike's Freemasonry. Christianity, he said, taught the doctrine of Fraternity, but repudiated that of political equality because it inculcated obedience to Caesar and to those lawfully in authority. [39]

According to Pike, the Samaritan Jews, using Kabbalistic data, characterized the "vulgar faith" by the figure of Thartac, a god represented with a book, a clock, and the head of an ass. This was because they believed Christianity was under the reign of Thartac, since its adherents preferred "blind faith and utter credulity . . . to intelligence and science. [40]

Concerning Heaven and Hell, Pike wrote: "The present is Masonry's scene of action—man is on earth to live, to enjoy. He is not in this world to hanker after another.

"The unseen can not hold a higher place in our affections than the seen," he declared, and added: Only those "who have a deep affection for this world will work for its amelioration. [41]

Ascetism, said Pike, is "unnatural" and "moribund." Those whose affections are transferred to Heaven, easily acquiesce in the miseries of earth. "Those given most decidedly to spiritual contemplation, and make religion rule their life are most apathetic toward improving this world's systems. They are conservators of evil and hostile to political and social reform." [42]

The writings of the Apostoles, Pike said, were only "articles of the vulgar faith." The real mysteries of knowledge handed down from generation to generation by superior minds were the teachings of the Gnostics . . . and in them [we find] some of the ideas that form part of Masonry." [43]

To Pike, Christ was not unique. The fundamental teachings concerning Jesus are commonly believed of Krishna, the Hindu Redeemer, he said. Born of a virgin, performing miracles, raising people from the dead. Krishna descended into Hell, rose again, ascended into Heaven, charged his disciples to teach doctrines and gave them a gift of miracles. [44]

Speaking of the Catholic Church, Pike wrote: "By what right . . . does the savage, merciless, persecuting animal endeavor to delude itself that it is not an animal?" [45]

In his commentary on the Council of Kadosh, Pike inferentially referred to the Holy Eucharist, and said:

The chief symbol of man's ultimate redemption is the fraternal supper of bread and wine. This fraternal meal teaches among other things "that many thousands who died before us might claim to be joint owners with ourselves of the particles that compose our mortal bodies, for matter ever forms new combinations: and the bodies of the ancient dead, the Patriarchs before and since the Flood, the Kings and common people of all ages, resolved into their constituent elements, are carried upon the wind over all continents, and continually enter into and form part of the habitations of new souls creating new bonds of sympathy and brotherhood between each man that lives and all his race.

"And thus the bread we eat, and the wine we drink tonight may enter into and form part of us the identical particles of matter that once formed parts of the material bodies called Moses, Confucius,

Plato, Socrates, or Jesus of Nazareth. In the truest sense we eat and drink the bodies of the dead. . . ." [46]

Over and over again, *Morals and Dogma* (MAD) emphasizes that Freemasonry is a religion based on the occult Jewish philosophy found in the Kabbalah.

The key to the true meaning of the symbols within the Temple is found in the occult philosophy of the Kabbalah, Pike said, and subsequently asserted that Masonry owes all its symbols and secrets to the Kabbalah. [47]

"It is the province of Masonry to teach all truths, not moral truth alone, but political and philosophical, and even religious truth," he said. [48] Masonry, he insisted is "the universal morality." [49]

And again: "The religious faith . . . taught by Masonry is indispensable to the attainment of the great ends of life. . . ." [50] Pike proclaimed that "every Masonic Lodge is a temple of religion; and its teachings are instruction in religion. . . ." [51]

The Degree Rose Cross teaches "the ultimate defeat and extinction of evil and wrong and sorrow by a Redeemer or Messiah yet to come, if he has not already appeared." [52]

Earlier commentators on Masonry have contended that Masonry is a State within the State. *Morals and Dogma* gives credence to that view by insisting that Masonry determines whether heads of State should stay in power.

"Edicts by a despotic power, contrary to the Law of God or the Great Law" of Nature, destructive of the inherent rights of man, and violative of the right of free thought, free speech, free conscience warrant lawful rebellion, he said [53] And, he noted, "resistance to power usurped is not merely a duty which man owes to himself and his neighbor, but a duty which he owes to his God.: [54]

If rulers have the Divine Right to govern, the true Masonic initiate will cheerfully obey, said Pike. [55]

The problem faced by both rulers and people is to know who has a "Divine Right" to govern; and how much freedom is permitted for speech and conscience in a state before rebellion is warranted. *Morals and Dogma* strongly indicates that Masonry alone will make such determinations.

Pike also makes clear that those in the lower degrees of Masonry are "intentionally misled by false interpretations" of the symbols of the Craft. "It is not intended," he said that Masons in the Blue Degrees (the first three degrees) "shall understand them; but it is intended that [they] shall imagine" they do. The true explanations of the

symbols are "reserved for the Adepts, the Princes of Masonry," he
said. [56]

Those are some highlights from a book that has been extolled in the
New Age magazine for over 60 years as the philosophic foundation
upon which Scottish Rite Freemasonry stands. While many members
of the Fraternity have found the book turgid and tedious, obviously
many others look upon it as a great source of wisdom. In January,
1950, the Scottish Rite Committee on Publications reminded members of the Craft that they were "expected to be leaders and teachers
of the people," and that the basic philosophy undergirding their efforts
must be *Morals and Dogma*. [57]

It can be little doubted that Pike had the pulse of Masonry. And
long prior to publication of his opus, the Supreme Council of the
Scottish Rite of the Southern Jurisdiction issued a circular which asserted: "Above the idea of country is the idea of humanity." [58]

A Mason has written that Masonry exists the world over "and is
susceptible of forming, at any moment, with its various Masonries, a
homogenous bloc, or mass, pursuing a common ideal. That ideal is
the emancipation of Humanity." [59]

One well-informed non-Masonic student of the Craft said that to
promote the Masonic concept of "the welfare of humanity" and elimination of "ignorance and prejudice" meant in practical terms Masonic
attacks on altar and throne. [60]

The same source also said the true purpose of Freemasonry is "the
fall of all dogmas and the ruin of all churches." [61]

The Grand Commander of Scottish Rite Masonry of the Southern
Jurisdiction revealed that Manuel Quezon, first President of the Philippines Senate and later the first President of the Philippine Commonwealth, declined to accept the "rank and dignity" of the 33rd degree
of Freemasonry, because he "feared, some way, sometime, that there
might be some obligation in accepting the honor which would be in
conflict with his allegiance to the Philippines." [62]

Albert Pike

The only monument to a Confederate general in the nation's capital
stands on public property between the U.S. Department of Labor
Building and the city's Municipal Building on D Street, N.W., between Third and Fourth Streets. It is a statue of Albert Pike, the grand

philosopher of Scottish Rite Masonry, who was indicted for treason for his activities during the Civil War.

Clad in a frock coat and weskit, wearing shoulder-length hair, the bewhiskered Pike is depicted holding in his left hand a volume of *Morals and Dogma,* his great Masonic treatise.

Chiseled into the statue's pedestal are words which purport to describe the man's abilities; poet, author, jurist, orator, philosopher, philanthropist, scholar and soldier. The sculpture gives no indication that Pike, as a Confederate general, was commander of a band of Indians who scalped and killed a number of Union soldiers during the Battle of Pea Ridge (Ark.). [63]

Military records show that Indians at the Battle of Pea Ridge conducted warfare with "barbarity." Adjutant John W. Noble of the Third Iowa Regiment said: ". . . from personal inspection . . . I discovered that eight of the men . . . had been scalped." [64]

Adjutant Noble added that the bodies had been exhumed and many showed "unmistakable evidence" of having been "murdered after they were wounded." [65]

First sergeant Daniel Bradbury swore he was present at the Battle on March 7, 1862 and saw Indians "doing as they pleased." The next day, he saw about 3,000 Indians "marching in good order under the command of Albert Pike." [66]

In a letter, dated March 21, 1862, Pike was admonished by D.H. Maury, assistant Adjutant General of the Trans-Mississippi District "to restrain [Indians under his command] from committing any barbarities upon the wounded prisoners, or dead who may fall into their hands." [67]

The New York Times reported that Pike had "seduced" the Indians into war paint." [68]

Pike was born in Massachusetts in 1809, but moved to Arkansas as a young man where he became president of the State Council of the anti-Catholic American Party.

In 1861, Pike wrote a pamphlet "State or Province, Bond or Free," addressed to the people of Arkansas following Abraham Lincoln's election to the Presidency of the United States, but prior to his inauguration. In the pamphlet, Pike said the border States should at once "unite with the states that have seceded and are yet to secede, meet them in convention, and aid in framing a Constitution and setting on foot a Government."

Then, he continued, there will no longer be a few seceded States, "but a new and powerful confederacy, to attempt to coerce which would be a simple fatuity. A war against it would be too expensive a luxury for the North to indulge in, and would, moreover, defeat its own purpose." [69]

Pike served as Commissioner to the Indians West of Arkansas in the Confederate States of America, and between July 10 and October 7, 1861 concluded Treaties of Friendship and Alliance with seven Indian nations on behalf of the Confederacy. The treaties gave certain tribes the unqualified right of admission as a State of the Confederacy and allowed each tribe a delegate in the Confederate Congress. However, President Jefferson Davis of the Confederacy urged that aspect of the treaties be deleted.

Subsequently, the Comanchees were "greatly astonished on being informed that they had made a treaty with enemies of the Government of their Great Father in Washington." [70]

That history of Albert Pike is rarely, if ever, discussed by Masons. He remains to them "an outstanding man," [71] a "great man, . . . a truly universal and creative genius, . . . an inexhaustible mine of inspiration, [and] a mental and spiritual giant." [72]

Other Integral Characteristics of Masonry

There are other distasteful characteristics integral to Masonry which are little noted, but deserve mention.

Prejudice

Masonry's "Landmarks," have been described by a Craftsman as "those peculiar marks of distinction by which we are separated from the profane world, and by which we are enabled to designate our inheritance as the 'Sons of light.' These landmarks are "unrepealable" and "can suffer no change." [73]

Among such inflexible laws of Masonry is Landmark No. 18, which lists qualifications for membership in the Craft. That Landmark says no man can be a Freemason unless he is "unmutilated" and "free-born." It is further stipulated that neither women, slaves, nor one born in slavery, are qualified for initiation into the rites of the Masonic Fraternity. [74]

In that connection, it is interesting to note that Albert Pike, writing of the Aryans who peopled the earth about 10,000 years ago, said:

"They were white men, . . . the superior race in intellect, in manliness, the governing race of the world, the conquering race of all other nations."

Continuing, he asserted: "The single fact that we owe not one single truth, not one idea in philosophy or religion to the Semitic race is, of itself, ample reward for years of study, and it is a fact indisputable, if I read the *Veda* and *Zend Avesta* aright." [75]

The *Veda* is the collection of sacred writings of the Aryans who invaded Northern India in 1500 B.C. The *Zend Avesta* is a compilation of the sacred writings and commentary thereon of the Zoroastrian religion of ancient Persia.

In his *Lectures on the Arya,* Pike noted the Yima (first of all men created, and the first with whom Ahru Mazda conversed) ultimately lived among people who had perfect stature and "no other marks which are the token of Anra-Mainyus, the Evil Principle, which he has made among men."

Regarding the "other marks," Pike said:

"By which it appears that deformity was considered as a mark put on man by the Evil One; and that Yima selected for his colonists only those in whom there was no physical defect." [76]

Perhaps that Zoroastrian view is responsible for Masons permitting only the "unmutilated" to "colonize" lodges of the Craft, as required by the Fraternity's Landmark 18.

Another example of Masonic prejudice was evidenced in a 1928 *New Age* review of a book, *Reforging America* by Dr. Lothrop Stoddard. The reviewer said the book's author "clearly demonstrates the necessity of America retaining its racial purity." The reviewer added: "[T]he influence of Masonry upon the author's philosophy is evident throughout the volume." [77]

Another article in the official journal of the Scottish Rite concerned the Indians of Mexico and purported to explain why so many revolutions have occurred in that country. The article said:

"The Indian, as such, is superstitious, immobile, a silhouette of stone. He breeds rapidly and would completely overrun the country and dominate by sheer force of numbers were it not for the fact that during each 'revolution' hundreds of Indians are killed or die from disease.

"The Indian of today in Mexico is the 'leftover', still native and Christian, God-fearing, a superstitious dominated being." [He is part of] a structure of ignorance, slavery and servitude . . . under the domination of the Church, whose sole idea was to maintain this servitude and ignorance." [78]

Commenting on the fact that Negro Masons have their own exclusive black Masonic organization, Grand Commander John Cowles explained that "most of the so-called colored Grand Lodges" trace their history to Prince Hall, a Negro who claimed that he was initiated in an English Army Lodge in Boston. Then the Grand Commander noted that "all regular Grand Lodges in the United States do not recognize any colored or Negro Masonry." [79]

Cowles addressed the same subject in 1947, but said it is not "because of their color" that blacks are not allowed into the lodges of "regular" Masonry. Rather, it is "the general characteristics of the race as it exists in this country and the apparent incompatible social reactions of the two races." [80]

The Grand Commander called attention to a photostatic copy of a joint letter in the files of the Supreme Council signed by the Grand Secretary of the Grand Lodge of Massachusetts and the Deputy of the Supreme Council of the Scottish Rite of the Northern Jurisdiction in Massachusetts, dated February 7, 1925, which allegedly says a black member was expelled from Freemasonry "on the technical ground that he had falsified as to the place of his birth; that . . . [he] had claimed to be an Indian, and that the Grand Lodge had evidence 'amply sufficient to prove that he was not an Indian at all, but a Negro, and other things to his discredit.' " [81]

Cowles said that on one side of the photostatic copy of the Massachusetts Grand Secretary's letter appears the statement: "The Masons could not afford to admit that they had initiated a Negro, so he was expelled upon the technical ground of fraud in naming his birthplace." [82]

In 1976, a Masonic affiliate organization for girls, the International Order of the Rainbow, suspended all Iowa chapters of the group because one local chapter endorsed membership of a 12-year-old black girl.

According to press reports, Michelle Palmer, whose father is white and mother is black, had been invited to join the Rainbow chapter in Indianola, Iowa, and was approved by the local assembly in October of that year. However, officials at the Rainbow's international headquarters at McAlester, Oklahoma ruled that all 136 Rainbow assemblies in Iowa must disband by the end of the year because they did not follow "rules and regulations."

It was explained that the organization took disciplinary action on the basis of an "unwritten law" which excludes blacks from membership. [83]

Subsequently, it was reported that a majority of the nation's 61 Rainbow assemblies voted to drop the so-called "unwritten law" which banned Negro girls from Rainbow. [84]

This Masonic racism persists to this day in both "regular" Masonry and Prince Hall Masonry, and the issue is rarely questioned in nominations to the judiciary or to other positions in government which require the strictest sense of fairness.

In 1979, *The Washington Star* carried an article by Robert Pear, the lead paragraph of which read: "Should a federal judge belong to a social club that excludes blacks—or women?

The article went on to note that the question occurred with "embarrassing frequency" in connection with President Jimmy Carter's nominees for federal judgeships, because so many of the candidates belong to racially exclusive "social clubs, eating clubs or other fraternal organizations.

Pear wrote: "The issue of white-only private clubs haunted Attorney General Griffin B. Bell at his confirmation hearings in 1977. He agreed to resign from the Piedmont Driving Club and the Capital City Club in Atlanta because, he said, 'the attorney general is so symbolic of equal justice under the law.' " [85]

Of course, even more the symbols of equal justice are the Justices of the Supreme Court of the United States.

The National Association for the Advancement of Colored People [NAACP] and the National Women's Political Caucus [NWPC], Pear observed in his *Star* article, "say judges should not belong to any clubs that discriminate on the basis of race, sex, religion or national origin." [86]

Interestingly enough, On May 6, 1983, Vice President George Bush addressed the all-black Prince Hall Grand Masters of Masons, at the invitation of Benjamin Hooks, president of the NAACP, and a Grand Mason secretary from Tennessee. [87]

Adding insult to injury, the State Supreme Court of New Jersey decided in 1986 that a low-level State-court employee, must step down as an officer of a local NAACP chapter in order to avoid the appearance of judicial involvement in political disputes.

The State Supreme Court also ordered the Monmouth County Superior Court attendant in question to resign from a taxpayers' group, a local mental-health board and four other groups. [88]

Earlier, the Maryland Senate enacted legislation to deny a tax exemption to Burning Tree Country Club because it discriminates against women. The amendment exempted the Masons, the Elks and

the Moose, because they were considered "charitable organizations."
[89]

Atheism

A careful reading of Masonic literature will make it evident that the
Craft rejects God of the Scriptures.

The basic Masonic law requires initiates never to be "a stupid atheist." But a knowledgeable Mason observed: "Let us not be deceived.
All atheists are not stupid." [90]

Pike, writing of atheism, said Nature is "self-originated, or always
was and had been the cause of its own existence." [91]

The test as to belief in God, he asserted, is whether the qualities
exist, "regardless of what name is given these qualities."

Real atheism, he said, "is the denial of existence of *any* God, of the
actuality of all possible ideas of God. It denies that there is any Mind,
Intelligence or Ens that is the cause and Providence of the
Universe. . . ." [92]

Joseph Fort Newton, one of the Fraternity's august theologians,
declared: "To enter our Lodges a man must confess his faith in God—
though he is not required definitely to define in what terms he thinks
of God . . ." [93]

Newton explained Masonic faith as follows: "Faith in the Universe
as friendly to fraternal enterprise . . . [I]t affirms . . . that man was
made for man." [94]

Another Masonic writer said: "man is divine, and his divinity is
within himself." [95] And yet another *New Age* writer declared:
"When we talk to God we are talking to ourselves, for God and Man
are one and the same through the ties of Love. . . ." [96]

Teacher of the World's Children

A previously noted quotation by Albert Pike (Page 47, above), is
important to recall. He said: "It is the province of Masonry to teach
all truths, not moral truth alone, but political and philosophical, and
even religious truth."

Indeed, shaping the minds of the world's youth has been an unremitting major activity of the Masonic Fraternity.

Historian Mildred Headings said the true purpose pursued by
French Masons is "the fall of all dogmas and the ruin of all
churches." [97] She also noted that the Fraternity successfully cam-
paigned in France to promote universal obligatory lay education and
the use of school texts with Masonic values. [98]

And what happened in France, has happened largely in America.

In 1915, the Scottish Rite urged that graduates of American public schools be given "preference in every appointment to public office." [99]

In 1920, during a special session held at Colorado Springs, Colorado, the Supreme Council of the Scottish Rite drew up a comprehensive education plan for the youth of the country. The plan called for sending all children through public schools for a certain number of years, and recommended the careful selection of school trustees and teachers, as well as supervisors of school textbooks and libraries in order to exclude "sectarian propaganda." [100]

The Masonic plan also urged the establishment of "a national department of public education headed by a secretary appointed as a member of the President's Cabinet." [101]

Almost immediately, the Craft's various journals propagandized in favor of the proposals which were generally embodied in legislation that through the 1920s and 30s was known as the Smith-Towner Bill, the Towner-Sterling Bill, and the Sterling-Reed Bill, reflecting the names of the Representatives and Senators who introduced the legislation. [102]

In 1922, the State of Oregon, with the Help of the Supreme Council and the Imperial Council of the Nobles of the Mystic Shrine [the group so beloved for its children's hospitals and circus presentations), was successful in lobbying for the passage of legislation which outlawed Catholic and other parochial schools in the State. [103]

The law was declared unconstitutional by the U.S. Supreme Court in 1925, in *Pierce v. Society of Sisters,* 268 U.S. 510, (See pp. 5-6).

The "apostle of free, public schools," Horace Mann, was a Freemason, and, according to his wife, was an enthusiastic advocate of the philosophy of religion, a philosophy which was "scientific, humanitarian, ethical, [and] naturalistic. . . ." Mann believed in "character education without 'creeds,' and in phrenology as a basis for 'scientific education.' " He held that "natural religion stands . . . preeminent over revealed religion . . ." [104]

In 1930, a Masonic writer said: "In America, public education is the right and duty of the state . . . For the time may come . . . when by unchecked operation of biologic law, and other considerations, Catholics will be a majority in these United States . . ." [105]

Four years later, another *New Age* contributor boldly proclaimed: "The practical object of Masonry is the moral, intellectual and spiritual improvement of the individual and society." [106]

But by 1935, the Masonic efforts to totally dominate the minds of American children had not come to fruition because, as a *New Age* editorial noted, eight of the 15 members of the House Committee on Education were Roman Catholics. That situation prompted the Scottish Rite journal to say: "Hence, so long as this condition exists in Congress there will be little opportunity for creating a Department of Education. [107]

It is now apparent, that if that handful of Catholic members of the House Education Committee had not prevailed, and subsequently been succeeded by equally steadfast Catholic Congressmen and Senators into the very early 1960s, every school child (including this writer) might have been propagandized with naturalism as the established national religion, long before the Masonically-dominated Supreme Court effectively imposed that curriculum on the nation's public school system when it outlawed Bible reading and school prayers in 1962 and 1963.

If the views of one Masonic writer are reasonably representative of the mind of Masonry, which they undoubtedly are, the likelihood of a Masonically-imposed naturalism on America's school children was clearly a possibility before mid-20th Century. The writer declared:

"The dramatic presentation of the 32nd degree of the Scottish Rite expresses a code of ethics which is essentially natural religion. . . . In this support of natural religion, Scottish Rite masonry presents an excellent example of what might be followed in our public schools . . . There can be no well-founded objection to the presentation of natural religion." [108]

Another recommendation for public school children was that they should be taught the "balance between good and evil." [109] Nine years later, the same theme was advanced in an editorial which called for strengthening "education for life . . . the knowledge of good and evil." [110]

The official organ of the Scottish Rite of the Southern Jurisdiction published an article in 1959 which said every Mason becomes a teacher of "Masonic philosophy to the community," and the Craft is "the missionary of the new order—a Liberal order . . . in which Masons become high priests." [111]

The article proclaimed that this "Masonic philosophy" which has brought forth a "New Order" had become a reality by "the establishment of the public school system, financed by the State, for the combined purpose of technological and sociological education of the mass of humanity, beginning at an early age in childhood." [112]

At the same time, another Craftsman asserted that the Fraternity "provided the major obstacle" to the growth of religious-oriented education. [113]

In 1968, a 33rd Degree Mason said: "The keynote of Masonic religious thinking is naturalism which sees all life and thought as ever developing and evolutionary . . ." [114]

The Bible, said Brother Leonard Wenz, "is not today what it once was." Current higher criticism, he observed, has "made obsolete the idea that the Bible is a unique revelation of supernatural truth." [115]

While the Court has outlawed public recitation of the Bible as a religious work in public schools, the "Americanism" program of the Scottish Rite has mandated that members of the Fraternity disseminate Masonic materials in public schools. [116] And the brethren take that role seriously.

In 1959, the Grand Commander said Franklin W. Patterson, 33rd Degree, secretary of the Scottish Rite Lodge at Baker, Oregon, succeeded in persuading the principal of the local high school to use Masonic-oriented texts in the local public schools. [117]. Also, the Scottish Rite bodies of Alexandria, Virginia "placed the *New Age* magazine in all public school libraries within their jurisdiction." [118]

In 1965, Grand Commander Luther A. Smith reported that Masonic booklets had been "distributed by sets to every room in every school" in the Charlotte, North Carolina public school system. The Superintendent of Schools for that jurisdiction made the Masonic propaganda "required reading." [119]

In 1965, Major General Herman Nickerson, 33rd Degree, Commander of the U.S. Marine Corps facility at Camp Lejune, N.C., was commended by the Supreme Council for introducing the Supreme Council's books on "Americanism" into the schools under his command attended by children of Marine Corps personnel. [120] In 1966, General Nickerson received an award from the Freedoms Foundation at Valley Forge, PA., for "his citizenship program at Camp Lejune. . . ." [121]

Subsequently, General Nickerson became Director of Personnel for the U.S. Marine Corps and on May 8, 1968 was the principal speaker when 17 West Point cadets "were obligated " as "soldier Masons," one month prior to being commissioned second lieutenants "to carry out our ideals in Viet Nam." [122]

George Washington University in the nation's capital has long had close ties to Freemasonry, and has been the recipient of its largess. Not only did it receive $1 million from the Masons in the 1920s, it has received additional funds from the Masonic International "High Twelve Clubs," the Masons of Louisiana, the National League of Masonic Clubs, and the Knights Templar [123]

When George Washington University restructured its Masonic-funded School of Government in 1966, it consolidated the Department of Government and Business and existing programs "at the U.S. Air Force Command and Staff School, Maxwell Air Force Base in Alabama, and the Industrial College of the Armed Forces (ICAF) at Ft. McNair, Washington, D.C."

The consolidation was effected only "after a conference was held with Grand Commander [Luther] Smith and his approval obtained." [124]

The ICAF is the highest and most prestigious of all federal educational institutions.

Moreover, Masonic influence is threaded through most college fraternities, and their rituals were written and insignia designated by Masons. However, only four college fraternities were founded exclusively for Masons: Acacia, founded at the University of Michigan in 1904; Square and Compass, founded at Washington and Lee University in 1917; Sigma Mu Sigma, (Tri-State College, in 1921); and the Order of the Golden Key, founded at the University of Oklahoma in 1925.

In 1952, Square and Compass merged with Sigma Mu Sigma, "to thoroughly indoctrinate the college men of America with the traditions of our American Masonic heritage." [125]

PART II

TARGET—THE CHURCH

3/ WARRING ON THE CHURCH—I

A cursory review of the social climate at the time State and federal laws were enacted to deny aid to "sectarian" institutions, sadly discloses those statutes really are musty memorials to appeasement of Know-Nothings, who once ruled America.

Those statutory stains of bigotry were designed primarily to prohibit equality of government assistance for Catholic parochial schools which were competing with the essentially Protestant public school system. Ultimately, those laws served as historic precedent to buttress arguments by the Court in subsequent decisions which outlawed nearly all public accommodation for traditional Judeo-Christian beliefs and values in public life.

Moreover, the Masonic Fraternity, an age-old militant enemy of the Church, strongly influenced the secret societies which formed the hard core of the Nativist and Know-Nothing movements that lobbied so successfully to impose those essentially anti-Catholic edicts upon the nation.

This was evident, not only by the secrecy Know-Nothings imposed on their members to conceal the organization's true purpose, but by Masonic membership of Know-Nothing leaders.

Nativism was characterized by the late Canon Anson Phelps Stokes as "the aggressive American Anglo-Saxon Protestant tradition," which goes back to the Reformation in England and came to America through the New England Puritans.

That tradition, he said, "developed the 'No-Popery' slogan as a protection against the feared overthrow of the English form of civil government." [1].

He noted that Nativism, coalesced under a variety of titles: the Native American Democratic Association; the Order of the Sons of

America; the Order of the Star Spangled Banner; the Order of Know-Nothings; the American Protective Association; and the Invisible Empire of the Knights of the Ku Klux Klan. [2]

A more accurate perspective on the groups mentioned by the former Canon of the Washington Cathedral was provided by Albert Stevens in his seminal book on the origins of secret societies in the United States. He found that the Masonic Fraternity is "the parent organization of all modern secret societies." [3]

Stevens traced the "germ" of American patriotic and political secret societies to the Loyal Orange institution, which "had Masonic antecedents." Its cardinal principle, he said, was "loyalty to the occupants of the British throne and opposition to the Roman Catholic Church." [4]

Orangeism appeared early in the United States, "and the members of earlier American patriotic secret societies (1840-1855) were pronounced 'Native Americans' and anti-Roman Catholic: The Orders of United American mechanics (Senior and Junior), Sons of America, Brotherhood of the Union, American Protestant Association, the Know Nothing party (Order of the Star Spangled Banner), and others, were conspicuous during the period referred to . . . others spreading into the American Protective Association movement, which had been conspicuous in American politics." [5]

However, anti-Catholic bias came to America long before the Know-Nothing movement. As Stokes observed, it was evident in the first colonial settlements.

Prior to the 19th Century, concern about the Church's inroads into America was demonstrated by stringent opposition to the Quebec Act, passed by the British Parliament in 1774 to institute a permanent administration in Canada. It was one of the "Intolerable Acts" complained of by the American colonists, and was directly alluded to in the "Declaration of Independence."

The Act, which contributed to the outbreak of the American Revolution, gave the French Canadians complete religious freedom. However the American colonists saw it as nullifying "many of the Western claims of the coast colonies by extending the boundaries of the province of Quebec to the Ohio River on the South and the Mississippi River on the west. The concessions in favor of Roman Catholicism also aroused resentment among Protestants in the Colonies." [6]

It was obvious, too, that the Act effectively extended the jurisdiction of the Bishop of Quebec into those western areas, a matter of some concern to the Protestant colonists.

Further evidence of the second-class status of Catholics in colonial

America was set forth in the early constitutions of Massachusetts (1780), New Hampshire (1796), New Jersey (1790), North Carolina (1776), and Vermont (1786), all of which expressly stated a preference for the "Protestant" religion. [7]

The pervasiveness of this opposition to all things Catholic was evident in an examination by Sister Marie Lenore Fell of more than 1,000 textbooks used in public schools during the period 1783-1860. Sister Marie pursued her research to determine the influence of these books on youth who later became "rulers of the country and molders of party politics." [8]

She found the "no Popery" cries, so common during the years preceding the Civil War, could be traced to the childhood training of the nation's leaders. [9]

Her investigations demonstrated that the Quebec Act was stressed in a number of school texts. [10]

Among those texts, Samuel Whelpy's *A Compend of History,* (which went through many editions between 1807-1856) asserted that the powers of the ecclesiastical state from the first part of the 7th Century were "carnal, sensual, and devilish." [11]

Whelpy also identified the Church of Rome with the woman, sitting on a scarlet-colored beast, who is called "the mother of harlots" in St. John's Apocalypse. He identified the beast as "the temporal powers which gave her support." [12]

Another text charged that Popery kept the people of Europe in ignorance by forbidding them to inquire into their duties, and commanded them to believe whatever priests told them. The ignorant people, the author wrote, would work for the priests and support large numbers of them in idleness. [13]

Conrad Malte-Brun's *A System of Universal Geography* (1834), depicted the Church in Catholic countries as prohibiting the dissemination of knowledge and of keeping the people in ignorance. [14]

This type of education, perpetuated through public auspices, shaped the future Church-State conflicts and fueled the attendant violence. It also assured that the fullness of the free exercise of religion would be denied to Catholics, who were by far the largest non-Protestant minority group.

Insult, Abuse, And Violence

The almost inexhaustible catalogue of insult, abuse and violence against one religious minority in America can only be highlighted.

On November 3, 1831, St. Mary's Catholic Church on Sheriff

Street, New York City, was deliberately set afire and totally destroyed with its furnishings and sacred vessels. No effort was made to fix responsibility by judicial inquiry. [15]

In 1836, Bishop John Purcell of Cincinnati deplored the caluminous writings against Catholics which were distributed everywhere. Above all, he was concerned because religious and political tracts were made available to children and imbued them with hatred and prejudice against the Catholic Church. [16]

Protestant preachers urged their members to preserve the nation from the blight of Romanism, asserting that the Valley of the Mississippi was to be either a sacred depository or sepulcher for their own religious and Christian principles, which now were endangered by the Roman Catholic Church. [17]

Among the most notable opponents of the rise of Catholicism in the West was the famous Boston Presbyterian clergyman, Rev. Lyman Beecher.

On August 11, 1834, following a series of anti-Catholic sermons by Beecher, the Ursuline Convent at Charlestown, a Boston suburb, was set afire and sacked by a mob. Even the cemetery was violated: graves were dug up, coffins were opened, and their contents exposed. [18]

In his best-selling book, *A Plea For The West,* the Boston clerical firebrand wrote: ". . . the conflict which is to decide the destiny of the West will be a conflict of institutions for the education of her sons, for the purposes of superstition, or evangelical light; of despotism or liberty." [19]

He insisted that the Catholic clergy, because of their "unlimited power" over the consciences of the immigrants, "would exert decisive political influence." He further warned:

"If we do not provide the schools which are requisite for the cheap and effectual education of the children of the nation, it is perfectly certain that the Catholic powers of Europe intend to make up the deficiency, and there is no reason to doubt that they will do it, until, by immigration and Catholic education, we become to such an extent a Catholic nation, that with their peculiar power of acting as one body, they will become the predominant power of the nation." [20]

Later, the Boston minister wrote in his autobiography: "Before I left (Boston), the tide had turned and Catholicism forever in New England must row upstream, carefully watched and increasingly understood and obstructed by public sentiment." [21]

On August 19, 1835, an editorial appeared in the *Detroit Journal and Courier,* a Whig publication, which said foreigners and Catholics were "chosen instruments of the demagogues to strengthen and perpetuate their ruinous influence over the people of this country." [22]

A public school teacher in Buffalo taught the children under his care that "the Catholics, no matter where they dwell, are considered lower in the scale of mental cultivation and refinement than the Protestant," and that "the degradation is due to their being deprived of the Bible by their priesthood." [23]

Author Carlton Beals noted that James Harper, head of Harper Brothers publishing house, was elected the first Know-Nothing Mayor of New York City, and the publishing house itself had set up a front firm, operated by two Harper employees, to publish the obscenely anti-Catholic tract, *The Awful Disclosures of Maria Monk.* The book was an overnight best-seller, and sold more than 300,000 copies prior to the Civil War. [24]

Samuel F.B. Morse, inventor of the telegraph, and a recognized painter of distinction, in his extraordinarily popular book, *Foreign Conspiracy,* pleaded for Protestants to lay aside their inter-sectarian feuds and awake to the menace of Catholicism. He urged them to: unite against Catholic schools; throw out all Catholic office-holders; and terminate lenient immigration and naturalization laws. [25]

In one periodical of the day it was remarked that abuse of Catholics had become "a regular trade," and the writing and publishing of anti-Catholic books were "a part of the regular industry of the country, as much as the making of nutmeg or the construction of clocks." [26]

New York Public School Controversy

By 1840, the religious war against Catholics took a turn for the worse. In New York City, Archbishop John Hughes requested the Public School Society to provide funding for schools under his jurisdiction similar to accommodations made for other religious groups.

The controversy focused on an 1813 law which directed the Free School Society of the City of New York (later called the Public School Society) to apportion educational funds to, among others, "such incorporated religious societies in said city, as now support or hereafter shall establish charity schools within the said city, who may apply for the same."

Shortly thereafter, a number of religious organizations were admitted to participation in the fund. For example, fifty children of Freemasons were taught from 1810 to 1817, by the Free School Society for an annual charge of six dollars per child. After that period, the Freemason's children were educated without charge. [27]

In 1821, Bethel Baptist Church received a portion of the fund, and legislation was passed the following year which provided additional money for that Church to cover the costs of buildings, training of teachers, and for "all other needful purposes of a common school education." [28]

In 1831, the Catholic Orphan Asylum participated in the program. But, nine years later, when the Catholic Benevolent Society applied for funds for parochial school students, because the religious curriculum in the public schools was incompatible with the consciences of Catholic students, the legislature passed a law which denied aid to any school which teaches "sectarian doctrine." [29]

Commenting on the incident, historian Ray Allen Billington said the Catholics had "a just cause for complaint against the Public School Society's monopoly over educational facilities in New York City."

He noted that the King James version of the Scriptures was read daily in all of the schools of the Society, and that the regular prayers, singing, and religious instruction were contrary to Catholic belief. The textbooks, particularly were the source of complaint, he said, because "all were blatently Protestant in sympathy and many were openly disrespectful of Catholicism." [30]

Archbishop Hughes requested the School Society to hold a public meeting so both sides of the issue could be aired. The Council agreed, and on October 29, 1840, the New York Ordinary stood alone to defend his position, while arrayed against him was "a whole field of talent gathered from the legal profession and the Protestant clergy."

Hughes spoke for three hours. The rebuttal lasted three whole days. In the climate of the day, it was not surprising that the Bishop lost his case.

Remarking on the outcome of the debate, Dr. Billington wrote: "It was obvious that prejudice was to rule rather than reason." [31]

Because State and City officials would authorize only the King James Bible and Protestant hymns and textbooks in the public schools, Archbishop Hughes urged a completely secular system of education devoid of all sectarian influence. Although a law was passed to accomplish that purpose, the Nativists controlled the educational establishment and the King James Bible remained firmly entrenched in public schools. [32]

To American Protestants there was only one Bible, and if Catholics objected to reading that version, they obviously must be opposed to the Sacred Book. [33]

That view was the flashpoint of the the conflict, and is a misperception which has continued to this day. [34]

The controversy inflamed passions in Philadelphia, Newark, Salem, Albany and Detroit; and propagandists pressed home the idea that all over the country Catholics were trying to gain control of the nation's educational system, in order to subjugate America, just as Beecher and Morse had warned. [35]

The situation greatly intensified in 1842, when a Canadian missionary priest visiting Carbeau, New York, became "justly angered" because a Bible Society distributed the King James version of the Scriptures to Catholics in the parish where he was staying. Over objections by the local pastor, the visiting priest publicly burned several copies of the Bible the Society had distributed.

This "Champlain Bible burning" incident, as it became known, quickly exploded into an issue which aroused national indignation, and convinced an increasing number of people to accept organized anti-Catholicism. [36]

The War Against Catholics Intensifies

At a meeting of the American Protestant Association in Philadelphia on November 22, 1842, ninety-four ministers, representing 12 denominations, signed a constitution which said the Papacy was in its "principles and tendencies, subversive to civil and religious liberty, and destructive to the spiritual welfare of men."

It was agreed that the only way to combat this situation was through united church action. The members pledged to further circulation of the Bible and anti-Catholic books, to "awaken the attention of the community to the dangers which threaten these United States from the assaults of Romanism." [37]

In such a combustible atmosphere, violence, literally, was only a stone's throw away.

• In November, 1844, three-days of rioting took place in Philadelphia, during which a cannon was fired point blank into St. Philip Neri Catholic Church. St. Michael's And St. Augustine's churches were burned, as were 30 Catholic homes. Official inquiry blamed the Papists [38]

• In 1846, during the War with Mexico, Catholic soldiers were not only required to attend Protestant services, but were forced to listen to denunciations of their faith. [39]

• In 1852, Pope Piux IX, like many world leaders, sent a block of marble as a gift to be installed in the Washington Monument, then under construction in the nation's capital. A mob broke into the shed where the block was stored, and stole it. Allegedly the Papal gift was thrown into the Potomac River, although there is no record it has ever been found. [40]

• In 1853, a Navy petty officer was put in chains for refusing to attend Protestant worship. Similar incidents took place in public almshouses. [41]

• In 1853, Archbishop Gaetano Bedini visited the United States *en route* to his post as Papal Nuncio to Brazil. Violence and blood-shed followed as he travelled to Boston, Baltimore, Cincinnati, Pittsburg, St. Louis and Wheeling. On Christmas Day, 1853, an attempt was made on the Nuncio's life by a mob of 600.

Those incidents were incited by Know-Nothing speakers and anti-Catholic attacks in the press. [42]

• On July 4, 1854, natives of Dorchester, Massachusetts celebrated the day by blowing up the Catholic Church of that city at 3 A.M.

Similar destruction of Catholic churches took place at Sidney and Massillon, Ohio, Brooklyn, and Saugerties, New York, Norwalk, Connecticut and Galveston, Texas.

During that same month, a Jesuit priest was tarred and feathered in Ellsworth, Maine. [43]

• On July 8, 1854, a Catholic church in Bath, Maine was burned to the ground after a man, called "the Angel Gabriel," lectured in that city for two days against Popery. [44]

• On July 10, 1854, there was a riot between "Americans and Irish" at Lawrence, Massachusetts, and several Catholic houses were "gutted." [45]

• Five days later, *The New York Daily Times* reported on a Know-Nothing riot at Buffalo, New York in which "seven or eight Irishmen's heads were broken, but no one was killed." [46]

• Also, during that year, the Supreme Court of Maine ruled that school authorities had a right to force the reading of the King James Bible on all children, even though that version of the Scriptures was contrary to Catholic beliefs.

The decision (*Donahoe v. Richards,* 38 Maine, 379) was the

leading judicial standard for the nation for the next 50 years.

• In 1859, a young student, William Wall, was expelled from school in Boston for refusing to read the Protestant version of the Bible and Ten Commandments. Upon his return to school, he was severely beaten for one-half hour by the school headmaster, McLaurin F. Cook, who commented to the class:

> "Here's a boy that refuses to repeat the Ten Commandments. I will whip him 'till he yields if it takes the whole afternoon."

After 30 minutes of such barbarity, the boy relented and did as he was directed. His father took the case to court, but the suit was dismissed by a Know-Nothing judge. [47]

Know-Nothing Power

The political power of the Know-Nothings was so great they claimed to control nearly half of the entire popular vote cast in the 1852 Presidential election. The Party carried municipal elections in Philadelphia, Baltimore, New York, San Francisco and New Orleans. [48]

The New York Daily Times made little effort to disguise its own affinity for the Know-Nothing movement. Not only did it regularly suggest that citizens of Irish descent were not truly Americans (as the above July 11, 1854 headline—"Serious Riot Between Americans and Irish at Lawrence, Mass"—suggests), but it editorialized in support of Know-Nothing candidates.

An editorial in November, 1854, attacked Fernando Wood, nominee of the "Soft Democrats," (those "soft" on the issue of slavery), as being "utterly unfit" to serve as Mayor.

The *Times* asserted that Wood had issued a statement denouncing Know-Nothings, although "it is known to thousands" that he "has been a member of the Order," and "acted as one of its Executive Committee." There was no further evidence to support the statement.

The editorial continued by praising Wood's opponent, "the Know-Nothing and Temperance candidate," James W. Barker.

There immediately followed another editorial titled, "James W. Barker," which claimed the newspaper had received a number of communications defending Barker against attacks that had been made about him.

Despite the *Times* endorsement, Barker lost. [49]

The *Times* seemed enthused by the 1854 election results, as indicated by an editorial headline which proclaimed: "The Victory—The Know-Nothing Movement." [50]

The editorial said the tremendous showing of the Know-Nothing Movement in New York State bears "abundant evidence of its *moral power*" [*sic*].

That movement, the *Times* continued, "rests partly upon hostility to Roman Catholicism," and partly upon jealousy of foreigners. No distinction was made regarding the difference, if any, between the two groups.

The editorial asserted that the "great mass of members of all the great Protestant sects regard Catholicism as far more dangerous than Slavery,—and all Catholics as subject in all things, civil and ecclesiastical, to the dictation of an absolute despot,—who has hitherto held all Europe in subjection, and who now seeks similar authority over the American Republic."

The commentary continued by noting that immigrant Irish citizens had established residence in nearly all communities of any size in the State, "and made themselves unpleasantly felt on the labor, religion, morals, and above all, on the politics of the place."

Emphasizing that Irish voters were not truly Americans, the editorial charged that politicians are "twice as careful to speak pleasantly to an *Irish voter* as to *an American*. [Emphasis added].

The *Times* commentary concluded on a curiously inflammatory note which seemed to sanction some undefined nefarious secret actions against the Irish; possibly even violence. It said: ". . . in a secret society, where no risks are run, the temptation to do something that shall '*fix* these Irish' is too strong to be resisted." [Emphasis by *Times*] [51]

Several days later, the *Times* headline trumpeted: "The Massachusetts Election—Great Know-Nothing Victory."

The headlined article, and a follow-up story, reported that every Congressional candidate supported by the Know-Nothing Order in Massachusetts had been elected to office, as had been the Governor, 342 of 349 members of the State House of Representatives, and all State Senators. [52]

In 1855, a man who later became a towering figure in Scottish Rite Freemasonry as Grand Commander and Grand Philosopher, Albert

Pike, spoke in Philadelphia at the national convention of the Nativist American Republican Party, of which he was an official. However, in his address to the gathering, which The *Times* called a Know-Nothing meeting, Pike said nothing significant. [53]

Governor Neils Brown of Tennessee, addressed the same meeting and said the religion of America, is Protestantism, and it must be protected.

Rome, he observed, "has now a Vatican, and a people who are organ grinders and paupers."

If Catholicism were established in the United States, he warned, the Pope would not only look after the souls of Catholics, but their politics. [54]

Although Pike said nothing significant at Philadelphia, several weeks earlier, on April 30, as President of the Arkansas State Council of the Know-Nothing American Republican Party, he addressed that State's Party members during their first annual convention.

He said he was fearful of foreign-born voters, who he identified as predominantly Catholic, and warned that the foreign vote comprised 30 to 51 percent of the electorate in eight major American cities.

Those cities, and their percentage of foreign voters were identified as: Philadelphia (30 percent); Louisville (32 percent); Boston (34 percent); Baltimore (40 percent); New York (46 percent); Cincinnati (47 percent); New Orleans (49 percent); and St. Louis (51 percent). [55]

Pike and his allies were quite perceptive. During the decade 1845-1855, over a million-and-a-quarter Irish immigrants arrived in the United States and doubled the Catholic population. Also, the German population, including a large number of Catholic immigrants from the Rhine, grew steadily from 1920 onward. [56]

In 1856, the *Times* reported that the National Executive Committee of the Republican Party had contacted the Know-Nothing American Party at its convention with a view toward a merger of the two political entities.

Mr. Elmore of Massachusetts, spoke to his brethren of the American Party, and expressed the hope that the overture by the Republican Party "would be well received, because [concert] of action was the only way in which they could destroy the opposition—Popery, Slavery and Rum." [57]

That effort came to naught, as the slavery issue became the dominant concern of the nation, and former President Millard Fillmore accepted the American Party's offer to be its standard bearer in the forthcoming election. [58]

The war against Catholicism abated with the growing national concern about slavery and the explosion of the Civil War. However, toward the end of the 1860s and the beginning of the 1870s, there were signs that the conflict was being renewed.

The post-War years saw a number of books in circulation attacking the Church. In 1871, for example, a book which included 72 cartoons by the famous artist, Thomas Nast, warned the North and South to beware of efforts by the Vatican to take over the American public school system. Nast's cartoons depicted Irish Catholics and Jesuits as monkeys and apes.

The cartoons and the book's text centered on "Miss Columbia," a figure representing the public school system. She warned, that while the North and South contended with each other, "those who have only come among us lately will usurp all your rights, and, in fact, it will only be the story of the camel over again, and you know such a monopoly as that would be intolerable to both of you." [59]

The Boston *Pilot* reported that by 1873 the militantly anti-Catholic Order of United American Mechanics controlled the entire Boston Police Department and were influential at City Hall. [60]

Further, other surviving Know-Nothing organizations professed the same aims as earlier days: to keep the Bible in public schools; to oppose Catholic schools, and any grants of public money to so-called "sectarian" institutions; and to oppose the election or appointment of Catholics to any public office. [61]

President Ulysses S. Grant, in an address to the Army of the Tennessee at Des Moines, Iowa, on September 29, 1875, said: "Encourage free schools and resolve that not one dollar appropriated for their support shall be appropriated to the support of any sectarian schools." [62]

The following year, in the Hayes-Tilden Presidential battle, the Republican Party's platform called for a Constitutional amendment prohibiting aid to "any school or institution under sectarian control."

In August of that year, Republican Congressman James G. Blaine of Maine introduced a resolution proposing a Constitutional amendment to accomplish what President Grant had advocated. But he added one codicil: "This article shall not be construed to prohibit the reading of the Bible in any school or institution." The proposal was defeated on strictly party lines. [63]

[It is significant that prior to the Civil War, only a few State Constitutions specifically prohibited public funding for religious institutions, although there were statutory proscriptions on such aid in several states prior to the War.] [64]

Blaine's Amendment served to emphasize the focal point of the controversy: all children were expected to be indoctrinated with a general Protestant concept of Christianity, focused on the King James version of the Bible. Those who rejected such indoctrination were considered "sectarian," and, therefore, ineligible to receive financial support from the State.

There can be little doubt that this extremely biased concept of "sectarianism" shaped and influenced a multitude of American legislators and jurists.

That success in proscribing freedom for Catholics and others, apparently led Masonic jurists later to proscribe all conventional religions. The logic was unassailable: if one religion could be proscribed, why not all religion?

Humanum Genus Exposes Masonry

In 1884, the simmering issue of secret societies commanded international attention. On January 14 of that year, *The New York Times* ran a lengthy editorial which noted that Pope Leo XIII was about to issue a major encyclical on Freemasonry.

The *Times* said the Pope "seems to have discovered [that] Freemasonry in this country and in England is a very different sort of thing [than in France and Italy].

"Anything more innocent than the fraternity, as it is in this country, could hardly be desired. . . .

"The Roman Catholic Church, in keeping its members outside the door of this innocent association, has committed a terrible mistake. . . ." [65]

Subsequently, the subject was mentioned briefly on page 1 of the *Times,* where it was noted that the Pope had submitted the encyclical to the College of Cardinals. No details of the document were provided by the *Times.* [66]

However, *The Milwaukee Catholic Citizen* ran a story, datelined Rome, April 16, which said the Pope's letter would defend "the City of God" against "the City of Satan."

Secret societies, the Milwaukee Catholic diocesan weekly said, are locked in a struggle against the Church, and "a grave peril threatens society." Earlier Popes "very properly excommunicated Freemasons."

Socialists, the Milwaukee paper asserted, have their "source of strength in Masonry." [67]

The *Citizen* ran the full text of the encyclical in its issue of May 17, 1884.

The Papal letter was far, far different than the *Times* had suggested and, in reality, expressed a strong condemnation of Freemasonry, as *The Catholic Citizen* had predicted. The Pope was particularly concerned about Masonry's efforts to control the education of youth.

Leo's attack was searing and devastating. He not only confirmed, in substance, what Robison and Barruel had written, but what Masonry's own writings admit.

The Pope said there is a battle raging between "the kingdom of God", and the "kingdom of Satan"; and that "partisans of evil, . . . led on or assisted by . . . Freemasons" are "boldly rising up against God Himself." [68]

He cited seven encyclicals issued between 1738 and 1865 in which various Pontiffs had warned "both princes and nations to stand on their guard, and not allow themselves to be caught by the devices and snares laid out to deceive them" by Masonry and allied secret societies. [69]

Leo said the Church knew about Masonry "by manifest signs of its actions, by the investigation of its causes, by the publication of its laws, and of its rites and commentaries, with the addition often of the personal testimony of those who were in the secret . . . [70]

Continuing, the encyclical noted that Masonry had been denounced by the governments of Holland, Austria, Switzerland, Spain, Bavaria, Savoy, and other parts of Italy.

Freemasonry, he said, was able "by means of fraud or of audacity, to gain such entrance into every rank of the State as to seem to be almost its ruling power." [71]

The Pope declared:

"Freemasons, like the Manichees of old, strive, as far as possible, to conceal themselves, and to admit no witnesses but their own members. As a convenient manner of concealment, they assume the character of literary men and scholars associated for purposes of learning. They speak of their zeal for a more cultured refinement, and of their love for the poor; and they declare their one wish to be the amelioration of the masses, and to share with the largest possible number all the benefits of civil life . . .

"Moreover, to be enrolled, it is necessary that the candidates promise and undertake to be thence foreward strictly obedient to their leaders and masters with utmost submission and fidelity . . . or, if disobedient, to submit to the direst penalties and death itself.

"As a fact, if any are judged to have betrayed the doings of the sect or to have resisted commands given, punishment is inflicted on them not infrequently, and with so much audacity and dexterity that the assassin very often escapes the detection and penalty of his crime." [72]

The ultimate purpose of Freemasonry, Leo said, is "the utter overthrow of that whole religious and political order of the world which the Christian teaching has produced, and the substitution of a new state of things in accordance with their ideas, of which the foundations and laws shall be drawn from mere naturalism." [73]

Fundamental to Masonry and to naturalists, he said, is that human nature and human reason "ought in all things to be mistress and guide." Sincere adherents of Masonry he continued, "care little for duties to God, or pervert them by erroneous and vague opinions. For they deny that anything has been taught by God; they allow no dogma of religion or truth which cannot be understood by the human intelligence, nor any teacher who ought to be believed by reason of his authority." [74]

Addressing specifically the issue of religious education, Leo said Masons imagine States "ought to be constituted without any regard for the laws and precepts of the Church." Moreover, the Pontiff asserted, Masons "teach the great error of this age—that regard for religion should be held as an indifferent matter, and that all religions are alike." [75]

He added: "With the greatest unanimity the sect of the Freemasons also endeavors to take to itself the education of youth. They think that they can easily mold to their opinions that soft and pliant age, and bend it whither they will . . . Therefore, in the education and instruction of children they allow no share, either of teaching or of discipline, to the ministers of the Church; and in many places they have procured . . . that nothing which treats of the most important and most holy duties of men to God shall be introduced into the instructions on morals." [76]

Once the fear of God and reverence for divine laws are taken away, the authority of rulers becomes despised, sedition is permitted, and popular passions are urged to lawlessness, the Pontiff asserted. With no restraint, he continued, "a change and overthrow of all things will necessarily follow."

This change and overthrow "is deliberately planned and put forward by many associations of communists and socialists; and to their undertakings the sect of Freemasons is not hostile, but greatly favors their designs, and holds in common with them their chief opinions." [77]

Freemasons, the Pope declared, "are prepared to shake the foundations of empires, to harass the rulers of the State, to accuse, and to cast them out as often as they appear to govern otherwise than they themselves could have wished . . ." [78]

The Papal catalogue of criminal activity by Freemasons was awesome and frightening. Surely such an indictment of an organization— which the *Times* had assured the public was an "innocent association"—merited an immediate, vigorous and forceful challenge by a newspaper with the stature and prestige of the *Times*.

Such a challenge to the Pope's statements, and a full exposition of Masonry's secret activities, was further warranted in view of the then current controversy in the United States over sectarianism in the schools, and the Pope's charge that Freemasonry "endeavors to take to itself the education of youth".

Masonic Influence In APA

Curiously, however, the *Times* never published even a brief excerpt of the encyclical, nor did it mention the subject again.

Nevertheless, the Papal indictment of Masonry was partially confirmed three years later when a new Know-Nothing secret society, with Masonic ties, captured the nation's allegiance, and intensified the war against the Church and Catholic education.

The new secret society, known as the American Protective Association (APA), was founded on March 13, 1887 at Clinton, Iowa by Henry Francis Bowers and six other men.

Bowers was "an enthusiastic Mason, a member of the Blue Lodge and the thirty-second degree of the Scottish rite." He insisted that the American Republic "was founded by Masons against the wishes of Rome." Moreover, he viewed the APA as an offspring of Masonry, "protecting the republican institutions the Masons had established. " [79]

Cementing the APA's bond to Masonry were life insurance policies on members of the former organization guaranteed by the Knights Templar and the Masons' Life Indemnity Company of Chicago. [80]

The APA's statement of principles said membership in the Catholic

Church "is irreconcilable with American citizenship," and that the organization was opposed "to the holding of offices in National, State, or Municipal government by any subject or supporter of such ecclesiastical power."

Another principle of the group held that religious liberty did not mean "any un-American ecclesiastical power can claim absolute control over the education of children growing up under the Stars and Stripes." [81]

That latter principle was identified as integral to Masonry by Pope Leo XIII in his Encyclical *Humanum Genus,* three years prior to the founding of the APA. [82]

Initiates into this secret Masonically-influenced order bound themselves to secrecy and took a solemn oath not to allow Catholics to enter the organization. They also swore never to employ a Catholic when a Protestant was available; and never to vote for or advocate a Catholic candidate for public office. [83]

Washington Gladden, in a 1894 issue of the *Century Magazine,* said the APA's proscription of Catholics for public office, enjoins its members "to violate the first principle of American constitutional liberty, which forbids discrimination against men on account of their religious belief," in that the Constitution declares "no religious test shall ever be required as a qualification to any office or public trust under the United States." [84]

Gladden also told how the APA circulated a false encyclical of Pope Leo XIII, which purported to assert that the United States belongs to him, and that U.S. citizens are absolved from their oath of allegiance to their country.

The false document also said the Pope was to take "forcible possession" of the United States, and *"it will be the duty of the faithful to exterminate all heretics found within the jurisdiction of the United States."* [Emphasis in original] [85]

That document and similar false statements relating to the Church, including a variety of alleged "oaths of papal leaders and garbled extracts of Catholic writings," were "used as campaign literature all over the land, in all manner of publications, and . . . their genuineness has been editorially asserted and defended in the organs of the order." [86]

Additionally there were tales of consignments of arms being sent to rectories all over the country, as Catholics drilled for war preparations in the basements of their churches. Yet, not a single instance of such wild imaginings, presented as facts, was ever corroborated. [87]

According to *The New York Times,* the APA was circulating a "Devils Catechism" in 1894, which purported to be a series of answers taken from canon laws and other authoritative statements of the Catholic Church.

Typical questions and answers were the following:

"Q. I infer from your argument that the Papal Government is laying its plans to obtain possession of the United States for the purpose of restoring the Roman hierarchy?"

"A. Undoubtedly."

"Q. Then it is the policy of the Roman Church to destroy the Government of the United States,—as it presently exists, by legislation—not by force?

"A. By legislation if possible; but, should legislation prove ineffectual or too tardy for the accomplishment of the object, then a resort to force has already been amply provided for." [88]

Commenting on the "Catechism," the *Times* said the questions and answers were "manufactured out of the whole cloth," but the APA "conspirators have become so accustomed to issuing forged documents that they make very little of this."

The *Times* further asserted: "It is with such material as this that the APA is arousing the 'noble American sentiment.' " [89]

The New York newspaper tied the APA to the Republican Party by noting: "Here in New York, . . . not a single active Republican politician has been found who would speak out against the APA . . ." [90]

While the *Times* rightly viewed the APA as an anti-Catholic extremist organization, it looked favorably upon the National League for the Protection of American Institutions (NLPAI), a high-powered lobby group which favored most of the restrictions on Catholic religious freedom advanced by the APA. In fact, the League was sometimes referred to as an "upper class APA."

Founded in 1889, its platform was "to secure constitutional and legislative safeguards for the protection of the common school system . . . and to prevent all sectarian or denominational appropriations of public funds." [91]

Rev. Thomas J. Morgan, a member of the Board of Managers of the League and Commissioner of Indian Affairs during the Administration of President Benjamin Harrison, explained to the *Times* the fundamental problem facing Catholics in America: they hold different views on the Christian religion. Morgan said:

"The Protestants are divided into numerous friendly divisions, agreeing to the great essentials of religious beliefs, but differing on minor points." [92]

Morgan was an ordained Baptist minister, and had served two terms as vice-president of the National Education Association (NEA). He had a reputation as being anti-Catholic. [93]

The Executive Secretary of the League was Rev. James M. King, pastor of the Union Methodist Church in New York City.

Honorary Vice Presidents of the organization included the well known writer, James Fenimore Cooper; David Starr Jordan, president of Stanford University; and Joseph Medill, owner and publisher of the *Chicago Tribune,* and a major influence in founding the Republican Party. Allegedly, he gave the Party its name.

Other members included such men of stature as Henry Holt, publisher; Henry C. Lea, historian; J. Pierpont Morgan, financier; Levi P. Morton, financier, and Vice President of the United States under President Benjamin Harrison; George L. Putnam, publisher; John D. Rockefeller, businessman and financier; Russell Sage, financier and founder of Western Union Telegraph; Charles Scribner, publisher; Cornelius Vanderbilt, railroad magnate; and Henry Villard, railroad magnate and founder of General Electric Company. [94]

The APA and the League (the latter just being organized at the time) were largely responsible for pushing through Congress the Enabling Act of 1889. That law required the Omnibus States admitted into the Union at that time to include in their Constitutions prohibitions on expenditure of public money for "sectarian" purposes.

The Omnibus States admitted that year were Montana, North Dakota, New Mexico, South Dakota, Utah and Washington. [95]

Typical of the tenor of debate on the issue was the following commentary by Mr. Medill's *Chicago Tribune:*

"Montana and Washington do not include or base their claim [for Statehood] upon their Indian population, but upon their American and white inhabitants. It is not right that new Mexico should enumerate her ignorant, mongrel, foreign-speaking Greasers in order to qualify on a representative basis for admission."

Five days earlier, the Tribune referred to New Mexicans as "weak, stagnant, mentally childish, unproductive rubbish, wretched and imbecile." [96]

The Congressional mandate to the Omnibus States was the first time the federal government took a position against "sectarian" institutions. However the word "sectarian" was never defined by the Act.

Certainly, as will be demonstrated, it was not the intention of Congress nor the League that the government should divorce itself from supporting and encouraging the advancement of Christianity. In fact, for the 312 years immediately prior to 1870, Indian education in this country was under the direction of religious missionary organizations. Then, in the late 19th Century, the federal government especially invited religious denominations to build schools for the Indians. [97]

However, the success of Catholic missionaries in educating the Indians apparently incited concern by the APA and the League. In 1891, for example, Catholic Indian missions received $356,957 from the federal government while all other religious organizations combined received only $204,993. [98]

The League, particularly, began petitioning Congress in 1889 to terminate "sectarian appropriations . . . for Indian education," while at the same time it prevailed upon Protestant organizations to withdraw from the Indian education program. Soon, the Catholic missionaries were the only "sectarian" groups involved in the effort.

Those efforts by the League made the Indian school policy an "issue" in the election of 1892. Some felt that a perception of anti-Catholicism in President Benjamin Harrison's Indian education program, under Rev. Thomas Morgan, resulted in Harrison's defeat by Grover Cleveland.

The APA, meanwhile, hung to the coattails of the League's efforts to end "sectarian appropriations," and was able to gain additional adherents. [99]

By that time, the APA had a new leader, William J. Traynor, a Mason, a member of the Independent Order of Good Templars, Deputy Grand Master of the Grand Orange Lodge of the United States, and a member of the Illustrious Order of the Knights of Malta. [100]

The State of Washington had the largest per capita membership (115,000 members in a total population of 395,589)—29 percent of the State's population. The APA State president, George Washington Van Fossen, was a Mason and organizer of the local Orange lodges. [101]

In June, 1897, *The New York Times,* commenting on House debate on an appropriations bill for Indians, noted that Congressman William S. Linton (R., Mich.) had lashed out at Catholics "who are engaged in educating the Indians, in schools which the Government has en-

couraged, with money that has, according to witnesses who are qualified to speak, been better expended than most of the money spent on
other denominational schools." [102]

Linton, a Mason and APA supporter, expressed concern that Catholic Indian Schools received approximately one-half more federal funding than all other Protestant Indian Schools combined. [103]

In rebuttal, Representative Thomas A. Weadock (D., Mich) said
the Catholic schools received more money because they were instructing a far greater number of pupils than the other religious organizations. The Michigan Democrat then observed that the APA "holds the
balance of power" in all Congressional Districts. He also called attention to APA oaths which are directed toward denying Catholic citizens
public office. [104]

Representative John Gear (R., Ia.) offered an amendment to cut off
funds for education in "sectarian" schools. However, that motion became embroiled in an uproar over who was pressing for such an
amendment. Finally, in response to cries for Gear to read a petition to
Congress from the National League for the Protection of American
Institutions, which called for the cut-off of such funds, the League's
petition, together with a list of all of its officers and supporters was
inserted in the *Record.* [105]

Ultimately the House passed the legislation without the amendments.

"Sectarian" Means "Non-Protestant"

Although the term "sectarian" was not defined during that House
debate, Rev. King of the League defined the term in his book, *Facing
The Twentieth Century,* He wrote:

> "Sectarianism is defined to be: 'the quality or character of a
> sectarian; adherence to a separate religious denomination.'
> "We have no established state church in the European sense,
> in this country . . .
> "Protestant is not the name of a sect . . . An institution or
> government may be Protestant and therefore not Roman Catho-
> lic, but it is not necessarily sectarian because its managers are
> Protestant, and it need not be sectarian because the majority of
> its managers are Roman Catholic." [106]

Rev. King, who, it has been shown, was singularly active in working for legislation which ultimately terminated public assistance for "sectarian" institutions, made it abundantly clear that he was strongly in favor of the government supporting his principles of Anglo-Saxon Christianity.

He wrote that while "sectarianism cannot become . . . the molder and conservator of our civilization, sectarian controversies ought not to be allowed to crowd out universal instruction in the unsectarian tenets and moral and religious principles of Christianity."

Continuing, he said: "The American civilization and free institutions rest upon unrestricted Christianity. A Hindoo writer puts it thus: 'The religion of Christ represents all that is noble in Western civilization, Western morality, science or faith.' " [107]

Christianized Anglo-Saxon blood, said King, "is the regnant force in this country; and . . . God is using the Anglo-Saxon to conquer the world for Christ by dispossessing feebler races and assimilating and molding others." [108]

All religions, he declared, "must have absolute liberty, restrained only when they antagonize the principles of our Christian civilization." [109]

King's view of the preferred position of Anglo-Saxon Protestantism in America was evidenced during House debate on the District of Columbia Appropriations bill in February, 1896.

Discussion on the floor developed that St. Ann's Infant Asylum, the Association of Works of Mercy, the House of the Good Shepherd, St. Rose Industrial School and St. Joseph's Asylum were considered "sectarian," because they were operated by members of religious orders of the Roman Catholic Church.

At the same time, the House approved use of public funds for the Young Women's Christian Home (YWCH) and the Hope and Help Mission (HHM).

With regard to the latter organization, its report showed that "at least 14 women and girls have been clearly converted during the last six months, and the aggregate of the year is at least 25." It also was admitted that all board members represented several Protestant denominations.

Addressing those facts about the HMM, Representative Joseph Cannon (R., Ill.) asked: ". . . if it is not a religious institution, then what is it?" [110]

Responding, Rep. William W. Grout (R., Vt.) said: "I do not understand the word 'Protestant' indicates a sect. I do not so understand at all . . ."

Congressman Elijah A. Morse (R., Mass.) rose in defense of funding the Protestant Hope and Help Mission. He said he agreed with his Republican colleague Grout, "in regard to what constitutes sectarianism."

"Surely," he said, "any institution supported by the different denominations of this country is not a sectarian institution." [111]

Later in that debate, Rep. John S. Williams (D., Miss.) wanted to know why appropriations were denied for Catholic organizations, but not denied to the Woman's Christian Association. He challenged the view that the WCA was not a "sectarian" institution by noting that no Jewish woman could belong, "by its very terms, and certainly no Catholic could consistently belong to it."

Rep. Morse replied: "The Women's Christian Temperance Association includes every Protestant Denomination, and it is entirely non-sectarian." [112]

When the Indian Appropriations Bill came before the Senate, in April, 1896, and debate ensued on an amendment to declare a settled policy to "make no appropriation whatever for the education of Indian children in any sectarian school," Sen. William V. Allen (Populist, Neb.) expressed concern about the infelicitous references during floor debate to the Catholic Church.

In connection with the amendment and the debate thereon, the Nebraska Senator demonstrated remarkable courage and decency by addressing his colleagues with the following remarks:

"I was in hopes that the time had passed in this country when sectarian bigotry would make its appearance in the Congress of the United States, and when any man could be moved to give utterance to sentiments that possibly he is not willing to express on all occasions in consequence of the particular or peculiar political situation existing at this time.

"I am not a Catholic. I am the son of a Protestant minister. Whatever religious education I have came from Protestant parents and teachers. But I supposed the time had come, . . . when no man is to be arraigned in this country in consequence of his religious faith, and when every man and woman may be permitted to worship God according to the dictates of his or her own conscience without being arraigned or charged with entertaining a belief that is hostile to the perpetuity of American institutions and American freedom.

"I know of no organization that has done more to bring about civilization in this country than the Catholic Church. I am not its advocate; I am not a member of it; and I cannot say that I have any more sympathy with it than I have for any other church. In fact, my sympathies go out to the church of my father and mother.

"[But] when the Pilgrims landed at Plymouth Rock they found the missionaries of this church scattered among the barbarous tribes of this country. They had preceded the landing of the Pilgrims and the landing of the immigrants at Jamestown. They were carrying the Gospel among the heathen of this country; they were devoted to the work of civilizing and bringing the Gospel of Christ to the uncivilized tribes inhabiting this country.

"We may disagree, as to church creeds, as to church government; we may disagree as to the proper construction to be placed upon certain passages of the Scriptures; but we certainly cannot disagree upon the question that the time has come in this country . . . when no man is to be proscribed, directly or indirectly, in consequence of any religious faith he may entertain." [113]

The amendment passed by a vote of 38 to 24, with 27 Senators not voting.

Sen. Allen was defeated in the next election.

Those prohibitions on aid to "sectarian" institutions were legislated at a time when Michigan Congressman William Linton referred to the election of 1894 as the "storm of 1894" which precipitated a "flood of ballots" [that] "swept members out of office for having voted such appropriations." [114]

Linton, a staunch Mason and APA supporter, was referring primarily to federal funding for Indian education of Catholic missionary societies.

At the same time, the Mason President of the APA, William Traynor, bragged that a sufficient number of APA supporters had been elected to the 54th Congress to insure passage of legislation "most dear to us." [115]

Among measures "dear" to the APA at that time were proposals to prohibit aid to "sectarian" institutions, either for education of Indian children or to support charitable organizations in the District of Columbia which the APA would view as "sectarian." [116]

That is the legislative history which established the meaning of "sectarianism." The term really meant "non-Protestant" when Congress first terminated public funding for "sectarian" institutions.

It is also worthy of note that the word "sectarian" was not defined in various acts which prohibited aid for such organizations or institutions at that time. [117]

The religion clause of the First Amendment, of course, makes no reference to "sectarian." It addresses the subject of "religion."

Meanwhile, during this period, the U.S. Catholic bishops were concerned about secret societies, but the prelates were reluctant to condemn such groups because of the general anti-Catholic climate of the time.

However, in 1892, the bishops of New York and Philadelphia did condemn the Odd Fellows, Knights of Pythias, Knights Templars, and Sons of Temperance.

At the same time, Fr. Aloysius Sabetti, a noted Jesuit theologian at Woodstock College in Maryland, sent to James Cardinal Gibbons of Baltimore, the Archbishop Primate of the United States, a study on secret societies by an American Jesuit colleague which found that no secret society, except the Freemasons, should be condemned unless it was proven that they worked against Church and State. [118]

The study was circulated among American bishops and forwarded to Rome for a decision. Two years later, the Vatican directed that the Odd Fellows, the Knights of Pythias, and the Sons of Temperance be condemned; however, the U.S. bishops chose to ignore the directive. In early December, 1894, Rome ordered the U.S. prelates to comply. [119]

Rome's attitude was not surprising. This was a period when the Church was concerned with an incipient heresy known as "Americanism," or a belief that the Church should alter its teachings on faith and dogma to better allow Catholics in the United States to conform to the world in which they lived.

That situation moved Pope Leo XIII to send a letter to Cardinal Gibbons on the subject of Americanism, titled *Testem Benevolentiae,* dated January 31, 1899.

Essentially the Papal letter condemned five specific errors held by many Church liberals in the States: rejection of external spiritual direction from the Vatican; preference for natural over supernatural virtues; rejection of religious vows as incompatible with the modern world; confounding license with liberty; and an unwarranted assumption that people in the modern era have received a greater outpouring of the Holy Spirit than did the Apostles, saints, and the faithful of earlier periods. [120]

That was the situation as the 20th Century began.

Attacks on Catholics abated, but never ceased; there was only a lull in the battle, although the federal government made no other significant efforts to proscribe Catholic institutions or activities.

However, the ferocity of the war against the Church intensified after William J. Simmons re-established the Ku Klux Klan at Stone Mountain, Georgia in 1915.

And from the Klan's putrescent swamp emerged a man who, arguably, played the most significant role of all in reversing the nation's long established policy of accommodating both traditional Trinitarian Christian beliefs and Old Testament convictions.

4/ THE CRAFT
AND THE KLAN

By the early 20th Century, attacks on Catholics had waned, and did not resume until shortly after Jews and Freemasons were singled out as threats to the nation.

First, it was charged in Congressional testimony that Jews were closely identified with Bolshevism and anarchism. Then, almost simultaneously, history's most distorted plagiarism, "The Protocols of the Elders of Zion," purported to reveal how Jews and Freemasons were conspiring to overthrow Christian Civilization as a prelude to joint world rule.

Prior to that bizarre imbroglio—which, it should be noted, never came close to exciting the hatred and bloodshed reserved for Catholics—the Church was gaining respect and adherents. Census data demonstrated that it accounted for over one-third of all religious denominations in the United States. [1]

In 1911, President William Howard Taft remarked that membership in the Roman Catholic Church is "assurance" of patriotic citizenship. The following year, the President's sister-in-law, Mrs. H.W. Taft, was received into the Catholic Church. [2]

The Klan Moves North

Three years later, Colonel William J. Simmons, an ardent admirer of the Ku Klux Klan of 1866-1869, under the leadership of Confederate General Nathan Bedford Forrest, re-established the Klan at Atlanta, Georgia in 1915, and called himself the Imperial Wizard.

According to a handbill he issued in 1917, titled "The ABC of the Knights of the Ku Klux Klan," [available in the Rare Book Division of the Library of Congress], the Klan advocated white supremacy, and was open only to "native born American citizens who believe in the tenets of the Christian religion." That viewpoint was strikingly similar to the philosophy of the Know-Nothings and the APA of previous periods.

A year earlier, it was apparent that a resuscitated Know-Nothing movement was taking nourishment in the North. *The New York Times* reported that a "secret oath-bound anti-Catholic order" (which refused to divulge its name) was operating in New York City as part of a nation-wide group organized specifically to oppose "political encroachments" by the Roman Catholic Church. The group's spokesman, Rev. William Hess, Pastor of Trinity Congregational Church, alleged that the Catholic Church intended to make the United States a "Catholic" country, and planned to "get control of the government."

Later that year, dissension arose in the organization's ranks and resulted in the New York adjunct separating itself from the national body. [3]

Although the group was extremely reticent about publicity, one of its spokesman bragged to the *Times* that it had been successful in efforts to defeat Martin H. Glen, candidate for Governor in the Empire State in 1914, because "he represented the Jesuit element" in American politics. [4]

In 1920, the Sons and Daughters of Washington, a group which bore an uncanny resemblance to the unidentified 1916 anti-Catholic organization, was formed in Brooklyn, New York to oppose Catholic political activities. It was characterized in the press as "a militant fighting organization for Protestantism,"

The august and powerful *Times* did not disagree with the goals of the Sons and Daughters of Washington, but faulted the organization for its egregious lack of tact. An editorial in that newspaper said the Sons and Daughters "show none of the discretion that characterized him whose name they have taken."

Hammering home the point, the *Times* said: "Only a minute fraction of it [i.e., discretion] would have enabled them to see that the war [World War I] is not yet remote enough to make attacks on the Knights of Columbus more than the forlonest of hopes. Our soldiers are under the impression that the Knights served them certainly as well as did any other agency of relief and support, and better than did several." [5]

Jews Attacked

But Catholics were not the sole targets of hatred. Jews were singled out for attack during the period 1919-1921.

Opposition to Jews developed as pressure built up in the United States to support a Zionist nation in Palestine for Jews who had been displaced by the Russian Revolution and World War I. The issue split the Jewish community itself.

Congressman Julius Kahn of California, for example, objected to President Woodrow Wilson's endorsement of an independent Jewish state in Palestine, principally, the Congressman said, because it incites "the division of one's affiliation with the country in which he lives," and creates "a divided allegiance." Kahn also said he was opposed to Zionists because they "believe in the foundation of a government which shall embrace both Church and State." [6]

At the same time, Rev. Dr. George S. Simons, who had been Superintendent of the Methodist Episcopal Church in Russia and Finland for the preceding 12 years, testified before a Senate committee investigating Bolshevism in 1919, and charged that chaotic conditions in Russia were due in large part to agitators from the east side of New York City who flocked to Russia immediately after the overthrow of the Czar.

The Methodist minister said that some of the New York people in Russia held high positions in the Bolshevist government, and that Bolshevists were responsible for wholesale murder of innocent civilians, outraging of young girls, and official starving of all who did not endorse Bolshevist teachings.

He identified those Bolshevists as "Yiddish agitators from the New York east side," and "apostate Jews, men who deny their God, and who have foresaken the religion and the teachings of their fathers."

His information was, he said, that 265 members of the Bolshevist Government "had come into Russia . . . from the east side of New York."

Rev. Simons also testified that "a large percentage of the Bolshevist agitators at work over here [the United States] are apostate Jews." [7]

Two days later, Louis Marshall, President of the American Jewish Committee, testified before the Senate committee He confirmed that some Bolshevists were apostate Jews, but complained that Rev Simons' statement was damaging to other Jews who oppose Bolshevism. [8]

In New York, Jewish leaders complained that two Episcopal Church clerics had charged that members of the Jewish race were in need of Americanization and Christianization. It was alleged that Rev. John L. Zacker told an Episcopal convention: "The Jews control the world, and if Christianity is to convert the Jews, it must be attempted at once." [9]

Rev. Thomas Burgess, Secretary of Christian Americanization of the Episcopal Church, replied that his Church's program was directed toward all "foreign born," including the "large number of Jews who have left the faith of their fathers." [10]

A little over one year later, Rabbis Joseph Silverman and Samuel Schulman condemned anti-Semitic attacks in various publications in the United States which were based on "The Protocols of the Wise Men of Zion." They said "The Protocols" allege that Jews and Free-masons "are in a great conspiracy to achieve world mastery." Among the publications cited by the Rabbis was auto magnate Henry Ford's *Dearborn Independent,* which had been serializing "The Protocols" for six months.

Dr. Silverman rightly pointed out that none of the publications furnished any evidence that an international secret political organization of Jews actually exists.

Continuing, he said anti-Semites "collect a few Jewish names, like Karl Marx, Bela Kun, Herezl, Trotzky and others, and cull a few sentences of their writings, divorced from their contexts," to show that Jews "are individualists, Socialists, Bolsheviki, Zionists and what not, who care only for the overthrow of all Governments in order to establish their own."

But, he observed, such people ignore that fact that the Zionists, Socialists and Bolsheviki, "who happen to carry Jewish names, are only a handful in comparison to the great bulk of Jewish people throughout the world who are not only not in sympathy with Zionism, Socialism, Bolshevism, but who actually denounce these attempts at separate forms of government."

The Rabbi declared that there never would be a Jewish nation or a Jewish army or navy with which to dominate the world. "In no nation of the world is there a Jewish vote," Dr. Silverman asserted. [11]

Henry Ford was attacked repeatedly for his publication of "The Protocols" [12]. Editorializing against "The Protocols," the *Times* said they were "about the strangest jumble of crazy ideas that ever found its way into print." [13]

The editorial added that "The Protocols" are of "unknown origin and accounted for only as having been put into the hands of the Russian Nilus by an unknown lady who obtained them 'in a mysterious way'. . . . [14]

The Conference of Jews issued a public statement on November 30, 1920 condemning the "Protocols," and characterized them as "a mere recrudescence of medieval bigotry and stupidity." [15]

Princess Catherine Radziwill, a Russian emigre writer who special-
ized in Russian and European matters, said she had seen the manuscript for the "Protocols" when it was being fabricated in 1884 by
General Orgewsky, head of the Third Section of Police of the Russian
State Department.

The General, she related, had sent agents to Paris to prepare the
fake documentation which would show that the Jews were responsible
for assassinating Alexander II, and "were planning a general conspiracy to destroy all the monarchies of the earth."

Continuing, she said the Czar's agents "searched old books, compiled citations from Jewish philosophers, and ransacked the records of
the French Revolution for abstracts of the most inflammatory
speeches." [16]

As it turned out, the Princess's recollection appeared to be accurate.

On May 8, 1920, there appeared in *The Times* (London) an article
"From A Correspondent" which called attention to a book, *The Jewish Peril, Protocols of the Learned Elders of Zion,* by Professor S.
Nilus. The correspondent called for an investigation of the book because it fostered "indiscriminate anti-Semitism . . . rampant in Eastern Europe," and "growing in France, England and America." [17]

Fifteen months later, *The Times'* Constantinople correspondent reported that the "Protocols"—which purported to evidence a Jewish-
Masonic conspiracy to destroy Christian Civilization by a universal
revolution which would usher in Jewish world-rule—were a plagiarism. The newspaper article clearly demonstrated that Nilus's work
was based largely on a book *"Dialogue aux Enfers entre Machiavel et
Montesquieu ou la Politique de Machiavel au XIX Siecle.* [Dialogue in
Hell between Machiavelli and Montesquieu, on the Politics of Machiavelli in the XIX Century].

The book, published at Brussels, Belgium in 1865, was authored
by a person identified on the title page as "un Contemporain," but
actually was Maurice Joly, a Parisian lawyer and publicist, who had
been arrested by Napoleon III's police and sentenced to 18 months
imprisonment. [18]

The Brussels book was "a very thinly-veiled attack on the despotism of Napoleon III in the form of 26 dialogues divided into four
parts," and the "Protocols" attributed to Nilus follow almost the identical order as the "Dialogues." of Joly. [19]

While the book by the Russian mystic Sergi Nilus was shown con-
clusively to be a plagiarism, many people obviously insist on continu-

ing the controversy, as is evidenced by approximately 100 books concerning the "Protocols" (pro and con), in several languages, listed in the card catalogue of the Library of Congress.

New York *World* Exposes Klan Anti-Catholicism

Exposure of the "Protocols" forgery pretty well ended serious anti-Semitism, although there were occasional attacks on Jews in such organs as *The Searchlight,* a Klan-influenced journal, which lashed out at "Jewish agitators" who were plotting a race war to destroy the Government, and "to overthrow all the Gentile governments of the world." [20]

But the motherlode which provided the Klan's enormous membership and great wealth was America's historic hatred of the Catholic Church. This was first evidenced in a series of 21 articles which began in the New York *World* on September 6, 1921, following three-months investigation of the Klan by that newspaper. The series simultaneously appeared in 17 other major dailies throughout the nation.

The first article in the series reported on the Klan's terrorism in the South, largely against Negroes. The Klan was exposed for having been involved in 21 tar and featherings; 25 beatings of individuals; 2 strippings and maltreatment of white women; 3 killings; and 18 warnings to prospective victims of Klan wrath. [21]

The series also reproduced a copy of a bogus oath which the Klan said was the actual oath taken by Fourth Degree members of the Knight of Columbus. The bogus oath began:

> "I _____, now in the presence of Almighty God, the Blessed Virgin Mary, the Blessed St. John the Baptist, the Holy Apostles, St. Peter and St. Paul, . . . and to you, my Ghostly Father, the superior general of the Society of Jesus, . . . declare and swear that His Holiness, the Pope . . . hath power to depose heretical kings, princes, States, Commonwealths and Governments, and they may be safely destroyed. . . ."

The fabricated oath further says the 4th Degree Knight will "wage relentless war, openly and secretly, against all heretics, Protestants and Masons . . . and that I will hang, burn, waste, boil, flay, strangle and bury alive those infamous heretics; rip up the stomachs and wombs of their women and crash their infants heads against the walls in order to annihilate their execrable race."

Continuing, the unbelievable document said the Knights would also wage war "secretly" using "the poisonous cup, the strangulation cord, the steel of the poinard, or the leaden bullet . . ."

Should the Knight prove false, the fake oath says he agrees to have his brethern "cut off my hands and feet and my throat from ear to ear, my belly opened and sulphur burned therein . . ."

The Knight then allegedly states that he will always prefer a Catholic to any other political candidate, especially a Mason.

Immediately following the fabricated text is a statement that the oath appeared in the Congressional Record on February 15, 1913 at page 3216. [22]

The World also set forth the real oath taken by Fourth Degree Knights, which is shown to be virtually the exact opposite of what the Klan libelously charged.

The true oath taken by members of the 4th Degree of the Knights of Columbus asserts:

> "I swear to support the Constitution of the United States. I pledge myself, as a Catholic citizen and Knight of Columbus, to enlighten myself fully upon my duties as a citizen and to conscientiously perform such duties entirely in the interest of my country and regardless of all personal consequences."

The Knight further pledges to preserve "purity of the ballot" and to "promote reverence and respect for law and order," and to practice his religion openly and to exercise public virtue "as to reflect nothing but credit upon our Holy Church. . . ." [23]

Moreover, in 1914, the "entire work, ceremonies and pledges of the Knights of Columbus were submitted to a Masonic Committee of the 32nd and 33rd degree Masons in California." Afterward, the Committee issued a statement certifying that the Knights' oaths were "intended to teach and inculcate principles that lie at the foundation of every great religion and every great State."

The Masonic Committee further stated that the alleged oath "is scurrilous, wicked and libelous, and might be the invention of an impious and venomous mind." [24]

Actually, anyone who was the least bit familiar with the solemn oaths taken by Masons would suspect that the bogus Knights of Columbus oath was written by a Mason. Such suspicion was well founded.

On September 18, 1921, an article in *The World* was headlined:

"Bogus K. of C. Oath An Old Plagiarism."

The article said the bogus Fourth Degree K of C oath circulated by the Klan is nearly identical in wording to an "oath first used by the Paris Illuminati, as they were called in 1786—the name being changed to Adepts in 1772 and Freemasons in 1778."

Continuing, the article said: "It was delivered in a cellar, back of a house in Rue Vaugirard in Paris, first in 1772, in a lodge attended by Jean Jacques Rousseau . . . Prince Louis Philippe . . . Jean Paul Marat . . . John Paul Jones, Emanuel Swedenborg and other conspirators, and was dictated by the celebrated charlatan Cagliostro. . . ."

The World article added: "The irony of the matter is that the K.K.K. assumes the oath to be of Roman Catholic origin and against the Masons, whereas it really is of Masonic origin against the Roman hierarchy and the French monarchy." [25]

The series of articles also likened the Klan to the APA. One article was headlined: "Ku Klux Klan As Venomous As The Old APA." The report concerned the "virulent attacks on Catholics and their Church" used by the Klan in recruitment efforts, particularly a "Do You Know? card on which is listed such questions as:

"That a secret treaty made by him [the Pope] started [World War I]? . . .

"That he controls the daily and magazine press?

"That he denounces popular government as inherently vicious . . .?

"That Knights of Columbus [members] declare they will make popery dominant in the U.S?" [26]

The Klan's concern for the good name of Freemasonry hinted at Masonic influence in the Ku Klux Klan. Certainly the bogus K of C oath was shown to have been of 18th Century Masonic origin.

Therefore, it was ironic to learn that *The World* worried about the Klan's secret oath which demanded "unconditional obedience to the as yet unknown constitution and laws, regulations . . . of the Knights of the Ku Klux Klan . . ."

The World also was disturbed by the "rigid secrecy" imposed upon Klan members "even in the face of death, in regard to any and all matters and knowledge" of the Klan.

The New York daily said it "has always in mind the potential danger to the United States from a secret organization bound together by such an oath, . . . and likely to draw into its ranks men of no regard for anything but the Ku Klux law and standards of conduct and ethics." [27]

The Craft And The Klan

What *The World* deplored about the Klan's "rigid secrecy," and the danger to society of men binding themselves by solemn oaths to accept or commit possible actions in the future which they were totally ignorant of when they took their oaths, is precisely the danger the Catholic Church always has seen in Freemasonry.

Indeed, it is remarkable that after three-months investigation by one of the nation's major newspapers, the 21-part series made no mention of the close bond between the Klan and Freemasonry.

After all, most of the Klan's major leaders were Freemasons. The organization's founder, Col. Simmons was a Mason, and a Knight Templar. Also, C. Anderson Wright, King Kleagle of the New York Klan and chief of staff of a Klan group known as Knights of the Air, was a 32nd degree Mason. Dr. Hiram Evans, who succeeded Simmons as Imperial Wizard, "for many years . . . was recognized as one of the most active men in Masonry, and is a 32nd degree Knight Commander of the Court of Honor . . . [who] had been devoting almost his entire time to Scottish Rite Masonry at the time the Klan was organized. . . ."

Israel Zangwill, a prominent London author, said he was told by a Jewish rabbi that Dr. Evans inducted him into the 32nd degree of the Masonic order. [28]

Further, initiations were held "in the Masonic Temple in New York City," and the Klan shared office space in Beumont, Texas "with the secretary of the Grotto, which, in a way, is a Masonic organization." [29]

Edward Young Clarke, a former publicity agent and fund raiser, who became Imperial Kleagle (salesman) for the Klan "realized the value of representing the Klan to be 'the fighting brother' of Masonry." Consequently, he issued orders that "none but men with Masonic affiliations" should be employed as Kleagles in the Klan's nationwide sales network.

Accordingly, he established the Great American Fraternity (GAF) in Georgia in 1920 as a nationwide sales organization composed of members of 13 secret societies believed to be hostile to the Catholic Church. Klan salesmen were instructed "in selling effective political anti-Catholicism to their brothers in their respective lodges."

Members of the GAF included the Freemasons, Junior Order of United American Mechanics, Independent Order of Odd Fellows, Guardians of Liberty, Order of the Eastern Star, Daughters of America, Rebekkahs, the Loyal Orange Institution, Knights of Luther, National Legion of Pathfinders, and the Order of De Molay. [30]

Although some Masonic spokesmen condemned the Klan, there were very few Masonic leaders who shared that view.

Charles P. Sweeney, writing in *The Nation* magazine in 1920, said if responsible Masons "exerted a tithe of the influence they possess, [they] could do more to stop the Know-Nothing program than any other single force." [31]

Imperial Wizard Simmons denied the authenticity of a report that the Masonic leadership in Missouri had condemned the Klan in 1920. He said he had addressed 3,500 people in the Shrine Temple at St. Louis in September of that year, and learned that the alleged Masonic condemnation "has been strongly denied." [32]

The Minneapolis *Daily Star* reported that most Klansmen in the city were Masons, while the State leaders included many popular Shriners.

In Wisconsin, the Klan leader was William Wiesemann, "a local insurance man who was prominent in Masonic circles."

Klan advertisements read: "Masons Preferred," and many Masons joined, as did a number of Milwaukee's Socialists.

A New York Klansman claimed that 75 percent of the Klan enrollment in that State were Masons. [33]

In Oregon, both Fred L. Gifford, head of the Klan in that State, and his secretary, Frank Parker were Masons. Delegates of an Oregon Klan front, the Good Government League, were Masons, Orangemen, Odd Fellows and Pythians. [34]

In 1924, an editorial in the Scottish Rite *New Age* magazine said the Rite holds "no brief for or against any organization outside of the Scottish Rite," and added the following observation: If Freemasonry follows the traditions of centuries, it "cannot dictate to any Mason what shall or shall not be his affiliations outside the lodge . . ."

The editorial then invited attention to a letter by the editor of the *Masonic Herald* that appeared in *The New York Times* on August 28, 1923. The letter said "genuine Masons—Masons who are such in their hearts—cannot be Klansmen, and cannot welcome with true brotherly love Klansmen into their lodges."

Commenting on the *Herald* editor's letter, the *New Age* said: "Possibly the editor of the *Masonic Herald* is prejudiced, but no Masonic

editor has any more right to speak pontifically for the Masonic fraternity than [a Catholic priest]." [35]

An article in the same publication commented: "One may not sub-
scribe to the Ku Klux Klan platforms in toto, but one may say of these
and similar anti-Catholic movements . . . this fellow hath the right
sow by the ear." [36]

Although most decent citizens were outraged by the Klan's rampant
bigotry, none of the Craft's Grand Lodges had taken "official action
in regard to the Klan." [37]

Nationally, "attacks on Masonry" in Italy "fired the Klan to renewed action and increased [its] membership" [38]

The above history strongly indicates that the Klan was a Masonic
front group. Certainly the Klan's venomous war on Catholics was in
keeping with a long tradition generally associated with the Masonic
fraternity.

The Klan In Action

In his article in *The Nation,* Charles Sweeney listed some of the
terrorism and murders attributed to the Klan:

- A sheriff in Waco, Texas, who stopped a parade of masked
men and demanded the names of the marchers was shot and
removed from office in proceedings "sponsored by the most influential citizens of his county."
- In Birmingham, Alabama, a "Klansman" who killed a
Catholic priest in cold blood on his own doorstep "was acquitted
at the 'trial' amidst the plaudits of the mob."
- In Atlanta, Georgia, members of the Board of Education
received letters threatening their lives when they hesitated to
consider a resolution to dismiss all Catholic public school teachers.
- In Naperville, Illinois, a Catholic church was destroyed by
fire two hours after a monster midnight Klan initiation in the
neighborhood.
- Imperial Wizard Simmons made clear that the Klan had
"given the world the open Bible, the little red school house, if
you please, the great public school system." [39]

The free publicity given to such a militant anti-Catholic organization by *The World's* widely publicized articles, coupled with Imperial
Wizard Simmon's testimony before the House Rules Committee only

served to advance the rapid growth of the Klan.

Simmons whetted the insatiable anti-Catholic appetite when he told the Committee there was available to the Klan "possibly the greatest existing mass of data and material against the Roman Catholics and Knights of Columbus." The material included "affidavits and other personal testimony attributing to the Roman Catholics and the Knights of Columbus in America more outrages and crimes than the Klan has ever been charged with."

Included in the material, he said, are charges of "murder, whipping, tar and feathers, and crimes of all natures." [40]

At the time the House Rules Committee hearings were underway, Congressman William Upshaw, a supporter of the Klan, introduced a resolution to investigate "each and every secret order in the United States." Ten days later the Committee called off further investigation of the Klan. [41]

Typical of Klan techniques in the North, in 1922, was an incident at Elizabeth, New Jersey. Five Klansmen marched into the Third Presbyterian Church and handed the pastor an envelope in which was enclosed a note and $25. The note expressed "appreciation "for the way the deacon's fund was administered by the church, and asserted that the Klan stood for "white supremacy, protection of women, . . . and separation of church and state."

Five days later, the church's pastor, Rev. Robert W. Mark, preached a sermon attacking the Knights of Columbus. He remarked that if he had to choose between joining the K of C and the Ku Klux Klan, he would select the Klan.

Rev. Mark said God intended the white race for leadership, but that he (Mark) did not advocate suppression of any race. With those words, he invited Rev. C.J. Turner, negro pastor of the Siloam Presbyterian Church, who was sitting in the front row, to join him on the platform. The two ministers stood side by side singing "America." [42]

Cathophobia (or morbid fear and hatred of the Catholic Church) was rapidly spreading across the nation. In November, 1923, for example, Lowell Mellett, a nationally prominent journalist, writing in the prestigious *Atlantic Monthly* magazine, recalled stories circulated during his boyhood in Indiana which alleged that Catholic youths were trained "to seize the whole country." The same stories were rampant, he said, when he returned to his hometown 30 years later. [43]

Mellett said the Klan was charged with being opposed to Jews,

Negroes and Catholics; however, he had heard "little concerning Jews and Negroes," but "heard much concerning the Catholics." He added: Very clearly, the crux of the Klan problem in Indiana is the Catholic Church." [44]

Some of Mellett's old friends, whom he characterized as "just some of the best citizens in Indiana," were Klansmen. They joined, he said, because they believed the Vatican "is soon to be moved to Washington, D.C.," and because they opposed the "fixed policy of the Church to keep its members down to a definite level of ignorance." [45]

One of the most serious charges against the Church, he remarked, is that it "is endeavoring to obtain control of the public schools." [46]

He charged that newspapers "have feared the Catholic Church," and agreed that was an article of Klan faith which "has a real basis." [47]

Mellett's answer to the Klan's problem with the Church was to investigate, not the Klan nor other secret societies which were viciously attacking the Church and her adherents, but rather to investigate the Church. Catholic churches, he said should "be forced open" to prove or disprove allegations "of buried rifles and ammunition" [48]

If adopted, that proposal, and a similar outrageous suggestion by Mellett, would have trampled the most basic religious and civil rights of Catholics.

His other suggestion was that a commission of inquiry be established to "call publicly for the presentation of every charge against the Catholic Church that any responsible person or group of persons might have to make, and then investigate the truth of these charges." [49]

Nowhere in the article did Mellett furnish evidence to support wanton Klan charges. Presumably, this outrageous assault on the rights of citizens was warranted merely because a group of friends, "just some of the best citizens in Indiana" thought it would be nice.

Curiously, he never suggested an assault upon the Klan or Freemasonry. In fact, he explicitly said the Klan and secret societies should not be investigated. The reality was, however, that abundant evidence had been presented over the years which detailed the serious danger emanating from both the Klan and Freemasonry.

Indeed, in the same issue of the *Atlantic Monthly* in which Mellett's article appeared, there was a letter from "A Citizen of Oklahoma"

who said the State was under the "secret rule of a hidden clique." He
noted that the civil offices of the State "are unquestionably in the
hands of the Klan; and that fact makes it impossible for the Governor
to oust these officials."

In that regard, the unidentified letter writer observed that the Governor was being considered for impeachment by the Klan and its many
sympathizers. The Klan, he remarked, "is the most dangerous force
at large in the country today." [50]

Strangely, however, Lowell Mellett was convinced that the Roman
Catholic Church was far more dangerous than the Klan.

By 1925, the Klan was being widely accepted as American as apple
pie. *The Nation* editorialized that the Klan "has become safe—and
uninteresting." [51]

On August 9, 1925, Imperial Wizard Hiram W. Evans led a march
of some 25,000 Klansmen and Klanswomen down Pennsylvania Avenue in Washington, D.C., in "their greatest national demonstration
and public show of strength," as 100,000 spectators cheered.

The "100 per cent Americans" knelt with heads bared at the Washington Monument to pledge allegiance to "one country, one language,
one school and one flag." [52]

Dr. A.H. Gulledge, national speaker for the Invisible Empire, advocated "race purity," and said Klansmen would fight in order that
"the State and Church be kept separate in America."

Continuing, he said Protestants intended to see that "they shall not
press down upon the brow of Uncle Sam the thorny triple crown of a
foreign potentate."

If the nation is to survive, he added, "it cannot remain half free
and half parochial schools." [53]

Dr. Gulledge prophesized: "Not until the sun shall hide its face or
the moon cease to shine or God resigns his throne in the heavens, or
until the white race becomes mongrelized, will the Ku Klux Klan
die." [54]

It should be emphasized that these Klansmen and Klanswomen
were not a bunch of stereotype Southern red-necks. These were militant anti-Catholic race supremists from Connecticut, Delaware, Michigan, New Jersey, New York and Ohio. Others were from Alabama,
Florida, Georgia, Oklahoma, Tennessee, Texas and West Virginia.

The following day, the leading daily in the nation's capital carried
an editorial titled, "An Impressive Spectacle," which said the demonstration "may indicate" the Klan was "turning from the un-American

principles of race and religious restriction and opposition that have
been its most striking characteristic," and is now "seeking to render
real and valuable service to the country."

The editorial said the march on Washington provided the Klan an
opportunity "to make itself a force for good without belying the
Americanism of which it bears the symbol." [55]

It was evident the Klan was growing more powerful, a point made
by William R. Pattangall, a Protestant, a Mason, former Attorney
General of Maine, and that State's leading Democrat politician, who
also was the Klan's "most distinguished victim." [56]

Pattangall said "Catholics and aliens have borne the brunt" of the
Klan's wrath. The Klan "menace," he said, "embraces the issue of
religious freedom, the issue of preserving equal opportunity to all
citizens, the issue of government by, of, and for *all,* rather than a part,
of the people."

The Klan, he noted, said: "Lincoln was assassinated by order of
the Pope, Mckinley killed by a Catholic, and Harding was poisoned by
the K of C." Further, "they [the Klan] solemnly read bogus statistics
to prove that 90 percent of the deserters in the World War were Catholics acting under orders of the Church!" [57]

The Maine Democrat said further: "The Klan seeks a secret hold
on legislators, judges and other officials. It uses that hold to enforce
its own demands . . . It . . . acts secretly in both parties, it tries
constantly for control—*secret control*—of elections, legislatures and
governments. . . ." [58]

Replying to Pattangall's article, Imperial Wizard Evans ignored
most of the charges leveled by the former Maine Attorney General.
Rather, Evans ranted against the Catholic Church which, he said,
"has always opposed the fundamental principle of liberty."

The Church, he declared, "is trying . . . to win control of the
nation," and Catholic politicians attempt to bring the Church into
politics. The Church, he went on, must show "that the need of intolerance against it has passed." [59]

Although *The New York Times* suggested that the Klan was in decline in 1926, its own statistics demonstrated the nationwide
Cathophope organization was quite robust.

The *Times* said there were 100,000 Klansmen in New York, who
were "fairly vigorous." Principal strongholds were Suffolk and Nas-
sau Counties on Long Island, as well as Westchester, Putnam, Dut-
chess, Rockland, Sullivan and Ulster Counties. The Klan also had
"considerable influence" in Buffalo, and had influence on elections in

Binghamton and Rochester. [60]

A sampling of membership in the Klan in other States indicated that the organization was rather strong. There were 50,000 in Connecticut, 150,000 in Kansas, 150,000 in Missouri, 60,000 in New Jersey, and 250,000 in Ohio. [61]

In Indiana, the public was scandalized to learn that D.C. Stephenson, former Grand Dragon of that State, was convicted of murdering a young woman and sentenced to life imprisonment.

Commenting on Stephenson, the *Times* said he "was the boss of the Republican Party in Indiana, and that through him the Klan was in control of offices and the process of government." [62]

After the Klan extended itself to defeat Catholic Democratic Presidential candidate Alfred E. Smith it went into decline for two major reasons: first, the United States Supreme Court upheld the Constitutionality of a New York anti-Klan law which required the Klan to give publicity to its regulations, oaths and memberships; [63] and second, the Great Depression, which began in 1929, made keeping or finding a job, and feeding the family, far more important than hating Catholics.

As it turned out, the 1928 general election proved to the Democratic Party that there was a "Catholic vote." Although Smith lost by 6.3 million popular votes to the Republican Herbert Hoover, the Catholic Democrat garnered 6.6 million more votes than did the 1924 Democratic standard bearer, John W. Davis. Smith also received 5.8 million more votes than did the 1920 Democratic Presidential candidate, James M. Cox.

Four years later, Franklin D. Roosevelt, with the crucial assistance of Catholic James E. Farley as Democratic Party Campaign Chairman, appealed to that Catholic vote and rode the Party to repeated victories during the next 16 years.

John F. Kennedy also appealed to that same constituency in 1960, and won a tightly contested election. Some political observers viewed that election as one of the most religiously intolerant political contests since the days of the Ku Klux Klan.

It is now time to assess the impact America's long history of anti-Catholicism has had on freedom of religion in this nation.

5/ FOOTSTEPS IN THE SAND

On February 19, 1930, during hearings on the nomination of Hugh M. Tate to serve as a member of the Interstate Commerce Commission, Senator Hugo L. Black (D., AL.), expressed the view that the Senate should not consent to the nomination. The Senator disagreed with Tate's position on business and labor matters, but less obviously known, was the fact that Tate, some years earlier, had tried to block Black from obtaining a government position in Alabama.

Explaining his opposition to the nominee, the future Supreme Court Justice said a man's past life had a definite impact on his beliefs and actions in the future. Senator Black said:

". . . as a general rule, a man follows in the future the course that he has followed in the past.

"Show me the kind of steps a man made in the sand five years ago, and I will show you the kind of steps he is likely to make in the same sand five years hence.

"Show me the course he was pursuing then, and unless there has been some great cataclysm which has absolutely changed his character, I will show you the course he is going to follow in the future." [1]

Available evidence confirms that Mr. Black's own footsteps on the high bench—particularly on the issue of equal religious rights for Catholics—generally follow "the course he was pursuing" in the past.

Senator Black was a product of an environment redolent with the odor of anti-Catholic bigotry. Attacks on the Church were a common occurrence in Birmingham, Alabama, where Black began practicing law in 1907.

In 1916, the local newspaper reported that membership in the Ku

Klux Klan exceeded the most optimistic expectations with more than 175 men applying to join the Klan at every meeting. [2]

In 1920, following discovery of a plot to destroy that city's two Catholic churches and adjoining schools, federal agents warned the pastors involved to employ armed guards to protect their property. [3]

It was a time when the people of Birmingham were led to believe Catholics "are plotting control of the city, state and national governments in the name of the Pope, that they seek the destruction of the public schools, and that they are a menace to the existence of the home as the basic unit of organized society." [4]

One of the principal groups promoting that vintage Know-Nothingism was the "True Americans," or "T.As.," which had proven enormously successful in denying employment to Catholics.

"If you didn't belong to the 'T.As.,' you were "suspect." in the eyes of those bigots who were dedicated to the "extermination of Catholicism." [5]

A Tombstone Becomes A Stepping Stone

That mind-set precipitated the murder of Father James E. Coyle in Birmingham on August 11, 1921, and the subsequent acquittal of his assassin.

The kindly and beloved 48-year-old priest, a native of Athlone, Ireland, had been pastor of St. Paul's Catholic Church for 17 years when he died from a gunshot wound, inflicted by an impoverished Methodist minister-barber, as he sat reading after dinner on the front porch of his old frame rectory. [6]

Father Coyle's murderer, Rev. E. R. Stephenson, was assigned to no regular church, but usually hung around the court house looking for couples to marry. He was referred to as "the marrying parson" by court house habitues. [7]

A local newspaper said the minister was angry with the priest because Stephenson's daughter was considering conversion to Catholicism, and was planning to marry Pedro Gussman, a Catholic Puerto Rican who was 12 years older than the young woman. [8]

Stephenson admitted that he had called the priest "a dirty dog," but said Father Coyle "struck me twice on the head and knocked me to my knees." At that point the parson said the priest "run his hand in his pocket, and I shot." [9]

Two hours after the murder, Ruth Stephenson telephoned her mother to announce her marriage to Gussman. [10]

On August 13, the minister was formally charged with murder in the first degree. On that day and the following day the press surprisingly reported that the impoverished defendant had conferred with a number of local attorneys, but had made no announcement concerning the selection of a specific lawyer. [11]

It is doubtful that many readers of the local papers at that time would have paid particular attention to a headline in the *Birmingham Age-Herald,* which appeared immediately under a photograph of mourners attending Father Coyle's funeral. The headline said: "Masons To Hold Conference." The brief news item noted that the Jefferson County Masons would hold their semi-annual meeting August 16-17. [12]

Meanwhile, at the priest's funeral Mass, Bishop Edward P. Allen of Mobile, deplored the dramatic change that had taken place in Birmingham during the past several years. Twenty-five years earlier, and up until 1915, he said, non-Catholics had always been cordial, broadminded, and got along well with their fellow Catholic friends and neighbors.

However, all that had changed, and he attributed the new attitude to the work of politicians and secret societies. [13]

The year 1915, of course, marked the resuscitation of the Ku Klux Klan by Col. William Simmons.

On August 14, Ruth Stephenson Gussman, the new bride, informed the press that she had been baptized into the Catholic Church at Our Lady of Sorrows Church by Father Kelly—not Father Coyle.

She also said her father had locked her in her room on the day she was scheduled to receive her First Communion. Additionally, she told the press that her parents were trying to force her to marry "a Mason who was divorced." [14]

On August 16, the new bride's father, who, it was universally agreed, was of very modest circumstances, announced that he had selected, not one attorney, but had engaged a battery of four lawyers. They were: Hugo L. Black, Crampton Harris, John C. Arnold and Fred Fite. [15]

Because of the Klan's proven close ties to Masonry, it may not have been entirely coincidental that the first day of the semi-annual meeting of the Jefferson County Freemasons, was curiously the very day the impecunious Rev. Stephenson finally decided to select a mass of legal talent to defend him from going to prison for the murder of a Catholic priest.

The preliminary grand jury trial of Stephenson was held on August

23 in the Court of Misdemeanors and Felonies.

Sheriff J.C. Hartsfield testified that there were no bruises noticed on the defendant, thus implying that the priest never struck his assassin. [16] However, his deputy testified that Stephenson had a lump on the side of his head. [17]

Another witness asserted that the defendant never complained about a head wound until the day after the murder. [18]

Testimony also developed that three shots were fired "as fast as you can pull a trigger." Witness A.L Easter saw Stephenson fire the first shot two feet from the porch steps. After the shooting, he said, the defendant rose from his knees and walked toward the courthouse. [19]

It was also disclosed that the man doing the shooting was below the man being shot. Father Coyle was killed by a bullet that entered near the left ear and passed out through the back of his head. [20]

No one testified that they saw the priest do anything, and no other weapon was introduced into evidence.

The testimony of the witnesses pointed to premeditated murder of the priest by Stephenson.

The preacher's daughter, Ruth Stephenson Gussman, testified that her parents made "many threats" in her presence about what they would do to the Catholic Church or to Father Coyle. She said:

> "We have had people there at the house—Masons—and they have all said that they wished the whole Catholic institution was in hell, if you will excuse me. My mother has said many a time that she wished she could set a bomb under the Catholic Cathedral.
> "My father asked me one time if I wanted to cause the death of Mr. Bender [a Catholic friend] and Father Coyle, and I would if I continued going to church." [21]

Following her testimony, Mrs. Gussman said she had received threats of being kidnaped, and that efforts were being made to send her to an insane asylum. She filed a petition in circuit court for an injunction to restrain city, county and State officials from molesting her in any manner. [22]

When the case went to trial before a jury in Criminal Court, a local journal noted that Stephenson entered the court smiling, "and seemed little concerned by the trial." [23]

Another reporter observed that one of the witnesses to the shooting was W.D. Chiles, and that the defendant's attorney, Black, elicited the fact that Chiles was the brother-in-law of Edwin McGinty, a Catholic. Also, another witness was probed by Black and found to be a Catholic. [24]

Black claimed self-defense and insanity for his client. At one point a witness testified that Rev. Stephenson seemed "nervous" and "abnormal." The prosecuting attorney interjected to say the word "abnormal" was vague, and could mean anything.

The presiding judge, William E. Fort, overruled the objection by stating that "abnormal" means "insane." The judge knew that, he said, because "I looked it up." [25]

Black put Ruth Gussman's husband on the stand. The attorney had the shades on the windows drawn, to emphasize the man's swarthy complexion, and addressed the jury: "I want you to look at this man."

Turning to the defendant, Black asked: "Were you aware that Gussman was a Puerto Rican?"

Stephenson responded: "You can call him a Puerto Rican, but to me he's a nigger."

Summing up, Black referred to Gussman's Spanish descent and commented: "He's descended a long way. "There are 20 mulattos to every Negro in Puerto Rico." [26]

In his closing argument, Black said:

"Who believes Ruth Stevenson has not been proselyted? A child of a Methodist does not suddenly depart from her religion unless someone has planted in her mind the seeds of influence . . . There is such a thing as imprisonment of the human will by influence, vice, and persuasion. When you find a girl who has been reared well persuaded from her parents by some cause or person, that cause or person is wrong.

"If the eyes of the world are upon the verdict of this jury, I would write that verdict in words that cannot be misunderstood, that the home of the people of Birmingham cannot be touched. If that brings disgrace, God hasten the disgrace." [27]

Although Ruth Gussman had testified before the grand jury that Masons were strongly opposed to the Catholic Church, and "said that they wished the whole Catholic institution was in hell," neither the prosecuting attorney nor Black questioned whether any of the jurors or witnesses were Masons.

Four hours after closing argument, the jury returned a "not guilty" verdict. Shortly thereafter, each juror filed past the defendant,

Stephenson, to shake his hand. Judge Fort discharged the jury with thanks and said they rendered an "honest verdict." [28]

Commenting on the results of the trial, the leading local newspaper ran an editorial which said: "Even those in Birmingham who have taken only such cursory interest in the case as impelled them to wish the law to take its regular course will find the verdict hard to understand." [29]

Ruth Gussman later wrote a letter to the editor of the same newspaper to protest that she had never been called to testify. She also repeated the substance of her testimony before the grand jury, noting particularly her parents' strident anti-Catholicism, and their desire to destroy the Catholic Church and Father Coyle. [30]

One newsman said his impression was that the prosecuting attorney and his staff "did not really want to convict Stephenson." The newsman suspected that the eyewitness had been deliberately held back until rebuttal, when new testimony would not be admissible. [31]

Virginia Van Der Veer Hamilton, has written that the Ku Klux Klan had done its work well. She said J. Fisher Rothermel, a reporter for the *Birmingham News* recalled that the Klan and similar organizations had raised a handsome sum to pay legal fees for Stephenson's defense. The jury foreman was a Klansman, according to James Esdale, Cyclops of the Robert E. Lee Klavern at the time of the trial, and Black and his law partner, Crampton Harris became members of the Invisible Empire. Harris served as Cyclops of the Robert E. Lee Klavern. [32]

Mrs. Hamilton also reported that Masons had close ties to the Klan. She noted that during an initiation ceremony of the Birmingham Klan in 1924, the speaker estimated that 1,125,000 Masons were Klan members, because they realized that "the Klan's ideals were identical with their own." [33]

A letter in Justice Black's files shows that William E. Fort, Sr., resigned his position as Judge of the Criminal Court (in Birmingham) to become Black's law partner. Another letter among those records shows that Judge Fort expressed his appreciation to Black for helping him obtain the position of Assistant United States Attorney. [34]

The New York Times reported that Fort was a fellow Klansman with Black. [35]

Pulitzer Prize journalist Ray Sprigle of the *Pittsburgh Post Gazette* said the large granite cross which marks the grave of Father Coyle in Elmwood Cemetery in Birmingham "is considered the stepping stone of Hugo L. Black's determined march to the United States Supreme Court." [36]

A Klansman Moves To U.S. Senate

Black's defense of Stephenson made him widely known throughout the State, in a trial that was the most famous in Alabama history. When the State's U.S. Senator, Oscar Underwood, came out against the Klan in the 1924 national election he was forced to leave public office. [37]

Underwood's remarkably courageous position made Black, who had joined the Klan in 1923, [38] a leading contender to replace the heroic Underwood in Washington.

Black had the support of the Alabama Klan, and to hold Klan support devoted part of his campaign to voicing opposition to Governor Al Smith, who was widely known to be a Catholic. [39]

Early in 1928, U.S. Senate Democrats voted 35 to 1 to support Senator Joseph T. Robinson's (D., Ark.) rebuke of his colleague Senator Tom Heflin (D. Ala.) for the latter's attack on Governor Smith. Senator Black, though present, was excused by the Democratic Caucus from voting. [40]

Black was under considerable pressure to voice his support for Smith after the New York Governor had been selected as the Democrats nominee for President of the United States. [41] The Senator's files contain numerous letters urging him to speak out for the Democrat nominee, but Black invariably replied that he felt his best course of action was to say nothing, although he insisted he was supporting the Party, and Smith. [42]

One letter, marked "Personal and Confidential," was from Senator Claude A. Swanson (D., VA.), who urged Black "to take the leadership in Alabama for the Smith ticket regardless of consequences."

Black replied: "I must admit that Governor Smith's statement on the prohibition [of liquor] question, which I considered to be wholly unnecessary, and his appointment of Mr. [John J.] Raskob, which I considered to be a supreme political blunder so far as the South is concerned, has made it difficult for us. His personal views on immigration have given aid and comfort to our ancient enemy [the Catholic Church?], and estranged many of our friends."

Continuing, Black said: "I am supporting the ticket. I must render that support by following the course which seems most effective for the interests of the party . . ." [43]

Shortly before the 1928 general election, *The New York Times* ran an article on the Ku Klux Klan and anti-Catholic propaganda. The article mentioned various defenders of Al Smith in Alabama, but Senator Black's name was not listed among those defenders. [44]

Following Smith's defeat by Herbert Hoover, the Montgomery *Advertiser* scolded Black for his "total indifference and neglect" of a party which had supported him in 1926. Black was faulted for adamantly refusing to make a statement urging support for the Democrat Party Presidential ticket. [45]

Dr. A. L. Stabler, Grand Knight of the Knights of Columbus in Alabama, said he didn't believe Black's support for Smith was very strong. The Grand Knight noted that he had been requested by Black to submit lists of names of Catholics to be considered for appointments in the Post Office Department, but he stopped sending the Senator such lists when he found none of his recommendations were acted upon. [46]

Further evidence of Black's strong opposition to the Catholic Church was provided in February, 1929, when the Senate considered a bill for the construction of naval vessels, and the matter became bogged down in the "Catholic Flag" argument.

Black's Senatorial colleague from Alabama, and a widely recognized anti-Catholic bigot, proposed an amendment to the legislation which said, "it shall be unlawful to fly any flag or pennant on the same staff or hoist above the flag of the United States."

The reference obviously was to the chaplain's flag, emblazoned with the Cross of St. Andrew, which flies over the Stars and Stripes when chapel services are in progress aboard ships.

Senator William Bruce (D., MD.)—who noted that he had been defeated by the Klan the preceding November—asked whether any church flags "except the Catholic flag" are ever flown above our national flag on our ships. Heflin said he knew of none.

Another Senator observed that "the church flag" is flown on naval vessels when church services are in progress to indicate "that God is over the Nation and over the Navy."

Heflin rejoined that he saw no necessity "for pulling the Stars and Stripes down to make room for anybody's flag above it. I want it to be first," he said.

Senator Bruce commented that Heflin called the chaplain's flag a "Catholic flag," and remarked that Heflin's amendment had its origin with the Ku Klux Klan.

The amendment was defeated by a vote of 10 to 68. Senator Black voted with nine other colleagues in support of Heflin's proposal. [47]

On December 27, 1929, Alabama Klan Grand Dragon James Esdale attacked the State Democratic Committee which barred candidates for office who failed to support the Democratic nominee in the last general election. Esdale said the Committee's action was so "unfair . . . so intolerant . . . so obedient to the Roman Catholic Church that it is being hotly contested by every Democratic Senator and Representative in Washington." Presumably Senator Black was among that group. [48]

In 1936, Senator Black left a footprint in the sand which showed a frightening proclivity to trample civil rights of the public at large, even by "subterfuge," if necessary, to impose his will. This was evident when, as chairman of the Senate Lobby Investigating Committee, agents of the Federal Communications Commission (FCC), accompanied by the Black Committee, used a subpoena to obtain files of Western Union, Postal Telegraph, and other communications companies. [49]

The subpoena was considered "vague," and effectively "a dragnet" which infringed on the constitutional rights of many private citizens who were in no way associated with the committee's inquiry. [50]

The issue went to the Supreme Court of the District of Columbia, where Crampton Harris, Black's former law partner and Cyclops of the Klan's Robert E. Lee Klavern, spoke on behalf of Black's committee as a friend of the court. Harris argued for an hour "the right of the committee to subpoena evidence without interference by the courts." The subpoena itself reportedly demanded the production of all telegrams addressed to anybody in the world, according to *The New York Times*. [51]

The Court's Chief Justice, Alfred A. Wheat, rebuked the action by Black's committee, enjoined the seizure of telegraphic correspondence, and restrained Western Union from delivering the files to the committee.

The Court said the "subpoena goes way beyond any legitimate exercise of the right of the subpoena duces tecus." [52]

The *Times* noted that the FCC had ruled, on April 15, 1935, that private telegrams and telephone records were inviolable. [53]

On April 6, 1936, the United States Supreme Court (*Jones v. Securities Exchange Commission*) rebuked Black's committee for conducting a fishing expedition, and characterized the committee's action to seize the telegrams and other communications as odious. [54]

Obviously, the gentleman from Alabama vigorously disagreed with the Supreme Court's view, and subsequently delivered a radio address in which he supported President Franklin D. Roosevelt's "court-packing" proposal. The Alabama Senator said:

"I naturally believe it is time to stop these judicial usurpations brought about . . . by the economic fallacies of a majority of the Supreme Court.

"A majority of our judges should not amend our Constitution according to their economic predilections every time they decide a case." [55]

The Court's Ku Kluxer

Clearly, Senator Black was a highly controversial figure, and his record in favor of trampling the civil rights of certain people made him a pariah in many civilized circles. Indeed, on the very day President Franklin Roosevelt sent the Alabama Senator's name "amid unusual secrecy" to the Senate as his nominee to replace Justice Willis Van de Vanter on the Supreme Court, Black had prepared a speech against an anti-lynching bill. The speech was not delivered because of his nomination, according to Representative Samuel D. McReynolds (D., Tenn.). [56]

The President's selection of Black, and the high-handed way he used the powerful machinery of the ruling Democratic Party to railroad the nomination through Congress, gave clear evidence that Mr. Roosevelt would pack the court with men of his philosophic persuasion on liberal social issues.

As soon as the nomination reached the Senate, Senator Henry Ashurst (D., AZ.), chairman of the Senate Judiciary Committee, requested unanimous consent to have Black approved immediately by the Senate without normal referral to committee.

Although that move was objected to by Senators Edward Burke (D., Neb.) and Hiram Johnson (R., CA.), the nomination was referred to the Judiciary Subcommittee and approved 5 to 1 on the same day it was received by the Senate. [57]

Of eight newspapers which commented editorially on the nomination, only two approved Black's selection. [58]

Curiously, legal scholars have given scant attention to a highly important fact about Black's position on the high bench, which was raised by Senators William Borah (R., ID.) and Warren Austin (R.,

N.H.). Senator Black was constitutionally incapable of being appointed to the Court. He was a member of Congress when that body enacted legislation increasing the compensation of Supreme Court Justices, and therefore could not be promoted to a position which paid more money than his position as a Member of Congress.

The Constitution (Article 1, Sec. 6) states:

"No Senator or Representative shall, during the time for which he was elected, be appointed to any civil office under the authority of the United States, which shall have been increased during such time."

The salary of Justices at that time had recently been increased by Congress to $20,000 per year, making it exactly double the salary of Members of Congress, who earned $10,000. [59]

Homer Cummings, Attorney General of the United States, and with Roosevelt and Black a fellow Mason, said the appointment was perfectly legal. Cummings, although responsible for checking the nominee's background before sending his name to the Senate, never bothered to do so. [60]

Senator Royal S. Copeland (D., N.Y.) called Black's nomination "an insult to the American people."

He added: "No man who was directly or indirectly connected with the Ku Klux Klan, or was the beneficiary of its sympathy or support is fit for a place on any impartial tribunal, and certainly not for a place on the Supreme Court bench."

The New York Senator said the nominee did not possess an "impartial mind," and questioned whether he was "able to administer even-handed justice to all who come before him regardless of religion or race." [61]

Nevertheless, Black had friends in high places. His nomination was consented to by the Senate with a vote of 63 to 16, on August 17, 1937 [62]

The following day, Black lunched with the President. As he left the White House, he assured newsmen he did not know when or where he would take the oath of office. However, about six hours later, the oath as a Justice of the United States Supreme Court was administered in virtually a secret ceremony by Charles F. Pace, financial clerk of the Senate. [63]

Normally, the oath is administered by the Chief Justice in the robing room on the day the new member first appears with the other

Justices. It seemed as though Mr. Roosevelt, and those who wanted a dramatic shift in the Supreme Court, knew they were on shaky ground with Black. Apparently, they wanted him locked into his position before the nomination could possibly be blocked.

But then, suddenly, the enormity of Black's bigotry was exposed in all its sordid deviousness by the *Pittsburgh Post Gazette.*

Black ostensibly resigned from the Klan in 1925 by means of a note written on stationery bearing the letterhead of the Klan's Office of the Grand Realm of Alabama. The note, addressed to J.W. Hamilton, Kligrapp [Secretary], dated July 9, 1925, said:

> Dear Sir and Klansman:
>
> Beg to tender you herewith my resignation as a member of the Knights of the Ku Klux Klan, effective from this date on.
> Yours I.T.S.U.B. [In the Sacred Unbreakable Bond],
>
> Hugo L. Black [64]

Black resigned, according to *The New York Times,* "so that he would be able to disclaim membership in the Klan if challenged on that score during the 1926 primaries."

The same *Times* article said he decided to resign following a conference with Klan officials after receiving a pledge of their support in the primaries. However, "the resignation was kept in the Klan archives and was never presented to J.W. Hamilton, Kligrapp of the Robert E. Lee Klan No. 1, to whom it was addressed, or made known to the Klan rank and file." [65]

Reporter Ray Sprigle said Black was welcomed back into the Klan at a great State meeting in Birmingham on September 2, 1926.

"I realize," Black told the assembled Klansmen, including representatives from other States, "that I was elected by men who believe in the principles that I have sought to advocate and which are the principles of this organization."

Black swore never to divulge, even under threat of death, the secrets of the Invisible Empire. And, he said,

> "I swear that I will most zealously and valiantly shield and preserve by any and all justifiable means and methods . . . white supremacy . . .
> "All to which I have sworn to by this oath, I will seal with my blood, be Thou my witness, Almighty God. Amen." [66]

Accepting the Klan's gold card, or "grand passport" of life membership, Black said:

> "This passport which you have given me is a symbol to me of the passport which you have given me before. I do not feel that it would be out of place to state to you here on this occasion that I know that without the support of the members of this organization, I would not have been called, even by my enemies, the 'Junior Senator from Alabama.' I realize that I was elected by men who believe in the principles that I have sought to advocate and which are the principles of this organization." [67]

Reporter Sprigle reported, on the basis of official files of the Alabama Klan, that Black preached alone, hailing the manifest destiny of the Invisible Empire as it moved irresistibly toward its goal of a white Protestant state, Southland and the Nation. [68]

The principles to which Black "sought to advocate" were reflected in a speech by the Imperial Wizard:

> "The Klan is scattered over the nation. The Catholic sentiment is hot in the big centers of the nation. And thus we are going to see whether the progress through the succeeding years of this century will be a progress through centralized hierarchical control of government and religions [note the plural], or whether we will have the great open spaces continue to provide the thought and the direction for this great free nation.
>
> "That is the Klan program. We are here to preserve America and to do it as a genuine fight, and I don't mean maybe . . .
>
> "No, the Catholic hasn't any chance to control Alabama. And the Negro hasn't any chance to control Alabama. . . ."

After the Wizard spoke, the Imperial Legal Adviser, William E. Zumbrunn, addressed the group. He said, in part:

> ". . . the man known as Al Smith, who seeks the Presidency of the United States, lowered the dignity of that high office by bowing the knee to a foreign potentate and kissing the ring upon his finger. Men, it is those conditions which the Klan is called upon to correct . . .
>
> ". . . America, the home of the free and the brave has been invaded by large hordes of foreigners that have neither the inclination nor the training to love our institutions and our flag, and

that power and that wave represented in the kultur of Catholicism across the water brings to America's shores the message of a Pope.

"The Catholic Hierarchy has been driven from every country on the face of the earth, save Mexico and America as a political machine."

Zumbrunn went on to deplore holding a Eucharistic Congress in the United States, an event which he said was a plan to make America the home of the Catholic Church and to challenge the Supremacy of the Klan.

Calling out to the throng, he asked if they were going to permit such an event to transpire, and the mob shouted back: "No! No!"

"Well, the Legal Adviser replied, "If you are not going to permit it . . . send back to the confines of Hades any man that lowers the dignity of the United States to kiss the ring of any foreigner." [69]

New York Times reporter Russell B. Porter showed Winston Williams of 7321 Third Avenue, South, in Birmingham, an affidavit which he had signed during preparation of the articles written for the *Pittsburgh Post-Gazette,* and asked the Alabamian whether the affidavit was correct. Williams agreed that it was.

He stated in the affidavit that he was a member of the Klan in Birmingham in 1926, that he attended the meeting at which Black is said to have received his life membership card, and that he heard Mr. Black accept the card in a speech in which he thanked Grand Dragon Esdale and the Klan for the honor of life membership and their support of his candidacy in the primary. [70]

With few exceptions, the revelations triggered by Sprigle's articles, which were picked up by the *Times* and other major dailies, caused a national uproar.

The Nation magazine, well known for its liberalism, supported Black vigorously, a position totally contrary to its articles some years earlier which deplored the pervasive bigotry in Alabama. One editorial in that publication said: "If we thought Justice Black were now a Klansman, in fact, spirit, deed, or idea, we should oppose him bitterly and without compromise."

But, the editorial continued, it saw nothing in his record that carried "even a whiff of the Klan smell." Rather, the magazine saw "a brilliant, militant, uncompromising liberal." [71]

The New York Times could not understand that viewpoint as set forth in *The Nation, The New Republic,* and other liberal journals. One editorial of the *Times* said:

> "Of what importance are old records of bigotry and religious persecution, compared with a Senator's vote on some new bill to curb industry or tax the rich? The New Liberalism, intent on economic issues, finds it easy to forgive some negligence in the matter of civil liberties. . . ." [72]

A week later, the *Times* again editorialized on the liberals exculpation of Black with the following words:

> "The so-called 'liberals' ignore the fact of Black's membership in the Klan and his fitness to serve. They revert to *argumentum ad hominum,* to wit: 'Who exposed Black? What [were] the political opinions of the persons who dug up the evidence against him" What were their motives?'
>
> "The editors of the liberal weeklies, and others making increasing use of the *ad hominum* argument, must be too intelligent to know they are not resorting to demagogy of a cheap and shameless sort. It is on all fours with Hitler's argument that a scientific discovery is worthless if it is made by a Jew." [73]

Black Evades The Issue

After his lifetime membership in the Klan was exposed, Black and his wife sailed to Europe. The furor in the press, however, would not die down. The continuing outrage of the American people, as expressed in the media, forced the new Justice, upon his return to America several weeks later, to deliver a nationwide radio address, ostensibly to explain his membership in the Klan.

However, the address was vintage Black. He never expressly repudiated the Klan, nor denied the accuracy of press reports concerning his Klan activity and the statements attributed to him. He never said he was sorry; never apologized. Rather, he attacked his opponents, and by innuendo, the Catholic Church, and any other religious people who project "religious beliefs into a position of prime importance" in public life.

To those who were aware of Black's attitude toward the Church, and to organized religion generally, it was striking to note his argument focused, not on the odious activities of the Klan, but rather on dangers inherent in diverse religious beliefs.

That fear of what sincere religious people can do in society later became a major concern of the Court upon which Black sat, beginning with the *Everson* decision in 1947, regarding freedom of religion in education, and progressing to the *Roe v. Wade* case of 1973, involving the sanctity of human life from the moment of conception.

In his radio address, Black said, in part:

"The Constitutional safeguard to complete liberty of religious belief is a declaration of the greatest importance to the future of America as a nation of free people. Any movement, or action by any group that threatens to bring about a result inconsistent with this unrestricted individual right, is a menace to freedom.

"Let me repeat: any program, even if directed by good intentions, which tends to breed or revive religious discord or antagonism can and may spread with such rapidity as to imperil this vital Constitutional protection of one of the most sacred human rights.

"I believe no ordinary manoeuvre executed for political advantage would justify a member of the Supreme Court in publicly discussing it. If however, the manoeuvre threatens the existing peace and harmony between religious or racial groups in our country the occasion is not an ordinary one. It is extraordinary." [74]

Black went on to say that while he was in Europe, "a planned and concerted campaign" to fan the flames of prejudice and calculated to create racial and religious hatred had taken place.

If such a campaign continued, he said, it will project "religious beliefs into a position of prime importance in political campaigns and . . . reinject our social and business life with the passion of religious bigotry."

Continuing, he declared:

"It will bring the political religionist back into undeserved and perilous influence in affairs of government . . .

"I believe my record as a Senator refutes every implication of racial or religious tolerance . . .

"I did join the Klan. I later resigned. I never rejoined. . . . I do not now consider the unsolicited card given me shortly after my nomination to the Senate as a membership of any kind in the Ku Klux Klan. I never used it. I did not even keep it."

Black said he had no sympathy "with any organization or group which anywhere or at any time arrogates to itself the un-American power to interfere in the slightest degree with complete religious freedom."

Concluding, he spoke a line that has become a classic statement identified with the prejudiced: "Some of my best and most intimate friends are Catholics and Jews." [75]

He never explained who had mounted an alleged campaign attempting to "fan the flames of prejudice calculated to create racial and religious hatred" during the brief period of his vacation in Europe.

He failed to indicate how such a purported effort differed in scope and intensity from the Klan's venomous program of religious and racial hatred which convulsed the nation for 22 years, and in which, the record shows, Black actively participated.

The new U.S. Supreme Court Justice did not define what he meant by "political religionist," nor did he explain how such a person or persons had acted adversely to the common good in the past. Neither did he tell why such individual(s) supposedly hold "undeserved and perilous influence in affairs of government."

Notably, he never categorically condemned the Klan nor its beliefs and practices.

Moreover, Black never explained the reason for taking his Supreme Court oath in secret, nor did he choose to reveal the content of that particular oath. Was it similar to the oaths he took as a Mason? Was it the oath of a Klansman?

In his nationwide radio address, he certainly made no solemn declaration or promise to renounce and vigorously oppose any Klan or Masonic bias against the Catholic religion which might be found on the bench or elsewhere; nor did he express an intention never to sit in judgment in cases in which his bias against the Catholic Church might be suspected.

In fact, the total impact of his broadcast was overwhelmingly negative, as evidenced by press reaction the following day.

The New York Herald Tribune editorialized that the Justice's conduct was "that of a coward, and added:

"The effort of Senator Black to suggest that he is the real protagonist of tolerance and that his enemies are intolerant is perhaps the greatest item of effrontery in a uniquely brazen utterance. Only a man heedless of the truth and a man afraid of his official skin could fall so low." [76]

The *Newark Ledger* said: "As he resigned from the Klan, he should resign from the Court. [77]

Negative editorials appeared also in *The Boston Herald, Boston Post, Hartford Courant, Worcester Telegram, Cleveland Plain Dealer,* and *Buffalo Courier.* [78]

The *Buffalo Evening News* said if Black continued on the bench, "every attorney representing a member of a group which the Ku Klux Klan terrorized can protest his sitting in judgment." [79]

The *Chatanooga Times* editorialized:

"One wanted so desperately to believe that Mr. Black would add: 'I have this day forwarded my resignation as an Associate Justice of the Supreme Court of the United States.' If that had been Mr. Black's contribution to the spirit of tolerance and of freedom, it would have made his speech an epochal event. Instead there followed the type of statement to be expected from a police court lawyer trying to obtain the dismissal of charges against a housebreaker by pleading that the defendant has always been kind to his family." [80]

And *The New York Times,* commented:

"Moral sense finds it increasingly hard to speak out in a world educated to the notion of a class morality and party morality. It is the ideologies against the humanities. It is the new morality by which Liberals may defend a Klansman on the Supreme Court because he is sound on the Administration's economic program . . .

"The new flexible moral code may even permit a good Liberal to look across the Atlantic and condone in one type of despotism the physical and spiritual brutalities which he condemns in another.

"The Liberal with a capital 'L' has pushed into the background the fine old word liberal with a small 'l'. The liberal mind was the open mind, and the liberal temper was the middle-of-the-road temper. The New Liberalism now covers men from the radical camps and the revolutionary camps, and they have brought with them their doctrinaire rigidities and their hard-boiled tactics.

"The former liberal approach to social problems was the moderate, gradualist approach . . . The new Liberalism hankers for the moral and technical shortcuts which the dictators employ as a matter of course." [81]

Despite the Constitutional prohibition on Senator Black's eligibility to serve on the Supreme Court (Article I, Sec. 6), and the overwhelming public opposition to his Klan background, the gentleman from Alabama served on the high bench for 34 years.

Had he changed his attitude toward the Church, so that there should be no suspicion that his opinions were tainted with prejudice in cases involving the religion clause? By no means.

With regard to the Christian Church generally, the Justice's own son wrote that his father—

". . . would make fun of the church . . . by hilarious imitation, singing through his nose songs like 'How tedious and tasteless the hours when Jesus came into my life . . .'" [82]

But the Roman Catholic Church, as in Black's Klan days, seemed to ignite in the Justice a particular animosity, according to his son, who wrote:

"The Ku Klux Klan and Daddy, so far as I could tell, only had one thing in common. He suspected the Catholic Church. He used to read all of Paul Blanshard's books exposing power abuse in the Catholic Church. He thought the popes and bishops had too much power and property. He resented the fact that rental property owned by the Church was not taxed; he felt they got most of their revenue from the poor and they did not return enough of it. But even then his favorite district judge was a man who had been a bishop's lawyer . . ." [83]

Hugo, Jr. also reported that his father suspected the Catholic Church was aspiring to be the State Church in the United States, and the Justice *"could not tolerate any sign of encouraging religious faith by state aid."* [84] [Emphasis added].

On the other hand, as so many of Justice Black's opinions evidence, he was determined to make the Supreme Court a haven for "the non-conforming victims of prejudice" [85], a facile phrase used by Hugo, Jr. to characterize his father's sympathy for non-believers in Judeo-Christian truths.

Indeed, the Justice "could not whip himself up to a belief in God or the divinity of Christ, life after death, or Heaven or Hell . . ." [86]

Unquestionably, Justice Hugo Lafayette Black spoke from experience when, in 1930, he said "a man follows in the future the course that he has followed in the past," and "the kind of steps a man made in the sand five years ago," show "the kind of steps he is likely to make in the same sand five years hence."

Perhaps the record of his activities would be even more dismal if he had not deliberately burned 600 volumes of his notes and papers. [87]

The Justice's son said that fifteen years prior to his death, his father "had made it clear to me exactly what papers he wanted destroyed." Moreover, that profound concern by the Justice to eliminate perhaps impolitic or other damning documents never left his mind. Hugo, Jr. wrote:

> "Practically the first thing Daddy wanted me to do once he was installed in the hospital was to go out and burn certain papers of his." [88]

In the Justice's *Papers* is a memorandum to his secretary (Frances Lamb), signed by Black, which says in part:

> "Hugo, Jr. will tell you what to do, that is to destroy them all. Hugo L. Black." [89]

In view of Justice Black's long history of prejudice against the Catholic Church, and Christianity generally, his majority opinion in a precedent Court decision on the issue of judicial bias appears to be the ultimate in contemptuous irony. He wrote:

> "A fair trial in a fair tribunal is a basic requirement of due process. Fairness of course requires an absence of actual bias in the trial of cases. But our system of law has always endeavored to prevent *even the probability of unfairness* . . . no man is permitted to try cases where he has an interest in the outcome . . . But to perform its high function in the best way 'justice must satisfy the appearance of justice.' " [90]

6/ CRAFT FIGHTS RELIGION CLAUSE HISTORY

Justice Hugo Lafayette Black arrived on the Court about the time Congress began considering major appropriations for education, including funds to assist students in Catholic and other religiously affiliated institutions. It was a period when the Craft desperately needed a member of the Fraternity on the high bench, such as Justice Black, who "could not tolerate any sign of encouraging religious faith by state aid." [1]

As will be demonstrated below, Brother Black did not let the Fraternity down. But his work was cut out for him.

For many years prior to the Alabama Senator's ascendancy to the high bench, Supreme Court decisions regarding religious freedom had been moving inexorably against the Craft's little known 1920 Colorado Springs plan to cast the minds of America's school children in a Masonic mold.

In 1899, for example, the Court held that there is no Constitutional bar against the government contracting with corporations affiliated with the Catholic Church, which perform public welfare services, "as long as the corporation is managed according to the law under which it exists."

Further, said the Court, contracts with such corporations can not be voided simply because their officers happen to adhere to "the doctrines of the Roman Catholic Church," or because the corporation's officials happen to wear distinctive religious garb. [2]

Again, in 1923, the Court ruled that the legislature of a State may not "interfere with . . . the power of the parents to control the education of their young." [3]

Just two years later, the same tribunal, in the *Pierce* case, struck down as unconstitutional the Masonically-crafted 1922 Oregon law which required every child in that State to attend public school. [4]

And in 1930, the Court held that children in nonpublic schools may be provided secular textbooks at government expense. [5]

Beyond those rulings by the nation's highest tribunal, the Masonic Fraternity was confronted with a number of State and federal historical precedents which evidenced a public will to protect and advance the religious values inherent in Christianity.

The Historic Record Of Religion In American Life

The national record in support of religion generally, and of Christianity in particular, was manifested—prior to the 1940s—in numerous official public acts. That reality was perhaps expressed best in 1892 by Mr. Justice David Brewer in his majority opinion in *Church of the Holy Trinity v. U.S.* He said:

> ". . . no purpose of action against religion can be imputed to any legislation, state or national, because this is a religious people. This is historically true. From the discovery of this continent to the present hour, there is a single voice making this affirmation. The commission of Christopher Columbus, prior to his sail westward, is from "Ferdinand and Isabella, by the grace of God, King and Queen of Castile," etc . . . The first Colonial grant to Sir Walter Raleigh was from Elizabeth, by grace of God . . . queen, defender of the Faith, etc. . . ." [6]

The Court went on to cite favorably a judicial decision in Pennsylvania which held that "general Christianity, is and always has been a part of the common law of Pennsylvania."

Continuing, Justice Brewer, speaking for the Court, also favorably cited an opinion by Chancellor Kent, Chief Justice of the Supreme Court of New York, who said (in *People v. Ruggles*):

> "The people of this State, in common with the people of this country, profess the general doctrines of Christianity, as the rule of their faith and practice; and to scandalize the author of these doctrines is not only, in a religious point of view, extremely impious, but, even in respect to the obligations due to society, is a gross violation of decency and good order . . .
>
> "The free, equal and undisturbed enjoyment of religious opin-

ion, whatever it may be, and free and decent discussions on any religious subject, is granted and secured; but to revile, with malicious and blasphemous contempt, the religion professed by almost the whole community, is an abuse of that right. Nor are we bound, by any expressions in the Constitution, as some have strangely supposed, either not to punish at all, or to punish indiscriminately, the like attacks upon the religion of Mahomet or the Grand Lama; and for this plain reason, that the case assumes that we are a Christian people, and the morality of the country is deeply ingrafted upon Christianity, and not upon the doctrines or worship of those imposters." [7]

State Constitutions

Justice Brewer was entirely accurate. State Constitutions extant at the time the religion clause was ratified, and for many years after, evidenced that the Christian religion, particularly Protestant Christianity, merited protection and encouragement by the State.

For example, the Constitution of New Hampshire, enacted the year after the religion clause of the First Amendment became effective, stipulated in Article VI:

"As morality and piety, rightly grounded on evangelical principles, will give the best and greatest security to Government, and will lay in the hearts of men the strongest obligations to due subjection; and as the knowledge of these is most likely to be propagated through a society by the institution of the public worship of the Deity, and of public instruction in morality and religion; therefore, to promote these important purposes, the people of this State have a right to empower the Legislature to authorize from time to time, the several towns, parishes, bodies corporate, or religious societies, within this State, to make adequate provision, at their own expense, for the support and maintenance of public Protestant teachers of piety, religion and morality. . . .

"And every denomination of Christian, demeaning themselves quietly and as good subjects of the State, shall be equally under the protection of the law; and no subordination of any one sect or denomination to another shall ever be established by law." [8]

The Constitution of Massachusetts (adopted in 1780) contained the same provision as did the New Hampshire Constitution for "public Protestant teachers of piety, religion and morality." Section VI of the Massachusetts Constitution required public office holders to declare a belief in "the Christian religion," and to have a firm persuasion of its truth" [9]

Also, the Constitutions of New Jersey (adopted in 1776), Delaware (adopted in 1792), Maryland (adopted in 1776), North Carolina (adopted in 1776), and Vermont (adopted in 1786) provided for equality among Protestants or Christians. [10]

Pennsylvania (adopted in 1790, and re-adopted in 1838) stipulated in Article 4: "No person, who acknowledges the being of a God, and a future state of rewards and punishments shall, on account of his religious sentiments, be disqualified to hold any office under this Commonwealth." [11]

Constitutional Conventions

Of the Thirteen Original States existing when the Constitution and its first Ten Amendments were adopted, only three proposed an amendment concerning religion. Those States were: Virginia, New York and New Hampshire.

Virginia's convention proposed: "That religion, or the duty which we owe to our Creator and the manner of discharging it, can be directed only by reason and conviction, and not by force and violence; and therefore all men have a natural, equal, and unalienable right to the exercise of religion according to the dictates of conscience; and that no particular religious sect or society ought to be favored or established by law, in preference to others." [12]

New York proposed an amendment very similar to Virginia's, except it did not define religion. The New York amendment read:

> "That the people have an equal, natural, and unalienable right freely and peaceably to exercise their religion according to the dictates of conscience; and that no religious sect or society ought to be favored or established by law in preference to others." [13]

New Hampshire proposed: "Congress shall make no laws touching religion, or to infringe the rights of conscience. [14]

Although North Carolina and Rhode Island did not recommend an amendment regarding religion, the Conventions in those States adopted declarations of principles which were identical to the amendment on religion submitted by Virginia. [15]

Maryland also did not propose an amendment, but a minority of the delegates urged the following language be added to the new U.S. Constitution: "That there be no national religion established by law;

but that all persons be equally entitled to protection of their religious liberty." [16]

Debates In The First Congress

On June 8, 1789, Representative James Madison of Virginia rose in the House chamber to offer amendments to the Constitution. He said:

> ". . . in article 1st, section 9, between clauses 3 and 4, be inserted these clauses, to wit: The civil rights of none shall be abridged on account of religious belief or worship, nor shall any national religion be established, nor shall the full and equal rights of conscience be in any manner, or on any pretext infringed . . ." [17]

Note that Madison recommended the amendment be inserted in the Constitution between prohibitions on bills of attainder, *ex post facto* laws, and suspension of *habeas corpus*. He did not propose that it be placed in Article 1st, section 9, before or after clause 7, which limits withdrawal of funds from the U.S. Treasury. Neither did he place it in Article I, section 10, which concerns acts prohibited by the States.

Note also, that Madison explicitly said he did not want "any national religion be established." The amendment reflected the sentiments of his colleagues in the Virginia Constitutional Convention (reported above) who urged that "no particular religious sect or society ought to be favored or established by law in preference to others."

On July 21, 1789, the proposal was referred to a select committee.

On August 15, 1789, the full House again considered the issue, at which time Madison proposed: "no religion shall be established by law, nor shall the equal rights of conscience be infringed." [18]

Rep. Peter Silvester, of New York, objected to the wording, saying he perceived the amendment to have a different construction than had been made in the committee. As worded by Madison, he thought the amendment might be construed to abolish religion altogether

Rep. Elbridge Gerry of Massachusetts said the amendment would read better if it were changed to say: "no religious doctrine shall be established by law."

Rep. Roger Sherman of Connecticut thought the amendment was altogether unnecessary. Congress, he said, had no authority whatever delegated to it to make religious establishments. [19]

Madison said his proposal prohibited Congress from establishing a religion, and enforcing the legal observation of it by law. Some State

Conventions, he observed, feared the power given by the Constitution to Congress "to make all laws necessary and proper to carry into execution the Constitution, and the laws made under it, enabled them to make such laws . . . as might infringe the rights of conscience, and establish a national religion . . ." [20]

Benjamin Huntington of Connecticut said he shared the views of Rep. Silvester that Madison's wording "might be extremely hurtful to religion." He hoped the amendment could be written in such a way as to secure the rights of conscience, and a free exercise of the rights of religion, but "that it not patronize those who professed no religion at all."

Subsequently, Madison withdrew his amendment. [21]

On August 17, 1789, Rep. Samuel Livermore of New Hampshire proposed that the amendment be changed to read: "the equal rights of conscience, the freedom of speech or of the press, and the right of trial by jury in criminal cases, shall not be infringed by any State." The amendment was adopted. [22]

On August 20, the House reconsidered the amendment and approved the following language proposed by Rep. Fisher Ames of Massachusetts: "Congress shall make no law establishing religion, or to prevent the free exercise thereof, or to infringe the rights of conscience." [23]

The Senate, on September 9, 1789, approved the following language proposed by Senator Oliver Ellsworth of Connecticut (who subsequently served as Chief Justice of the U.S. Supreme Court from 1796 to 1800): "Congress shall make no law establishing articles of faith or a mode of worship, or prohibiting the free exercise of religion; or abridging the freedom of speech, or of the press." [24]

Finally, on September 24, 1789 Conferees of the House and Senate agreed on the clause as it reads today: "Congress shall make no law respecting an establishment of religion, or prohibiting the free exercise thereof . . ." [25]

From the comments made in debate it is apparent that the the religion clause was intended to prohibit the National Government from establishing a single religion and enforcing the observation of it, or its tenets, by law. At the same time, the Founding Fathers agreed that religion is very important to the American people and the Government should protect their right to practice their own religions freely.

But of equal importance during House debate was the exposition of another critical facet of the religion clause: that was the view of the Founding Fathers toward those who practiced no religion at all.

When Benjamin Huntington asserted that the Government should "not patronize those who professed no religion at all," there is no record that his point was disputed. Indeed, the general thrust of those reacting to his statement was in the affirmative.

The concern of Huntington and his colleagues, Peter Silvester, and Elbridge Gerry was prompted by Madison's proposal that "no religion shall be established by law . . ."

Because of the substantial opposition to his proposal, Madison withdrew it.

Worth noting, too, is that the Constitution itself concludes with: "Done in Convention, . . . the seventeenth day of September, *in the year of our Lord one thousand seven hundred and eighty-seven* . . ." [Emphasis added.] [26]

Federal Legislation

Article III of the Northwest Ordinance of 1787 (passed by the Continental Congress), ordained: "Religion, morality and knowledge being necessary to good government and the happiness of mankind, schools and the means of education shall forever be encouraged. [27]

The present Federal Government, formed under the Constitution of 1787, continued the same policies. Territorial land sold by the Federal Government stipulated that sections were to be reserved for schools and religious purposes. [28]

The Act of June 1, 1796, regulated grants of land appropriated for the military services and for the Society of the United Brethren for Propagating the Gospel Among the Heathens. That Act required the Surveyor General to survey several tracts of land "formerly set apart by an ordinance of Congress of the 3d September, 1788, for the Society of the United Brethren for propagating the Gospel among the heathen; and to issue a patent or patents for the said three tracts to the said society for the uses and purposes in the said ordinance set forth." [29]

The record shows there was no objection by any member of Congress, including James Madison, who helped to shape the religion clause of the First Amendment. Although the Act of 1796 was approved by voice vote, Madison was recorded as present for a quorum call in the House that day, and presumably was available to object to the measure. [30]

In 1798, an Act establishing the government of the Mississippi Territory contained the same provisions as the Northwest Ordinance of 1787 [31]

In 1803, the territorial government of Ohio was authorized by Congress to sell all or part of the lands appropriated by Congress "for the support of religion within the Ohio company's and John Cleeves Symmes' purchases . . ."

That federal legislation was re-enacted in 1826 and 1833. It was not rescinded until 1968. [32]

In fact, the national policy on land grants for education between 1820-1865 placed no restriction on participation by private or church schools. [33]

The Supreme Court noted that "before 1895 the Government for a number of years had made contracts for sectarian schools for the education of the Indians" [34].

In 1852, the U.S. Senate issued a report in response to repeated expressions of concern about abolishing military chaplains.

The report said the "establishment of religion" meant "the connexion with the State of a particular religious society by its endowment at the public expense, in exclusion of, or in preference to any other, by giving to its members exclusive political rights, and by compelling the attendance of those who rejected its communion . . . or religious observances. [35]

In 1888, mission schools in Alaska received $112,000. The denominational breakdown was: Episcopal, $30,000; Catholic, $25,000; Moravian, $25,000, Presbyterian, $15,000; Swedish Evangelical, $15,000, and Reformed Episcopal, $1,000. [36]

Finally, private sectarian schools shared in all Federal emergency programs in the Great Depression of the 1930s, and in war emergency programs in the 1940s. [37]

Messages and Addresses of Presidents

In his well known Farewell Address, President George Washington said:

> Of all the dispositions and habits which lead to political prosperity, religion and morality are indispensable supports . . . [L]et it simply be asked where is the security for prosperity, for reputation, for life—if the sense of religious obligation desert? . . .
>
> [A]nd let us with caution indulge the supposition that morality can be maintained without religion." [38]

Although nearly all Presidents referred to Almighty God, Providence, our Creator, etc., in their inaugural addresses, Presidents John Adams, William Henry Harrison, James Buchanan and Abraham Lincoln specifically noted the nation's identification with Christianity. [39]

Days Of Thanksgiving And Prayer

Days of prayer, thanksgiving and fasting go back to the early days under the Constitution. A Day of Prayer And Thanksgiving was proclaimed by George Washington in 1789, and similar proclamations were made intermittently until 1815.

It was not until Jan 4, 1861 that another Day of Prayer was proclaimed by President Lincoln. Three similar proclamations were made that same year, followed by similar invocations in 1864 and 1865.

Again there was a hiatus until the United States was on the brink of war, and President Franklin D. Roosevelt set aside a Day of Prayer. Similar Days were annually marked until 1945. Another interruption followed until 1952, when the practice of reserving a Day of Prayer was resumed. Days of Prayer have been proclaimed annually since that time.

Thanksgiving Day was first established officially in 1863, and has been marked every subsequent year. [40]

It also is worthy of note that President James Madison sent a Message to Congress on June 1, 1812 recommending that Members consider entrusting the "just cause [the War of 1812] into the hands of the Almighty." [41]

Just over two months later, Madison again urged the nation to render to "the Sovereign of the Universe and the Benefactor of Mankind the public homage due to His holy attributes." The President sought God's "merciful forgiveness and His assistance." Mr. Madison further asked that God inspire all nations with "a love of justice and of concord, and with a reverence for the unerring precept of our holy religion to do to others as they would require that others should do to them . . ." [42]

Earlier Supreme Court Decisions

In addition to the previously cited Supreme Court decision in *Church of the Holy Trinity,* the high bench has identified the United States as a Christian nation on several other occasions. Also, Justice Joseph Story, a recognized authority on the Constitution, who was appointed to the Supreme Court by James Madison, expressed the same opinion in his *Commentaries on the Constitution.*

Terret v. Taylor: This 1815 case concerned an effort by the State of Virginia to turn over to public officials glebe lands of the Episcopal Church which had been confiscated during the Revolutionary War. Justice Story, speaking for a unanimous Court said:

> "The legislature could not create or continue a religious establishment which would have *exclusive* rights and prerogatives, or compel the citizens to worship under a stipulated form of discipline, or to pay taxes to those whose creed they could not conscientiously believe. But the free exercise of religion cannot be justly deemed to be restrained by aiding with equal attention the votaries of every sect to perform their own religious duties, or by establishing funds for the support of ministers, for public charities, for the endowment of churches, or for the sepulture of the dead." [43]

In his *Commentaries,* which were a major formative influence on American jurisprudence, Justice Story wrote:

> ". . . it is impossible for those who believe in the truth of Christianity as a divine revelation to doubt that it is the especial duty of government to foster and encourage it among all the citizens and subjects. This is a point wholly distinct from that of the right of private judgment in matters of religion, and of the freedom of public worship according to the dictates of one's conscience." [44]

> "Every American colony from its foundation down to the revolution, with the possible exception of Rhode Island, did openly, by the whole course of its laws and institutions, support and sustain, in some form, the Christian religion, and almost invariably gave a peculiar sanction to some of its fundamental doctrines. And this has continued to be the case in some of the States down to the present period, without the slightest suspicion that it was against the principles of public law or republican liberty."

> "Probably at the time of the adoption of the Constitution, and the amendments to it, the general, if not universal sentiment in America was that Christianity ought to receive encouragement from the State so far as was not incompatible with the private rights of conscience and the freedom of religious worship.

> "The real object of the [First] Amendment was not to countenance, much less to advance Mahometanism, or Judaism, or

infidelity by prostrating Christianity; but to exclude all rivalry among Christian sects, and to prevent any national, ecclesiastical establishment [be given] the exclusive patronage of the national government." [45]

Vidal v. Girard's Executors (1844)

The Supreme Court was presented with a controversy involving the will of Girard, who established a school for white males. The will stipulated that no ecclesiastic, missionary or minister of any sect was to hold any position at the school or even to visit it. By implication, the will excluded all instruction in the Christian religion.
The Court said:

". . . we are compelled to admit that although Christianity be a part of the common law of the state [Pennsylvania], yet it is so in this qualified sense, that its divine origin and truth are admitted, and therefore it is not to be maliciously and openly reviled and blasphemed against, to the annoyance of believers or the injury of the public . . .
"It is unnecessary for us, however, to consider what would be the legal effect of a devise in Pennsylvania for the establishment of a school or college, for the propagation of Judaism or Deism, or any other form of infidelity. Such a case is not to be presumed to exist in a Christian country; and therefore it must be made out by clear and indisputable proof . . .
"Where can the purest principles of morality be learned so clearly or so perfectly as from the New Testament? Where are benevolence, the love of truth, sobriety, and industry, so powerfully and irresistibly inculcated as in the sacred volume? . . .
"It has hitherto been thought sufficient if [a charitable donor] does not require anything to be taught inconsistent with Christianity." [46]

Mormon Church v. United States (1889)

The case involved Mormon belief in polygamy, which the Court said was "a blot on our civilization." Continuing, the Court declared:

"It is contrary to the spirit of Christianity and of the civilization which Christianity has produced in the Western world." [47]

U.S. v. Macintosh (1931)

The case involved a Canadian immigrant who balked at taking up arms to defend the United States, because the requirement conflicted with his religious beliefs. In handing down its decision, the Court remarked:

"We are a Christian people *(Holy Trinity Church v. United States . . .),* according to one another the equal right of religious freedom, and acknowledging with reverence the duty of obedience to the will of God . . ." [48]

That is the rather formidable public record of support for religion and Christianity by the three branches of government, dating from the time the religion clause was proposed, drafted and ratified—until 1947.

The Masonic View Of The Religion Clause

Despite that historic record, impressive as it is, it proved woefully inadequate to deter Masonry from imposing its philosophy of Kabbalistic Gnosticism upon the nation, beginning at the elementary school level.

How did it happen?

The key to effecting that Masonic goal was to sweep aside the reality of history by "interpretation" of the Constitution.

"Law," said one Masonic author in 1933, "is largely in the interpretation and not in the text . . ." [49]

Two years later, a powerful member of the Craft, President Franklin D. Roosevelt, in his January 6, 1937 Message To Congress, commented: "The vital need is not an alteration of our fundamental law, but an increasingly enlightened view in reference to it." [50]

The President's remarks were made as he was attempting to implement his "court-packing" plan. It also was the time when Justice Hugo L. Black took a seat on the Supreme Court.

In 1941, another member of the Craft, Justice Robert H. Jackson, wrote that the Constitution and its amendments "are what the judges say they are." [51]

Brother Jackson candidly admitted that he, and those who shared his viewpoint on the Constitution, succeeded in their efforts to shape that charter of liberty by influencing the choice of "forward-looking" Justices. [52]

Although not noted by Mr. Jackson, it so happened those Justices, like President Roosevelt and Justice Black, were, in overwhelming numbers, members of the Masonic Fraternity.

Meanwhile, beginning in 1935, and continuing through the mid-1940s, the *New Age* carried on a massive propaganda campaign against State assistance for transportation of children to Catholic schools. [53]

Five years later, that effort was expanded by the Scottish Rite to include opposition not only to prayer and Bible reading in public schools, but also to released time for religious instruction of students at such schools. [54]

Blueprint For Court's Re-Direction

Of even more interest, is the fact that the Scottish Rite journal, and the Grand Commander of the Southern Jurisdiction, advanced arguments against aid to religious education which appeared to be, curiously, like blueprints for the line of reasoning the Masonically-dominated Court would soon follow in its "interpretation" of the religion clause.

The Masonic mode of interpreting the religion clause of the Constitution began in earnest in 1935.

In November of that year, the *New Age* ran a commentary opposing aid to parochial schools. In support of that position, the magazine advanced the argument that such assistance was contrary to James Madison's "Memorial and Remonstrance," which said, in part:

> "Because it is proper to take alarm at the first experiment on our liberties . . . The freemen of America did not wait till usurped power had strengthened itself by exercise, and entangled the question in precedents . . . Who does not see that . . . the same authority which can force a citizen to contribute three pence only of his property for the support of any one establishment, may force him to conform to any other establishment in all cases whatsoever?" [55]

About a year-and-a-half later (April, 1937), Elmer Rogers, editor of the *New Age* and executive assistant to Grand Commander of the Scottish Rite of the Southern Jurisdiction, appeared as a witness before the House Committee on Education to oppose legislation which would authorize federal funds for education. Speaking for the Grand Commander, Rogers said the Craft feared some of the funds might be diverted to Catholic schools.

To support his position the Masonic official called attention to a statement by a Rev. Thomas E. Little, a man who shared the Scottish

Rite viewpoint on education, and whose statement cited the same quotation from Madison's "Memorial and Remonstrance" as had appeared in the *New Age* 17 months earlier. [56]

Also in his testimony, Rogers called attention to four prior Supreme Court decisions which, in his view, confirmed that the Court had found State aid to religion to be unconstitutional. The cases cited were: *Watson v. Jones,* 13 Wallace 679 (1871); *Davis v. Beason,* 133 U.S. 333 (1890); *Reynolds v. United States,* 98 U.S. 145 (1878); and *Quick Bear v. Leupp,* 210 U.S. 50 (1908). [57]

In April, 1940, a *New Age* editorial expressing opposition to aid for "sectarian purposes," said Madison's "Memorial and Remonstrance" and Jefferson's bill for Establishing Religious Freedom [in Virginia] "were the principles and precedents out of which was formed the Bill of Rights." [58]

The Masonic Argument In Perspective

Madison Jefferson, and Virginia

Madison's "Memorial and Remonstrance" (written in 1785), and Jefferson's Bill for Establishing Religious Freedom (written in 1786) concerned religious freedom in one State, Virginia, several years prior to the time the religion clause was proposed, composed, approved and ratified.

Neither document was discussed during debates in the Constitutional Convention, nor were they ever mentioned during discussions when the religion clause was being crafted by members of the House and Senate.

Jefferson, it might be noted, was in France when the First Amendment was discussed in Congress and adopted by the people.

Madison, as the record of House debate on that clause shows, was unsuccessful in having any of his proposed language on the subject accepted by his colleagues. Indeed, he withdrew his last proposal for fashioning the clause.

During House debate on the religion clause, the person in the First Congress who proposed language most closely resembling the wording of that provision as we know it today was Congressman Fisher Ames of Massachusetts, not James Madison of Virginia. [59]

Further, Madison and Jefferson's own State, Virginia, not only was the reluctant and last State to ratify the first Ten Amendments to the Constitution (on December 15, 1791), but members of the Virginia legislature expressly declared that the religion clause permits the use of tax money "for the support of religion or its preachers." That view is evident in *The Journal of the Virginia Senate* (1789), which states:

> "We the underwritten members of the majority on that question deem it incumbent on us [to express] . . . our objections to those articles [i.e., amendments] . . .
>
> "The third amendment [the present First Amendment to the Constitution] recommended by Congress does not prohibit the rights of conscience from being violated or infringed; and although it goes to restrain Congress from passing laws establishing any national religion, they might, notwithstanding, levy taxes to any amount for the support of religion or its preachers; and any particular denomination of Christians might be so favored and supported by the general government as to give it a decided advantage over the others, and in the process of time render it powerful and dangerous as if it was established as the national religion of the country." [60]

Earlier Court Decisions: Reynolds, Beason, Watson

The *Reynolds* and *Beason* cases were concerned with bigamy and polygamy, practices commonly engaged in by Mormons at that time as a matter of religious belief, despite the fact that having a plurality of wives was a statutory crime.

The common consensus against polygamy was so widespread in "a Christian nation" that it was condemned by Congressional statute, judicial decisions, and Presidential statements.

Presidents James Garfield and Grover Cleveland condemned polygamy in their Inaugural Addresses of 1881 and 1885, respectively. [61]

Thus, that particular religious belief was strongly opposed by the three branches of government, clearly demonstrating that there are limits to the free exercise of religion under the Constitution.

Actually, as the following discussion of the Court's decisions in the cited cases evidences, the high bench consistently demonstrated uninterrupted support for Christian values and beliefs.

In the *Reynolds* case, George Reynolds, a Mormon, had been charged with committing bigamy in the Territory of Utah, where the act was a crime according to federal law.

In rendering its decision, the Court established two Constitutional principles: First, it provided a definition for the word "religion" in the First Amendment; and, second, it ruled how "free" the "free exercise" of religion really is.

The Court noted that the word "religion" is not defined in the Constitution. Consequently, it was necessary to look elsewhere to find the meaning of the word in "the history of the times in the midst of which the provision was adopted."

The Court then cited Madison's "Memorial and Remonstrance" where he demonstrated "that religion, or the duty we owe the Creator," was not within cognizance of the civil government.

The high bench also observed that Jefferson's Bill for Religious Freedom, approved by the Virginia legislature, defined "religion" exactly as had Madison in his "Memorial." [62]

Further, the Bill said civil government can only interfere with religious belief "when principles break out into overt acts against peace and good order."

That provision of the Bill, said the Court, provides "the true distinction between what properly belongs to the church and what to the state."

The Court also referenced Jefferson's reply to an address he received from the Danbury, Connecticut Baptist Association. He told the group the religion clause, in his view, built "a wall of separation between church and state."

Explaining, he said he was convinced man "has no natural right in opposition to his social duties."

Addressing its own understanding of those historic documents, the Court declared: "Congress was deprived of all legislative power over mere opinion, but was left free to reach actions which were in violation of social duties or subversive to good order."

Continuing, the opinion noted that polygamy has always been "odious among the northern and western nations of Europe and, until the establishment of the Mormon Church, was almost exclusively a feature of the life of Asiatic and of African people. At common law, the second marriage was always void . . . and from the earliest history of England polygamy has been treated as an offense against society."

The Court said English ecclesiastical courts, as well as civil courts, punished polygamy, and that by the statute of James I, the penalty for polygamy was death. [63]

In *Davis v. Beason,* the Court conceded the right to religious belief, but cautioned that the First Amendment prohibits legislation for "the support of any religious tenets, or the modes of worship of any sect."

Despite that holding, the Court strongly supported the Christian concept of the marriage bond, thus tacitly recognizing that the Constitution protects that particular Christian belief.

The decision observed that bigamy and polygamy are crimes "by the laws of all civilized and Christian countries." [64]

Continuing, the majority ruling said:

"Certainly no legislation can be supposed more wholesome and necessary in the founding of a free, self-governing Commonwealth, fit to take rank as one of the coordinate States of the Union, than that which seeks to establish it on the basis of the idea of the family, as constituting in and springing from the union for life of one man and one woman in the holy estate of matrimony; the sure foundation of all that is stable and noble in our civilization; the best guaranty of that reverent morality which is the source of all beneficent progress in social and political improvement. And to this end, no means are more directly and immediately suitable than those provided by this [statute] which endeavors to withdraw all political influence from those who are practically hostile to its attainment." [65]

The *Watson v. Jones* case was concerned with property rights of religious societies. The Court affirmed the obvious when it emphasized it had no jurisdiction on questions of church discipline. The high bench said "total subversion of . . . religious bodies" would be effected if any member of such society aggrieved by the church's "decisions could appeal to the secular courts and have them reversed." [66]

The Court enunciated what *Reynolds* later affirmed. It said: "In this country the full and free right to entertain any religious belief, to practice any religious principle, and to teach any religious doctrine— which does not violate the laws of morality and property, and which does not infringe personal rights—is conceded to all. The law knows no heresy, and is committed to the support of no dogma, the establishment of no sect." [67]

The above excerpts abundantly manifest that the decisions in both *Reynolds* and *Beason* supported the Christian beliefs and practices regarding marriage.

Further emphasizing that position was the Court's reference to the northern and western nations of Europe, which were Christian, as was England and its "ecclesiastical courts." The Asiatic and African people, referred to in Beason, were largely non-Christian, and mostly Muslim.

In *Beason,* too, the Court spoke with approval regarding the attitude of "Christian countries" toward marriage. It also praised the concept of "family" springing "from the union for life of one man and one woman in the holy estate of matrimony." Certainly, such a view of marriage has been unique to Christianity (see Matthew 19: 6-12).

But the Court went a step beyond. It supported the right of Congress to pass, and the President to sign into law, an Act which withdrew "all political influence from those who are practically hostile" to the Christian view of marriage.

There also is the matter of the "religion" protected by the First Amendment. In both *Reynolds* and *Beason,* the Court accepted the definition which says "religion" in the religion clause means a philosophy or view of life which recognizes the existence of "our Creator," as well as a "duty" owed to that Being. That viewpoint is consistent with the Court's opinions in *Vidal v. Girard,* in 1844, and *Holy Trinity,* in 1892. It also mirrors the interpretation of Mr. Justice Story in his *Commentaries.* [68]

Obviously, Masonic spokesmen and their philosophical allies can cite isolated words or phrases culled from earlier Court decisions to suggest that precedent Court rulings support their view of the religion clause. However, when those citations are placed in context they serve to reaffirm and illuminate the fact the Supreme Court—up until the time it was packed with Freemasons in the 1940s—had consistently enunciated a view which held that basic Christian values are to be protected by the government because that is the will of the people, and because it is in the bests interests of society at large.

7/ DEFUSING THE PAROCHIAL AID BOMB

By the 1940s, the rush of events and precedents by the three branches of government enhancing religious equality, seemed to militate strongly against Masonry's efforts to control America's educational agenda.

The growing Catholic membership in Congress particularly worried Scottish Rite leaders and, as was noted above, militated against the Fraternity's efforts to enact its own federal education legislation. In fact, it seemed that a rapidly growing sense of fairness and equity was moving inexorably toward granting federal aid to non-public school students.

For example, in 1940, the Fraternity opposed a pending Congressional proposal which would allow States to make available to parochial school children "any services of health, welfare, books, reading materials, or transportation . . . that may be made available" through federal funding for children in public schools. [1]

The *New Age* said such legislation demonstrated that "many of our legislators are succumbing to the desire to hold office" by supporting aid to non-public schools." [2]

"The G.I. Bill Of Rights."

However, the major educational skirmish lost by the Fraternity was enactment of the Servicemen's Readjustment Act of 1944, popularly known as "The G.I. Bill Of Rights."

The new law provided a wide range of benefits for returning veterans, including virtually free education in the school of the returning serviceman's choice—even in religious seminaries. It was a devastating blow to Masonry's efforts to deny government assistance to "sectarian" institutions.

The Craft and its allies were particularly outraged by a unique aspect of the law which empowered the Administrator of Veterans Affairs to provide aid directly to religiously-affiliated schools, which otherwise were barred from receiving tax support by State statutes or constitutional provisions. [3]

Opponents of that aspect of the "G.I. Bill" rightly suspected the "State by-pass" provision would set a precedent for appropriating federal funds for Catholic and other religiously affiliated schools.

Surprisingly, however, the hearing record which preceded debate and enactment of the legislation fails to show that any Masonic Supreme Council official testified for or against the legislation. [4]

Nevertheless, Craft sentiment was clearly evident during floor debate on the measure. The strong undercurrent of opposition to the State "by-pass" provision paralleled Masonic thinking on the issue.

In fact, a substitute bill, introduced by Rep. Graham Barden (D., N.C.), a Mason, was almost identical to the proposal approved by the American Legion, and the House Committee on World War Veterans—except that Barden's Bill eliminated the power of school selection by the Administrator.

However, not once during the rather protracted debate in the House and Senate on the legislation was it ever suggested that providing funds to religiously-affiliated institutions violated the religion clause of the First Amendment. [5]

During House debate , Rep. Fred Busbey (R. IL.) asked his colleague, Walter Judd (R., MN), about the possibility of veterans attending theological seminaries. Judd replied that they should be allowed to do so as long as the schools are properly equipped and staffed. [6]

Senator Ernest McFarland (D., AZ.) said: "it is important that the veteran be given the privilege of choosing his own school. This is in accordance with the American system which has prevailed during all these years . . . No man should be compelled to attend a school which is not his own choice." [7]

Rep. William Cole (R., N.Y.) asked why the Administrator was authorized to designate certain schools. Rep. John Rankin (D., Miss.), floor manager of the legislation, replied that there "might be some private schools that the public authorities would not want to recognize." [8]

Rep. Thomas Abernethy (D., Miss.), commenting during an extensive discussion about federal usurpation of State control of education, said the legislation "is a veterans' bill," and returning servicemen and women "may select free of even the most infinitesimal dictation of any individual, a school of his choice." [9]

Rep. Edith Nourse Rogers (R., Mass.), said the committee bill gave no control over "private or religious schools or institutions" to any State or State agency.

On the other hand, she observed, the Barden substitute proposal "gives the State agency control over such institutions." That aspect of the Barden Bill, she said, "poses for consideration of Congress the question of academic freedom and individual initiative." [10]

Rep. Asa Allen (D., LA.) pointed out that the committee bill was intended to guarantee "the greatest liberty of choice and the greatest possible liberty of action." After all, he continued, "that is democracy. Is that not what the boys are fighting for?" [11]

Lengthy debate occurred regarding a letter each Congressman had received from Dr. Cloyd H. Marvin, president of George Washington University. The letter, dated May 11, 1944, was written on behalf of the Conference of Representatives of Educational Associations, and urged defeat of the committee bill and passage of the Barden Bill.

In his letter, Dr. Marvin said he and his group favored the Barden Bill "because we cannot maintain two systems to interfere with regular education policies."

The Barden Bill, as Mrs. Rogers and others had noted, would almost certainly prohibit veterans from attending Catholic or other religiously affiliated schools.

Surprisingly, among the 21 groups co-signing Dr. Marvin's letter was the National Catholic Education Association. [12]

The final vote on the "G.I. Bill" showed that the Congressmen faced a political dilemma. They were caught between the pressures brought by Masonry (and the hardly indistinguishable pressures exerted by the Educational Establishment) on the one hand, and countervailing pressure from the general public and veterans groups on the other.

The Senate voted 50 to 0 for the bill. However, nearly half of the 96 Senators failed to vote for the legislation, even though it had 81 co-sponsors. [13]

The House voted 388 to 0 for the bill, with 41 Representatives not voting. [14]

Certainly, it was virtually impossible to oppose assistance to men and women who were serving the nation at a desperate hour, many of whom were being wounded or killed in battle in Europe and the Pacific.

The Catholic populace had a a particularly vital stake in the legislation. For years, Masonic subterfuge had been successful in denying Catholic students an equitable share in tax benefits. Now, when the Catholic population of the United States was a mere 18 percent, it was reported, on August 31, 1943, that "the religious preference of American soldiers was 31 percent Catholic." And, according to the *National Catholic Almanac,* the "distribution of Catholics was probably higher in the Navy and Marine Corps than in the Army." [15] It was inconceivable that the National Legislature would deny educational benefits in the schools of choice for those profoundly patriotic men and women.

Meanwhile, the public and the Congress was largely ignorant of the fact that Dr. Marvin, the man who exerted so much pressure to substitute the anti-Catholic Barden Bill, was a 33rd degree Mason, who presided over a university which received $1,000,000 from the Scottish Rite to operate a school of government that specializes in foreign affairs. [16]

In addition to contributions from the Scottish Rite, Dr. Marvin has noted that George Washington University also receives substantial contributions from the National League of Masonic Clubs, The High Twelve International, and the Knights Templars, all of which are Masonic groups. [17]

Masons, Dr. Marvin said, serve the nation by making recommendations relative to the "character, mental capacity, and social attitudes of those who should be set aside by our society for leadership." [18]

Parochial School Aid At The Threshold

In December, 1944, six months after the "G.I. Bill" became law, an Advisory Committee to the House Education panel issued a report recommending federal funds for private colleges and universities.

Commenting editorially on the Committee report, *America* magazine said: ". . . since existing State laws forbid State allocation of funds to private institutions, arrangements will be made to pay federal funds directly to institutions and individuals." [19]

Soon thereafter, on January 9, 10, 1945, legislation sponsored by the National Education Association (NEA)—an organization that historically has been closely tied to Scottish Rite Freemasonry—was introduced in the House and Senate. It provided substantial funds for public education, but made no provision for assisting non-public schools.

The Senate version became the dominant proposal, known as S.181. Among its principal sponsors was Senator Lister Hill (D., Ala.), a Mason, and the man who replaced Sen. Hugo L. Black, when the latter went to the Supreme Court. [20]

At a January 23rd conference on education sponsored by *The New York Times,* Sen. Hill said his bill stood a better chance of passage "than at any other time in the many years it has been introduced." [21]

On January 31, Elmer Rogers, executive aide to the Sovereign Grand Commander of the Scottish Rite of the Southern Jurisdiction, and associate editor of the organization's publications, appeared before the Senate Education and Labor committee to express opposition to S.181. He told the Senate panel the bill "does not give . . . assurance" that parochial schools could not receive government benefits. [22]

The Scottish Rite official referred to a study by Fordham University's Institute of Educational Research which found that direct appropriations of public money to Catholic schools would be legal. [23]

Rogers then made reference to selective excerpts from Pope Leo XIII's Encyclical Letter *Humanum Genus* [but the Scottish Rite official never mentioned that the Papal letter was against Freemasonry, nor that it detailed Masonry's long revolutionary history, and its particular dedication to controlling education in every nation].

The excerpts chosen by Rogers purported to show that Catholic Church teaching is incompatible with the Constitution of the United States. [24]

Rogers invited attention to the identical Supreme Court opinions cited in his 1937 testimony before the House Committee on Education: *Davis v. Beason, Watson v. Jones, Reynolds v. U.S.,* and *Reuben Quick Bear v. Leupp.* [25]

As an interesting sidelight, the hearings revealed that an ostensible pro-public school group apparently served as a front for Scottish Rite Freemasonry.

General Amos Fries, appearing on behalf of a one-thousand-member group, called Friends of the Public Schools, testified in opposition to federal aid to education. During a colloquy with Sen. William Fulbright (D., Ark.), the General said his organization distributed approximately 32,000 copies of its bulletin. Explaining, under Senatorial questioning, how a small organization could distribute its publication in quantities 32 times larger than the organization's membership, Fries disclosed that the "principal contributor" to his organization was the Supreme Council of the Scottish Rite of the Southern Jurisdiction. [26]

He provided the Committee with a typical Bulletin issued by his group. Bulletin No. 79 (undated) listed under the heading, "What We Have Opposed," the following: "(f) taking time out . . . of school . . . to send children, whose parents request it, to different sectarian religious centers for instruction in the tenets of their particular religion." [27]

Less than a month after the hearings concluded, Senators James Mead (D., N.Y.) and George Aiken (R., Vt.) introduced S. 717, a related education aid bill. Unlike its predecessor, S. 181, the new measure, would provide aid to parochial schools. The legislation was largely drafted and sponsored by the American Federation of Labor (AFL).

One key aspect of the Mead-Aiken Bill was a State "by-pass" principle, similar to the educational provisions of "The G.I. Bill of Rights." The new proposal established a five-man National Board of Apportionment, appointed by the President, with consent of the Senate. A related provision required each State to notify the Board whether State law prohibits use of public funds in non-public schools. If such was the case, the Board would appoint a trustee (nominated by the State Governor) to receive and allocate funds to non-public schools. [28]

Enter Justice Black

The Mead-Aiken Bill apparently triggered a startling reaction from a man who had a rather long record of anti-Catholicism; a man who "would make fun of the church," in general; who "suspected the Catholic Church," in particular; and a man, above all, who "could not tolerate any sign of encouraging religious faith by state aid." That man was Justice Hugo L. Black. [29]

Black's Papers show, that within a month following introduction of the Mead-Aiken Bill, he wrote a "Dear Lister" letter to Sen. Lister Hill, to which he appended Issue No. 61, of the *Scottish Rite News Bulletin*, dated April 5, 1945. The letter said:

"You will doubtless be interested in this document insofar as it may affect you personally, and because it may also affect the fate of your Federal Aid to Education Bill."

Black went on to note that the last page of the Scottish Rite publication contained five educational principles favored by the Supreme Council. The first principle, he noted, reads:

"The American public school, non-partisan. non-sectarian, efficient, democratic, for all of the children of all the people." [30]

Black did not repeat the fifth Masonic principle on the list, which appears on the last page of that issue of the Bulletin—and regularly appears in most Scottish Rite publications. That principle says:

"5. the entire separation of Church and State, and opposition to every attempt to appropriate public moneys—federal, state or local—directly or indirectly, for the support of sectarian or private institutions." [31]

The letter to Sen. Hill continued by noting that articles in the April 5 edition of the *Bulletin* "appear to be in conflict with the spirit if not with the letter of this expressed Council policy." All of them, he said, "are against Federal aid intended to bring about the type of schools described in principle 1."

Black said articles in the *Bulletin* suggest that the editors "do not oppose political appointments as such, but merely those made by the Federal Government."

The former Alabama Senator also noted that the Hill Bill was based on the premise that the "American public school" cannot be "efficient, democratic for all of the children of all of the people." unless there are funds available to make them such, and that some of the States are unable without federal assistance to provide adequate funds to maintain such schools.

Continuing, he said: "Without challenging this premise at all, the Editors of the [*Bulletin*] make artificial State boundary lines sacrosanct and argue against making the entire wealth of all of America available for educational use for 'all of the children of all of the people.'

"This leads me to believe that the Supreme Council favors a course which the publishers of the Bulletin are betraying. They have gathered together a group of articles which use all the old cliches of numerous tax dodgers' leagues which exalt individual wealth above individual educational opportunities of the children.

"You know the influence of the Scottish Rite Masons in Alabama and elsewhere. If you and others do not challenge this activity, you will hear from it later in connection with the passage of your Bill and future elections. My belief is that this Bulletin runs counter to the basic precepts of Masonry. If I thought that the Scottish Rite organization had dedicated its efforts along the lines indicated by the Bulletin, I should immediately resign my membership which has been held for more than 25 years.

"My guess is if you will talk to Elmer Rogers you will find that the policies emphasized in the Bulletin chiefly represent the views of one man who happens to hold a position of influence there. If I were not on the court, I should challenge them immediately, and I hope that someone else will do so." [32]

Justice Black's *Papers* contained no response from Senator Hill. Efforts to obtain permission from Senator Hill's daughter, Mrs. Henrietta Hubbard, to review her father's *Papers* for any response that might have been made to Justice Black's letter, met with negative results. [33]

On April 23, Black wrote to Rogers, referencing the "last few issues" of the *Bulletin,* and the articles opposing federal aid to education. As he had to Sen. Hill, so to Rogers, he called attention to the first principle favored by the Fraternity, the public school "for all of the children of all of the people," a statement which he underlined. He asked his friend, Rogers, to inform him whether or not the "Supreme Council" has taken a position against federal aid to education. [34]

Rogers responded to Black on April 27. He informed the Justice that he had referred his letter to the Grand Commander, who "asked that I reply as follows:"

The rather formal response simply noted that the Fraternity had "for many years" favored a Department of Education, but recent legislation began to carry appropriations for millions of dollars, and the Supreme Council "feared that such appropriations would lead to federal control of education." [35]

In the same file in Black's *Papers* is a copy of issue No. 62 of the *Scottish Rite News Bulletin,* dated April 20, 1945. The lead article by Rogers, titled, "More About Senate Bill 717," notes that if the Mead-Aiken Bill was enacted "it would, in effect, annul those provisions in state constitutions which prohibit their legislatures from aiding sectarian schools out of public funds." [36]

The fact Black admitted he had read "the last few issues" of the *Bulletin* makes it clear that he knew precisely what the Scottish Rite position was.

But Black pursued the subject further. On April 30, he wrote to A.B. Andrews at the Scottish Rite Masonic Temple, Birmingham, Alabama, to inquire whether the Alabama Scottish Rite was working to defeat Congressional legislation to provide educational aid to the States.

Black added: "In my present position I do not desire to become involved in any controversy over pending legislation." [37]

No reply from Andrews could be located among Black's *Papers*.

Black's letters to Sen. Hill, Rogers, and Andrews seemed curious. As a man who admitted reading Masonic publications, and as a member of the Craft for 25 years, it is reasonable to assume that he was aware that Freemasonry had been pressing for federal aid to public education since the 1920s. Moreover, he expressly favored Senator Hill's anti-parochial school bill, and emphasized public school "for all the children of all the people." Moreover, the Scottish Rite's five principles, to which he alluded, demonstrated that the Craft was a staunch supporter of public schools.

It was clear, too, that Black was interested in bringing to bear "the influence of Scottish Rite Masons," and suggested that Sen. Hill "talk to Elmer Rogers . . . who happens to hold a position of influence . . ."

It is curious, too, that Black said "If I were not on the Court, I should challenge them immediately, and I hope that someone else will do so." It is curious, because almost immediately after saying that, he took the initiative to write to two Masonic officials to question the Scottish Rite position opposing aid to education.

Moreover, Black's ethics as a sitting Justice are certainly suspect for initiating a letter of support to one of the chief sponsors of a bill which would provide government assistance to public schools only. A further breach of judicial ethics was his condemnation of an organization which opposed the legislation. His behavior also is questionable for suggesting a "challenge" to a powerful group which ostensibly was opposing the legislation.

Actually, the April 5 *Bulletin* must have made it clear to Black that Brother Rogers was opposing only legislation which would aid Catholic schools. Nowhere did Black himself indicate that he supported equitable aid to non-public schools.

A front page article in the April 5, 1945 *Scottish Rite News Bulletin* by Rogers stated:

"The bill's scheme to make public funds available to sectarian schools treats with contempt the principles set forth in Madison's Memorial of 1784 and the same principles affirmed later by Thomas Jefferson in his Act for Religious Freedom in the Legislature of Virginia, to say nothing of the curse that sectarian schools supported by public funds has inflicted upon man.

"The enactment of S. 717 would reverse the declaration of Congress in Indian school matters which stated it to be the settled policy of the Government hereafter to make no appropriations whatever for education in any sectarian school. Moreover, in this connection, S. 717 ignores the decision of the United States Supreme Court in the case of *Reuben Quick Bear v. Leupp* (210 U.S. 50, 1908) which held, in part, that the general appropriations Act of 1895, 1896 and 1897 forbid contracts for the education of Indians in sectarian schools out of public funds . . ." [38]

The Assault On Parochial Aid

A week after Justice Black's letter to Sen. Hill, the Senate Education and Labor Committee began a second series of hearings on the education legislation, focusing mostly on objections by Masons and the Educational Establishment to the Mead-Aiken bill.

On April 11, Matthew Woll, Vice President of the AFL and chairman of that organization's Committee on Education, appeared before the Committee and said any education legislation considered by Congress must be "without prejudice to any child."

After noting that the AFL had fought anti-Negro discrimination, he observed:

"But discrimination is not limited to racial issues. Religious prejudice also gives rise to discrimination."

Citing the *Cochran* textbook case, he said the Court held that "all children . . . should be helped to get an education." [39]

But Senator Forrest Donnell (R., MO.), a 33rd Degree Mason and former Grand Master of the Grand Lodge of Missouri, was relentless in his questioning of anyone who favored aid to parochial schools. He insisted that the State "by-pass" provision was "subterfuge to avoid the provisions of the State constitutions."

Woll replied that "it does circumvent State law openly. That is not subterfuge." [40]

The following colloquy ensued:

Senator Donnell: It would be for the purpose, however, of enabling the distribution of funds by an official appointed by the Governor of a State in which the law would prohibit the distribution by the State.

Mr. Woll: Haven't we been doing that before?

Senator Donnell: This is the purpose, is it not, of that provision?

Mr. Woll: Haven't we been doing that before?

Senator Donnell: Would you mind answering that question? That is the purpose of that provision, is it not?

Mr. Woll: Certainly it is. Haven't we done that heretofore with the N.Y.A. [National Youth Administration], in distributing moneys this way?

Senator Donnell: I am not certain as to whether that has been done or not.

Mr. Woll: It has been done heretofore. [41]

The following day, George L. Googe, Southern Representative of the AFL appeared before the Senate Committee to complain that statements about "Union of church and state," and "Destruction of the free public school system," are "Shibboleths," and "empty phrases."

He noted that the ROTC (Reserve Officer Training Corps) program at public and non-public schools and colleges did not lead to the destruction of the free public school system.

The present danger, he insisted, is not from the church taking over the State, but "the growing power of the State over the conduct of the individual human being."

Stateism, he said, is "a pure Hegelian concept—is the very basis of nazism, which is on the march in this country." [42]

Sen. Donnell vigorously pursued his questioning of Googe, and would repeatedly interrupt the witness before the labor official could finish his statement; or the Senator would interrupt him with: "Just answer my question." [43]

The Missouri Republican said the Continental Congress made land available for "religious" purposes only on a couple of occasions, and it did so because the government was desperately in need of money. In trying to press home an admission of that view on Selma Borchardt, vice president of the American Federation of Teachers, AFL, and a vigorous proponent of aid to non-public school students, the labor official replied:

"I am always at a loss to interpret pressures at a long distance. When I am close at hand and can see them operating, as in the case now being heard, I have little difficulty in interpreting such pressures." [44]

On May 4, 1945, The Scottish Rite's Elmer Rogers again testified on behalf of the Grand Commander and himself. The Grand Commander, in a statement read by Rogers, affirmed the truism known since the States established their public school systems: ". . . the American public school system, without being denominational in its instruction, is yet one of the primary Christian institutions existing in the world today." [45]

Rogers' own statement was preceded by a listing of the same five principles regarding education which apparently had impressed Justice Black. [46]

The Grand Commander's aide opposed S. 717 because "sectarian schools would become among the nonpublic schools, the principal beneficiares of Federal aid. Such a status would ultimately destroy not only the free independent character of our public schools but would establish in our national life an interdependence of state and church." [47]

Once again, he said aid to parochial schools would be contrary to Madison's "Memorial and Remonstrance" and Jefferson's Act for Religious Freedom in the Legislature of Virginia. And, he added, it would ignore the principles of the U.S. Supreme Court in *Quick Bear v. Leupp.* [48]

Continuing, Rogers seemed to echo a sentiment voiced nearly eight years earlier by Justice Black during his nationwide broadcast to answer critics who were outraged by his membership in the Ku Klux Klan. Rogers, said:

"The enactment of S. 717 would be a powerful lever in the hands of sectarian interests to force States and communities to separate the school taxes paid by these interests from the general school taxes, and turn them over to their schools.

"Because of the baneful effects of a dominant sectarianism in education, such action would ultimately destroy our popular government." [49]

Continuing the same thought he referred to the Board to be established by S. 717 to "by-pass" the States whose laws prohibited distribution of government funds for religious-oriented schools, Rogers said it "would be, naturally, subject to great pressures from both public and nonpublic schools.

". . . each group would contend for the most it could get and thus give rise to much wrangling.

"Moreover, the fight between the two kinds of nonpublic schools, sectarian and nonsectarian, would be always tense, to say nothing of a like feeling that would arise as between the various religious denominations for their respective shares. All of this will throw religion and education into State and National politics with that acrimony and vindictive jealousy that always characterizes such issues." [50]

Rogers' concluded by attempting to demonstrate that education in Catholic schools leads to criminality. His source for such an assumption was an article written by "the former Roman Catholic bishop," Dr. L.H. Lehmann, and published in *Converted Catholic Magazine,* January, 1945.

The article, by Lehmann was based ostensibly on a detailed survey made by Fr. Leo Kalmer, O.F.M., and purported to show that the percentage of Catholic prisoners in State prisons frequently was higher than the Catholic percentage in the population of the States in which the prisons were located. [51]

However, Sen. James E. Murray (D. Mont.) inserted in the record a report he received from Dr. Mary E. Walsh, assistant professor of sociology, Catholic University of America.

Dr. Walsh's report showed that ex-bishop Lehmann did not accurately reflect the information in the study he cited for his statistics. The study, titled, "Crime and Religion," by Fr. Leo Kalmer, and others, showed that after parole laws went into effect in various States prisoners identified themselves with various religions. Membership in a church, it seemed, was helpful in getting a parole in that it indicated the prisoner was better than the system suggested; also, the prisoner had the chaplain, as well as others affiliated with the prisoner's religion to take an interest in his parole.

Using Kalmer's study, Dr. Walsh demonstrated that identification of prisoners with various church groups, "suddenly rocketed" immediately following enactment of the parole law. [52]

Further, Dr. Walsh showed that in prisons at that time, "merely hypothetical" preference for religion suffices to be identified with a

hypothetical" preference for religion suffices to be identified with a
particular church, even if the prisoner never had set foot inside a
church.

Finally, the Catholic University professor demonstrated that Fr.
Kalmer's statistics showed—contrary to Lehmann's allegation—that
"the percentage of those prisoners who 'attended public schools only'
was higher than the percentage who 'attended Catholic schools
only'." The respective percentages were 35.85 for criminals identifying themselves with public schools, and 20.82. for those criminals
who claimed affiliation with the Catholic religion. [53]

However, despite the two volumes of Senate testimony, Congress
temporarily shelved the issue on December 12, 1945, after the House
Education Committee voted (10 to 9) not to report out legislation
identical to the NEA-sponsored bill under consideration by the Senate.
[54]

Nevertheless, a fact not to be overlooked is that every Member of
Congress takes an oath to uphold and defend the Constitution of the
United States. In that regard, thirteen of the eighteen members of the
Senate Committee on Education and Labor were lawyers, including
Sen. Donnell, and Sen. Wayne Morse (R. OR.). Indeed, the latter had
served as dean of the University of Oregon Law School prior to his
election to the Senate. Yet, during the hearings on aid to church-
schools, no Member of Congress, and particularly no member of the
Senate Education and Labor panel, ever claimed that federal aid to
church-related schools was unconstitutional. [55]

Moreover, just about that time, re-affirmation of the Constitutionality of such assistance was further evidenced by a recommendation of a
prestigious panel appointed by President Franklin D. Roosevelt. The
Advisory Committee on Federal Aid to Education said education legislation should be directed toward "the benefit of pupils both in public
and non-public schools." [56]

Meanwhile, it is not known whether Senator Hill acceded to Justice
Black's urging and decided to "challenge" Brother Rogers. However,
subsequent to the date of Black's letter to the the Alabama Senator, the
New Age ran a series of editorials under the eye-catching headline:
"Unofficial, Read, Think, Study." The editorials warned the Brother-
hood of a purported imminent danger of a union between Church and
State,—a principle staunchly opposed by Masonry, as Black had re-
minded Sen. Hill.

The Masonic journal also commented on the need to oppose such a possibility, particularly in view of alleged efforts along those lines by the Roman Catholic Church. [57]

Congress Presses On

As for Congress, it continued to be occupied with the education issue.

Sen. Hill and several of his colleagues introduced legislation in mid-1946 to aid public school students only, ignoring the needs of church school students.

Addressing the issue of aid to students in the latter schools, Senators Murray, Aiken and David I. Walsh (D., Mass.) issued a joint statement, which said:

"We have considered this problem very carefully and we have concluded that such a fear is groundless. If it were not, we would be the first to oppose such aid.

"Another tenet of our democratic belief, which we hold to be just as sacred and important as the separation of Church and State, is that of freedom of religion. Such freedom should not be limited by imposing, in effect, certain penalties on those who faithfully carry out the practice and teachings of their religion.

"In this connection, too, we must recognize that the Government does not wish to supplant the duty of parents in the instruction and training of their children, but merely wish to supplement and facilitate it." [58]

Although Congress continued to address the subject for the remainder of 1946 and into 1947, no general aid to education legislation was passed until eighteen years later, when the Elementary and Secondary Act of 1965 was approved. That Act also denied to parochial school students full participation in benefits bestowed by the law.

However, long before 1965, the Court, on February 10, 1947, handed down its ruling in the *Everson* case, which effectively doomed expenditures of public funds to any significant degree for church schools.

Everson Wends Its Way

On the eve of the Court's *Everson* decision, the Masons clearly had a problem.

The historic record on the issue of government support for the Christian religion and for Christian moral education was overwhelmingly against the Masonic viewpoint. More importantly, it appeared that in the very near future some form of federal financial assistance would be provided on an equitable basis to church schools.

Clearly, the Fraternity was in need of a *deus ex machina*—a Masonic miracle. And it happened.

The *Everson* case went before the Supreme Court of New Jersey on October 5, 1943. It involved a New Jersey law which authorized the Township of Ewing to pay for the transportation of students to all schools, including Catholic schools. On September 13, 1944, the Court ruled the law unconstitutional, a decision noted by the *New Age*. [59]

Nowhere in its opinion did the New Jersey Supreme Court make reference to Madison's "Memorial and Remonstrance" nor to Jefferson's letter to the Danbury Baptist Association in which he erected "a wall" separating Church and State.

Subsequently, the Board of Education entered an appeal before the New Jersey Court of Errors and Appeals, and the case was argued before that tribunal on May 21, 1945.

Interestingly, the brief filed by the attorney for the Prosecutor-Respondent (Arch Everson) paralleled arguments used by the Scottish Rite's Elmer Rogers. Specifically mentioned was Jefferson's Act for Establishing Religious Freedom, and the identical passage from the "Memorial and Remonstrance" which Rogers had cited in a 1935 and 1940 *New Age* commentary, as well as in his testimony before the House Education Committee in 1937. [60]

A friend of the court brief was filed by the American Civil Liberties Union (ACLU) in support of Mr. Everson. The ACLU attorneys called the Court's attention to an excerpt from the *Reynolds* decision relative to Jefferson's "wall of separation" statement [61]

The Court was unimpressed. Nearly five months later it reversed the New Jersey Supreme Court and ruled that the school transportation law violated neither the Constitution of New Jersey nor the Constitution of the United States. [62]

A petition for re-argument before the New Jersey Court of Appeals was denied on November 29, 1945. However, a little more than two months later, on February 5, 1946, the Chancellor and Presiding Judge of that Court authorized an appeal to the Supreme Court of the

United States. On May 6, 1946, the latter tribunal issued an order noting probable jurisdiction. [63]

Curiously, the arguments made by Mr. Everson's attorney in his brief to the U.S. Supreme Court did not reiterate the arguments advanced by his attorney in the lower Court of Errors and Appeals. Rather, those earlier arguments in the New Jersey court were advocated on Mr. Everson's behalf before the U.S. Supreme Court by the ACLU in another friend of the court brief.

That brief listed virtually all the citations against aid to church schools which had been made years earlier by Elmer Rogers of the Scottish Rite. Common to the ACLU brief and Rogers published statements were references to the "Memorial and Remonstrance," Jefferson's Act for Religious Freedom, Jefferson's reply to the Danbury Baptists, *Davis v. Beason,* and *Reynolds v. United States.* [64]

8/ *EVERSON:* MASONIC JUSTICE BUILT ON SAND

On February 10, 1947, Justice Hugo L. Black rendered the majority opinion for a Masonically-dominated Court in the *Everson* case. It was a farrago of shallowness, gross inaccuracies, and wishful thinking. The majority and minority opinions in the case, taken as a whole, are built on sand.

A careful reading of that landmark case clearly shows it is curiously compatible with the views of Scottish Rite Masonry, and to the personal philosophy of people like Justice Black—a man who, in his son's words, "could not whip himself up to a belief in God or the divinity of Christ, life after death, or Heaven or Hell."

It was a decision crafted for those, again like Black, who "could not tolerate any sign of encouraging religious faith by state aid."

The majority opinion did properly recognize that "legislation intended to facilitate the opportunity of children to get a secular education" can serve a public purpose. The Court also conceded that reimbursement of parents, in order that their children may "ride in public busses to and from school rather than run the risk of traffic and other hazards," is Constitutionally permissible (but not mandated on the basis of equity). [1]

However, the Court perceived a more serious question. That was whether transporting children to church schools "constitutes support of a religion by the State." If the New Jersey law is invalid for that reason, the majority continued, "it is because it violates the First Amendment's prohibition against the establishment of religion." [2]

Black's majority opinion emphasized the role of Virginia in providing leadership to engraft a Bill of Rights on the Constitution. In that State and elsewhere, he observed, people reached the conviction that "individual religious liberty could be achieved best under a government which was stripped of all power to tax, to support, or otherwise to assist any or all religions, or to interfere with the beliefs of any religious individuals or group". [3]

That viewpoint, the Court said, was embodied in Madison's "Memorial and Remonstrance," and led to the State of Virginia enacting Jefferson's Bill for Religious Liberty which forbade the State to compel "a man to furnish contributions of money for the propagation of opinions which he disbelieves." [4]

Madison and Jefferson, the Court continued, played leading roles in "the drafting and adoption" of the religion clause which had the same purpose as the Virginia Bill for Religious Liberty. The decision also asserted that the Court's majority opinion on the interpretation of the religion clause had previously been voiced by the high bench in *Reynolds, Watson, and Beason.* [5]

Continuing, the majority said Madison in the "Memorial" eloquently argued "that no person, either believer or non-believer, should be taxed to support religious institutions of any kind." [6]

The State, said the Court, "cannot exclude individual Catholics, Lutherans, Mohammedans, Baptists, Jews, Methodists, Non-believers, Presbyterians, or the members of any other faith, *because of their faith, or lack of it,* from receiving the benefits of public welfare legislation." [7]

Concluding, Justice Black said:

> "the 'establishment of religion' clause . . . means at least this: Neither a state nor the Federal Government can set up a church. Neither can pass laws which aid one religion, aid all religions, or prefer one religion over another . . . No tax in any amount, large or small, can be levied to support any religious activities or institutions, whatever they may be called, or whatever form they may adopt to teach or practice religion . . . In the words of Jefferson, the clause against establishment of religion by law was intended to erect 'a wall of separation between church and State.' *Reynolds v. United States supra* at 164."

That last statement is pure Black, and pure Masonic. It reads suspiciously like Scottish Rite Principle No. 5 regarding education (which was included in the letter Justice Black sent to his fellow Mason, Sen. Lister Hill on April 5, 1945, when the Senator was running up against the likelihood of Congress approving—as it had for World War II veterans—legislation which would provide aid to church schools.

Scottish Rite Principle No. 5 states:

"5. The entire separation of Church and State, and opposition to every attempt to appropriate public moneys—federal, state or local—directly or indirectly, for the support of sectarian or private institutions." [8]

Justices in the minority were outraged by the majority opinion. The lyrics of the ruling did not match the melody of the thought on a Court dominated seven to two by Justices who were Freemasons, and two others who shared a Masonic philosophy.

In a separate dissenting opinion, Justice Robert H. Jackson, a 33rd Degree Mason, said:

". . . the undertones of the opinion, advocating complete and uncompromising separation of Church from State, seem utterly discordant with its conclusion yielding support to their commingling in educational matters. The case which irresistibly comes to mind as the most fitting precedent is that of Julia who, according to Byron's reports, 'whispering "I will n'er consent,"' consented'." [9]

Justice Jackson expressed concern that Catholic schools were mandated in conscience for Catholics by Canon Law. He said "the whole historic conflict in temporal policy between the Catholic Church and non-Catholics comes to a focus in their respective school policies."

Catholic education, he continued, "is the rock upon which the whole structure rests, and to render tax aid to its Church school is indistinguishable to me from rendering the same aid to the Church itself." [10]

Although he failed to pursue the true crux of the school conflict, Justice Jackson did allude to it by noting that governing authorities had long ago established a public school system which was "consistent" with a general Protestantism. [11]

However, he immediately contradicted himself in the next sentence by asserting that the public school was "organized on the premise that secular education can be isolated from all religious teaching." [12]

The truth is, prayer and Bible reading were integral to the "Protestant" public school system in the United States until the Supreme Court's *Engel* decision in 1962, and its *Schempp* ruling in 1963—a period when Masons dominated the Court by a six-to-three ratio.

Actually, once education was mandated by law, all that Catholics, Lutherans, Christian Reform, Orthodox Jews, and others who established church schools, ever expected from their government was equality of opportunity to freely exercise their religion. It was a view they shared with James Madison, who wrote in his "Memorial,"

"A just government . . . will be best supported by protecting every citizen in the enjoyment of his Religion with the same equal hand which protects his person and his property; by neither invading the equal rights of any Sect, nor suffering any Sect to invade those of another . . ." [13]

Commenting on the Constitutional rights of those who believe in a conventional religion oriented to God and Christ, Justice Jackson asserted that the State "may not spend funds to secure religion against skepticism."

At the same time, he characterized public welfare benefits for church school children as a Constitutionally impermissible "reward [for] piety," or compensation "for adherence to a creed." [14]

In saying that, the Justice exhibited a peculiar antipathy toward conventional religion—particularly Christianity and Catholicism—which has become common to members of Court from the time of *Everson.*

According to the rationale of the Court, citizens who were not affiliated with a church or religion, "non-believers," skeptics, and atheists, for example, were free to propagate their a-theist (without God) values and philosophy in the public schools.

In that connection, six years after the *Everson* decision, Professor Wilber K. Katz of the University of Chicago observed:

". . . naturalistic philosophy involves religious assumptions quite as much as supernaturalistic philosophy. To call supernaturalism a philosophy, and on that basis exclude one and embrace the other is a form of self-deception." [15]

If Justice Jackson's first point regarding the rights of religion and skepticism are true, then the Constitution has been designed to shield only skepticism and non-religion, while leaving conventional religion defenseless.

But such a position is totally contrary to the meaning of the religion clause, as evidenced by its genesis and development. Further, such a viewpoint negates the "privileges and immunities" clauses of the Fourth and Fourteenth Articles of the Constitution, as well as the equal protection provision of the latter Article.

The Justice, however, did point to the flash-point of the perduring school controversy.

That flash point centers on the conviction, held by a great many citizens, that their tax money for education is being used to secure skepticism against conventional religion in public schools. Those citizens are unable to understand how such a system of injustice can be perpetrated by decisions of the Supreme Court of the United States, beginning with *Everson.*

As for Justice Jackson's second point, public welfare benefits for church school children are not a reward for piety, nor compensation for adherence to a creed. Such benefits are a right in equity under the Constitution when States mandate education for all children between certain ages. Mr. Jackson's sense of justice effectively penalizes citizens for holding beliefs that differ from his own; or, as James Madison said, "whose opinions in Religion do not bend to those of the Legislative [or Judicial?] authority." [16]

Further Preference For Non-Belief

But the assault on belief involved far more than Justice Jackson's views. The minority opinion in *Everson* by Justice Rutledge, joined in by Justices Burton, Frankfurter and Jackson, was equally militant in defense of Non-belief—a value system with which the Masons and Unitarians on the high bench were not at all uncomfortable.

Just as the Scottish Rite's *New Age* magazine, seven years prior to the *Everson* decision, had insisted that Madison's "Memorial and Remonstrance" and Jefferson's Bill for Religious Freedom "were the principles and precedents out of which was formed the Bill of Rights," so agreed the Court. Indeed, Justice Rutledge included the "Memorial" as an appendix to his opinion. [17]

The thrust of Rutledge's minority opinion was that citizens who wish religious instruction mixed with secular education do not have the same protection of the Constitution as do others who prefer secular education alone, devoid of any reference to a Supreme Being and eternal truths. [18]

Justice Rutledge said:

"Like St. Paul's freedom, religious liberty with a great price must be bought. And for those who exercise it most fully, by insisting upon religious education for their children mixed with secular, by terms of our Constitution the price is greater than for others." [19]

That viewpoint clearly conflicted with the views of Madison, the man Rutledge relied upon so heavily to buttress his own understanding of the religion clause. The *Everson* minority placed themselves in the position of defending their own Establishment, a position differing little from the Religious Establishment in Virginia which Madison so vigorously opposed. In that connection, Madison said:

> "it violates equality by subjecting some to peculiar burdens; so it violates the same principle, by granting to others peculiar exemptions." [20]

The minority's advocacy of second class citizenship for people supporting and attending church schools, also constituted a repudiation of the words "Equal Justice Under Law," which are chiseled in stone above the main entrance of the U.S. Supreme Court Building in Washington, D.C.

But most amazing was the fact that cursory examination of some key citations noted by the minority to support its position are non-existent!

For example, Justice Rutledge, after citing extensively from the "Memorial and Remonstrance" (often finding very little support for his position), wrote:

> "In view of this history no further proof is needed that the Amendment forbids any appropriation, large or small, from public funds to aid or support any and all religious exercises. But if more were called for, the debates in the First Congress and this Court's consistent expressions, whenever it has touched on the matter directly, supply it."

He then referred to Congressional debates on the religion clause and found only "sparse discussion, reflecting the fact that the essential issues had been settled."

The minority opinion then referred to "the only enlightening reference" which, "shows concern, not to preserve any power to use public funds in aid of religion, but to prevent the Amendment from outlawing private gifts inadvertently . . ."

That statement is followed by a footnote which references a colloquy between Madison and Representative Huntington during debate on the religion clause in the First Congress. At that time, Madison proposed that "No religion shall be established by law . . ."

Justice Rutledge, rightly noted that Huntington objected, because he feared the words might be "extremely hurtful to the cause of religion." However, the minority opinion curiously failed to quote Huntington's remarks which immediately follow those quoted by Rutledge. And, from Justice Rutledge's viewpoint, that is understandable.

Huntington continued by saying he "hoped the amendment [proposed by Madison] would . . . not . . . patronize those who professed no religion at all." [21]

Rutledge then said Madison suggested the word "national" be placed before "religion." That word-change, Rutledge declared, would "not only again [disclaim] intent to bring about the result Huntington feared but also showing unmistakably that 'establishment' meant public 'support' of religion in the financial sense. 1 Annals of Congress 731." [22]

Once again, Justice Rutledge was more than misleading, he was totally inaccurate. In explaining his proposed addition of the word "national" before the word "religion" Madison—

> "feared one sect might obtain pre-eminence, or two combine together, and establish a religion to which they would compel others to conform. . . . if the word national was introduced, it would point the amendment directly to the object it was intended to prevent." [23]

Nowhere in that response by Madison is it shown—as the minority opinion asserts—"unmistakably that 'establishment' meant public 'support' of religion in the financial sense."

More importantly, Justice Rutledge failed to note a crucial aspect of that proposal by Madison. As the Annals record: he "withdrew his motion." [24]

Pressing on, and using questionable facts, Justice Rutledge said *Reuben Quick Bear v. Leupp,* 210 U.S. 50 (1907) is the Supreme Court's "decision most closely touching the question" of appropriation of public funds to aid or support any and all religious exercises. In that case, Justice Rutledge said, "it was stated also that such a use of public moneys would violate both the First Amendment and the specific statutory declaration involved . . ." [25]

In reality, there is no mention of the First Amendment in *Quick Bear* in the context used by Rutledge.

The case concerned the use by Sioux Indians of their own money from a "Treaty Fund" to educate Sioux children under contract with the Bureau of Catholic Indian Missions.

The Court held that Indians may use their own money to educate their children "in the schools of their own choice because the Government is necessarily undenominational, as it cannot make any law respecting an establishment of religion or prohibiting the free exercise thereof." [26]

Further, while the Court recognized the fact that Congress had terminated appropriations for education of Indians in sectarian schools in 1895, the high bench also observed that subsequent public appropriations for Indian education in such schools was entirely possible.

Addressing that specific issue, the Court, in *Quick Bear,* said: ". . . the effect of the legislation was to make subsequent appropriations for education mean that sectarian schools were excluded in sharing in them, *unless otherwise provided."* [emphasis added] [27]

The Court never hinted that future funding of Indian children in sectarian schools would violate the First Amendment. Rather, it recognized that Congress might at some future time "otherwise provide" appropriations for Indian education in sectarian school.

Once again, the minority opinion was gravely misleading.

Justice Rutledge also argued that providing State funds for church schools would lead to national strife, as different groups vied for public funds. He said:

"Public money devoted to payment of religious costs, educational or other, brings the quest for more. It brings too the struggle of sect against sect for the larger share or for any. Here one by numbers alone will benefit most, there another. That is precisely the history of societies which have had an established religion and dissident groups . . .

"Exactly such conflicts have centered of late around providing transportation to religious schools from public funds . . . [28]

To buttress the allegation that public appropriations for church schools would bring "the struggle of sect against sect," Rutledge cited sections 8 and 11 of Madison's "Memorial and Remonstrance". However, those paragraphs contradict the very point Rutledge was attempting to establish.

Both citations express opposition to a single Church establishment, and call for equality among the various religious sects. A single establishment, simply by definition, would not tolerate a variety of "sects."; a plurality of church schools. There would be only one "sect," and one church school.

Sec. 8 of Madison's "Memorial" says:

> "A just government . . . will be best supported by protecting every citizen in the enjoyment of his Religion with the same EQUAL hand which protects his person and his property: by neither invading the EQUAL rights of any Sect, nor suffering any Sect to invade those of another." [Emphasis added. *Everson,* p. 68].

And Sec. 11 of the "Memorial" expresses total opposition to the secular arm intruding into religious affairs by prohibiting public expression of religious opinion that is contrary to the State-imposed value system. Madison called for the free exercise of religion for all sects. He opposed the very monolithic public school system with its "group think" which Rutledge and his colleagues mandated.

Madison said:

> ". . . Torrents of blood have been spilt in the old world, by vain attempts of the secular arm to extinguish religious discord, by proscribing all difference in Religious opinions. Time has at length revealed the true remedy. Every relaxation of narrow and rigorous policy . . . has been found to assuage the disease. [America] has exhibited proofs, that EQUAL and compleat liberty, if it does not wholly eradicate it, sufficiently destroys its malignant influence on the health and prosperity of the State . . . [Emphasis added. *Everson,* p. 68].

Actually, the statement by the minority, while not accurately reflecting the views of Madison, does echo the views of Justice Black, and Elmer Rogers of the Scottish Rite.

In testimony delivered before the Senate Education and Labor Committee—shortly after Justice Black had initiated correspondence with Senator Hill and with the high Masonic official—the latter expressed opposition to Congress providing equitable educational benefits for students in both public and church schools. He said:

". . . each group would contend for the most it could get and thus give rise to much wrangling.

"Moreover, the fight between the two kinds of nonpublic schools, sectarian and nonsectarian, would be always tense, to say nothing of a like feeling that would arise as between the various religious denominations for their respective shares. All of this will throw religion and education into State and National politics with that acrimony and vindictive jealousy that always characterizes such issues." [29]

And those views of Rogers were strikingly similar to sentiments expressed by Justice Black when he was commenting on his membership in the Ku Klux Klan before a nationwide radio audience in 1937. At that time Black said:

". . . any program, even if directed by good intentions, which tends to breed or revive religious discord or antagonism can and may spread with such rapidity as to imperil this vital Constitutional protection of one of the most sacred human rights . . .

"[It will project] religious beliefs into a position of prime importance in political campaigns and . . . reinject our social and business life with the passion of religious bigotry.

"It will bring the political religionist back into undeserved and perilous influence in affairs of government . . ." [30]

The "Religion" Of The Religion Clause

A central theme of both the majority and minority in *Everson* focuses on the rights of non-believers under the religion clause; yet the basic documents used by the Court to support its position—Madison's "Memorial" and Jefferson's Bill for Religious Freedom—never mention "non-believers." That is not to say that Christian citizens, whose church affiliations, values and beliefs have overwhelmingly dominated this nation throughout its entire history, have not accorded rights to non-believers under the Constitution. Manifestly, they have.

However, to put the First Amendment in perspective, it is essential to understand what precisely the word *religion* in the Amendment refers.

That meaning is readily discernable by reviewing the wording of the proposals on the subject submitted by the States immediately prior to the time the religion clause was drafted. The applicable State proposals define *religion* exactly as it is defined by Madison in his "Memorial," and by Jefferson in his Bill for Religious Freedom in Virginia.

Those sources stipulate that *religion* is the "duty which we owe to our Creator and the manner of discharging it." [31]

That precise definition was recognized and accepted by the Supreme Court in *Reynolds, Beason* and *Macintosh,* in 1878, 1890, and 1931, respectively—many years prior to the *Everson* decision. [32]

Indeed, after reading 74 pages of a judicial decision regarding the religion clause, it seems odd that the Court avoided any mention of the historically acceptable definition of religion.

It is odd, because the *Everson* court repeatedly referred to Madison's "Memorial," Jefferson's Bill, and, to a lesser extent, *Reynolds* and *Beason.* (Interestingly enough, the *Everson* Court never referred to *Macintosh*).

Clearly, that historic definition excludes "non-believers" and atheists, a view reinforced by Congressional debate when the clause was being drafted, and by earlier Supreme Court rulings and Constitutional commentary. [33]

Under that definition, the religion clause places its protective mantle over those who recognize a Supreme Being, and who also believe they have a duty toward that Being.

But Madison was even more emphatic about the need for the State to recognize and protect that sacred relationship between man and God. In the first section of his "Memorial" he said:

> Before any man can be considered as a member of Civil Society, he must be considered as a subject of the Governor of the Universe: and . . . every man who becomes a member of any particular Civil Society [must] do it with a saving of his allegiance to the Universal Sovereign." [34]

That view illuminates the unanswered point in the debate on the issue of government involvement in education. Once the State mandates education for children between certain ages, it is prohibited—by the judicially accepted concept of the term "religion" in the religion clause—from forcing children to accept education in schools where the teaching is not compatible with their religious beliefs; and, indeed, where the children may be ridiculed for their conscientious understanding that there is a God, and a "duty" which must be discharged toward Him, even in the classroom. Madison recognized that truth when he observed that a person's first allegiance is to "the

Universal Sovereign. It is an allegiance, he insisted, which takes precedence over any man's membership in civil society.

To Justice Jackson, any State effort to equitably accommodate youthful citizens by invoking that judicially accepted meaning of religion, would be an "award for piety," or "compensation for adherence to a creed."

At the same time, Justice Rutledge, who was quite selective in his citations from Madison's "Memorial," never conceded that children who insist on "a saving . . . allegiance to the Universal Sovereign" have any Constitutional right to discharge their duty to Him in the classroom. As far as Justice Rutledge was concerned, any child who had such ideas must be willing, under the Constitution, to pay a price "greater than for others" who do not concede the meaning of religion defined by Madison and Jefferson—a meaning accepted as *the* Constitutional definition of religion by three prior Supreme Court decisions.

Those viewpoints by the Court in *Everson* (and its progeny) effectively mandate a philosophy in public school classrooms that is completely compatible only with the views of non-believers—a group not covered by the Constitutional definition of "religion." That definition of "religion" applicable to the religion clause had been accepted from the time the clause was written, and was confirmed several times by the Court prior to its dominance by members of the Masonic Fraternity.

The *Everson* decision clearly was a novel departure from the entire history of the origin and development of the religion clause. As post-1947 decisions involving the clause demonstrated, *Everson* marked a turning point in the public perception of the role of religion in public life.

That historic 1947 decision—based largely on a collection of arguments first advanced by spokesmen for Scottish Rite Freemasonry—began a trend in jurisprudence which elevated the Masonic religion of Kabbalistic Gnosticism to a preeminent position in a nation that historically is rooted in Christianity.

Reaction To *Everson*

The record detailed above provides sufficient documentation to support the view that the Court essentially enunciated a philosophy gestated in the Lodge.

That perception is reinforced by a letter Justice Black received from Professor Peter Masten Dunne of the University of San Francisco, protesting the *Everson* rationale. Professor Dunne wrote:

"The American people have always aided religion in many different ways and they have aided all religions. For your enlightenment on what is good Americanism, read the Annals of the Congress of the United States, volume one, where the debate on the wording of the First Amendment is given. It becomes evident from a study of this record that the framers of the Amendment wanted religion to be aided; they feared the very interpretation which you have so illogically given." [35]

In the margin of the letter, opposite the words "volume one," and extending down the page, appears a hand-written note: "Get Vol. 1 and let's see what was said." [36]

The note indicates that the *Annals of Congress,* which records the debate on the religion clause, was never seen by Justice Black.

The Court's decision was attacked by the Council of Bishops of the Methodist Church as a "departure" from the American principles of separation of church and state. [37]

On May 9, 1947, *The New York Times* reported that the Southern Baptist Convention warned Baptist institutions against accepting Government grants for construction or equipment because it weakens separation of Church and State.

Dr. J. M. Dawson, executive secretary of the Joint Conference Committee of American Baptists deplored a "drift toward the union of Church and State." Baptists, he said, "protest Federal or state appropriation of tax funds for sectarian purposes." [38]

In connection with the published position of the Baptists, it is worthy of note that Justice Black received another letter, this one from Mr. C.E. Crossland of Lakeland, Florida, who thanked the Justice for his majority opinion in the *Everson* case.

Mr. Crossland enclosed pages 429 and 485 of the minutes of meetings of the Lakeland City Commissioners which showed the city gave $25,000 in public funds for a Baptist children's home; and also gave 15 city lots to the Florida Baptist Institute where "Baptist ministers could be instructed." Mr. Crossland said he had nine such files, seven of which related to Baptists receiving government funds. [39]

Also, Sen. George Aiken, commenting on the issue of aid to religious schools, said it "has been met over and over again with such legislation as the G.I. Bill of Rights, and it can be met again."

He added: "The old argument of separation of church and state falls down, when under the G.I. Bill of Rights, the United States is paying today to educate priests, Protestant ministers and Rabbis." [40]

McCollum Reinforces *Everson* Philosophy

Just over one year after its controversial *Everson* decision, the Court decided *McCollum,* a case involving released time for religious instruction in public schools. Again, it was a situation Scottish Rite Masonry had protested for a long time.

Reaffirming *Everson* philosophy, Justice Black, speaking for the majority, struck down an Illinois State law which permitted released time. The rationale again was predicated on Jefferson's "wall . . . which must be kept high and impregnable." [41]

Justice Black repeated his view that "Neither a state nor the Federal Government can set up a church. Neither . . . aid one religion, aid all religions . . . No tax in any amount . . . can support religious activities or institutions . . ." [42]

Both *McCollum* and *Everson* drew strong opposition from the Catholic Bishops of the United States. At their annual meeting in 1948, the prelates said secularism is "the most deadly menace to our Christian and American way of living."

The bishops characterized the Court's interpretation of the religion clause as "novel," and said Jefferson's "wall" was merely a metaphor. Continuing, the Catholic churchmen said it would be an "utter distortion of history and law" to establish a national policy of "indifference to religion." [43]

Everson's Enduring Impact

The "wall" erected by the *Everson* decision has been left standing by the Court in case after case, beginning with *McCollum* and continuing into the the 1980s. However, a modest counterattack against that judicial attachment to a vagrant phrase became evident within the judicial system, beginning in the 1970s. [44]

In addition to outlawing released time, the Court over the years has: established secular humanism and other non-theistic beliefs as "religion"; [45] prohibited vocal prayer, devotional Bible reading, and recitation of the Lord's Prayer in public schools; [46] banned aid for sectarian purposes to colleges where the curricula was permeated with religious teaching and exercises, and at which clerics dominated the boards of trustees; [47] proscribed public funding of salaries for teachers' at parochial schools, as well as State-funded instructional materials in such schools; [48] prohibited public funding for maintenance and repair grants at parochial schools, while also denying tuition reimbursement and tuition tax deductions for education at such schools. [49]

Further, the Court prohibited State funding for instructional materials and equipment, counseling, testing services, together with speech and hearing therapy in church schools. [50] Also, the Court ruled as unconstitutional a Kentucky statute which authorized posting the Ten Commandments (purchased with private contributions) on the walls of public school classrooms in the State. [51]

Michigan and New York were prohibited from providing enrichment classes in mathematics, art, and music taught by public school teachers to nonpublic school students in classrooms leased from church schools; [52] and an Alabama statute authorizing a one-minute period of silence in public schools for meditation or prayer was declared to violate the religion clause of the First Amendment. [53]

Moreover, the curious concern about religious strife endemic to equitable state funding of church schools—a perception which reflected the thinking of Justice Black when he defended his Ku Klux Klan membership in a nationwide broadcast in 1937, and a viewpoint voiced later by the Scottish Rite's Elmer Rogers in Congressional testimony, and by Justice Rutledge in his minority *Everson* opinion—became judicial boilerplate in numerous Supreme Court religion-clause decisions.

Justice Frankfurter's concurring opinion in *McCollum,* (joined by Justices Jackson, Rutledge and Burton), recalled "fierce sectarian opposition, to the barring of tax funds to church schools;" and credited Horace Mann with saving the common school "from being rent by denominational conflict."

The concurring opinion also cited a passage from mid-19th Century *Girard* decision, but quoted it out of context to suggest there was a consensus in the 1840s opposing religious instruction in public schools. It was a totally erroneous and misleading statement by Justice Frankfurter. [54]

Justice Arthur Goldberg included a reference to the potential for national discord because of religious beliefs in his opinion in the *Schempp-Murray* decision. And the national hazard associated with religious beliefs again loomed up in Justice John M. Harlan's opinion in the *Allen* case. [55]

In 1969, Professor Paul Fruend said, "political division on religious lines is one of the principal evils that the first amendment sought to forestall." [56]

Justice Harlan emphasized the identical theme the following year in the *Walz* case, as did Chief Justice Burger in the 1971 *Lemon* decision. And the threat of national violence associated with funding of church schools was echoed once more by Justice Lewis Powell in his majority opinion in *Nyquist* two years later; as it was by Justices Stewart, Brennan, Douglas and Marshall in their joint opinion in the *Meek* case of 1975. [57]

That train of conjecture by the highest tribunal in the land about an unfounded *potential* for national discord and strife was strange indeed, particularly since only conventional religion was indicted as the source for such fears. However, in the *Girard* case, the Court referred to public policies "connected with religious polity, in a country composed of such a variety of religious sects as our country." It was then declared that the Court had no right to inject itself into potential disputes on the issue unless an actual case was before it.

Rather than conjecture about potentialities, the Court said:

"We disclaim any right to enter upon such examinations, beyond what the state constitutions, and laws, and decisions necessarily bring before us." [58]

The post-*Everson* Court's train of conjecture is rather bizarre because (a) there is no history to support such conjecture since the demise of the Ku Klux Klan; and (b) the Court never evidenced such fears about strife and conflict precipitated by legislation and Court decisions that provided open housing, school busing, and other civil rights laws, which in modern times did, in fact, frequently ignite serious rioting and bloodshed across the nation.

How Religion Clause Cases Came To Court

Some who were adults prior to 1947 have expressed wonderment at the sudden explosion of religion-clause cases taken up by the Supreme Court following the *Everson* decision.

Based upon the record, it is obvious that many, if not all of the religion clause cases, beginning with *Everson,* were brought to the Supreme Court by Freemasonry and its allies.

For example, the preceding pages established that Scottish Rite Masonry had expressed its opposition to: public busing of children to parochial schools; released time religious education in public schools; every form of religious expression in those schools; as well as "the entire separation of Church and State, and opposition to every attempt to appropriate public moneys—federal, state or local—directly or indirectly, for the support of sectarian or private institutions."

It also has been demonstrated that all of those Masonic concerns were largely resolved by the Court to the satisfaction of the Craft when that tribunal was dominated by Masons. Moreover, the opinions by the Justices in those cases paralleled a unique series of arguments that had been first advanced by a representative of the Supreme Council of Scottish Rite Masonry.

The next question is: how did it happen?

One Masonic author disclosed in 1959 that Masonry "provided the major obstacle" to the growth of religious-oriented education in America.

Two months later, another member of the Craft commented: "The action of judges who were Masons in defending the liberties of the people from the encroachment of a power-hungry despot, oligarchy, bureaucracy [i.e., the Catholic Church] . . . has been uniformly commendable." [59]

In 1966, the Grand Commander of the Scottish Rite of the Southern Jurisdiction, explained how Masonic activity in religion clause cases is initiated. He said:

"The first thing to do is to find taxpayers who will allow their names to be used to take the case to court." [60]

The Grand Commander's remarks were prompted by the Craft's success in pursuing a case in Maryland which ultimately resulted in denial of public funds for three church colleges: Western Maryland, a Methodist institution; and Notre Dame and St. Joseph's, both of Maryland and both Catholic (St. Joseph's subsequently closed its doors). [61]

Continuing, the Grand Commander said the motivating force in the Maryland case, was the Horace Mann League, aided by Protestants and Others United for Separation of Church and State (POAU), and the Scottish Rite Supreme Council itself. [62]

Both POAU (presently known as Americans United (AU)) and the Horace Mann League are Masonically supported and influenced organizations. [63]

Additional victories by the Craft occurred when former California Governor Earl Warren, a 33rd Degree Mason, became Chief Justice in 1953.

Two years after Brother Warren assumed his exalted position on the high bench, Brother Henry C. Clausen of California, 33rd Degree (who later became Sovereign Grand Commander of the Scottish Rite), reminded the Fraternity of Brother Warren's philosophy toward education. He recalled a 1936 annual message made to the Brethern by then Grand Master Warren of the Grand Lodge of California. At that time, Earl Warren said:

> ". . . the education of our youth . . . can best be done, indeed it can only be done, by a system of free public education. It is for this reason that the Grand Lodge of California, ever striving as it does to replace darkness with light, is so vitally interested n the public schools of our state . . .
>
> "By destroying prejudice and planting reason in its place it prepares the foundation of a liberty-loving people for free government . . ." [64]

"Darkness and Light" are old Masonic code words for the beliefs of conventional religious groups, particularly teachings of the Roman Catholic Church, as opposed to the beliefs of Freemasonry and naturalists. The "prejudice" to be destroyed, is, again, Catholic and other conventional faith and belief.

Grand Commander Clausen was not lax in using the courts to ban State aid for religous education. In 1968, he filed a brief before the Supreme Court on behalf of the appellants in *Flast v. Cohen*. [65]

Florence Flast, chairperson of the New York State PEARL (a militant anti-church school coalition), argued that federal funds had been expended unconstitutionally for sectarian schools under the federal Elementary and Secondary Education Act. Chief Justice Warren ruled that the coalition had "standing" to bring the suit to the Court. [66]

The Chief Justice, according to Masonic dogma, was subordinate, in Masonic activities, to the Sovereign Grand Commander of Scottish Rite Freemasonry. Prohibiting aid to religious education certainly is a well-documented Masonic activity.

The *New Age* viewed Chief Justice Warren's ruling as "a signal victory" for the doctrine of separation of Church and State. [67]

Other Masonic interests that submitted briefs supporting Flast and PEARL were POAU and the late Senator Sam Ervin (D., N.C.), a 33rd Degree Mason. [68]

Further evidence of Scottish Rite involvement in bringing cases before the Supreme Court was set forth in a report by the Supreme Council's Committee on Education and Americanism. The report said "almost without exception, in most [efforts to oppose aid to church schools] you will find strong activity on the part of individual Scottish Rite Masons." [69]

The Committee urged Masons: (1) to join organizations such as Americans United, and Americans for Public Schools in order to oppose aid to parochial schools; (2) to educate each Master Mason on the importance of the issue; (3) to elect legislators opposed to aid to such schools; (4) to lead men and women to repulse efforts to obtain aid for religious-affiliated schools; (5) to encourage formation of lawyers committees to monitor legislation and recommend legal steps to "strike down" unconstitutional laws; and (6) to distribute Masonic propaganda "through public and private schools and libraries." [70]

In 1976, the same Supreme Council committee observed that courts alone can not deny subsidies to church schools, nor can they initiate action on their own. The courts, said the panel report, "must wait for others to bring cases before them," a situation which "requires people and money."

At that point, the report said: "It can be done; it has been done."

Examples were cited including the Grand Commander's efforts to challenge tax credits for education in California in 1976, as well as litigation in six other States, including the *Horace Mann* case in Maryland. [71]

Not cited was Grand Commander Clausen's brief filed in the 1971 *Lemon* case, in which he argued: "The American [Catholic] Church officials are merely executing and voicing those directives from Rome. Control is in Rome, regardless of the American hierarchy, on subjects such as birth control, dogma or education." [72]

After reviewing arguments, the Court, in its *Lemon* decision, apparently accepted the substance of the Grand Commander's argument. It noted that Catholic schools constituted "an integral part of the religious mission of the Catholic Church," and added:

"We cannot ignore the dangers that a teacher under religious control and discipline poses to the separation of the religious from the purely secular aspects of pre-college education. the conflict of functions inheres in the situation." [73]

Commenting on the Court's ruling in that case, the Grand Commander saw it as "a tremendous vindication for the often-expressed views of the Supreme Council of the Scottish Rite. . . ." [74]

Secularizing Religious Colleges

Of particular interest is the Court's decision in the *Horace Mann League* case which denied State funding to church-related colleges, because it shows how a single Court ruling effectively emasculated the religious mission, not only of the church related colleges involved in the case, but many others across the nation.

In that 1966 case, the Maryland Court of Appeals (the State's "Supreme" Court) found the stated purposes of Notre Dame College of Maryland "are deeply and intensely religious."

The theory of Catholic education, the court observed, utilizes "prayer, Holy Mass, and the sacraments, as the "unifying forces." Moreover, the Maryland tribunal found that students' lives are "lived in a Catholic atmosphere which assumes that earthly life is to be lived . . . in terms of a preparation for the future life with God." To that end, it was determined that the college "harmonizes" its entire program "with the philosophy and theology of the Catholic Church." [75]

The Court also noted that the governing board of the college was controlled by a Catholic religious order whose members are completely committed to Catholic discipline and educational philosophy. Further, those who administer the college were found to be comprised of people who were almost entirely priests or Religious; and the faculty was chosen on the basis of commitment to the Roman Catholic objectives and ideals of the college which are overwhelmingly Catholic. Additionally, "more than 97 percent of the whole student body is Catholic." [76]

Finally, it was noted that St. Joseph's College had purposes which "seem to be even more strongly religious than Notre Dame . . ." [77]

Within one year of that decision (which was upheld by the U.S. Supreme Court, 387 U.S. 97), a number of Catholic colleges and universities, notably the University of Notre Dame at South Bend, Ind., replaced almost all of the priests, brothers and nuns on their

Boards of Directors with lay personnel. The Catholic ambience of those educational institutions also was toned down considerably.

Ten years later, the Masonically influenced Horace Mann League brought to the Supreme Court a related case, involving most of the same schools.

The Court, now found the ostensibly Catholic colleges of Notre Dame of Maryland, St. Joseph's, Mount St. Mary's, and Loyola of Baltimore were not "pervasively sectarian." Despite "formal affiliation with the Roman Catholic Church," they are "characterized by a high degree of institutional autonomy." None of the four "Catholic" institutions "receives funds from, or makes reports to the Catholic Church;" and "no instance of entry of Church considerations into college decisions was shown." [78]

The Court further found attendance at religious exercises is not required, and "encouragement of spiritual development is only 'one secondary objective' of the college." Further, "religious indoctrination is not a substantial purpose or activity of any of these defendants," and there is "no 'actual college policy' of encouraging the practice" of prayer. [79]

Interestingly enough, in his dissenting opinion, Justice John Paul Stevens noted "the pernicious tendency of a state subsidy to tempt religious schools to compromise their religious mission without wholly abandoning it." [80]

By the 1980s, the common practice of Catholic colleges and universities muting or abandoning Catholic teaching and discipline, in the service of Mammon, blossomed into a lively dispute between the so-called American Catholic Church and the Holy See.

Melding The Craft And The Court—A Summary

Freemasonry, throughout its entire history, has relentlessly fought the religious beliefs of Christianity, and with equal tenacity opposed the use of public funds for Christian religious education.

In the United States, the Craft historically had been enormously successful at the State level in thwarting efforts to provide equity in distribution of funds for schools serving a public purpose. At the national level, too, the Fraternity had some success, even though the federal government was only minimally involved in education. But by the 1930s, the national government began to be increasingly involved in assisting church related institutions.

From a Masonic point of view, that situation became even more ominous in 1944, when Congress approved the "G.I. Bill of Rights," and thereby, without a recorded dissenting vote, authorized World War II veterans, at government expense, to attend the school of their choice, secular or religious.

The "G.I. Bill," as Sen. Aiken noted, resulted in the federal government "paying . . . to educate priests, Protestant ministers and Rabbis."

Further, in the immediate post-war period, Congress was moving actively toward providing equitable assistance for students in public and church-related elementary and secondary schools.

At no time during discussions of measures involving aid to church schools, including the G.I. Bill of Rights and other legislation debated in Congressional Committees prior to *Everson,* did any Congressman or Senator—most of whom were lawyers—suggest that such legislation violated the Constitution, the fundamental law of the land which they solemnly swore to uphold and defend.

The entire legal history of federal support for church institutions performing public services, demonstrated that such government accommodations were clearly Constitutional, and indeed, had been upheld repeatedly by the Supreme Court.

With that background, it was evident any change in the situation would have to be effected by the Supreme Court, despite substantial Court precedents upholding federal laws which accommodated, on an equitable basis, religious institutions performing public functions.

Meanwhile, a little noticed propaganda campaign was being advanced by members of the Masonic Fraternity. That effort insisted: law "is largely in the interpretation and not in the text;" and that the Constitution and its amendments "are what the judges say they are."

By 1941, an ardent Freemason President succeeded in having members of the Craft dominate the Court. At least one member of that body, Justice Hugo L. Black was known to be militantly anti-Catholic, as evidenced by his membership in the Ku Klux Klan, his votes in Congress, and his own son's testimony that he "suspected the Catholic Church," and "could not tolerate any sign of encouraging religious faith by state aid."

Within days after legislation had been introduced in Congress to provide equitable aid for both public schools and nonpublic schools, Justice Black wrote a letter to Senator Lister Hill, a fellow Alabamian, a Brother Mason, and the principal sponsor of legislation which would aid public schools only. Justice Black called the Senator's attention to a list of five Masonic principles concerned with education favored by the Scottish Rite of Freemasonry.

Principle No. 1 advocates the public school "for all of the children of all of the people." Principle No. 5 calls for "The entire separation of Church and State, and opposition to every attempt to appropriate public moneys . . . directly or indirectly, for the support of sectarian or private institutions."

The Justice urged Sen. Hill to get in touch with officials of the Scottish Rite for the purpose of having them support the Senator's legislation, a measure which would assist public schools only. Indeed, the Justice himself contacted Masonic officials to inquire of the Fraternity's position on aid to public schools.

The legislation foundered. However, within two years of Justice Black's letter to the man who succeeded him in the Senate, the Masonically dominated Court made it absolutely certain that Congress would be unable to include church schools in educational funding legislation.

The high bench declared it unconstitutional to provide public funds to directly assist or encourage religious education.

And the Justices based their decision—not on the true meaning of the religion clause of the First Amendment—but on the meaning of Jefferson's Bill for Religious Freedom, applicable only to the State of Virginia. [81]

That is the record of Masonic Justice. And it is built on sand.

Statutory law and the American Bar Association's "Canons of Judicial Ethics" require that judges be completely impartial in their decisions, and that there should be no suspicion that their verdicts are tainted with bias.

The Supreme Court put it well in 1954 when it ruled:

"A fair trial in a fair tribunal is a basic requirement of due process. Fairness of course requires an absence of actual bias in the trial of cases. But our system of law has always endeavored to prevent *even the probability of unfairness.* To this end no man can be a judge in his own case and no man is permitted to try cases where he has an interest in the outcome. . . . But to perform its high function in the best way 'justice must satisfy the appearance of justice.' *Offutt v. United States,* 348 U.S. 11, 14."

That majority opinion was written by Justice Hugo L. Black. [82]

9/ Warring On The Church—II

Masonry's cosmic battle plan always has massed its primary attack against the Roman Catholic Church, while subordinating general Christian beliefs as secondary targets of opportunity.

As an integral part of this war between the religion of Masonry and the religion of Christianity, the Craft has consistently endeavored to lure practicing Catholics and other Christians onto its membership rolls in order to subvert the Church.

A *New Age* article explained the irreconcilability between the religion of the Church and the religion of the Craft, as follows:

> "In each system, the controlling ideal has to do with the ultimate destiny, the final goal, of humanity; and in each system the urge is strong to bring every power and resource to bear in an effort to realize that ideal. . . ."

The article went on to say Masonry rejects the Kingdom of Heaven as an other-world kingdom, but believes the Kingdom of God "is to be established among men by the evolution and development of man himself. . . ." [1]

The Catholic Population Threat

During the years immediately following World War II, the Craft became deeply worried about the explosive growth of the Catholic Church in the United States. And understandably so. Table 1 shows the Catholic population of this country doubled during the 20 year period 1940-1960, soaring from 20.4 million adherents to 40.8 million. Moreover, between 1955-1960, fifty-six percent of the total population growth in the entire nation was in the Catholic sector. Overall,

Table 1

GROWTH OF U.S. CATHOLIC POPULATION IN RELATION TO TOTAL NATIONAL POPULATION INCREASE, 1940-80*

1	2	3	4	5	6	7	8
Year	U.S. Pop. (000)	U.S. Pop. Increase (000)	Percent (%) U.S. Pop. Increase	U.S. Cath. Pop. (000)	U.S. Cath. Pop. Growth (000)	Percent (%) U.S. Cath. Pop. Growth	Cath. Growth As Percent (%) U.S. Pop. Increase (Cols. 6:3)
1940	132,000	—	—	20,400	—	—	—
1945	139,800	7,800	5.6	23,900	3,500	14.6	45.0
1950	151,100	11,400	7.5	27,700	3,800	13.7	33.0
1955	164,600	13,500	8.2	32,500	4,800	14.8	36.0
1960	179,400	14,800	8.2	40,800	8,300	20.3	56.0
1965	193,200	13,800	7.1	45,600	4,800	10.5	35.0
1970	203,800	10,600	5.2	47,800	2,200	4.6	21.0
1975	214,900	11,100	5.2	48,700	900	1.8	08.0
1980	226,400	11,500	5.1	49,800	1,100	2.2	09.0

*Figures rounded to nearest hundred.

U.S. population figures are from the *Statistical Abstract of the United States, 1982-83*, U.S. Department of Commerce, Bureau of the Census, U.S. Government Printing Office, Washington, D.C., 1982, Table 7, p. 9.

U.S. Catholic population figures are from *The World Almanac*, 1941-1981. During that period the *Almanac* was published 1941 through 1951 by the *New York World Telegram*; subsequently it was published by the *New York World Telegram and Sun*. Since 1968 it has been published by Newspaper Enterprise Association, New York.

See also *Historical Statistics Colonial Times To 1957*, Part I, Department of Commerce, Bureau of Census, Washington, D.C., 1960, Series H 538-543, "Membership of Selected Religious Bodies: 1790 to 1957," p. 228-229. Catholic statistics in that Series go back only as far as 1891, at which time Catholics numbered 8,277,000. However, that religious body is not known to have been larger than that estimate during the preceding years.

the two decade period from approximately the time of U.S. involvement in World War II until 1960, Catholics accounted for 42.5 percent of the national population growth.

That eye-catching expansion of Catholics in a nation that had long been Protestant and secularist was even more impressive from a historical standpoint. It took 427 years—from the time Ponce de Leon first set his foot on the coast of Florida, until 1940—for Catholics to number 21 million people. And then, in less than one generation, that number of Catholics doubled.

Moreover, the vast majority of adherents to that religion were concentrated in 19 States with 283 electoral votes. Their percentage of the total population of those States ranged from 64 in Rhode Island to 21 in California. [2]

Clearly, if such a trend continued, Catholics would become a majority. Even if it did not continue, their political clout would be enormous.

But the surge of Catholics in the population did not maintain, as Table 1 shows. One reason for this tapering off was a decline of immigrants from Catholic countries, and action by Congress to severely cut back on the number of immigrants from Europe. But the more important reason, was acceptance of artificial birth control by a majority of Catholics.

Nevertheless, the strong Catholic growth worried Scottish Rite Freemasonry.

In 1945, the Grand Commander urged the Pope to lift the ban on the Church's ages-old condemnation of the Masonic Fraternity. [3]

In 1950, a Knight Templar was telling *New Age* readers that Catholicism, not Communism nor Socialism, was the real worry, because Catholics were winning elections. [4]

A 1952 *New Age* editorial complained that a bill pending in Congress would "open floodgates" for some 300,000 refugees—a preponderance" of whom "are Roman Catholics," [5]

The Scottish Rite leadership evoked the old specter about the Church, its parochial schools, fraternal and veterans organizations being "based on a difference in sectarian faith and teachings [and] are . . . creative of a grave disunity among our people." [6]

It was another effort to evoke the same alleged explosive threat to national unity inherent in the free exercise of beliefs held by Catholics and other committed Christians.

That specter loomed first in Justice Black's 1937 national radio broadcast as he railed against those who made an issue of his Klan membership. The same alarm was sounded by Scottish Rite Masonry's Elmer Rogers, and, repeatedly, by the Supreme Court.

Always, according to those alarmists, the hovering threat of national discord and potential violence is inherent in any government effort to equitably accommodate Catholics and other committed Christians to freely exercise their religious beliefs in a State-mandated education system. Curiously, the Court never has found the advancement of non-theistic beliefs a cause for alarm and potential revolution and violence.

Pursuing the issue of religious discord, the *New Age* reported, in 1954, that the National Council of Churches was profoundly concerned about the "growing factor of Catholic power in our national life," and that the Catholic hierarchy had become "more aggressive in the political arena, especially in the fields of medicine, education and foreign policy. . . ." The hierarchy, it was claimed, "is on the march as never before in more than 50 years." [7]

It was also said the Catholic Church insists upon pressing for a policy of "out-breeding the 'non-Catholic world,' " and thus attempts to control democracies. [8]

One Masonic author said the Catholic population had grown from a missionary territory in 1910 to 31 million adherents in 1958. He called for a "resistance movement" to prevent imposition of Catholic Church policies "upon our schools, hospitals, government and family organizations." [9]

Roman Catholic values, the author asserted, are "in direct opposition to the laws of our country, with regard to "official religion, divorce, marriage, birth control, education, sterilization, and therapeutic abortion."

The same article said many of "our conscientious, thoughtful, freedom-loving Catholic citizens" ask themselves:

" 'Can one at the same time be a good Catholic and a loyal American citizen?' " [10]

Catholics Help Masons

The idea that "conscientious, thoughtful, freedom-loving Catholic citizens" would help Masonry make fundamental changes in the Church was a view which persisted in the *New Age* for many years, and proved to be quite accurate.

As far back as 1926, the *New Age* carried an article which said the Craft should encourage its members to be active in Christian churches. Every member "should cast his lot with the Church—to help vitalize it, liberalize it, modernize it and render it aggressive and efficient—to do less is treason to your country, to your Creator, and to the obligation you have promised to obey." [11]

However, it was not until the 1940s that the *New Age* began reporting success in persuading Catholics to look favorably toward the Craft.

In March, 1949, the magazine carried an editorial which said Masonic anti-Catholicism is directed, not against the individual Catholic, but against the system with which he, unfortunately is identified. However, the editor continued, when the individual Catholic "gets spunk enough to tell his hierarchy what he wants done," and makes them do it, instead of "grovelling under fear and threats," then the individual Catholic will find himself welcomed by his fellow citizens as part of the American scene—a culture that is white, Protestant and Anglo Saxon." [12]

Another editorial in the same publication said Masons must educate Americans about Roman Catholics and "recover and maintain our integrity as a political national sovereignty, free from theocratic interference by the Romish-Church State. . . . Help will come from lay Roman Catholics and many priests. . . ." [13]

In 1955, the *New Age* ran a three-part series of articles which discussed the view that Catholicism is incompatible with democracy, and that Catholics should "repudiate" the anti-democratic doctrines of their Church. [14]

The article by Harold Rafton, previously appeared as a pamphlet published by the Beacon Press, the publishing arm of the Unitarian Universalist Church, an organization which has always been closely allied with Freemasonry.

Rafton said there is hope for America if Catholics in this country cleanse the Church of its anti-democratic doctrines, and organize small groups in each parish to "request frequent itemized accountings of all the money received by their parish church." Until such a report is made by the pastor, the article admonished, Catholics should not contribute to their parish. [15]

He characterized refusal to contribute to support of the Church as "a mortal sin," which "*no just God will condemn them to Hell merely for wanting to know how their money is spent.*" [Emphasis in original] [16]

Discussing small parish groups, the article said members of those groups should "obtain the right to cooperate in drawing up their church budget, to pass on the desirability of individual items and to keep expenditures within the financial resources of the parish. The motto should be, 'no taxation without representation.' They may thus be able to curb expensive building programs the Church may have planned, but for which the Catholic layman can ill afford to pay." [17]

Other points made in the article were:

- Parishioners should gain control of Church property.
- Parishioners should insist that lay Catholics sit on parochial school boards, and make sure "no taint of any anti-democratic doctrine" is "taught in the religious courses or in any other subject."
- Let the laity choose their clergy rather than be "dependent for their positions on a foreign source" and follow its bidding.
- When the above are accomplished, Catholics can "demand the elimination of anti-Democratic Catholic doctrines." [18]

Concluding, Rafton said: "When that happy day comes," non-Catholics will be able to assure their Catholic fellow citizens "that the tension between us will disappear like snow in the warm sun." [19]

Rafton's call was echoed four years later by the Grand Commander of Scottish Rite Masonry. Catholics, he said, should manage and control the Church so there would be no more demands for tax support for parochial schools "because most of the children would be attending public schools; the obnoxious Catholic 'Medical Code' for nurses, doctors and hospitals, and opposition to birth control would have been abolished . . . and the Church's propaganda barrage for the election of a Roman Catholic President would subside. Liberty, Equality and Fraternity would be a reality in America." [20]

Like the constant rush of water on a stone, the Masonic campaign apparently was making an impression within the Church itself.

In 1961, the *New Age* called attention to a column by Msgr. George W. Casey in the *Boston Pilot,* the Archdiocesan weekly organ, which urged closing of parochial schools to eliminate Catholic "separation and inbreeding." The Monsignor also reportedly called for an end to novenas which are conducted "for palpably profit motives . . ." [21]

Subsequently, it was reported that "many Roman Catholics" are now opposed to parochial schools which "segregate Roman Catholics into scholastic enclaves, a medieval concept which . . . is bad for the Church and bad for the Nation." [22]

The same report said Richard Cardinal Cushing of Boston opposed financing of Church-related schools, and that some Catholic school administrators desire to break away from their traditional structure "which requires that their schools be directed by parish pastors controlled by the hierarchy." [23]

In 1971, the Grand Commander invited attention to a controversial book, *Are Parochial Schools The Answer?* by Mary Perkins Ryan, which recommended severe cutbacks in parochial schools. About the same time, the Masonic chieftain reported, a Catholic lay group met at La Jolla, California where the president of the organization declared: "We are against putting tax funds into a secret organization that never divulges what it does with its money or documents the need for financing." [24]

The striking aspect of the Rafton series of articles, as well as subsequent articles and commentaries in the *New Age* was that the changes recommended for the Catholic Church, in America, actually were adopted.

Specifically: powerful lay-dominated parish councils were established throughout the United States, and members of these bodies immediately demanded a full accounting of parish income and expenditures.

As a result, school personnel were given salaries to begin competing, at first modestly, with tax-paid public school personnel. Accordingly, tuitions were increased dramatically.

Previously, it had been common for parochial school employees to work more for the glory of God, and less for material wealth. Moreover, parish communities had been more amenable to bearing the full costs of parochial education, or, alternatively, tuition costs were kept very nominal. It had not been unusual for tuition costs to be in the $50 per-year range, and additional children in the same family were given very low group rates.

The increased tuition, which began running to high three and low to mid-four figures, forced a growing number of Catholic children into public schools where religion was not a subject for discussion, except as those schools imposed a secularist value system. That development had long been an avid desideratum of Masonry.

Although Church property has remained under control of the local ordinaries, new church buildings no longer were distinguished by inspirational architecture, and interior appointments were jettisoned.

Sacred tabernacles, where God Himself in the Blessed Sacrament reposed—the very focal point of every Catholic church—were removed to side altars or sacristies. Beautiful marble altars often were torn out, as were altar rails at which the faithful for centuries had reverently knelt to adore and receive the Sacred Host. Statutes of Saints were largely dispensed with, as were the silent, flickering flames of vigil lights, symbolic of prayers rising after the petitioner had left the church. Stations of the Cross, by which Catholics fervently recalled Christ's last Passion, were often discarded; so, too, were novenas, the Rosary, Exposition of the Blessed Sacrament, and Benediction. The carnage wreaked in the Church called to mind Psalm 73 (Douay):

> "Remember thy congregation, which thou hast possessed from the beginning . . .
> See what things the enemy hath done wickedly in the sanctuary . . .
> As with axes in a wood of trees, they have cut down at once the gates thereof, with axe and hatchet they have brought it down.
> They have set fire to thy sanctuary: they have defiled the dwelling place of thy name on earth."

And there was more. A new emphasis was given to democratic procedures in a Church which, from its founding, had been hierarchical and authoritarian. Indeed, it was evident that the old heresy of "Americanism," condemned at the turn of the Century by Pope Leo XIII, was again under way. A concerted effort was being made to establish an American Catholic Church, as distinguished from the Roman Catholic Church in America. The new emphasis would tailor the traditional teachings of the Roman Catholic Church to the consensus of the American people, rather than to the orthodox teachings of the Holy Father and the Church's Magisterium.

The most evident sign of consensus morality was the massive opposition by a small army of theologians and other priests and nuns—as well as millions of laity—to Pope Paul VI's Encyclical Letter, *Humanae Vitae,* which stipulated that the Church will not change its consistent teaching that artificial contraception is sinful.

Like the Reformation of the 16th Century, the Church's liturgy placed a new emphasis upon the the Bible as it subdued preaching about the efficacy of the Sacraments, particularly weekly or monthly Confession. Sin faded almost into oblivion. All who said "Lord, Lord" were saved.

As in Protestantism, so in the new Catholicism, there "was a tendency to minimize liturgy and to stress preaching by the ministry and the reading of the Bible."

A growing belief became manifest among theologians and laity that individual conscience is the valid interpreter of Scripture. Also a growing nationalism and a revivification of the 15th Century conciliar movement—the attempt to establish the superiority of the ecumenical council over the Pope—became apparent.

Another episode which indicated Masonic philosophy had its effect on influencing ages-old Catholic thought was the action by Catholic colleges and universities to establish lay control over their institutions in order to obviate denial of funds by federal, State, and local governments and foundations. [25]   Academic freedom superceded obedience to Church teaching.

A parallel effort to lure Catholics into the Fraternity was a propaganda campaign which claimed that many members of the Catholic clergy had been won to Masonry's banner over the years, most notably Pope Pius IX.

According to an editorial in the *New Age,* the Pontiff, when a priest on assignment in Chile, joined the Fraternity in 1823 under his pre-Pontifical family name, Giovanni M. Ferretti. However, the editorial said he was expelled March 27, 1874. [26].

Pius IX reigned from June 21, 1846 until February 7, 1878, and had issued a number of condemnations of Freemasonry. Even the *New Age* said the Pontiff's "Syllabus of Errors," which was an integral part of his Encyclical Letter, *Quanta Cura* (published December 8, 1864) "is the most dogmatic attack on freedom ever penned by a human being." [27]

Actually, Pius IX published four other Encyclicals opposing Masonry beginning with *Qui Pluribus,* issued November 9, 1846, shortly after he was elected Pope. He also "attributed Masonry to Satan." [28]

The Church's Rapprochement With Masonry

A review of Catholic publications over a 40-year period shows development of a gradual change in Catholic thought toward Freemasonry that ranged from outright condemnation at the beginning of the period studied, to a slow but sure tendency toward acceptance of membership in the Fraternity as a brotherly thing to do, particularly because Masonry in America is different than in Europe and Latin America.

In 1934, Father James Magner wrote that Catholics are forbidden to join the Craft because it "has the characteristics of a religious sect . . . with its own religious symbolism derived from the Old Testament, and its own ritual."

Continuing, the priest said, Masonry historically "has identified itself" as a social and political body whose aims are "hostile to the rights of the Catholic Church." It is "the outstanding proponent of secularism," and many of the severest persecutions" of the Church in modern times "have come from Masonic sources." [29]

In 1938, the Jesuit national weekly, *America,* ran a commentary which said Masons in the United States were 'rather conservative' and "not rabidly anti-Catholic." However, the commentary continued, the Craft was undergoing a "most insidious change" by which U.S. Masonry was being endangered by "a most secret impenetration of the Orient from Paris," particularly in the cities of New York and Washington, D.C. [30]

In 1949, a prominent student of Masonry, William J. Whalen, said the Church traditionally had condemned the Craft primarily because of its naturalism "which undermines the Christian faith and promotes indifferentism and contempt for religious authority." But, he noted, Masons in the United States "do not attack the Church with the vigor and relish" of their brethern in Europe." [31]

The *New Age* reported that during Easter Week, 1950, priests in Montreal, Canada warned parishioners against joining Masonry under penalty of excommunication.

The report said Father M. Cordovani, a Dominican and Master of the Apostolic Sacred Palaces in Rome, wrote in *Le Devoir,* a Montreal daily, that "a movement is on foot" to bring about a reconciliation" between the Church and that portion of Masonry which is considered "not to be antagonistic" toward Catholicism. Such a reconciliation, said the priest, is "an impossibility." [32]

The same editorial said the *Masonic Light* of Huntingdon, Quebec, reported that Father Joseph Bertheloot, S.J., had written three books on the urgency of concluding an accord with Masonry and Catholicism. The *Light* said, it was hardly conceivable that the Jesuit priest "would publish such views as he expresses without having received the approval of his superiors." [33]

The editor of the Quebec Masonic journal commented: "[W]e are frankly mystified that the Dominican Cordovani should express an opinion so diametrically opposed to that of Father Bertheloot!"

Addressing that latter remark, the *New Age* said: "We are not mystified at these interplays of attitudes by the heads of the leading orders of the Roman Catholic Church toward the Masonic Fraternity." But, said the *New Age,* Fr. Bertheloot's wish "can never be had." [34]

Continuing, the Scottish Rite editorial said "the greatest harm" could be done to Masonry in the event a number of Catholics joined the Fraternity who were not "true Masons at heart." The editorial added: "much depends upon the early ethical rearing of a candidate for the Craft." [35]

As it turned out, Father Cordovani, was completely accurate in his prediction, and his prophetic understanding of the situation became evident rather quickly.

Just the next year, for example, the Jesuit weekly, *America,* carried an editorial which said Catholics in the United States "used to be much agitated about the anti-Catholicism of American Freemasons." But, said *America,* Northern Masons (as distinct from the Scottish Rite of the Southern Jurisdiction) have demonstrated friendliness and fairness in dealing with Catholics, and "have largely dropped the issue." [36]

Explaining the putative friendliness and fairness of the Northern Masons, the Jesuit editorial cited the fact that President Franklin D. Roosevelt, a Mason, had selected two Catholics for his first Cabinet, and also pointed out that Catholic students were treated on an equal basis in the National Youth Administration program, as well as under the World War II veterans assistance program, generally referred to as the "G.I. Bill of Rights." Moreover, Roosevelt had appointed his own personal representative to the Vatican, said *America.* [37]

On the other hand, the Jesuit editorial deplored the "incessant anti-Catholicism of the Scottish Rite Freemasons of the Southern Jurisdiction, particularly in the field of education. It was then suggested that "our Northern Masonic friends" look into the close tie between Southern Masonry and anti-Catholic, anti-Negro policies—or, the editorial concluded, "is it only Southern.?" [38]

Apparently, *America's* editorial writer was not well informed about President Roosevelt. For example, *The New York Times* noted in 1932 that the Vatican daily, *L'Osservatore Romano* had charged that Communism, in league with Freemasons, was at the bottom of the religious troubles in Mexico. It was a conflict in which the national law limited the Catholic people to one priest for every 100,000 members of the faithful. [39]

Roosevelt was appealed to repeatedly, and in vain, by the Knights of Columbus to take action which would relieve the persecution of Catholics in Mexico. In February, 1935, the Knights wrote a letter telling the President they had "documentary proof of the tearing down of crucifixes . . . and the shooting of Catholics and priests on the steps of churches." [40]

On December 17, 1935, the Knights wrote a letter to Mr. Roosevelt protesting his lack of action, not only on behalf of Catholics in Mexico, but also his decision to ignore the closing of Baptist missions and Mormon temples in that country. The letter pointed out that other U.S. protests concerning acts of discrimination against religious groups in foreign lands resulted in the United States making representations to the governments involved in 1833, 1870, 1876, 1893, and 1903 [41]

The Jesuit editor also overlooked the fact that Roosevelt was an ardent Scottish Rite Mason of the Southern Jurisdiction and, in 1933, in the regalia of the Georgia Grand Lodge of Masons, raised his son, Elliot, to the degree of Master Mason at Architect Lodge 519 in New York City. [42]

The senior Roosevelt's Southern Masonic affiliation came about in connection with his visits to Warm Springs, Georgia where he regularly went for treatment of his polio condition.

The President also was a member of the Northern Jurisdiction's Lodge No. 8 in New York City, a Knight Templar a 32nd Degree Mason, and a member of the Mystic Shrine. [43]

There was more commentary in *America* on Freemasonry in 1956. An article in the Catholic weekly stated that Fr. Bertheloot "never entertained any illusions" and did not seek acceptance by the Church of Masonic positions which were "doctrinally or psychologically out of the question." Nevertheless, the article said, it was hard to believe that Bertheloot's efforts have had no impact at all upon the course of this historic conflict." [44]

Jesuit involvement in the Church's apparent rapprochement with Masonry took an interesting turn when the Scottish Rite's Grand Commander, Luther Smith, revealed that during a visit to Rome, Italy, in 1957, he found a Masonic group sponsored by Jesuits was attempting to organize there. [45]

The following year, the national Jesuit weekly ran an article in which a priest scolded the Church for lack of tolerance which prevented him from advancing into the higher degrees of Freemasonry.

Father Walter M. Abbott, S.J., wrote that he was the grandson of a 32nd Degree Mason, and was entitled as a youth to belong to several organizations allied with Masonry.

He said that as far as the Craft was concerned it "would not have prevented me from entering the Masonic order itself when I reached 21," even though he and his father had become converts to Catholicism. [46]

However, the priest noted, his entrance into the Jesuit order prevented him from becoming a 32nd Degree Mason, although he could advance as far as the 17th Degree.

Fr. Abbott said all Christians should be against Masonry because "Masonic oaths are violations of the Second Commandment of God." At the same time, he insisted that the secrets sworn to by Masons concern "only trivial things" in the early Masonic degrees. [47]

He expressed the view that the Papacy in its numerous condemnations of the Fraternity referred primarily to Grand Orient Freemasonry, although he provided no citations from the Papal documents which supported that allegation. [48]

The article further substantiated why the Church has exhibited a lack of tolerance toward the Craft. Father Abbott said Masonry, "in its basic degrees, is at least indifferent to Christianity, and probably inimical to it." Moreover, he observed that in the 30th Degree ritual a papal tiara is pierced by a sword and trampled upon—and not only the tiara, but a royal crown as well. [49]

In 1961, Father Michael Riquet, S.J., appeared before a group of 500 Masons to argue that the Fraternity and Catholics are "separated brothers." [50]

Efforts by the Jesuits to bring Masonry into the Catholic Church were abetted by Father John A. O'Brien of the University of Notre Dame. He began meeting with Masonic leaders after he had read that the Grand Commander of the Northern Masonic Jurisdiction had "banned all political material" in Scottish Rite publications under his jurisdiction as a reaction to the mass of anti-Catholic mail which was flooding Boston during the Presidential campaign of John F. Kennedy.

The Northern Masonic chieftain reportedly declared that if a Catholic was willing to die for his country, his faith "should be no barrier" to serving as commander-in-chief of the military as President of the United States.

After reading that comment, Fr. O'Brien sent the Masonic leader a note of "gratitude and commendation." As a result, a friendship developed between the two men which "was destined to have far-reaching consequences." [51]

On January 18, 1961, Albert N. Hepler, Jr., 33rd Degree, of South Bend, Indiana, telephoned the Notre Dame priest to say the Grand Commander of the Northern Jurisdiction and other members of the Supreme Council of Masonry wished to meet the cleric at a motel on the Notre Dame campus where the Masonic group happened to be staying.

The priest said that visit led to several similar gatherings, and soon leaders of the Knights of Columbus began meeting with the Masons. [52]

In 1965, Bishop Leo A. Pursley of Fort Wayne-South Bend addressed a group of Masons at the Scottish Rite Temple in South Bend, Indiana. During his remarks, the prelate said: . . . with honest effort to achieve mutual understanding, with a growing sense of the bonds that unite us . . . we can all bear witness to the truth in which we believe. . . ."

Bishop Pursley was introduced by Father O'Brien's Masonic friend, Albert Hepler, who said the meeting was "an attempt to display our appreciation for what they [the Fathers of Vatican Council II] have done . . . to help set the wheels of action rolling . . . that someday we may truly go together as the sons of God." [53]

O'Brien himself began speaking at Masonic gatherings, as did Bishop Robert Joyce of Burlington, Vermont, Richard Cardinal Cushing of Boston, and John Cardinal Cody of Chicago. [54]

Meanwhile, on December 6, 1964, Pope Paul VI, at Vatican II, agreed to make it easier for Roman Catholics who had become Freemasons to be reconciled with the Church. This was to be accomplished simply by a Catholic Mason going to Confession to any priest, explaining the reasons for the penitent's membership in the Craft, and asking for absolution. Previously, membership in the Masonic Fraternity had been considered a reserved sin which caused automatic excommunication, and could be absolved only by a bishop or the Pope himself. [55]

Father O'Brien pressed on. In September, 1966, he commented: "Surely the time has come for the Church in the U.S.A. to establish a commission for dialogue with the leaders of Masonry with a view toward removing any obstacles to Catholic membership therein."

He characterized as "unfortunate, unnatural and pathological" the fact that Catholics could not be active members of the nation's largest fraternal organization. It was his view that the Church soon would "re-examine the causes and circumstances of its ban against Catholics joining a Masonic lodge." Freemasonry in America, he insisted, is "far from being the enemy of religion, [but rather is] a mighty and powerful ally of religion." [56]

The Notre Dame priest, not surprisingly, was supported by the Jesuits at *America* magazine. A 1967 editorial in that publication, titled "Milestones in Ecumenism," argued that Church laws against Catholics joining the Craft "are the reaction of the Church to European Masonry, the history and objective of which have fully merited condemnation."

Continuing, the Jesuit journal asserted: "Since American Masonry has demonstrated its willingness and eagerness to collaborate with Catholic organizations on matters of mutual concern, a revision of Church law on the subject of membership in the Masons is very much in order. . . ." [57]

But that argument did not convince one knowledgeable reader of the Jesuit weekly. Responding to the *America* editorial, William J. Whalen wrote the editor:

> "By what stretch of the imagination would Catholic cooperation with, or membership in, an oath-bound secret society, such as Freemasonry, constitute a 'Milestone in Ecumenism' . . .? Does not ecumenism refer to the reunion of Christian churches and communions?
>
> "Are you aware that American Freemasonry is strictly segregated, and that even if Catholics were allowed to join, those Catholics who are Negroes would be refused initiation by the 16,000 regular lodges?" [58]

But Mr. Whalen's letter was in vain. Responding to an inquiry from John Cardinal Krol, Archbishop of Philadelphia and president of the National Conference of Catholic Bishops (NCCB), Franjo Cardinal Seper, Prefect of the Sacred Congregation for the Doctrine of the Faith, wrote from the Vatican on July 19, 1974 that "various situations of each country did not permit the Holy See to change [Canon Law]," and such legislation would remain in force until the new Canon Law was published.

Continuing, the letter from the Vatican said:

> "As for particular cases, it is appropriate to recall that penal law must always be interpreted restrictively. One can therefore teach with certainty and apply the opinion of the authors stating

that Canon 2335 [pertaining to Catholic membership in Freemasonry] concerns only Catholics who belong to *associations acting against the Church.* [Emphasis added].

"It is still, and in all cases, forbidden for clerics, religious and members of secular institutes to belong to a Masonic association." [59]

It was apparent that the Jesuits and Father O'Brien of Notre Dame had won their case. Catholics could join Masonic lodges in the United States because, either the specific argument of the editors of *America* magazine and the Notre Dame priest, or a similar one, had been accepted by the Sacred Congregation at the Vatican. That argument held that Freemasonry is different in the United States and other geographic locales than it is in other Masonic "associations acting against the Church" in Europe and elsewhere.

The rationale for permitting Catholics to join an oath-bound Fraternity whose philosophy has consistently been diametrically opposed to 2,000 years of Church belief and teaching is inexplicable, unless one believes that Freemasonry has penetrated the Vatican itself.

The Roman Catholic Church is the one institution in all the world that has understood and fought that international secret society for 250 years. To believe the Craft is different in the United States than elsewhere is to ignore totally two-and-one-half centuries of historic evidence, current Masonic documents, and the wording of rituals attendant to Masonic initiation ceremonies.

Certainly, Masons in the United States are required to take solemn oaths never to divulge the Craft's secrets. Those oaths before fellow lodge members are accompanied by grave promises to accept cruel and unusual punishment, including death itself, if a brother should divulge any secrets of the Order. Under such circumstances, how can any bishop, pastor or confessor truly be certain that Masonry in the United States differs from Masonry in Europe or elsewhere?

Moreover, as has been evidenced in the preceding pages, Scottish Rite Masonry's Grand Philosopher, as well as many other high-ranking members of the Fraternity, have stated that the Craft is the successor to the Ancient Mysteries, and the Universal Morality based upon Kabbalistic Gnosticism.

Further, the Fraternity considers itself "not merely . . . the handmaid of religion, but the original deposit of secret, sacerdotal science upon which all the world's great faiths have been erected." [60]

The Craft also has been defined as "a sacramental system, possessing like all sacraments, an outward and visible side [explained as its ceremonial doctrine and symbols], and an inward, intellectual and spiritual side, which is concealed. . . ." [61]

Not to be overlooked by those interested in preserving the integrity of the Church is the fact that the Fraternity meets in "temples" and "cathedrals," and the formal headquarters of the Scottish Rite of the Southern Jurisdiction is referred to by the ecclesiastical term, "See."

Also, Masons view the Bible as a symbol of the Book of Nature, or the code of human reason. [62] At lodge meetings the "square is superimposed upon the Bible, in order that Masons "may ever be guided by reason, and that even the Book of Religion shall be read only in the light of reason and exact knowledge." [63]

Yet, despite those readily available facts, a number of Catholic bishops in the United States suddenly rushed to apologize for the Church's centuries old view of, and implacable opposition to, Freemasonry.

On March 28, 1976, the late Terence Cardinal Cook, Archbishop of New York, appeared as the principal speaker at a gathering of 3,000 Masons attending their annual breakfast in that city. The New York Ordinary characterized the meeting as a "joyful event" on the "road of friendship" between the Roman Catholic Church and Freemasonry.

He "lamented" past estrangements over a period of 238 years between "your ancestors" and "some clerics," and said whatever had happened in the past "should not stand between us and the future." [64]

In its report on the meeting, *The New York Times* said "many Roman Catholics are affiliated with the Masonic fraternity today." [65]

Later that year, the Vatican daily, *L'Osservatore Romano*, published an article by Dominican Father Georges Cottier, consultant to the Vatican's Secretariat for Non-Believers, in which the priest attacked dissident Archbishop Marcel Lefebvre of Econe, Switzerland, because the Swiss prelate and his followers "see in the motto of the French Revolution, 'Liberty, Equality, Fraternity,' the essence of all the evils of the modern world and the expression of its apostasy."

Such people, the Vatican consultant said, seem unaware that "Liberty, Equality and Fraternity" have become part of the Church's agenda, and had been endorsed in conciliar documents on religious liberty, ecumenism, and the Church [66] Unfortunately, Fr. Cottier never listed the various conciliar documents in which the Masonic motto, or its equivalent, might be found.

Manifestly, Catholics were affiliating with Masonry, and it is reasonable to assume that Masonry had penetrated the highest levels of the Church.

This was clearly evident when the Grand Master of Italian Masonry, Lino Salvini, stated in a 1978 telephone conversation with a reporter for the National Catholic News Service (NC News) that there are "very fine relations between the Church and the Masons." The Grand Master added: we have priests and even bishops" who are members of the Craft. [67]

In the United States, Bishop Louis Gelineau of Providence, Rhode Island, was presented with the Grand Master Award on March 5, 1981 by Rhode Island's Grand Lodge of Masonry for "best exemplifying the principles of Freemasonry."

The Providence prelate said he had permitted Catholics to join the Masons, although each request was decided on an individual basis. [68]

On March 13, 1984, Religious News Service (RNS) reported that the editor of *The Oklahoma Mason,* James Maynard, was at that time a Master Mason and a Roman Catholic.

The report also said Maynard had been initiated into the Order of DeMolay (the youth arm of Freemasonry) on February 17, 1974, after he "got the green light" from his pastor.

Subsequently, Maynard rose to become head of the Oklahoma State Chapter of DeMolay. His deputy was Bruce Gros, who was studying to be a Catholic priest in the Tulsa diocesan seminary. [69]

Obviously, pastors had been permitting Catholics to enter Masonry some years before Cardinal Seper's letter to Cardinal Krol on July 19, 1974, concerning the moral liceity of Catholic membership in the international secret Fraternity.

In that connection, it will be recalled that the Vatican Prefect informed Cardinal Krol that the existing Canon law then in force [which prohibited membership of Catholics in the Masonic Fraternity] would remain authoritative (in most instances) "until the new Canon Law is published."

The new Canon Law was published in Advent, 1983, and pointedly did not mention Freemasonry at all.

The old law (Canon 2335) read: "All those who enroll their names in the sect of Freemasons or similar associations which plot against the Church or the legitimate civil authorities incur by this very fact the penalty of excommunication, absolution from which is reserved simply to the Holy See."

The new Code (Canon 1374) reads: "A person who joins an association which plots against the Church is to be punished with a just penalty; one who promotes or takes office in such an association is to be punished with an interdict." [70]

Notably absent from the new Code is any mention of "Freemasons," plotting against "the legitimate civil authorities," or "excommunication."

Those sympathetic to Masonry apparently had done their job well. The new Canon clearly authorized the entry of Catholics into Masonry if pastors or bishops determined that a lodge did not plot against the Church, or, indeed, if an individual Catholic was convinced such was the case.

Moreover, the new law, by omitting any objection to plotting against "the legitimate civil authorities," as the prior law had stipulated, tacitly suggested that the Church did not object to Catholics engaging in revolutionary activities. Such activities are virtually integral to Liberation Theology, a new mind-set which has been devastating the Church in Central and Latin America.

However, simultaneous with the issuance of the new Code, the Sacred Congregation for the Doctrine of the Faith, now under the leadership of Joseph Cardinal Ratzinger, issued a Declaration which had the effect of modifying the new Canon law. The Declaration said Masonic membership is a serious sin that denies to Catholics "the right to approach Holy Communion."

The document also affirmed that the Church's "negative position on Masonic associations . . . remains unaltered," because the Craft's principles "have always been regarded as irreconcilable with the Church's doctrine." Catholic affiliation with the Masonic Fraternity, Cardinal Ratzinger said, "remains prohibited by the Church." [71]

Several weeks later, an unsigned editorial concerning Catholic membership in Freemasonry, appeared on the front page of *L'Osservatore Romano*. Vaticanologists viewed the editorial as having been written by Cardinal Ratzinger, particularly in view of its many references to SCDF, an abbreviation for the Sacred Congregation for the Doctrine of the Faith.

The editorial's condemnation of Masonry was expressed with a vigor reminiscent of that found in Leo XIII's *Humanum Genus*. Four times the document stated that Christianity and Freemasonry are fundamentally "irreconcilable." The second paragraph of the document said the Church long had held Masonry to be "responsible for subversive activity" against the Church.

Some Catholics, it was observed, believe Freemasonry does not impose any "principles" of a religious or philosophic nature, but rather bonds men of goodwill to "humanistic values comprehensible and acceptable to everyone." Commenting on that view held by some Catholics, the editorial cautioned that Masonry's obligations are "of an extremely binding nature," reinforced by a "rigid rule of secrecy." Such a climate of secrecy, the Vatican editorial said, "entails above all the risk of becoming an instrument of strategies unknown to them." [72]

Moreover, the *L'Osservatore* editorial pointed out, it is "not within the competence of local ecclesiastical authorities to give a judgment on the nature of Masonic associations which would imply a derogation from what has been decided above." [73]

Once again, Rome condemned membership in Masonic organizations, and the message prompted the U.S. hierarchy to issue a statement which broadly supported Cardinal Ratzinger's view.

On April 19, 1985, the Committee for Pastoral Research and Practices of the NCCB, under the chairmanship of Bernard Cardinal Law, Archbishop of Boston, issued a confidential report to all Catholic bishops. The report said Freemasonry is "irreconcilable" not only with Catholicism but with all Christianity. A background study accompanying the Committee's statement, sharply criticized the "pseudo-Islamic ritual" of the nation's 600,000 members of the Shrine, an adjunct of Masonry. [74]

Despite the Church's most recent pronouncements on Catholic-Masonic relations, a question remains as to how those statements have impacted upon Masonic influence in the Church, particularly in view of the conflict between Canon law and the Directive by the Sacred Congregation for the Doctrine of the Faith. The evidence suggests that Freemasonry has gained the upper hand, at least momentarily, in this protracted conflict between two ages-old, implacable enemies.

PART III

TARGET—THE STATE

10/ WARRING ON THE STATE

The idea that a relative handful of men have conspired for years to rule nations and the world according to their philosophy is difficult for many people to grasp.

Yet, most thoughtful people will concede that Hitler, Mussolini, Tojo and Stalin pursued that very idea and precipitated incalculable carnage.

Cecil Rhodes believed "the absorption of the greater portion of the world under our [English] rule simply means the end of all wars." To accomplish his goal of world domination under English rule, Rhodes drew up the first of six wills in which he stipulated that a secret society was to carry out his scheme. [1] Later, he conceived of world domination in federation with the United States, using "a secret society gradually absorbing the wealth of the world." This plan is the "meaning of his last will and the plan behind his scholarships." [2]

That secret organization envisioned by Rhodes became the Round Table Group of England, the "real founders of the Royal Institute of International Affairs . . . the Institute of Pacific Relations," and the "godfathers" of the Council on Foreign Relations (CFR). [3]

Communism has long been recognized as a separate secret conspiratorial movement to control the world. On the other hand, Christianity is a completely open, non-secret conspiracy to bring all men to salvation through Jesus Christ.

So what of Freemasonry?

One knowledgeable member of the Craft said: "The nature of Freemasonry and of its traditions is responsible for the difficulty the historian encounters in evaluating the influence which the Fraternity has exercised on the development of the Enlightenment . . . and all other progressive ideologies . . ." [4]

The "nature" and "traditions" of Masonry refer to the Fraternity's secrecy. The great advantage of secrecy, in addition to advancing Masonry's cause, is that it permits Masons and their supporters to use no other argument than ridicule to dismiss charges that the Masonic Order subverts Church and State—charges which have consistently been brought against the Fraternity by various Popes and heads of states.

Secrecy, said Albert Pike, "is indispensable to Masonry." [5]

In that connection, Masonry has 25 "landmarks," or canons which are "unrepealable," and can "never be changed." [6] Landmark no. 23 concerns "secrecy of the Institution." It admonishes initiates that to change or abrogate such a requirement of confidentiality "would be social suicide, and death of the Order would follow its legalized exposure." Continuing, the same Landmark notes that Freemasonry has lived unchanged for centuries as a secret association, but as an open society, "it would not last for many years." [7]

One wonders why the organization must be so secret. Why would openness bring "death of the Order"? Why would it "not last for many years" if its secret activities were unmasked? Certainly, that landmark suggests the Craft is something more than a fraternal and charitable organization. Why hide good works?

The answer is: Freemasonry in America and elsewhere is far more than a fraternal organization. It never hides its charitable endeavors. But its secret work, is something else entirely. And that secret work frequently has involved subversion of the existing political order in any given State.

In 1884, Pope Leo XIII declared that Freemasonry uses "every means of fraud or of audacity, to gain . . . entrance into every rank of the State as to seem to be almost its ruling power." [8]

Just over 100 years later, an unsigned article appeared in the authoritative Vatican newspaper, *L'Osservatore Romano,* regarding Masonry. The article was described by an official of the Congregation for the Doctrine of the Faith as a Vatican "policy position." It said Masonry was much more than an association of men of good will; that the Craft involves moral obligations for its members, a rigid discipline of mystery and a climate of secrecy that brings to members the risk of becoming the instruments of strategies unknown to them. [9]

The hold of the Craft on initiates is almost total. One member of the Fraternity said Masonry is one of the few organizations that is "able to change the relationships created by nature," such as family relationships.

To "produce the desired result," Masons must take vows and make "a complete surrender" to the Masonic institution. ". . . there can be no reservations" to the new league. [10]

Freemasonry, another Craftsman observed, "is—and must be—a political force . . . the whole spirit of the Order, and especially of the Scottish Rite, is a propulsion to political action." [11]

One Grand Commander commenting favorably on Masonic support for revolutions in different parts of the world noted:

> "They were charged in the Lodges with teachings that enabled them to become individual champions of democratic progress and of religious and civil liberty." [12]

Masonry's mark is embedded in the Great Seal of the United States [13], and the official seal of the Supreme Court of California was marked with numerous Masonic symbols during the period 1850-1873. [14]

The Fraternity's activities in the American Revolution, Mexico, and the States of New York, Massachusetts and Pennsylvania, as well as Albert Pike's work in the Civil War were noted in Chapters one and two.

Masonry In The Civil War

The Craft's relationship to any nation was clearly explained at the time of the Civil War in an 1861 letter from the Grand Lodge of York Masons in Pennsylvania to their counterparts in Tennessee. The letter said:

> "Masonry is as old as government. It constitutes a government in itself . . .
> "Masonry is a sovereignty and a law unto itself . . . It knows nothing but the principles and teachings of its faith.
> "The proud position [of Masonry is to] stand aloof from the rise and fall of empires, the disturbances in States, the wars of contending nations, and rebellions and revolutions in commonwealths or among people . . .
> "The claims of a brother are not dissolved by war . . . the tie once formed, is only sundered by death. [15]

The same letter said: "By the ancient Constitutions of Masonry, a brother, even when engaged in rebellion against his country, is still to

be considered as a Mason; his character as such being indefeasible."
[16]

During the War of Secession, as the War Between the States is
sometimes called, the Union Government was seriously concerned
about several secret subversive groups which operated in the North
and South during the Civil War. Although military records did not
formally identify any of those organizations with Freemasonry, the
groups shared characteristics common to the Masonic Fraternity. Like
Masonry, those secret units—

- Operated under a "Supreme Council" with a chief execu-
tive at State level known as the "Grand Commander." [17]
- Maintained a rigid secrecy about their activities. [18]
- Held formal meetings in "lodges" and "temples. [19]
- Restricted membership of the "vulgar herd" to the basic
"mysteries" of the group [20]
- Bound members by oaths which demanded blind obedience
to superiors. [21]
- Threatened awesome bodily mutilations and death if oaths
of secrecy were violated. [22]
- Utilized passwords, hand grips, and signs of distress to
protect the secret societies and their members. [23]

The Deputy Grand Commander of one of the secret societies,
Charles E. Dunn, of the Order of American Knights (OAK), insisted
that President Lincoln had "usurped" powers and thereby forfeited all
claim to support from members of the Order. Moreover, said Dunn,
action taken to force Lincoln's "expulsion" from power "is an inherent right" which belongs to the Order, and is "not revolution." [24]

Dunn's statement is quite similar to the following words found in
Albert Pike's *Morals and Dogma:* "[R]esistance to power usurped is
not merely a duty which man owes to himself and his neighbor, but a
duty which he owes to his God." [25]

Secret agent William Taylor of the Union's Provost Marshal's office
reported on an OAK Lodge meeting he attended, presided over by Dr.
John Shore, a St. Louis physician. During the meeting, attended by
149 Lodge members, it was announced that General Albert Pike had
"promised arms and equipment" for a military company then being
formed by the Lodge. [26]

Subsequently, in a sworn statement, Dr. Shore denied membership
in OAK or any other secret political organizations. However, Shore
did admit membership in Masonry, and said his obligations to Ma-

sonry are "most assuredly" sacred and "of paramount consideration."

In response to the Provost Marshal's question whether, "under oath" he was permitted to reveal the secrets of Masonry before a court of justice, Dr. Shore replied: "I am not." [27]

A Fourth Degree member of OAK, Green B. Smith, in a sworn statement, said an oath of the Order was "paramount to every other oath."

Smith further indicated that the OAK might well have had Masonic roots when he noted that the Order "extends back to the Revolution of 1776, having had a previous existence up to the Rebellion." [28]

OAK was organized in 1863 by Clement L. Valandigham, a Democratic Congressman from Ohio. The Order was known also as the Order of the Sons of Liberty and the Knights of the Order of the Sons of Liberty. [29]

Valandigham died June 17, 1871. His funeral was "under the direction of the Masons," and "many members of the Masonic fraternity" escorted his remains to his late residence. [30]

According to the Judge Advocate General of the Union Army, the OAK Order engaged in the following activities:

- Aided soldiers to desert and protected deserters.
- Worked to undermine portions of the Army
- Furnished lawyers to find "some quasi-legal pretext" to help soldiers leave the Army.
- Imbucd military camps with a spirit of discontent and disaffection, and "whole companies were broken up."
- Members of the Order who were drafted into the Army "were instructed . . . to use their arms against their fellow soldiers, rather than the enemy, or, if possible, to desert to the enemy."
- Assassinations and murders were carried out which were "discussed at the councils of the Order." [31]

President Andrew Johnson And Masonry

After Albert Pike had been tried and found guilty of treason for his activities during the Civil War, Benjamin B. French, a 33rd Degree Mason and member of the board of directors of the Supreme Council of the Scottish Rite, wrote a letter, dated July 1, 1865, to President Andrew Johnson (also a Mason) urging him to pardon Pike. Additional appeals on Pike's behalf were made to the President by Masons from different parts of the United States. [32]

On April 20, 1866, the Scottish Rite Supreme Council met in

Washington, at which time the Masons' Sovereign Grand Inspector General, T.P. Shaffner of Kentucky wrote to the Attorney General of the United States to request that Pike be pardoned. Two days later, the President's military aide wrote to the Attorney General, and "by order of the President," directed him "to send to this office [the White House] warrant for pardon of Albert Pike of Arkansas." [33]

The following day, April 23, 1866, officials of the Supreme Council, including Pike, "visited the President at the White House," and the President handed pike "a paper constituting a complete pardon for his part in the Civil War." [34]

Nine months later, a list of "pardoned rebels," including Pike, was released to the press. The list showed the names of the pardoned individuals and the person or persons, if any, who had spoken on behalf of the pardonedee. The entry for Pike read:

"Albert Pike, rebel Brigadier-General; by Hon. B.B. French, Col. T.P. Shaffner, and a large number of others." [35]

In March, 1867, the House Judiciary Committee began an investigation into charges by some Congressmen that Johnson should be impeached. Later, when the committee finally issued its report, a key charge against the President was that "he pardoned large numbers of public and notorious traitors . . ." [36]

Shortly after the impeachment investigation began, Pike and General Gordon Granger met with President Johnson at the White House for approximately three hours. Subsequent to that meeting, General Granger was summoned before the Judiciary Committee where he was asked to disclose the substance of the conversation with the President. The General told the committee:

"They [President Johnson and Pike] talked a great deal about Masonry. More about that than anything else. And from what they talked about between them, I gathered that he [Pike] was the superior of the President in Masonry. I understood from the conversation that the President was his subordinate in Masonry. That was all there was to it . . ." [37]

On June 20, 1867, the President received a delegation of Scottish Rite officials in his bedroom at the White House where he received the 4th through the 32nd Degrees of the Scottish Rite "as an honorarium." [38]

Later that month, the President journeyed to Boston to dedicate a Masonic temple. Accompanying him was General Granger and a delegation of the Knights Templar.

Addressing a crowd of well-wishers at a Boston hotel, President Johnson said he came to the city "for two reasons, one of which was to visit the State of Massachusetts. There is another [reason] it is true, to which I shall not allude on this occasion." [39]

On June 25, *The New York Times* page one lead story was headlined: "Masonic Celebration," and provided many details of the history and growth of Masonry in Massachusetts. Strangely, however, no mention was made of the investigation of the Fraternity by the Massachusetts Legislature in 1834 which reported Freemasonry was "a distinct Independent Government within our own Government, and beyond the control of the laws of the land by means of its secrecy, and the oaths and regulations which its subjects are bound to obey, under penalty of death." [See *supra*, p. 35]

Actually, the *Times* was so obviously overwhelmed by the Masonic event that four of the seven columns on page one of the June 25th issue of that newspaper were devoted to extolling Masonry.

The New York daily said the 16,000 marching Masons, resplendent in their regalia, were so impressive that "a finer looking body of men has never before been seen in this city or elsewhere." [40]

At the Masonic temple, the President was accompanied by General Granger, Benjamin B. French and T.P. Shaffner.

During his address to the gathering, the President disclosed the other reason he came to the State of Massachusetts. He said:

> "I should not have visited Massachusetts, at least on the present occasion, had it not been for the order of Masonry. I came in good faith for the express purpose of participating and witnessing the dedication of this temple today to Masonry, and as far as I could, let it be much or little, to give my countenance and my sanction." [41]

Clearly, Scottish Rite Freemasonry had a friend in President Andrew Johnson.

Masonry And The Philippine Insurrection

Conventional wisdom says the Philippine Insurrection of 1896 was ignited because of native opposition to the power of the Catholic

Church in the Islands. The revolutionary fire was fueled by the writings of Jose Rizal, augmented by the political leadership of Emilio Aguinaldo. [42]

Subsequently, during the Spanish-American War, Commodore George Dewey furnished arms to Aguinaldo and urged him to rally the Philippine people against the Spanish. However, when the United States succeeded Spain as the ruling colonial power, Aguinaldo led a new revolt that became largely a guerrilla action, and "cost far more money and took far more lives than the Spanish-American War." [43]

That is the conventional thumb-nail account of events in the Philippines at the turn of the Century, but it is quite superficial and misleading. In reality the Philippine Insurrection was orchestrated by Freemasonry, and while Emilio Aguinaldo indeed led that revolution, he did so as a dedicated member and tool of the Craft.

That insight into Philippine history was suppressed by the United States Government for 45 years, until it finally was revealed by historian John T. Farrell in 1954. [44]

The United States Government concealed the real history of the Insurrection, according to a National Archives pamphlet, because of a "reluctance to publish facts that might prove injurious to ex-revolutionists, Federal officials, and military personnel." Also some people felt the War Department report "expressed a personal viewpoint and was not an objective study of Philippine affairs." [45]

Captain John R.M. Taylor, author of the War Department's suppressed report, noted that lodges of the Masonic Grand Orient of Spain were established in the Philippine Islands around 1890, and proselytes from those lodges formed the Katipunan, a Tagalong Masonic revolutionary organization. [46]

The Katipunan was the outgrowth of a series of nine associations formed by a revolutionary clique to seek independence for the Philippines. To accomplish that purpose, the clique mounted a systematic attack on the monastic orders in the Islands to undermine their prestige, "and to destroy their influence upon the great mass of the population." [47]

A 1898 "Memorial" from the Dominican Fathers to the Spanish Government said:

> "In consequence of the teaching of the Freemasons, the voice of the parish priest has no longer any effect on numbers of the natives, especially at Manila and in the neighboring provinces . . .

"The Freemasons . . . have recommended the war against us." [48]

And the Spanish commander of Manila's Civil Guard, Olegario Diaz, wrote on October 28, 1896:

"It is fully proven that Masonry has been the principal cause of the trouble in these islands, not only from the advanced and irreligious ideas scattered about, but more by the foundation of secret societies of a distinctly separatist character." [49]

Commander Diaz also said the Grand Master of the Spanish Grand Orient sent Masons to establish native Masonic lodges of exclusive Tagalong character. Within five years, 180 Tagalong lodges had been established in the Philippines. [50]

The Masons planned and carried out a "brutal and shameless campaign" against monastic Orders and constantly ridiculed religion. Later, this campaign acquired a political character, which included attacks on the central government and the authorities in the Archipelago. [51]

Jose Rizal established a secret society called the Philippine League to which only Masons were admitted to membership. Its purpose was to educate the people in liberal ideas and ultimately armed rebellion.

The League was governed by a Supreme Council. The founders of the organization "took a solemn oath on a human skull, which they afterward kissed, and signed a document of agreement with their own blood, making the necessary incision in one of their arms." Further, every initiate "was bound to carry on the propaganda by every means in his power . . . and under severe penalties to guard the secret oath, to report everything they knew to the League, and to obey their superiors blindly." [52]

Organizers of the Katapunan and members of its first Supreme Council also were members of Rizal's Philippine League. [53]

One section of the oath taken by members of the Katapunan asked:

"Do you swear before Our Lord Jesus that you will be able to assassinate your parents, brothers, wives, sons, relatives, friends, fellow townsmen or Katipunan brothers should they forsake or betray our cause?" [54]

Punishment for disobeying Katipunan directives—which included all Philippine people "whether they want to be or not"—was sobering. It consisted of being buried alive and then having the murdered person's possessions—including his family—taken by members of an organization called the "mandudicut." That punishment was decreed by Emilio Aguinaldo, the Katipunan Supreme Leader and dictator. [55]

Information about some of the operations of the Katipunan was furnished by a member of the organization, Teodoro Patino, a printer for *Diario de Manila,* a local daily. Patino gave the information to his sister, who was a student at the Catholic college at Lauban, operated by the Sisters of Charity. The girl told the Mother Superior, who later interviewed the printer. The Mother Superior told Patino to pass the information to Father Mariano Gil, his pastor, which he did.

As a result, documents were seized at the *Diario,* a number of members of the Katipunan were arrested, and numerous letters and other material were found which corroborated Patino's statement.

Further corroboration was provided by a report of Isabelo de Los Royes, who gathered most of his information in prison from a Katipunan member. [56]

The U.S. War Department document includes a report by the Civil Governor of Manila, Manuel Luengo to the Spanish Colonial Minister. The report, dated October 1, 1896, includes "An Extraordinary Document of Philippine Masonry, Giving Instructions To Be Carried Out At The Outbreak Of The Rebellion." The "Instructions" say, in part:

> "Fourth. While the attack is being made on the Captain-General and other Spanish authorities, the men who are loyal will attack the convents and behead their infamous inhabitants. As for the riches contained in said convents, they will be taken over by this G.R. Log. [i.e., Grand Regional Lodge] . . .
>
> * * *
>
> "Seventh. The bodies of the friars will not be buried, but will be burned in just payment for the crimes which during their lives they committed against the noble Filippinos for three centuries of hateful domination."

Names listed at the end of the "Instructions" are shown as "President of the Executive Committee, Boliva. The Vice Grand Master, Gordiano Bruno. The Grand Secretary Galileo." [57]

Captain Taylor said other documents show the names actually are pseudonyms for President Andres Bonifacio; Vice Grand Master, Pio Valenzuela; and Grand Secretary, Emilio Jacinto.

Bonifacio seized the leadership of the Katipunan in January, 1896, and turned the Masonic Supreme Council of that organization into the insurgent government of the Philippines, with himself as dictator. [58] Emilio Aguinaldo succeeded him.

The American Connection With Philippine Masonry

Insurgent Record No. 8 lists letters found in the papers of E.A. [Emilio Aguinaldo] which show that a Masonic Lodge called "Patria" was used to cover insurgent intrigues in October, 1899.

Insurgent Record No. 9 is a copy of an undated letter from Juan Utor y Fernandez, a 33rd Degree Mason, to U.S. Army Chaplain Charles Pierce, relative to the establishment of a newspaper to be named "Patria." The letter to Chaplain Pierce says the "brothers [i.e. Freemasons] who put their confidence in me . . . [believe that] by your and my cooperating with our brother American Masons, and especially with the good will and wishes of Senor Otis, may cause the happy day [of peace] to arrive . . ."

Continuing, Fernandez said he expected the cooperation of "the most worthy General Otis, and our brothers . . ." [59]

Another letter by Fernandez, now shown as editor of *La Patria Democratic Daily,* to Don Ambrosio Flores, dated October 8, 1899, introduces the bearer of the letter, one Senor Giselda, who has with him a copy of *La Patria.* The letter urges Flores to read and provide Ferandez with an opinion of the publication. Fernandez's letter added:

> "I am in relation with some American brothers of impor-
> tance, and if we can give, secretly, a Masonic character to the
> peace we perhaps shall succeed in guaranteeing it from attack in
> the future since you know, dear brother, that England and the
> United States are the two countries in which the Masonic institu-
> tion has most respect and weight." [60]

According to a letter received by Aguinaldo from *La Patria,* the newspaper was established, apparently with the approval of the American General, Otis, "to inaugurate a frank campaign against the annexationist sentiment" being advanced by two other Masonic dailies.

The writer, Aurelio Tolentino, said he had formed an association with seven people, "and indeed we told General Otis of it through Mr. Pierce, a Protestant clergyman in the confidence of said General . . . The General approved our political plan and, as a result, we published our first number on the 16th of September last." [61]

The letter continued by noting that Tolentino and some colleagues had founded "Patria" Masonic Lodge "to which no one in favor of autonomy belongs in spite of some having applied for admission." The object of his group, he said, is to work for his government and to "better consolidate the laws of Liberty, Equality and Fraternity." [62]

The references to "Senor Otis" and "General Otis," suggest that the man belonged to the Masonic Fraternity. Although the General is not further identified in the War Department report, General Elwell S. Otis, was at the time U.S. Army Commander in the Philippines, and Director of Civil Government. [63] Also, Harrison Gray Otis, owner and publisher of *The Los Angeles Times,* served as a Brigadier General in the Philippines during the Spanish American War. [64]

Of the two, it would seem that Major General Elwell S. Otis, as head of Civil Government, would have been the General most closely involved in authorizing the establishment of a newspaper in the Islands.

As for Aguinaldo, he and other Masons organized the Triagle Magdole which later became the Magdolo Lodge. The proclamation of the first Philippine Republic took place on the porch of Aguinaldo's home, an edifice which also served as the Magdolo Lodge. [65]

In January, 1955, Aguinaldo said: "It cannot be denied that the Filipino Revolution against Spain was the work and glory of Freemasonry in the Philippines." [66]

Masons also were "instrumental in working for the grant of Philippine independence by the United States." [67]

Additional evidence of Masonic influence in the Philippines surfaced following World War II.

First, shortly after the War's close, Federal Reserve regulations prohibited organizations and individuals from sending abroad more than $500. However, in response to pressure exerted by General Douglas MacArthur (a prominent Freemason), the Federal Reserve Bank of Richmond, Virginia, authorized Grand Commander John Cowles of the Scottish Rite's Southern Jurisdiction to send $5000 to the Philippines to rebuild and restore Masonic property. Shortly thereafter, the Federal Reserve authorized another $15,000 to be sent by Masons to the Islands, followed by another $100,000 sent by the

Brethern in California. [68]

Secondly, the Craft was successful in amending legislation designed to rehabilitate property of churches and other religious organizations lost or damaged due to the War, so that it covered Masonic property. The Masonic amendment added the words "any corporation or *sociedad anonima*" [i.e. secret society] organized pursuant to the laws in effect in the Philippine Islands at the time of its organization.

As a result of that legislation (Public Law 79-370), eighty percent of the cost of repairs for Scottish Rite Temples in the Philippines was underwritten by U.S. taxpayers. [69]

Interestingly enough, in May, 1955, a claim for recovery of World War II loss and damage to Catholic property in the Philippines was disallowed. [70]

Finally, it should be noted that one Philippine statesman made known his serious reservations about demands the Fraternity imposes upon its initiates.

Brother Manuel Quezon, former President of the Philippine Commonwealth, although selected for advancement to the 33rd Degree, declined the dubious honor, because "he feared some way, sometime, that there might be some obligation in accepting the honor which would be in conflict with his allegiance to the Philippines." [71]

Masonry And World War I

Some sources attribute World War I to Masonic intrigue. However, according to a *New Age* editorial, the War was precipitated by a "secret treaty" between the Vatican and Serbia, which would have annexed Serbia to the Vatican State and imposed canon law on that non-Catholic country. When the treaty became known, the editorial continued, Archduke Franz Ferdinand, "Roman Catholic heir to the Austro-Hungarian throne [and] known to be a secret party to the policy embodied in the treaty," was assassinated by Gavrilo Princep. [72]

Not mentioned by the Scottish Rite journal was the fact that the alleged assassins of the Archduke were members of the "Black Hand," a South Slav revolutionary organization which was a progeny of Freemasonry. [73]

During the trial, Princep testified that his colleague, Ciganovitch, "told me he was a Freemason;" and, on another occasion, "told me that the Heir Apparent [Franz Ferdinand] had been condemned to death by a Freemason's lodge." [74]

Moreover, another of the accused assassins, Chabrinovitch, testified that Major Tankositch, one of the plotters, was a Freemason. [75]

Communism And Freemasonry

The legacy of World War I was the Russian Revolution and the scourge of International Communism, both of which had Masonic influence.

James H. Billington, in his penetrating treatise on the history of modern revolution, documents the intimate ties between Freemasonry, Illuminism and modern revolutions. Of Freemasonry. He says:

> "So great, indeed, was the general impact of Freemasonry in the revolutionary era that some understanding of the Masonic milieu seems an essential starting point for any serious inquiry into the occult roots of the revolutionary tradition." [76]

Billington notes that the "masonic lodges of Geneva provided the ambiance" in which the early 19th Century revolutionary, Filippo Giuseppe Buonarotti—the "first apostle of modern communism"— formulated "his first full blueprint for a new society of revolutionary republicans: the Sublime and Perfect Masters." Both the society's name and the three levels of membership proposed for it "had been adopted from Masonry." [77]

The *New Age* observed that after 1825, many Russian Masons exiled themselves to France where lodges operating in the Russian language were sponsored by the Grand Orient. Some of the exiles later returned to Russia, and organized lodges in St. Petersburg and Moscow. Later, additional lodges were organized in the early 20th Century and had "an avowedly political aim and view; namely, that of the overthrow of the autocracy." [78]

The Scottish Rite monthly added: "The first Revolution in March, 1917 is said to have been inspired and operated from these lodges and all the members of Kerenski's government belonged to them." [79]

The Craft And Spanish Communism

The Craft's empathy with Communism was evident in Spain. In 1927 fraternal relations were "resumed between the U.S.S.R. and the Spanish Scottish Rite. [80]

Four years later, King Alfonso XII was forced into exile, and Masons, Communists, Socialists and Anarchists came into power. The

Catholic Church was disestablished, and education was secularized. In June, 1931, the "Bulletin" of the Supreme Council of the Scottish Rite in Spain boasted:

"The new Republic . . . was the perfect image molded by the gentle hands of our doctrines and principles. There will not be effected another phenomenon of a political revolution more perfectly Masonic than the Spanish one." [81]

By 1933 a conservative reaction had set in, but the Marxist-Masonic group returned to power and governed from 1935 to 1939 when they were toppled, precipitating the Spanish Civil War.

With the ouster of the Marxists-Masons, the *New Age* pleaded repeatedly for Americans to support the Spanish Loyalists. People were urged to write their Congressmen to repeal legislation passed in 1937 which embargoed shipments of munitions and war materials to the Marxist government of Spain. [82]

In February, 1939, the *New Age* called attention to a meeting of two groups in Washington, D.C. which took opposite positions on aiding the Masonic-supported Marxists in Spain.

One group was the National Conference to Lift the Embargo Against Republican Spain. The other, called Keep the Embargo Committee, was supported by Monsignor [later Archbishop] Fulton J. Sheen, notable Catholic orator, author, and authority on Communism.

In his address at Constitution Hall before Keep the Embargo Committee supporters, Msgr. Sheen identified the Loyalists as "Red Spain," and urged "all those who believe in freedom, democracy and religion to join in a protest against the 'Reds' supporting the Loyalist cause in this country." [83]

The pro-Loyalists met at the Masonic Almas Shrine Temple. Included among the speakers at that rally were Lieutenant Colonel John Gates, representing Friends of the Abraham Lincoln Brigade, and Herbert Biberman, motion picture director. [84]

[Interestingly, several years later, the *New Age* published a list of organizations considered by the Attorney General of the United States as "subversive" to the national security interests of America. Included in the list was the Abraham Lincoln Brigade, which was cited as a Communist Party front organization]. [85]

The Scottish Rite monthly journal also noted that Spain's Nationalist Army of 1936-1939 "marched to war singing the battle song of Rafael del Riego, an unsuccessful revolutionary (and a Mason)." [86]

The Masonic publication also said five cabinet members of the Loyalist government were Masons, as were five leading generals. However, a British history of the Spanish Civil War suggested that all the General officers of the Loyalist Army were Masons. [87]

Communist China And Masonry

In 1925, the New Age reported that a Chinese secret society [tong] "pretended" to be Masonic in 1903-1904, in order to secure protection of American Masons, which was forthcoming. However, the real object of the *tong* was to overthrow the Manchu dynasty. [88]

That report was clarified some years later when it was explained that the Hoon Bong, or Red Society of China, was founded by Hoong Hsieu Chuan, some of whose "educators were Masons." And "[a]ided by such friends, Hoong formed a secret society to oppose the then ruling Manchu Dynasty . . .

"The Hoong Bong contributed materially to the overthrow of the Manchu Dynasty . . ." [89]

Prior to World War II, Masons praised militant Chinese Communist leader, Chou En Lai, who was extolled as the person largely responsible for negotiating the Sian Agreement of 1936 which terminated the Chinese civil war.

A Masonic writer said the Agreement "indicates that the Red Army of China represented an agrarian movement based on a patriotically inspired program . . . If from this war emerges a real democracy for China, there will be no occasion for the old Red Army to again come to life as such. It can be merged into a government that believes in fair representation of all classes, and is in that process now." [90]

More direct American identification with Chinese Masonry occurred in 1943 when John Stewart Service instituted the Fortitude Lodge at Chunking. [91]

Mr. Service was a diplomatic adviser to General Joseph Stilwell and General Albert Wedemeyer in China during World War II. Commenting on that situation, journalist M. Stanton Evans has written:

"In that position he [Service] maintained a running fire of criticism against America's only ally Chiang Kai-shek, contrasting his 'Kuomintang' regime unfavorably with that of the Chinese Communists." [92]

On June 7, 1945, the Federal Bureau of Investigation (FBI) arrested Service and five others for alleged violation of the Espionage Act. However, he was not indicted; although in 1951, the U.S. Civil Service Commission's Loyalty Review Board found "there is reasonable doubt as to his loyalty," and he should be "forthwith removed from the rolls of the Department of State." [93] Nevertheless Service remained with the Department until his resignation in August, 1962.

Masonry, Communism And The Catholic Church

In 1948, Grand Commander John Cowles said religion "is freer in Russia today than it is in Roman Catholic Spain." [94]

By 1950, the Scottish Rite feared the Catholic Church would "capture the United States" and turn it against Russia. This grandiose plan supposedly was to be accomplished by using the U.S. government and its resources "to annihilate Russia and Russian opposition to the Pope." [95]

During the years immediately following World War II, the Scottish Rite Masons repeatedly insisted that the Catholic Church is far more dangerous than Soviet Communism.

Catholicism, not Communism nor Socialism is Masonry's immediate worry, the *New Age* said. [96]

"How much longer are the free peoples of the Western World going to submit to resistance being confined to Russia, while they lift neither voice nor fist to strike the even more insidious force of the Vatican Church-State?", a *New Age* editorial asked. [97]

Minimization of the threat of Communism and magnification of an alleged threat posed by the Catholic Church was a consistent theme of the *New Age* during the mid-1950s. [98]

Freemasonry, Nazism And Fascism

The unremitting antagonism of the Scottish Rite toward the Roman Catholic Church is well documented. Therefore, it is surprising to find the official publication of that Rite testifying to the Church's early opposition to Hitler, at a time when the Craft itself was currying favor with the Nazis.

In 1931, the *New Age* reported: "the Hitlerites are facing stiff opposition from a newly organized group headed by five leading bishops of the Roman Catholic hierarchy in Germany." [99]

Continuing, the article said:

"The anti-Fascist stand on the part of the Catholic Church was first asserted by the Bishops of Bavaria and Silesia, who in official statements virtually excluded members of the Nationalist Socialist Party from the church. At the present time, [other Catholic bishops] have succeeded in virtually lining up the entire Catholic population of the republic against the Hitlerites.

"In a statement, the Bishops charge the Fascisti with preaching hatred and racial religion . . ."

Some pages later, an editorial criticized the bishops for "engaging in politics". [100]

Eight years later, the *New Age* found that when the Nazi revolution came to Germany, Albert Einstein looked first to the universities, then to editors of newspapers, and to individual journalists to speak out against Hitler's engulfing tyranny. But his efforts were in vain, because those elements in German society were silenced. Einstein added:

"Only the Church stood squarely across the path of Hitler's campaign for the suppression of truth . . . [T]he Church alone has had the courage and persistence to stand for intellectual truth and moral freedom." [101]

In its efforts to curry favor with Hitler, one Mason wrote in the *New Age*: "I do not belong to Hitler, as I do not know his opinion about Masons, but he seems to be an honest man and therefore his movement has become strong. It is not the intention of the Hitlerites to expel the Jews. We have Jewish families in Germany who came with the Romans and settled here peacefully for centuries . . . the Hitlerites are opposed to the lower class elements which have immigrated here from foreign countries, importing Bolshevistic ideas . . . [102]

In 1933, various German Masonic lodges changed their names, in an effort to avoid being closed down by Hitler. Also, many lodges broke relationship with foreign Masonic groups to demonstrate their German nationalism and to indicate they were merely fraternal organizations. [103]

Commenting on the situation, *The New York Times* noted that German Masonic lodges were adopting Christian names. One called itself the National Christian Order of Frederick the Great, which prompted the *Times* to editorialize: "Neither Frederick nor his close chums Voltaire and Catherine of Russia have hitherto figured as conspicuous Christians." [104]

German Masonry also was "pleading for the admission of its members to the Nazi Party." By-laws of the Fraternity were changed to stipulate: "This order professes a German Christianity which has much in common with the primitive sun worship. The order's symbols are the sun and the cross." [105]

Eligibility for membership in German Masonry became limited to those Christian who can prove pure Teutonic descent for three generations. [106]

But the Nazis were not the only subjects of Masonic sychophancy. The *New Age* discloses:

"Masons adhered to Fascism at the beginning and even contributed toward the march on Rome. Freemasonry, officially, was never hostile to Fascism until Il Duce, influenced by the Vatican, prepared a bill against secret societies, *forgetting to include in it the Society of Jesus,* which is the most secret society in the world." [Emphasis in original]. [107]

By 1934, Masonry's efforts to temporize with the Nazis proved unsuccessful. Acting on Hitler's orders, Hermann Goering dissolved all the lodges, including those which purported to be Christian. [108]

Although the *New Age* had been somewhat ambivalent about the war against the Axis Powers prior to 1939, it's militancy on the issue galvanized after the Duke of Kent, brother of the reigning king, George VI, was selected as the Grand Master of the Grand Lodge of England in 1939. That action by the English Masons continued an unbroken tradition of intimate association between Freemasonry and English royalty that goes back to 1737. [109]

By late summer, 1940, the *New Age* became a strong advocate of U.S. involvement in the war, at first urging direct aid to England, but later pressing for direct American entry into the war. [110]

An editorial called the Brotherhood to "rally to the support of England, not alone because that country is the last stronghold of Freemasonry in Europe . . ." The editorial said the "enemies" of the Craft "would have reason to respect the military power its influence could marshal in this country," if it chose to do so. [111]

Nevertheless, the American people were strongly opposed to sending their youth to fight on foreign soil. The strong division of opinion on the subject was evident by the one-vote margin with which the House approved legislation in September, 1940, calling for a military draft. And by the summer of 1941, the first draftees were chanting

"OHIO," meaning: "Over the Hill in October"—or a massive flight from military service once the troops had served one year of compulsory military duty.

As the public sentiment became increasingly divided on involvement in Europe, the *New Age* continued to press for U.S entry into the War. Finally, the issue was settled when the Japanese bombed Pearl Harbor on December 7, 1941.

Meanwhile in Europe, the Masonic Brotherhood continued to operate in "secret circles in the private security of locked homes to carry on their Masonic work," according to Brother Meyer Mendelsohn, a French refugee who emigrated to the United States. [112]

Brother Mendelsohn's statement was confirmed and elaborated upon in an unusually candid and lengthy letter written by a German Mason to the Commanding General, Headquarters, U.S. Forces European Theatre, in connection with a request that Freemasons be legally permitted to assemble.

Masonry's Political Orientation Confirmed

The writer of the letter, Wilfrid Schick, a resident of Munich, and "speaker for my comrades," urged the European Commander to reopen the *Symbolische Grossloge von Deutschland,* which he characterized as a philosophical lodge organized on an international basis to serve "the idea of the general world chain." [113]

Herr Schick told how Lodge members during the War used "appropriate manoeuvres" and "skillful tactics of the freemasons" to destroy or otherwise secure all Craft documents relating to membership and operation of the Grand Lodge. Those tactics, he said, destroyed the "outward organization" of the Grand Lodge, while allowing the Brotherhood to work in the "smallest circles" to carry on a "quiet, permanent struggle" against "the power of suppression." [114]

The Bavarian Mason asked that the U.S. military officials utilize the civilian radio network to help him in locating other German Masons. [115]

Confirming that Masonry avoids all conventional religious beliefs, Brother Schick also made it clear that Masonry's interest in "education" extends far beyond formal schooling at elementary through university levels. Such "education" also includes the inculcation of Masonic philosophy into political party doctrines.

In that regard, he said the basic beliefs of "true freemasonry," center on the "eternal, inborn rights of every individual . . . and the avoiding of all dogmatic and intolerant bindings . . ."

It was vital, he insisted, that Freemasonry be expanded in Germany in order "to maintain the exclusivity" which is "absolutely necessary to create . . . a highly qualified freemason leader class."

Every Freemason, he continued, must be granted the right to participate in politics "without limitation" in order to "win influence on the public life and on the governmental administration, with the assistance of political parties."

Important to that effort, he stated, is the necessity to make "a concentrated penetration of . . . party doctrines with freemason ideas."

The "real sphere" of the Lodge, he added, is "to fulfill an educational mission." [116]

The Bavarian Mason also confirmed that Masonry uses the same deceptive techniques which were first revealed in connection with Adam Weishaupt's Bavarian Illuminati.

Brother Schick said the Craft must propagate the ideas of world Freemasonry by using "a number of institutions for education." Such institutions, he continued, "will have to be created as the first elements to the real lodges." He proposed, as did Weishaupt, that the institutions be "in the form of societies for politics, economic politics, for art and sciences, etc." Those types of "institutions," he observed, would appeal to the best class of people, including youth. [117]

Schick confirmed that the Catholic Church is a particular obstruction to Masonry's success. He said, in the "occidental cultural sphere [i.e., Europe, North and South America] only the Catholic Church" stands as an opponent of Freemasonry by appealing to the "dogma-*bound*" people, while Masonry appeals to the "dogma-*less.*" [118]

The Bavarian Craftsman made it clear that Freemasonry's principles of "love of the mother-country and duties as a citizen" must never be wrongly understood. "Superordinated to all," he insisted, "is the duty . . . towards the all-uniting community of fellow-freemasons of the democratic world." [119]

Finally, Brother Schick insisted that any attack on the "natural rights of humanity" by "the schools of religion or political dogmatists" must never be tolerated, but rather strongly "opposed . . . with active fighting . . ." [120]

U.S. Military Opposes Masonry

Herr Schick had to wait two months for a reply from the military commandant. Finally, on December 10, 1945, he was notified that

Freemasonry could not be reactivated, because the Intelligence Division (G-2) found Freemasonry to be "a secret organization and . . . their meetings should be prohibited." [121]

The question of revival of the German Masonic Order was raised again by General Lucius Clay, Commander of the Office of Military Government, in a message to General Joseph McNarney, Commander of the European Forces. McNarney replied by secret cable: "Policy this headquarters is to prohibit application of German Masonic Order at this time. Previous application for permission to reestablish was unfavorably considered . . . Decision based on the grounds that the Masonic Order is a secret organization and also on the uncertain security situation." [122]

A memorandum by the legal division of the Office of Military Government (OMG), Germany, dated April 1, 1946, noted that members of the Hohenzollern family were Freemasons and that the Craft "flourished" under the Weimar Republic. Under the Nazis, the memorandum, said the lodges were viewed as "a centre of international conspiracy to destroy Germany," and were, accordingly, dissolved. [123]

That memorandum served as a background document for another memorandum written by General Clay to the War Department on June 27, 1946 relative to a German-American Club in the U.S. Zone known as the Cosmopolitan Club.

General Clay noted that the Club was dissolved because Prince Louis Ferdinand, a grandson of Kaizer Wilhelm, was a close friend of Captain Merle A. Potter, director of Military Government at Bad Kissingen, who also was the organizer and president of the Club.

Prior to his World War II service, Potter had been a movie critic for the *Minneapolis Journal* for 17 years. He described the Club as a Kiwanis-type organization, and said no discussion of politics was permitted during Club meetings. The organization reportedly was comprised of professional men and business executives.

However, Potter was reassigned following dissolution of the Cosmopolitan Club, "because of the poor judgment exercised by Captain Potter in having Louis Ferdinand as a member of the Club and his personal friend."

The memorandum added: "We fully recognize that the association of a Military Government Officer with a member of the Hohenzollern family will be misunderstood at home, in Germany, and by our allies." [124]

On July 3, 1946, Major General H.R. Bull, Chief of Staff, U.S. Forces European Theatre, informed Clay that he (Bull) and General McNarney were concerned about security problems associated with secret social organizations. At the same time, he said "penetrating" such groups by Counter-Intelligence Corps (CIC) agents "would be of doubtful practicable" value. Nevertheless, the Chief of Staff was concerned about the secret social clubs, because fraternizing under "the cloak of secrecy . . . might well be abused." Accordingly, General Bull said he and General McNarney recommended that any directive allowing meetings of social groups and secret societies be "deferred indefinitely." [125]

Masonry Wins Again

However, despite that recommendation, the Allied Military Government for Germany approved reactivation of the German Grand Lodge of Freemasonry on July 23, 1947. [126]

By October, 1947, Captain Potter had been promoted to Major, and became adviser to the Chief of Staff on American-German relations.

On October 8, Potter wrote a letter to the Military Government of Germany reporting on a conference which took place September 23-27, 1947, which was attended by twelve American-German Social Discussion Clubs. A summary of the minutes of that conference showed that those attending had discussed formation of a United States of Europe. The topic was characterized as "a subject of outstanding discussion." [127]

The conference mentioned by Major Potter appeared to be uncannily similar to Herr Schick's proposal for establishing "institutions for education" in Masonic philosophy, such as "societies for politics, economic politics, for art and sciences, etc."

In that regard, the idea of a United States of Europe, and the concept that Masonry "had no nationality" was advanced in the French lodges. [128]

As a matter of fact, early in the War years, Masonic spokesmen had viewed World War II as a turning point for the Fraternity, and spoke of the "world government" expected to be established at the conclusion of the War to help usher in a "newer phase of evolutionary progress." [129]

A Czech Mason said the struggle for the freedom of man began with the American and French Revolutions, and World War II "is the climax of a world ideological struggle which started at the end of the 18th Century. It is the struggle of the New Age against the Middle Age." [130]

Masonry In Japan

Meanwhile, on the other side of the world, Masonry had gotten off to a rather slow start.

In 1893, Japanese law empowered police to attend and superintend any organized group meeting, and to break up any such gatherings if the police determined there was any reason for doing so. Secret meetings were prohibited.

Because of that situation, Scottish Rite Masons in Japan contacted the Grand Commander in Washington, D.C. and urged him to explain the situation to the President of the United States and the Secretary of State. Apparently that was done, and Japanese law was not enforced against U.S. Scottish Rite Masons. [131]

However, in 1936, the Japanese Government became alarmed at what it called the "mysterious world organization" known as Freemasons, and "secretly investigated the Craft." [132]

The concern was not surprising. At that time, the Masonic "Club" of Kobe, Japan, had been in existence for 65 years as the Japanese branch of Freemasonry. It was viewed as "a secret society of Judea which has been picturing a phantasm of a mysterious world." Branches of the "Club" were located in Kobe, Yokahama, Tokyo, and in Korea. [133]

The Kobe Masonic Club came into existence in strict privacy. The Club was made up of several lodges, such as the Rising Sun Lodge, and the Lodge Hyogo and Osaka (Scottish). Most of the leading foreign residents from England, America, France, Switzerland, Sweden and Denmark "secretly affiliated themselves with the Club," which had as a "principal object . . . to "bring about a world revolution." [134]

In October, 1942, the *New Age* ran an article by one of 10 Freemasons who had returned to the United States from Japan. The anonymous author of the article told of the thoroughness with which the Japanese Government investigated Freemasonry. "Nothing has been left undone or unseen by them within the capabilities of those in charge," he said.

It was also noted that "the innermost secrets of the confidential files" of the Craft in Japan were taken by the government authorities.

Concluding, the article stated:

">. . . it behooves all of us first to gain victory and then to bear in mind the significance of that great legend so well known—*Ordo Ab Chao*." [135]

The words *"Ordo Ab Chao"* mean Order From Chaos, and are the motto of the Scottish Rite's 33rd degree.

A book titled, *On The World-Wide Secret Society,* written by Jiro Imai, assistant professor of literature at Tokyo Imperial University, said that Freemasonry "was a most dangerous and subversive secret society." In reply, Dr. Sazkuzo Yoshino wrote that "the League of Nations was created with the genuine spirit of Freemasonry." [136]

Nevertheless, the International Rotary Club of Japan "was ordered dissolved as an outer organ of Freemasonry." Also, Rotarians faced charges by Army officers that the organization had received secret orders for the destruction of the country, and were sending information to their enemies. The Japanese Rotarians were further accused of conspiring with Freemasonry against Japan's national policies."

Boy Scouts, too, were declared an arm of Freemasonry. [137]

However, the status of Masons Rotarians and Boy Scouts were changed dramatically with the defeat of Japan in World War II.

General Douglas MacArthur, Supreme Commander in Japan, informed George M. Saunders, 33rd Degree, Imperial Recorder of the Shrine of North America, that the Occupational Government under MacArthur was molded on the precepts of Freemasonry. [138]

The five-star General recommended to the Masonic Supreme Council that his aide, Major Michael Rivisto, be named deputy in Japan. And so it was done: Rivisto became the first Master of the Tokyo Lodge.

Count Tsuneo Matsudaira, former President of the House of Councillors, said he knew Masonry very well. He added: "Japanese misunderstanding and prejudice toward Freemasonry was one of the main causes of the last war."

The Japanese official said further that Freemasonry "will undoubtedly be a social revolution in Japan." [139]

One member of the Fraternity, after noting that General MacArthur, a 33rd Degree Mason, had reopened Masonic lodges in Japan, commented:

"Most of the Generals of the Occupation and many men of

lesser rank who were in key positions were Masons. The Japanese have since concluded that Masonry had some connection with the success of the Occupation." [140]

Moreover, the Sovereign Grand Commander of the Scottish Rite pointed out that all except one successor to General MacArthur as Far East Commander were "all active masons and members of the Scottish Rite." Those officers were Generals Matthew Ridgeway, Mark Clark, John Hull and Lyman Lemnitzer. [141]

PART IV

TARGETING MEN FOR THE FRATERNITY

11/ HOW IT'S DONE

Some men gravitate naturally to Freemasonry because of its Gnosticism and commitment to revolution, but the vast majority are attracted to the Fraternity by its external glitter.

The Lure

The following item in *The New York Times* typifies the favorable publicity which surrounds meetings of the Shriners—the so-called "fun-loving" adjunct of Masonry which is open only to men who are Knights Templar or who have received the 32nd degree in a Scottish Rite consistory.

> KANSAS CITY, MO., July 5 (UPI)—Arab sheiks swished in flowing robes, Keystone Kops cavorted on tricycle-sized motor scooters, the cavalry chased the Indians, trumpeters tooted, horses pranced and motorcycles chugged—craziness prevailed on the downtown streets today. [1]

The Shriners are well known for their ability to evoke laughter and spread happiness among young and old. They also are universally admired and respected for sponsoring hospitals which specialize in caring for children.

My own experience at a 1965 Shriner's parade in Washington, D.C. left my wife and me so impressed by the Arab sheiks, Keystone Kops, marching bands, clowns and choirs—and the immense joy and pleasure they all brought to our small children—that we were strongly persuaded to believe the Catholic Church's age-old condemnation of the Masonic Fraternity, must certainly be misguided.

Consequently, it was shocking later to learn that behind the festive facade and the children's charities lurked a more profoundly selfish purpose. Adam Weishaupt suggested the reason for such activities nearly 200 years ago when he instructed his Illuminees:

"We must win the common people in every corner. This will be obtained chiefly by means of the schools, and by open, hearty behaviour. Show condescension, popularity, and toleration of their prejudices, which we, at leisure, shall root out and dispel." [2]

In 1945, a member of the Craft put it this way: "the major job of the Masonic Fraternity is the creation of a healthy and enlightened public opinion." And, he added: All other Masonic activities are "incidental" to the real purpose of Freemasonry, which is "the creation and maintenance of a public opinion that will sustain the kind of world that we all wish to live in." [3]

Public relations activities are the life-blood of Masonry, because the Craft's policy ostensibly forbids extending invitations to join the Fraternity. Rather, men who are attracted to the Craft must themselves request entry into the Lodge. This claim is often true, but it is well known that the Fraternity frequently expends considerable effort to invite persons of rank and distinction to accept entrance into the Secret Brotherhood. Two such trophies bagged by the Brotherhood were President William Howard Taft, and General Douglas MacArthur. They are typical examples of prominent individuals who were made Masons "by sight; that is, they did not request entry into the Fraternity, the Brotherhood imposed itself upon them, and elicited their consent to be identified with the Craft.

In 1968, the Scottish Rite Grand Commander clearly explained the technique for luring men into the Fraternity. He said Masons are "bound by age-old policies and traditions to refrain from inviting or making a direct appeal to individuals to apply for membership." So, to incite a desire to join the Craft, the Brotherhood must attract attention to the organization "in such a way" that the profane will initiate inquiries "as to how they might . . . become Masons."

Continuing, the Masonic chieftain said "tact, diplomacy, and skillful salesmanship will bring opportunities." In that regard, he mentioned a Masonic film, "In The Hearts Of Men," which had impressed many profane [i.e., non-Masons] by the number of "distinguished Americans [who] were Masons." Commenting further, the Grand Commander said:

"Crippled children's hospitals throughout the country, and the knowledge that Masons are largely responsible for them, has induced many outsiders to petition for the degrees of Masonry. The same can be said about education programs of the Supreme Council in support of the public schools and Americanism." [4]

And he added: "It comes down to this: Responsible citizens of the United States want to help causes and institutions that are unselfishly working for the good of our country and humanity."

Pressing home the need for luring men into the Fraternity, the Commander said the Brethren must be "recognized as strong advocates of Masonic participation" in such publicly accepted entities "as public schools, scouting, youth organizations, YMCA, Salvation Army, and libraries." [5]

Albert Pike placed in perspective how the Fraternity uses Masons who are nationally prominent public figures. He wrote: "Masons do not build monuments to [George] Washington, and plume themselves on the fact that he was a Mason merely on account of his Masonic virtues. It is because his civic reputation sheds glory upon the Order." [6]

Professor Renner, one of the Marianen Academy scholars who gave a written deposition about his knowledge of the Illuminati, said the Order bound adepts by subduing their minds "with the most magnificent promises, and assure . . . the protection of great personages ready to do everything for the advancement of its members at the recommendation of the Order." [7]

Moreover, the professor said, the Order (which, incidentally has much in common with modern Freemasonry) enticed into its lodges only those who could be useful: "Statesmen . . . counsellors, secretaries . . . professors, abbés, preceptors, physicians, and apothecaries are always welcome candidates to the Order." [8]

Although the Craft popularized the phrase, "Brotherhood of Man Under the Fatherhood of God," in reality, it "was never intended for the multitude." [9]

Masons who believe the Craft is a "social and fraternal order," are operating under an "erroneous impression," and become "a distinct liability" to the Fraternity. [10]

It is truly surprising that thousands of men are lured into joining an organization about which they know almost nothing. Advertising experts call it "selling the sizzle and not the steak."

A 1950 *New Age* editorial remarked on the phenomenon by observing that the applicant for membership in the Craft "does not know in advance the vows he must take or the principles to which he will pledge allegiance. Yet, in spite of such a handicap, hundreds of person every year make application to join a Masonic Lodge." [11]

Why do they do so? The editorial explains that the major reason is because a man's acquaintances and friends are members of the Fraternity, "and, if they have found Masonry in accordance with its reputation for good in the community, then he feels justified in the faith that nothing will be asked of him which could not be proclaimed to the world with propriety." [12]

But the editorial did not find it necessary to report that, once inside, the initiates are bound by solemn oaths, and stern promises of mutilation and death if they reveal Masonic secrets. However, even if the Brotherhood's secrets are revealed, they are dismissed as untrue by the general public, because so many honorable men are associated with the Fraternity.

But what are the Fraternity's secrets? Why must members bind themselves so solemnly and agree to accept mutilation and death if the secrets are revealed? If the organization is simply fraternal, charitable and dedicated to good works, surely such extreme measures are totally uncalled for.

The obvious conclusion is that the Secret Brotherhood is hiding something so serious that decent men would never join it if they were fully informed in advance of its activities and purposes.

Targeting The Candidates

Masons obviously are very choosy about who makes up the "Brotherhood of Man" in the lodge rooms across the world. Craft leaders insist that it is "very important" for its investigating committees to scrutinize those who seek admission into the Fraternity. It is particularly important to determine the "religious views" of the candidates, as well as their "habits, associates, how they spend [their] leisure time, and whether [they are] financially able to become a Mason." [13]

As part of the selection process, the candidate is personally interviewed by the investigative committee in the presence of his wife, in order to "ascertain that the financial condition of the family is such" that the man will be able to pay dues to the Craft without financial strain. [14]

Masonic investigating committees check references provided by the candidate, and make inquiries of his co-workers. Moreover, Brothers who work in government law-enforcement agencies are contacted, and usually "are extremely cooperative." [15]

The Brotherhood's own investigating agency is known as the Masonic Relief Association [MRA], "a great agency for information concerning all types of investigations of the character of individuals seeking the good offices of the Fraternity, and all that is necessary is to make use of it . . ." [16]

The Binding Oaths

Once the candidate has been lured or targeted, he is formally initiated into the Fraternity amid occult signs and symbols of the Mystery Religions and, incongruously, the Holy Bible. The candidate for the Apprentice Degree, by direction, sinks to the floor on his bared left knee, his right knee forming the angle of a square. His left hand holds the Bible, square and compass, and his right hand rests on those Masonic symbols. Now the candidate proclaims in a loud voice before the Master of the Lodge and the assembled Brethren:

"I, _____, of my own free will and accord, in the presence of Almighty God, and this Worshipful Lodge, erected to Him, and dedicated to the holy Saints John, do hereby and hereon most solemnly and sincerely promise and swear, that I will always hail, ever conceal, and never reveal any of the arts, parts, or points of the hidden mysteries of Ancient Free Masonry, which may have been, or hereafter shall be, at this time, or any future period, communicated to me, as such, to any person or persons whomsoever, except it be to a true and lawful brother Mason, or in a regularly constituted Lodge of Masons; nor unto them until, by strict trial, due examination, or lawful information, I shall have found him, or them, as lawfully entitled to the same as I am myself. I furthermore promise and swear that I will not print, paint, stamp, stain, cut, carve, mark or engrave them, or cause the same to be done, on any thing movable or immovable, capable of receiving the least impression of a word, syllable, letter, or character, whereby the same may become legible or intelligible to any person under the canopy of heaven, and the secrets of Masonry thereby unlawfully obtained through my unworthiness.

"All this I most solemnly promise and swear, with a firm and

steadfast resolution to perform the same, without any mental
reservation or secret evasion of mind whatever, binding myself
under no less penalty than that of having my throat cut across,
my tongue torn out by its roots, and my body buried in the rough
sands of the sea, at low water mark, where the tide ebbs and
flows twice in twenty-four hours, should I ever knowingly violate this my Entered Apprentice obligation. So help me God,
and keep me steadfast in the due performance of the same." [17]

More than 150-years-ago, former President John Quincy Adams,
commenting on Freemasonry, said it was "vicious in its first step, the
initiation oath, obligation and penalty of the Entered Apprentice" degree. He opposed the oaths because they are: extra-judicial and contrary to the laws of the land; violate Christ's precept to "swear not at
all;" impose a commitment to keep undefined secrets unknown to the
person swearing the oath; impose a penalty of death for violation of
the oath; and prescribe a mode of death that is "cruel, unusual and
unfit for utterance form human lips." [18]

The Entered Apprentice oath is, of course, the first of many oaths
Masons voluntarily agree to utter. Moreover, the punishments threatened become increasingly severe as the initiate progresses through the
various degrees.

From the outset, the new Mason learns that almost none of the
Craft's teachings originated with Christianity, but rather in "China,
four thousand years ago," and in the "priesthood of ancient Egypt,
and the Jews of the Captivity." [19]

Repeatedly, his attention is directed toward the Mystery Religions;
to the fact that early man "found God in nature," and is told of the
ceremonies of ancient Egypt, the mysteries of Eleusis, and the rites of
Mithras. [20]

The nascent Mason immediately learns that the Masonic attraction
for the feast of St. John the Baptist (June 24), and St. John the Evangelist (December 27) has nothing to do with Christianity, but refer to
the summer and winter pagan festivals of the sun. [21]

He is subtly reminded to forget his early religious upbringing because his initiation "is an analogy of man's advent from prenatal darkness into the light of human fellowship, moral truth, and spiritual
faith. Masonic initiation, he is informed, is an "opportunity for spiritual rebirth." [22]

Again, the neophyte Mason is warned that he has become affiliated
with a strange organization which literally sets itself apart from the

rest of society. He is told the lodge "is a world unto itself; a world within a world, different in its customs, its laws, and its structure from the world without . . ." [23]

One does not have to be elevated to the 32nd Degree to understand that Masonry holds unique religious beliefs that are totally contrary to conventional religion.

On pages 50 and 51 of his handbook, a thoughtful Apprentice Mason will understand that Man is God. This is made clear as the booklet develops the thought that beautiful stone statues are created simply by knocking away with hammer and chisel the stone that is not needed from the statue that was in the rock "all the time." He is reminded: "The kingdom of heaven is within you," and man "is made in the image of God." In the very next sentence the new Mason is instructed to recall the analogy of the sculpted statue, which is produced simply by "a process of taking away" to reveal the "perfection . . . already within." [24]

A moment's serious thought will tell the Apprentice Craftsman that the Grand Architect who shapes the Universe is not God of the Old and New Testaments, but MAN—"the perfect man and Mason," who, until he was shaped from a "rough stone" to become a "perfect stone," had concealed his image as God by the excresencees of religious beliefs and familial and national loyalties. Heaven is not above, it is within the Masonic man, who, has the ability to create Heaven on earth.

As he moves up the Masonic ladder, the candidate for the Second (Fellow Craft) Degree makes the following commitment:

". . . binding myself under no less penalty than of having my breast torn open, my heart plucked out, and placed on the highest pinnacle of the temple there to be devoured by the vultures of the air, should I ever knowingly violate the the Fellow Craft obligation . . . " [25]

In the Third Degree (Master Mason), the candidate is threatened—

". . . under no less penalty than that of having my body severed in two, my bowels taken from thence and burned to ashes, the ashes scattered before the four winds of heaven, that no more remembrance might be had of so vile and wicked a wretch as I would be, should I ever knowingly, violate this my Master Mason's obligations . . ." [26]

The Master Elect of the Fifteen (Tenth Degree) says:

". . . I consent to have my body opened perpendicularly, and to be exposed for eight hours in the open air, that the venomous flies may eat of my entrails, my head to be cut off and put on the highest pinnacle of the world, and I will always be ready to inflict the same punishment on those who shall disclose this degree and break this obligation . . ." [27]

The Knight Kadosh (30th) Degree symbolizes the Fraternity's raging battle against Church and State. The Grand Master approaches a table on which are three skulls. One is adorned with a papal tiara, a second wears a regal crown, and the third is festooned with a laurel wreath. The Grand Master stabs the skull with the papal tiara, as the candidate repeats: "Down with Imposture! Down with crime!" The Master and the candidate then kneel before the skull adorned with the laurel leaf and say: "Everlasting glory to the immortal martyr of virtue." Passing to the crowned skull, the pair chant: "Down with tyranny! Down with crime!"

The candidate takes a second oath to "strive unceasingly . . . for the overthrow of superstition, fanaticism, imposture and intolerance."

He takes a third oath in which he accepts and consents "to undergo the sentence which may be pronounced against me by this dreaded tribunal, which I hereby acknowledge as my Supreme Judge."

The fourth oath taken by a Knight Kadosh focuses again on the "cruel and cowardly Pontiff, who sacrificed to his ambition the illustrious order of those Knights Templar of whom we are the true successors." Then all present trample upon the papal tiara, as they shout: "Down with imposture." [28]

In the 31st Degree, the candidate agrees that the Masonic ideal of justice "is more lofty than the actualities of God." [29]

The 32nd Degree teaches that "Masonry will eventually rule the world." [30]

Symbolism

Early in their service to the Craft, the Brethren learn the art of symbolism is crucial to carrying on the Fraternity's work in a profane world. One Mason said all words used in Masonry are symbolic, and the initiate must learn "the symbolic meaning of true religion . . . of true philosophy, true morality and true brotherhood." [31]

Another Craftsman said a full understanding of Masonic symbols
"can only be obtained by a study of Eastern mysticism—Cabbalistic,
Pythagorean, and such." [32]

In 1968 the Brotherhood was informed:

"The symbolism of Masonry has many shades of interpretation which each Mason must evaluate for himself in accordance
with his own individual nature. Masonic rituals are the 'idioms'
of an ancient symbolic language, a language which expresses
ideas, more so than words. It is said that seven magical keys
conceal the innermost secrets of Freemasonry within the volume
of Sacred lore upon the Masonic altar. These sacred truths are
variously interpreted by different individuals within the Lodge.

". . . Each Mason on the journey of exploring life through
Masonic Ritual finds *his* Truth.

* * *

"The Freemason, the *ritualist,* is the all-inclusive manipulator
of nature's finer forces within himself.

"Freemasonry is much more than an *exact* ritual alone. It is
also an exact *formula* through which we together, but differently,
may be enabled to make progress, slowly but surely . . ." [33]

One authority on the Fraternity said symbolism attracts the Masonic candidate and fascinates the initiated. It trains Masons to consider the existing institutions religious, political and social—as
passing phases of human evolution. It also allows the Craft to conceal
its real purposes. [34]

Father Hermann Gruber noted that the Great Architect of the Universe and the Bible are of utmost importance to the Brotherhood,
because symbols are explained and accepted by each Mason according
to his own understanding.

The official organ of Italian Masonry, for example, emphasized the
Great Architect as representing the revolutionary God of Mazzini, the
Satan of Carducci, God as the fountain of love, or Satan, the genius of
the good, not the bad. In reality, the German Jesuit observed, Italian
Masonry in those interpretations was adoring the principle of Revolu-
tion. [35]

Typical of that revolutionary orientation within Masonry are the
initials I.N.R.I. Inscribed on the Crucifix above Christ's head, they
mean to the Christian: Jesus of Nazareth, King of the Jews. But in
Masonic symbolism they stand for *Igne Natura Renovatur Integra—*
Entire Nature Is Renovated By Fire. [36]

It is important to note also that a substantial portion of Masonic communication is passed from "mouth to ear." As one Craftsman observed: "One of the principal avenues for keeping Masonry active is the manner of instructing from mouth to ear, from generation to generation." [37]

Masonry And The Media

Masonry obviously wields enormous influence in world media. Historian Mildred Headings said Masons influenced at least 47 periodicals throughout France, off and on, during the late 19th and early 20th Centuries. [38]

In the United States, in 1920, the Scottish Rite established a news service for "furnishing accurate and gratuitous information to newspapers. [39]

In 1924, the Grand Commander informed the Brethren: "Through the activities of our state organizations, the *New Age* Magazine, our clip service and News Bureau, we are stimulating the public interest and furnishing much valuable material to speakers and writers, and thereby can reasonably claim much credit" for the growing interest in favor of compulsory education by the state. [40]

Two years later, the Grand Commander was able to report to the Brethren: ". . . it is safe to claim that the majority of daily publications seem very friendly in their attitude toward the Craft." [41]

It was not only small town newspapers which looked with approval on the Fraternity's activities. The *New Age* reported that "many members of the National Press Club are Masons, not a few of them very prominent Masons." [42]

Also it was noted that a number of Christian Science officials have been Masons, and the *Christian Science Monitor* "devotes considerable space to Masonic activities throughout the world." [43] Indeed, during the 1930s, the Monitor ran a regular column regarding Freemasonry's routine activities.

Prominent Masons in the media included: Charles P. Taft, founder and publisher of the *Cincinnati Times Star;* [44] Roy W. Howard, chairman of Scripps-Howard newspapers, United Press, and Newspaper Enterprise Association (NEA); [45] Ogden Reid, editor of the *New York Herald Tribune;* [46] Richard H. Amberg, publisher of the St. Louis *Globe Democrat;* [47] and James G. Stahlman, president of the *Nashville Banner.* [48]

In 1987, *The Wall Street Journal* published an editorial castigating Senator Patrick Leahy (D., Vt.) for questioning Masonry's segregation policies in connection with membership in the Fraternity by a prospective judicial candidate Judge David Sentelle. The editorial stated:

"The problem is that Sen. Leahy's smoking gun is loaded with blanks. One phone call would have told Sen. Leahy that the Masons don't discriminate against blacks. The Masonic Services Association in Washington, D.C., says membership is open 'without regard to race, color or religion.' Blacks founded their own lodges a century ago, but now many belong to predominately white lodges, as Judge Sentelle said.

"The group also provides a membership list. This includes George Washington, both Roosevelts, Harry Truman, a total of 15 of 40 presidents. Eight of nine justices who signed *Brown v. Board of Education* were Masons, including Earl Warren and William Douglas. About 75 congressmen also belong, including liberal Sens. Robert Byrd (W. Va. Mountain Lodge No. 156), Mark Hatfield Oregon Pacific Lodge No. 50) and Arlen Specter (Pa. E. Coppe Mitchell Lodge No. 605). [49]

The author wrote a letter to the *Journal* the next day to say the editorial was "wide of the mark." The letter continued by making the following points:

"The fact is a basic Masonic 'landmark' (which cannot be repealed) stipulates that only men who are neither crippled, slaves, nor born in slavery are eligible for membership in the Masonic Fraternity. The latter criterion has excluded Negroes from regular Masonry, and prompted them to form their own 'clandestine' branch, known as Prince Hall Masonry, to which Justice Thurgood Marshall belongs."

The letter also noted that the Senator's challenge must be an historic first "or at least the first such legislative challenge to Masonic philosophy since the early 19th century" when committees of the legislatures of New York, Pennsylvania and Massachusetts found Masonry to be a distinct threat to both government and religion.

It also was observed that similar findings have been published over 200 times by various Popes beginning in 1738. Moreover, the letter recalled that many other Christian denominations have similarly indicted Freemasonry, as has Scotland Yard. In conclusion, The letter said:

> "Indeed, between 1941-1971, the Supreme Court was dominated by Masons in ratios ranging from 5 to 4 (1941-1946; 1969-1971) to 8 to 1 (1949-1956). During that 30-year-period, the Court erected "a wall" separating things religious from things secular. It was an epoch when prayer and Bible reading were derascinated from public education and when decision after decision succeeded in prohibiting any State financial assistance to religious schools.
>
> "Despite the facade of prominent national personalities who are boasted of by the Craft, as well as parades, circuses and hospitals, Masons have succeeded in having their religion dominate American society." [50]

Although the letter contained information that is little known to the public at large, it was never published; however, its receipt at the *Journal* was acknowledged privately to the writer.

Almost two months later, *The Washington Times* ran an "op-ed" piece on the same subject, which argued in support of Masonry along lines almost identical to the position set forth earlier by the *Journal*. The article was written by a man named Blair Dormney, a Washington, D.C. attorney and free-lance writer who was identified as a non-Mason. [51]

On the very day the article appeared, this writer sent a letter to the editor of the *Times* to make (more briefly) the same points as were made in response to the *Journal's* editorial. Again, although receipt of the letter was acknowledged, it was never published. [52]

Of course, editors are free to choose which letters to print, but it seems strange that both the *Journal* and the *Times* base their arguments largely on what a Masonic organization says about its own Fraternity, and fail to report the known history of the Brotherhood or facts set forth in counter arguments which are readily verifiable.

And so men are attracted to Masonry by its favorable public image and by knowing they are Brothers with Presidents, statesmen, justices, Congressmen, Senators, prime ministers, generals, admirals, captains of industry, journalists and other shapers and molders of history. Yet, some become disillusioned and separate themselves from the Craft, only to find Masons often "retaliate against members who quit by trying to get them fired from their jobs and otherwise harassing them." [53] Several former members of the Fraternity said they moved from their residences after leaving the lodge, and some asked that their names not be used by newspaper reporters because they feared reprisals." [54]

One former Mason called attention to the oath of a Master Mason, which says in part:

> "I furthermore promise and swear that I will not cheat, wrong or defraud a Lodge of Master Masons, or a brother of this degree . . . I swear that I will not violate the chastity of a Master Mason's wife, his mother, sister or daughter, knowing them to be such . . ."

Anokan Reed, a former top-level York Rite Mason pointed to the morality of such oath by commenting: "It's OK to seduce another man's daughter, or steal his car, as long as he's not a Master Mason . . . In the higher degrees, Masons deny the reality of evil." [55]

Reed, a former 13th Degree York Rite member, said he joined a lodge in Kokomo, Indiana when he was in his 20s, because his boss, a Mason, guaranteed he would "move up in the steel mill" if he joined. After becoming a Mason, Reed was promoted to a supervisory position, for which, he admits, he was not qualified. [56]

The former York Rite Mason moved from Kokomo to avoid harassment after being expelled from the Fraternity for challenging the Craft's secrecy. [57]

Masonry And Politics

Writing of Freemasonry's dominance of the public life of France during the Third Republic (1870-1940), historian Mildred Headings, said the Fraternity established a firm and determined policy that nothing should occur in that country "without the hidden, secret participation of Masonry."

With that goal in mind, the Craft made a concerted effort to have as many Masons as possible in parliament, the ministries, and in other official capacities. As a result, "the public power, the national power [was] directed by Masons." [58]

To demonstrate the political power of Masonry in France during that period, Ms. Headings noted that in 1912, for example, 300 of the 580 members of the House of Deputies (52.7 percent) were Freemasons, as were 180 of 300 Senators (60 percent). [59]

What of the United States? The preceding pages of this book have disclosed how Masonry dominated public policy in a number of individual States, and, nationally, through the Nativist, Know-Nothing, APA, and Ku Klux Klan Movements. But if Masonic dominance of the national legislature is used as a criterion for the strength of Freemasonry in France, the same criterion applied to Masonic membership in the United States Congress shows the Fraternity's control of public life on this side of the Atlantic has been much more pronounced than in France.

In 1923, for example, 300 of 435 members of the U.S. House of Representatives (69 percent) were members of the Craft, as were 30 of 48 members of the US. Senate (63 percent). [60] Six years later, 67 percent of the entire U.S. Congress was comprised of members of the Masonic Brotherhood. [61]

Although Masons continued to hold a dominant position in the House and Senate in 1941, their proportion of the total membership dropped to 53 percent in the Senate and 54 percent in the House. In 1957, a "typical" member of the 85th Congress was a Mason. [62]

Subsequently, Congressional membership in the Masonic Fraternity seemed to be less pronounced, so that by 1984, for instance, only 14 Senators (14 percent) identified themselves as members of the Craft, as did 51 House members. [63]

Those figures, however, are not entirely accurate, because some public figures do not always announce their membership in the Craft. Typical of such coy Masons in public life is Congressman Jack F. Kemp (R., N.Y). The former football star and Presidential candidate does not list his Masonic affiliation in the biographical sketch he provided for the 1983-1984 Official *Congressional Directory;* nor does it appear in the routine *curriculum vitae* handed out by his office. However, the *Buffalo News* reported in 1986 that Rep. Kemp is "a member of Fraternal Lodge, F&AM, in Hamburg, New York; a member of Palmoni Lodge of Perfection, 14th Degree; Palmoni Council, Princes of Jerusalem, 16th Degree; Buffalo Chapter of Rose Croix, 18th Degree; and Buffalo Consistory, 32nd Degree." In September, 1987, the Supreme Council of the Scottish Rite of the Northern Jurisdiction singled him out to receive the 33rd Degree of that Rite in Boston in September, 1987. [64]

But it has not been the Legislative Branch alone in the United States which has been subjected to strong Masonic influence. The Craft's control of the Supreme Court already has been explored; and although Masonry's authority has not been as pronounced in the Executive Branch as in the two others, the secret Brotherhood has had good representation among Chief Executives. Fifteen of 39 Presidents have been members of the Craft, some of whom have been much more ardent in their attachment to the Fraternity than others.

In addition to George Washington and Andrew Johnson, among more recent Presidents who have been Masons are Franklin D. Roosevelt, Harry S. Truman, Lyndon B. Johnson and Gerald R. Ford.

Of Roosevelt, the Grand Lodge of New York remarked in its official publication that if world Masonry ever comes into being, historians will give much credit to the period when Franklin Delano Roosevelt was President. [65]

President Harry Truman, a Past Grand Master of the Grand Lodge of Missouri, was quoted as saying: "Although I hold the highest civil honor in the world, I have always regarded my rank and title as a Past Grand Master of Masons as the greatest honor that has ever come to me." [66]

Following President Truman's death in 1972, the Scottish Rite Grand Commander hailed the Missouri-born Chief Executive as "a devoted son" of the Fraternity," and "the first President of the United States to have been coroneted an Inspector General Honorary of the Thirty-third Degree (1945)." [67]

Masons serving in Cabinet posts under President Roosevelt were Henry Morganthau, Secretary of the Treasury; Homer Cummings and Robert H. Jackson (later a Supreme Court Justice), Attorneys-General; Daniel Roper and Jesse Jones, Secretaries of Commerce; George Dern, Secretary of War; and Claude Swanson and Frank Knox, Secretaries of Navy.

Among Masons in President Truman's Cabinet were James F. Byrnes and George C. Marshall, Secretaries of State; Tom Clark, Attorney General (and later Supreme Court Justice); Fred Vinson, Secretary of Treasury (and later Chief Justice); Louis Johnson, Secretary of Defense; Clinton Anderson, Secretary of Agriculture; and Henry Wallace, Secretary of Commerce. Mr. Wallace also served as Vice President during Franklin D. Roosevelt's third term.

During World War II, under both Presidents Roosevelt and Truman, the Chairman of the Joint Chiefs of Staff, General George C. Marshall; the Commander of the U.S. Fleet, Admiral Ernest King; and the Chief of the U.S. Army Air Corps, General Henry H. Arnold—were all members of the Masonic Fraternity.

Freemasons serving under President Dwight D. Eisenhower (a

non-Mason) were Sherman Adams, his Chief of Staff; Christian Herter, Secretary of State; Douglas McKay, Secretary of Interior; and Robert B. Anderson, Secretary of Treasury. [68]

The Fraternity's Disguised Power

It must be emphasized that many members of the Fraternity do not disclose their Masonic affiliation, as Congressman Kemp's *curriculum vitae* indicates. That aspect of the Craft's operations was made clear in a 1962 *New Age* editorial, which said:

> "That a man is a Mason is something only another Mason can know, and the secret of the Master Mason can be simply and subtly communicated amongst eavesdroppers without the slightest awareness of non-Masons. [It] is [part of] the continuing and ancient charm of the age-old rituals and rites." [69]

The same editorial said: "Masons set the basic policies of our society. Yet the order is not political, and its purposes are not public. It is religious . . ." [70]

And one member of the Craft pointed out that there are at least 160 organizations (which he did not identify) that require their members to also be initiates into the Masonic Fraternity. [71]

In 1948, the *New Age* boasted that some ten million adults were linked directly, or were indirectly associated with the nation's three million Master Masons. The Scottish Rite publication estimated that "between one in five and one in 10 of the adult thinking population come directly within the circle of Masonic influence . . ." [72]

A candid statement on Masonry's dedication to imposing its philosophy on the nation, often through men who hold positions of national leadership, was set forth two years later by a high-ranking member of the Brotherhood. He said:

> "Any teaching which is completely antagonistic to all that we consider sacred, in religion, in morals and in government, is subversive of those fundamentals, and on them we depend for our very existence as a Craft. Our first duty, therefore, becomes one of self-preservation, which includes defense of those principles for which we stand and by which we live. This duty cannot be discharged by complete silence on the subject, and this view,

it is encouraging to note, is today shared by most of those who speak Masonically in the United States."

Significantly, the writer concluded by noting that some men who were leading the nation at that time were also "leaders of the Craft." He declared:

"This nation was nurtured on the ideals of Freemasonry; . . . *most of those who are today its leaders are also members and leaders of the Craft.* They know that our American Democracy, with its emphasis on the inalienable rights and liberties of the individual, is Freemasonry in government . . ." [73]

Perhaps typical of how leaders of the Craft work within the government was the cancellation in 1955 by the Senate Judiciary Committee of a hearing to openly explore and discuss the real meaning of the religion clause of the First Amendment. It is possible such a hearing might have been considered discussion of a "teaching which is completely antagonistic to all that we consider sacred."

At any rate, the *New Age* reported that the Senate committee had announced in August that it would commence hearings on the religion clause of the First Amendment beginning October 3. The Masonic publication also made clear that it was opposed to such hearings. Subsequently, the magazine reported: "On September 30, hasty announcement was made by the Chairman of the subcommittee, Sen. Thomas C. Hennings, Jr., of Missouri, that public hearings on the religion clause would be postponed."

The late Sen. Hennings was a 33rd Degree Mason. [74]

In 1960, the Grand Commander related how the federal government was used to help consolidate two lodges in Italy into one Supreme Council. The situation developed as a result of Italian dictator Benito Mussolini taking over the Masonic Temple in Rome. Following his assassination, the Temple's ownership passed to the Italian government, a transaction upheld by Italian courts. The courts also ruled that the Italian Masons owed 100 million *lire* in interest and back rent.

U.S. Masons organized American Friends for Justice for Italian Freemasonry, under the leadership of Admiral William H. Standley. A deadline for payment of the 100 million *lire* was set for February 18, 1960; however, "a sympathetic hearing" was given to the U.S. Masons by Secretary of State Christian Herter, a 33rd Degree Mason," and the deadline was extended 90 days. Moreover, while the Temple remained in the possession of the Italian government, Masons were given the right to certain portions of the building for 20 years, beginning in July, 1960. The 100 million *lire* debt was reduced by four-fifths, so the Craft was required to pay only 20 million at the rate of 1 million per year for two decades. [75]

Secretary Herter received the Gourgas Medal of Masonry, which is awarded by the Fraternity "in recognition of notably distinguished service in the cause of Freemasonry, humanity or country." [76]

In 1976, the Grand Commanders of the Scottish Rite bodies of the Southern and Northern Jurisdictions honored a number of the Masonic Congressmen. During the ceremonies it was made clear that "much credit must go to the Brethren in governmental positions." It was also stated "that good, dedicated, patriotic men can determine the fate of a nation and contribute to the fulfillment of Freemasonry's high ideals." [77]

Among the Fraternity's "high ideals" is prohibiting government support to children attending religious educational institutions. In that regard, a Washington newspaper column ran two items which were separated in time by eight months, but clearly reflect how Masonry's agenda can be accomplished within the government even if the President of the United States seems to hold a contrary view.

The unsigned column, "Alice in Potomac Land," reported on April 5, 1983:

> "Not many lobbyists have the ability to alter public policy like Timmons and company. Its top dogs, Bill Timmons and Tom Korologos, are not only veterans of the Nixon/Ford Administrations, but also helped the Reaganites in the 1980 campaign. They have the luxury of picking and choosing their clients. So, when they move into the area of family issues, you know that more is afoot than a [Sen.] Jesse Helms filibuster . . .
>
> "And then word reached us that Timmons has been using his old contacts at 1600 Pennsylvania Avenue to bring about a meeting between President Reagan and Henry Clausen, the head of the Masonic Order. The purpose of the chat is to talk the Old Man out of his support for tuition tax credits, which the Masons adamantly oppose. "

Just over eight months later, on December 13, 1983, the same column ran the following item:

> "Those folks who were active in the fight for tuition tax credits said all along that White House legislative affairs director

Ken Duberstein didn't have his heart in the struggle, even though his boss, the President was leading the charge. Now they think they know why.

"Mr. Duberstein is leaving the administration to join Timmons and Co., the high-powered lobbying firm. Conservatives feel that Mr. Duberstein was so intent on moving out of government into the big bucks that he didn't want to risk his marketability by twisting arms for conservative causes." [78]

The Military And Masonry

The Masonic Fraternity has been working within military units for many years. The officer cadre of Masonry in the armed forces is known as the Sojourners Club. [79]

However, the Craft recognizes that secret organizations uncontrolled by the military itself are not looked upon favorably by military commanders. In that regard, one Craftsman noted that lodges have been closed "owing to the disapproval of military authorities." [80]

The same source suggested one method of enhancing acceptance of a Masonic lodge within the military is to appoint officials, such as regimental commanders, as First Masters of Regimental Lodges. [81]

An example of penetrating military organizations with Masonic philosophy was discussed in a 1945 *New Age* editorial. The item concerned the California College in China, formerly of Peiping, but operating in "exile" in California. The editor said:

"This is one of the educational institutions to the support of which the Supreme Council Southern Jurisdiction contributes. W.B. Pettus, 33rd Degree, who is connected with the college, writes: 'Many of us in California College in China do not forget . . . that our college Foundation here in this state really had its beginning in the Scottish Rite Temple in Los Angeles'."

The editorial continued by noting the "wartime object" of the College:

". . . it is important that the officers of the Army and Marine Corps should be trained for their service in the Far East in institutions guided by similar principles which accord with those things for which our Scottish Rite stands. This is true of California College in China, and I am glad that during 1945 we are to be training some 360 officers of the Army, and a comparable number of Intelligence officers of the Marine Corps." [82]

Another sobering 1968 report concerned a group of 17 West Point graduates who, one month before being commissioned second lieutenants, were "obligated" as "soldier Masons . . . to carry out our [i.e., Masonry's] ideals in Vietnam."

The ceremony of obligation was attended by 457 people (135 had to be turned away), and the principal speaker was Lt. General Herman Nickerson, 33rd Degree, Chief of Staff for Manpower and Director of Personnel of the U.S. Marine Corps. [83]

The report gave no indication whether "Masonry's ideals in Vietnam" were the same as those of the United States. For an organization that has long been identified as "a State within the State," a fomenter of revolutions, and the successor-custodian of the Mystery Religions, it was a rather significant omission.

AFTERWORD

AFTERWORD

America has lost its way.

And it has done so, as the preceding pages have documented, through the determined and protracted efforts of an international secret society which has largely operated as "a state within a state."

The late historian Christopher Dawson wrote: "The great civilisations of the world do not produce the great religions as a kind of by-product; in a very real sense, the great religions are the foundations on which the great civilisations rest. [1]

To a great extent, the United States, in its art and architecture, its morals and music, and in its national and foreign policies, impresses many as a civilization in decline. And the argument is here made that this is happening because the fundamental Christian ethic which shaped the nation is being rapidly eroded. The body politic is largely sustained by the lingering fragrance of an abandoned Faith.

But the record shows the vast majority of the American people did not voluntarily abandon their Christian vitality: it taken was from them by a series of artificially grounded decisions concerning the religion clause of the First Amendment at a time when the Court was dominated by Justices who were Freemasons.

One of those men, Justice Hugo L. Black, was a member not only of the militantly anti-Catholic and anti-Christian Masonic Order, but of its adjunct, the notorious Ku Klux Klan.

Moreover, he is known to have expressed his interest in "advancing liberal religion," could "not tolerate any sign of encouraging religious faith by state aid," and initiated a campaign to have the Masonic Fraternity support legislation which would aid public schools only. [2]

The Masonic Fraternity immersed itself in a relentless attack on government practices which suggested minimal accommodation of traditional religions. The Craft did so by bringing before the courts case after case challenging these various aspects of minimal State toleration of and cooperation with traditional religious practices. It was Supreme Court decisions on those cases which eroded the Christian patina that was a hallmark of the United States.

The evidence set forth in this book has only scratched the surface of the Masonic iceberg which threatens the bark of Peter and the Ship of State.

The remarkable thing is the State—which is mandated to "insure domestic tranquility . . . promote the general welfare, and secure the blessings of liberty to ourselves and our posterity"—has been seriously derelict in challenging Masonic rule in America.

Repeatedly, the Masonic Fraternity has been found to be dangerous to Church and State. These findings have been made and publicized by numerous Popes, heads of State, several legislatures, various church denominations, and Scotland Yard. Yet, the United States Government which has the authority and the ability to investigate this secret world-wide organization—an anachronism in a free and open society—has studiously failed to investigate the Craft or to question its initiates who serve in key positions in government.

In 1921, a leading newspaper, *The World* (New York), after concluding a 20-part series on the danger of the Ku Klux Klan (which was closely identified with Masonry) worried about the Klan's secret oath, an oath which demanded "unconditional obedience to the as yet unknown constitution and laws, regulations. . . . of the Knights of the Ku Klux Klan."

The newspaper also was disturbed by the "rigid secrecy" imposed on Klan members "even in the face of death."

The World said it "has always in mind the potential danger to the United States from a secret organization bound together by such an oath . . . and likely to draw into its ranks men of [*sic*] no regard for anything but the Ku Klux law and standards of conduct and ethics." [3]

The fact is, Freemasonry also has secret, blood-curdling oaths, and demands of its initiates "unconditional obedience to the as yet unknown constitution and laws, regulations" of the Craft.

Almost immediately after that article appeared, the Rules Committee of the U.S. House of Representatives conducted several days of hearings on the activities of the Klan, at which *The World's* editor was the first witness. However, the hearings were suddenly concluded following a proposal by a member of Congress to investigate all secret societies which, of course, would have included the Freemasons.

In 1923, the State of New York approved a statute which said, in part, every membership corporation and association, "having a membership of twenty or more persons, which corporation or association requires an oath as a a prerequisite or condition of membership . . . shall file . . . a sworn copy of its constitution, by-laws, rules, regulations and oath of membership, together with a roster of its membership and a list of its officers for the current year . . ."

Another section of the same law stipulated that any person who joined such a group or remained a member, with knowledge that the entity "failed to comply with any provisions of this article, shall be guilty of a misdemeanor." [4]

The Freemasons, Grand Army of the Republic, the Odd Fellows (a Masonic adjunct) and the Knights of Columbus were exempt from the legislation.

The Klan, in court, objected to the law. They argued that the statute deprived them of liberty, under the due process clause, in that it prevented them from exercising their right of membership and association.

The Court responded that "membership in the association . . . must yield to the rightful exertion of the police power."

Continuing, the Court said: "There can be no doubt that under that power, the State may prescribe and apply to associations having an oath-bound membership any reasonable regulation calculated to confine their purposes and activities within limits which are consistent with the rights of others and the public welfare."

The information mandated by the law to be furnished "will operate as an effective or substantial deterrent from the violations of public and private right to which the association might be tempted if such a disclosure were not required." [5]

Regarding the requirement that the Klan register and have its activities examined, the Court said the State "May direct its law against what it deems the evil as it actually exists without covering the whole field of possible abuses." [6]

As for specifically excluding the Masons and Knights of Columbus, the Court said: "These organizations and their purposes are well known, many of them having been in existence for many years. Many of them are oath-bound and secret. But we hear no complaints against them regarding violation of the peace or interfering with the rights of others." [7]

Of course, the secret work of Masonry is not at all "well known," but the long history of complaints against it by such respected sources as numerous Popes, heads of State and various legislatures should suggest that a thorough investigation of the Craft clearly is in order.

In a minority opinion in the New York Supreme Court's Appellant Division, Judge Davis noted that the Masons were "bitterly assailed and charged with all sorts of crimes and delinquencies," but that "natural moderation and good sense" prevailed, and "no legislation was required in the interest of public safety or welfare to suppress" Masonry.

At the same time, Judge Davis conceded that there "can be no doubt that societies having principles subversive to the government or peace and good order may be banned and their members forbidden to meet." [8]

This book has offered substantial data which demonstrates that Masonry is a society "having principles subversive to the government or peace and good order" of the nation and of those citizens who wish to freely exercise their religion.

Scottish Rite Masonry's Grand Philosopher, Albert Pike, in his magnum opus, *Morals and Dogma*—which is given to each initiate into the Fourth Degree—makes this statement:

> "Masonry teaches that the Present is our scene of action, and the Future for speculation and trust . . . [Man] is sent into this world not to be constantly hankering after dreaming of, preparing for another . . .
>
> "The Unseen cannot hold a higher place in our affections than the Seen and the Familiar . . .
>
> "Those only who have a deep affection for this world will work resolutely for its amelioration. Those who under-value this life naturally become querulous and discontented and lose their interest in the welfare of their fellows . . .
>
> "The earth, to the Mason, is both the starting place and goal of immortality." [9]

To indicate the type of mentality to which such a philosophy appeals, it is instructive to read how closely Brother Pike's sentiment was expressed some years later by a leader of another sinister organization. That man said:

> "We don't want people who keep one eye on the life in the hereafter. We need free men who feel and know that God is in themselves."

The latter statement was made by Adolph Hitler. [10]

Obviously, the government, which alone has the ability to probe deeply into Masonry, will never challenge the Craft, because many members of Congress owe their seats to the Fraternity. However, the public can do something to neutralize the one organization that has lead the assault on the Christian religion, and has a long history of involvement in fomenting discord, dissension and revolution. Members of the public can—

- Conduct independent research into all aspects of Freemasonry by reading books about the Craft; searching libraries, lodges, attics, and government documents available through the Freedom of Information Act.
- Make membership in the Masonic Fraternity a criterion for assessing the qualifications and philosophy of candidates for public office.
- Urge State legislators as well as Congressmen and Senators to conduct public investigations of the Fraternity and expose its oaths, penalties and purposes.
- Insist that "secret societies" be subjected to scrutiny and that its records and membership be made available to the public.
- Demand to know why there must be "secrets" in an open society if an organization is merely a charitable and fraternal group.

Of critical importance is prayer. "For our wrestling is not against flesh and blood but against principalities and powers; against rulers of the world of darkness; against the spirits of wickedness in high places." (St. Paul's Letter to the Ephesians, 6:12).

Appendix A

UNITED STATES SUPREME COURT JUSTICES WHO WERE FREEMASONS

Years	No. of Masons	JUSTICES					
1789	2	John Jay	John Rutledge	**Willaim Cushing[1]**	James Wilson	**John Blair[2]**	
1790-91	2	do	do	**do**	do	**do**	James Iredell
1791-93	2	do	Thomas Johnson	**do**	do	**do**	do
1793-94	3	do	**William Paterson[3]**	**do**	do	**do**	do
1795	3	**John Rutledge[4]**	do	**do**	do	**do**	do
1796	4	**Oliver Ellsworth[5]**	do	**do**	do	**do**	do
1796-97	3	do	do	**do**	do	Samuel Chase	do
1798	3	**do**	**do**	**do**	Bushrod Washington	do	do
1799-1800	3	**do**	**do**	**do**	do	do	Albert Moore
1801-1803	3	**John Marshall[6]**	**do**	**do**	do	do	do
1804-05	3	**do**	**do**	**do**	do	do	William Johnson
1806	2	**do**	Henry Livingston	**do**	do	do	do

Years	No. of Masons	JUSTICES								
1807-10	3	**do**	do	**do**	do	do	do	**Thomas Todd**[7]		
1811	2	**do**	do	Joseph Story	do	do	do	do		
1812-22	2	**do**	do (Died 1823)	do	do	Gabriel Duval	do	do		
1823-25	2	**do**	Smith Thompson	do	do	do	do	do		
1826-28	2	**do**	do	do	do	do	do	**Robert Trimble**[8]		
1829	1	**do**	do	do	do	do	do	John McLean		
1830-34	2	**do**	do	do	**Henry Baldwin**[9]	do	do	do		
1835	2	**do**	do	do	**do**	do	James Wayne	do		
1836	1	Roger Taney	do	do	**do**	Philip Barbour	do	do		
1837	2	do	do	do	**do**	do	do	do	**John Catron**[10]	John McKinley
1838-40	2	do	do	do	**do**	do	do	do	**do**	do
1841-44	2	do	do	do	**do**	Peter Daniel		do	**do**	do
1845	2	do	Samuel Nelson	Levi Woodbury	**do**	do	do	do	**do**	do
1846	1	do	do	do	Robert Grier	do	do	do	**do**	do
1847-50	1	do	do	do	do	do	do	do	**do**	do

Appendix A (continued)

Years	No. of Masons	JUSTICES									
1851-52	1	do	do	Benjamin Curtis	do	do	do	do	do	do	
1853-57	1	do	do	do	do	do	do	do	do	John Campbell	
1858-61	1	do	do	Nathan Clifford	do	do	do	do	do	do	
1862	2	do	do	do	do	Samuel Miller	do	Noah Swayne[11]	do	David Davis	
1863-64	2	do	do	do	do	do	do	do	do	do	Stephen Field
1864-65	2	Samuel Chase	do	do	do	do	do	do	do	do	do
1865	1	do	do	do	do	do	do	do	Died	do	do
1866-67	1	do	do	do	do	do	do	do		do	do
1867	1	do	do	do	do	do	Died	do		do	do
1867-70	1	do	do	do	William Strong	do	Joseph Bradley	do		do	do
1870-72	1	do	do	do	do	do	do	do		do	do
1872-73	1	do	Ward Hunt	do	do	do	do	do		do	do
1874-76	1	Morrison Waite	do	do	do	do	do	do		do	do
1877-80	2	do	do	do	do	do	do	do		John Harlan[12]	do
1880-81	3	do	do	do	William Woods[13]	do	do	do		do	do
1881-82	3	do	do	Horace Gray	do	do	do	Stanley Matthews[14]		do	do

Years	No. of Masons	JUSTICES								
1882-87	4	do	**Samuel Blatchford**[15]	do	do	do	do	do	do	do
1888	3	do	do	do	Lucius Lamar	do	do	do	do	do
1888-89	3	Melville Fuller	do	do	do	do	do	do	do	do
1889	2	do	do	do	do	do	do	David Brewer	do	do
1890	2	do	do	do	do	do	do	do	do	do
1890-92	2	do	do	do	do	Henry Brown	do	do	do	do
1892-93	2	do	do	do	do	do	George Shiras	do	do	do
1893	2	do	do	do	Howell Jackson	do	do	do	do	do
1894-95	1	do	Edward White	do	do	do	do	do	do	do
1895-97	1	do	do	do	Rufus Peckham	do	do	do	do	do
1898-1902	1	do	do	do	do	do	do	do	Joseph McKenna	do
1902-03	1	do	do	Oliver Holmes	do	do	do	do	do	do
1903-06	1	do	do	do	do	do	William Day	do	do	do
1906-1909	2	do	do	do	do	**William Moody**[16]	do	do	do	do
1909-10	2	do	do	do	Horace Lurton	do	do	do	do	do

Table columns under heading **J U S T I C E S**

Years	No. of Masons									
1910-1911	2	Edward White	Charles Hughes	do	do	Joseph Lamar	do	**Willis Van Devanter**[17]	do	do
1912-1914	2	do	do	do	do	do	do	**do**	**Mahlon Pitney**[18]	do
1914-16	2	do	do	do	James McReynolds	do	do	**do**	do	do
1916-21	3	do	Louis Brandeis	do	do	**John Clark**[19]	do	**do**	do	do
1921-22	4	**William H. Taft**[20]	do	do	do	do	do	**do**	do	do
1922	3	do	do	do	do	George Sutherland	Pierce Bulter	**do**	Edward Sanford	do
1923-25	2	**do**	do	do	do	do	do	**do**	do	do
1925-30	2	**do**	do	do	do	do	do	**do**	do	Harlan Stone
1930-32	1	Charles E. Hughes	do	do	do	do	do	do	Owen Roberts	do
1932-37	1	do	do	Benjamin Cardozo	do	do	do	do	do	do
1937-38	1	do	do	do	do	do	do	**Hugo Black**[21]	do	do
1938-39	2	do	do	do	do	**Stanley Reed**[22]	do	do	do	do
1939-40	3	do	do	Felix Frankfurter	do	do	**William Douglas**[23]	do	do	do
1940-41	3	do	Frank Murphy	do	do	do	do	do	do	do

Years	No. of Masons	J U S T I C E S								
1941-42	5	Harlan Stone	do	do	James Byrnes[24]	do	do	do	do	Robert Jackson[25]
1943-44	5	do	do	do	Wiley Rutledge[26]	do	do	do	do	do
1944-46	5	do	do	do	do	do	do	do	do	do
1946-49	7	Fred Vinson[27]	do	do	do	do	do	do	Harold Burton[28]	do
1949-53	8	do	Sherman Minton[29]	do	Tom Clark[30]	do	do	do	do	do
1953-55	8	Earl Warren[31]	do	do	do	do	do	do	do	do
1955-56	8	do	do	do	do	do	do	do	do	John Harlan[32]
1956-57	7	do	William Brennan	do	do	do	do	do	do	do
1957-58	6	do	do	do	do	Charles Whittaker	do	do	do	do
1958-62	6	do	do	do	do	do	do	do	Potter Stewart[33]	do
1962-65	6	do	do	Arthur Goldberg	do	Byron White	do	do	do	do
1965-67	6	do	do	Abe Fortas	do	do	do	do	do	do
1967-69	6	do	do	do	Thurgood Marshall[34]	do	do	do	do	do
1969-70	5	Warren Burger	do	do	do	do	do	do	do	do
1970-71	5	do	do	Harry Blackmun	do	do			do	do

Appendix A (continued)

Years	No. of Masons											
1971-75	3	do	do	do	do	do	do	do	do	do	**do**	Lewis Powell
1975-81	2	do	do	do	do	do	**do**	**do**	do	William Rehnquist	**do**	do
1981-84	1	do	do	do	do	Sandra O'Connor	do	do	John P. Stevens	do	**do**	do

Names in boldface denote Masonic membership.

1 *Ten Thousand Famous Freemasons* by William R. Denslow, Board of Publication, Transactions of the Missouri Lodge of Research, St. Louis, 1957, 3 vols. Vol. 1, p. 275. *Justices of the Supreme Court Identified As Masons* by Brother Ronald E. Heaton, The Masonic Service Association, Washington, D.C., 1969, p. 12.

2 *Ten Thousand, op. cit.,* vol. 1, p. 102, *Justices Identified, op. cit.,* p. 5.

3 *Ten Thousand, op. cit.,* vol. 3, p. 315. *Justices Identified, op. cit.,* p. 24.

4 Appointment not confirmed by the Senate. Identified, op cit., p. 24.

5 *Ten Thousand, op. cit.,* vol. 1, p. 20. *Justices Identified, op. cit.,* shows Ellsworth only as an "Applicant" in 1765, p. 14.

6 *Ten Thousand, op. cit.,* vol. 3, p. 139. *Justices Identified, op. cit.,* p. 19.

7 *Justices Identified, op. cit.,* shows that Justice Todd withdrew from Masonry in Dec., 1811, p. 31.

8 *Ibid.,* p. 32.

9 *Ten Thousand, op. cit.,* lists Justice Baldwin's name only, p. 5. *Justices Identified* states that he withdrew from Masonry in 1809, p. 3.

10 *Ten Thousand,* vol. 1, p. 193. *Justices Identified* states that Justice Catron was "not on the roll" at the time of his death in 1865, p. 9.

11 *Ibid.,* p. 29.

12 *Ten Thousand,* vol. 2, p. 184. However, we learn that he was "probably" an Entered Apprentice in 1858, but that his name "disappears from the list of Enter Apprentices . . . after 1867." *Justices Identified,* p. 16.

13 "Demitted" (i.e., resigned) from Masonry sometime after 1854. *Ibid.,* p. 37.

14 *Ten Thousand,* vol. 3, p. 152. *Justices Identified,* p. 20.

15 *Ten Thousand,* vol. 1 p. 105. Justice Blatchford was "stricken" from the rolls of his lodge in 1873. *Justices Identified,* p. 6.

16 *Ten Thousand,* vol. 3, p. 221. *Justices Identified,* p. 22.

17 *Ibid.,* p. 33.

18 "Demitted," April, 1923. *Ibid.,* p. 25.

[18]"Demitted," April, 1923. *Ibid.*, p. 25.

[19]*Ten Thousand*, vol. 1, 0. 219. *Justices Identified*, p. 11.

[20]*Ibid.*, p. 30 Justice Taft was cited, *ibid.*, as being very active in Masonic affairs.

[21]*Ibid.*, p. 4.

[22]*Ibid.*, p. 26.

[23]*Ibid.*, p. 13.

[24]*Ibid.*, p. 8.

[25]*Ibid.*, p. 17.

[26]*Ibid.*, p. 27.

[27]*Ibid.*, p. 7.

[28]*Ibid.*, p. 34.

[29]*Ibid.*, p. 21. Justice Minton became a convert to Catholicism and "demitted" Jan. 8, 1946.

[30]*Ibid.*, p. 10.

[31]*Ibid.*, p. 35.

[32]

[33]*Ibid.*, p. 28.

[34]*New York Times*, August 25, 1979. Justice Marshall is a member of the Black "Prince Hall" branch of Freemasonry.

Appendix B

The Depth Of George Washington's Masonry

Masons regularly allege that "the Father of our Country," President George Washington, was one of the most illustrious and active members of the Craft. However, the historic record indicates he only had tenuous ties to Masonry, probably because it was a potent political force in the 18th Century.

The subject became an issue in the 1970s when the Disabled American Veterans (DAV) distributed a booklet which stated that the nation's first President was "not a very active" member of the Fraternity. The DAV also suggested that Masonry attempts to capitalize on Washington's nominal membership to bring unwarranted merit to the international secret society.

The Grand Commander of the Scottish Rite of the Southern Jurisdiction attempted to rebut the Veteran's position, but his documentation, in reality, tended to confirm the DAV's charge.

The Scottish Rite chieftain noted that Washington became a Freemason at the Fredericksburg, Virginia Lodge on August 4, 1753, and visited that lodge later the same year, and again in 1755.

However, the Grand Commander's record shows that it was not until 1776—23 years later—that Washington participated in any Masonic activity. At that time, he marched in a Masonic procession in Philadelphia.

The following year, he celebrated "St. John's Day" with a military lodge in New York, and did the same thing later that year with a New Jersey military lodge.

[There are two "St. John's" Days. One ostensibly refers to St. John the Baptist (June 24), and the other, St. John the Apostle and Evangelist (Dec. 27). Actually, in Masonry the days refer to solar worship and represent the summer and winter solstices, when the sun is at its greatest distances from the celestial equator—a turning point.]

Continuing his catalogue of Washington's purported devotion to the Masonic Fraternity, the Grand Commander cited brief visits by the President to various lodges, and incidents when he simply walked in Masonic processions on five separate occasions between 1781 and 1797.

It was also noted that numerous communications from Masons proposed that Washington receive various awards and commendations.

The Grand Commander called attention to the Alexandria, Virginia Lodge receiving a painting of the First President executed by William Williams of Philadelphia, on order of the Alexandria Lodge, a portrait for which Washington sat.

With regard to that situation, the Founding Father, responding by letter, dated July 3, 1792, to a request from Governor Henry Lee of Virginia that the President sit for a portrait, Washington said he was "heartily tired" of sitting for portraits, and had "resolved to sit for no more of them . . . except in instances where it has been requested by public bodies . . . and could not, without offense, be refused."

Williams had been refused a sitting by Washington, and subsequently offered the Alexandria Lodge the finished portrait of the President if the Masons would request the President to sit for the artist.

The Lodge approved the proposal on August 29, 1793, and the portrait was completed at Philadelphia in September, 1794. It now is proudly displayed by the Alexandria Lodge.

See: The Grand Commander's Message: "Exposing The Debunkers," *New Age*, February, 1973, pp. 2-11.

The Writings of George Washington, op. cit., volume 32, p. 93, note 59.

Appendix C
The Ancient Mysteries

For more than one-thousand years, the Mystery Religions were familiar in the ancient Mediterranean world. In the Graeco-Roman region, they dominated from the invasion of the East by Alexander the Great in 334 B.C. until Constantine, the first Christian emperor, founded Constantinople in 327 A.D. [1]

These cults—of which Masonry is the modern day successor—were predicated upon Gnosticism, a belief in a spurious "knowledge" of the origin, control and destiny of the universe. This "knowledge" supposedly originated in Egypt or Chaldea, and was handed down through an ancient message transmitted secretly by a chain of initiates. [2]

The "mysteries" were for a select few, who were bound by solemn oaths not to reveal the cult's rites. These religions were strongly opposed by the early Church as "strange doctrines" and "myths" that "come from the devils." In his First Letter to Timothy, St. Paul urged the Church under his jurisdiction to have "nothing to do with the pointless philosophical discussions and antagonistic beliefs of the 'knowledge' [i.e., Gnosticism] which is not knowledge at all." [3]

Actually, as St. Paul noted in his Letter to the Colossians, the "Mysteries" were distorted shadows of the the real "mystery" hidden for the ages and generations: the reality of Christ, the Redeemer and Savior promised long ago to mankind, who offers salvation to all men who believe in Him [Col. 2:6-18].

Charles Heckethorn, in his penetrating analysis of secret societies, noted that in prehistoric times man possessed a true knowledge of nature and her workings. That is why the "mysteries' of the most distant nations had so much in common. The common knowledge among different races and peoples was transmitted from a common source. [4]

Heckethorn said this prehistoric knowledge "was gradually distorted by perverse interpretations" and embroidered by fanciful creations of man's brain. [5]

Originally, the sun, moon and stars were seen as outward manifestations of the power of the Eternal Life. However, the multitude was more interested in satisfying material wants and "hence arose the personification of the heavenly bodies and terrestrial seasons depending upon them." Gradually, the human figure, which originally had been a symbol, came to be looked upon as the representation of an individual being that had actually lived upon earth. Thus was born Chrisna, Fo, Osiris, Hermes, Hercules and other "divine" beings. [6]

In all the "mysteries" there was a superior being who suffers death and recommences a more glorious existence. Everywhere there is a grand event of mourning followed immediately by the most lively joy. Moreover, the doctrine of the Unity and Trinity was common to all ancient doctrines, as was the "prototype of the Christian dogma in which a virgin is seen bringing forth a Savior, and yet remaining a virgin." To the primitive people that mystery is seen as Virgo in the Zodiac, and the "savior" brought forth is the Sun [7]

Also, in all the "mysteries," light was represented as born out of darkness—thus Kali, Isis, Ceres, Proserpine, represent the night from whose bosom issues life, and into which the life returns.

The cross, too, in all the mysteries, symbolized purification and salvation. [8]

These various aspects of the "mysteries," as St. Paul noted, particularly the common theme of a "Savior," demonstrate a faint glimmering of the truth of Divine revelation which was revealed by Jesus Christ. [9]

Another aspect of the "mysteries" included a requirement that candidates for membership pass through seven caves or ascend seven steps, or be transported through the seven planets—a theme which is a reflected in modern Masonic initiations [10]

One Mason observed that the religious symbols painted upon the walls and tombs of ancient Egypt tend to make a Freemason "almost believe he is witnessing a scene at an initiation," as he notices the apron, grips, signs, postures and symbols and other features common to Masonic lodges so vividly displayed. [11]

Another member of the Craft said Sun worship "was the foundation from which has been gradually elaborated the various mysteries and cults which gave us Masonry as we find it today." [12]

This same source said the cults of Dionysus or Bacchus developed from phallic worship. That cult held speculative and secret opinions of the unity of God and immortality of the soul. It also had "signs and symbols and practices similar to those found in Freemasonry . . ." [13]

The Phrygians worshiped the Magna Mater (the Great Mother), sometimes identified as Ma or Cybele, the fecund mother of all things. In the wild orgies of worship associated with that mystery religion, some devotees voluntarily wounded themselves and, becoming intoxicated with the view of blood, with which they sprinkled their altars, they believed they were uniting themselves with their divinity. Others sacrificed their virility to the gods. [14]

St. Augustine wrote that, as a young man, he "took pleasure in the shameful games which were celebrated in honor of the gods and goddesses," including Cybele. On the day consecrated to her purification, "there were sung before her couch productions so obscene and filthy for the ear . . . so impure, that not even the mother of the foul-mouthed players themselves could have formed one of the audience."

Continuing, he said, "the lewd actions and filthy words with which these players honoured the mother of the gods, . . . they could not for very shame have rehearsed at home in presence of their own mothers. [15]

Effeminate men were consecrated to the Great Mother, and in the rites of Liber (the god of the seed of fruits and animals) the devotees worshiped "the private parts of a man." [16]

During the ceremonial rites dedicated to the Great Mother, a young man stood beneath a platform upon which a steer was slaughtered and showered himself with the animal's blood. After the blood bath, the gore-covered mystic offered himself to the veneration of the crowd. The ceremony was known as the taurobolia. St Peter's Basilica in Rome stands on the very spot where the last taurobolia took place at the end of the fourth century. [17]

The Egyptian goddess Isis, was honored especially by "women with whom love was a profession." Juvenal referred to her as a procuress, and her temples "were frequented by young men in quest of gallant adventures." [18]

The morals of the cult of Isis and Osiris were viewed by the Roman community at large as very loose, and the mystery surrounding it excited the worst suspicions. Additionally, its secret societies were suspected of easily becoming "clubs of agitators and haunts of spies."

Consequently, the Roman Senate had the altars dedicated to these mysteries torn down on five separate occasions, 59 B.C., 58 B.C., 53 B.C. and 48 B.C. [19]

The celebrations associated with the worship of Isis included the "Finding of Osiris," a ceremony commonly used in Masonic initiations. In the ceremony, Osiris is killed by an opponent's attack, after which the former is buried. The attacker is vanquished by Horus, the son of Isis and Osiris, and the dead father is restored to life. [20]

Astrology—a practice condemned in both the Old and New Testaments—influenced the Mysteries of Mithra. [21]

Persia introduced dualism as a fundamental principle of religion, and deified the evil principle. It was taught that both evil and the supreme deity must be worshiped. Also, Persian Mithraism preached absolute fidelity to its oaths. And like Masonry, it preached fraternity. "All the initiates considered themselves as sons of the same father owing to one another a brother's affection. [22]

This dualism taught that the world is the scene of perpetual struggle between two powers that share mastery. The true believer was constantly in combat with evil in order to bring about the triumph of Ormuzd. [23]

The Persian Mazdeans brought the dimension of magic to their rites and made their "mysteries" a reversed religion with a liturgy focused on the infernal powers. "There was no miracle the experienced magician might not expect to perform with the aid of demons. . . . Hence the number of impious practices performed in the dark, practices the horror of which is equaled only by their absurdity: preparing beverages that disturbed the senses and impaired the intellect; mixing subtle poisons extracted from demoniac plants and corpses already in the state of putridity; immolating children in order to read the future in their quivering entrails or to conjure up ghosts . . ." [24]

These were some of the "Ancient Mysteries" about which Freemasons boast of being the modern successors.

These mysteries are based on myths. There never was a real Mithra, nor a Great Mother, nor an Isis nor Osiris.

That is why the "Mysteries" passed from the scene with the advent of Christianity. The new religion could boast of a Founder of unique holiness and power who actually lived among men and women. His teachings were new, arresting, different, and promised salvation not to the select few, but to all mankind.

The ethical ideals yearned for by men through the ages, and the Redeemer and Savior spoken of through unnumbered generations, became incarnated upon earth. True God and True Man entered history, and the world has not been the same since. Indeed, history is divided by all that happened in the world Before Christ and in the Years of Our Lord—B.C. and A.D. [25]

Notes   Amazing Discovery

1. *Everson v. Board of Education,* 330 U.S. 1 (1947).
2. *Ibid.,* pp. 15-16.
3. *McCollum v. Board of Education,* 333 U.S. 203 (1948).
4. *Torcaso v. Watkins,* 367 U.S. 488 (1961)
5. *Engel v. Vitale,* 370 U.S. 421 (1962); *Wallace v. Jaffree,* No. 83-812 (1985).
6. *Abington Township v. Schempp,* 374 U.S. 203 (1963).
7. Joseph P. Lash, "The World Of Felix Frankfurter," *The Washington Post,* "Outlook" section, Washington, D.C., August 10, 1975, p. 1.
8. "The Papers of Felix Frankfurter," Manuscript Division, Library of Congress, Washington, D.C., last box.
9. *Ibid.,* letter undated, but apparently prior to the Court's 1922 term.
10. *Ibid.,* box 225.
11. *Ibid.,* box 70.
12. Joseph P. Lash, From *The Diaries Of Felix Frankfurter,* New York, W. W. Norton and Co., 1975, p. 342.
13. "Frankfurter Papers," box 125, "Hugo Black Correspondence."
14. Harlan B. Phillips, *Felix Frankfurter Reminisces,* New York, Reynal and Company, 1960, pp. 290-291.
15. *Ibid.,* p. 13.
16. "Frankfurter Papers," box 99, letter dated January 22, 1944.
17. *Pierce v. Society of Sisters,* 268 U.S. 510 (1925).
18. *Meyer v. Nebraska,* 262 U.S. 410 (1923).
19. "Frankfurter Papers," box 125. Frankfurter's letter to the *Times* appeared in the June 6, 1925 issue, p. 6.
20. "Frankfurter Papers." box 125.
21. *Ibid.,*
22. *The Holmes-Laski Letters, The Correspondence of Mr. Justice Holmes and Harold J. Laski, 1916-1935,* Mark De Wolfe Howe, ed., Cambridge, Mass., Harvard University Press, 1953.
23. *Ibid.,* p. xiii.
24. *Ibid.,* p. 3.
25. *Ibid.,* p. 88.
26. *Ibid.,* p. 476.

27. *Ibid.,* p. 77.

28. *Ibid.,* p. 631.

29. *Ibid.,* p. 1450.

30. *Ibid.,* pp. 79-80.

31. "Frankfurter Papers, box 19, letter from Acheson, February 2, 1953.

32. For example, see his *Reason and Civilization,* London, Victor Gollancz, Ltd., 1944, p. 195, *ff.* where he expressed strong opposition to any Christian concept of society. The Church and Christianity, he said, offer "freedom only in a prison house."

In his *Studies in Law and Politics,* New Haven, Conn., Yale University Press, 1932, p. 163, Laski said *it is difficult to overestimate the significance of the judiciary* in the modern State. He pointed out that in countries, such as the United States, which are governed by written constitutions, judges "are the appointed interpreters and *masters* of the constitution" [emphasis added].

33. "Frankfurter Papers, ACLU folder, box 125. The same folder contains a number of ACLU pamphlets and other printed matter for the years 1925, 1928, and 1931. Frankfurter is listed as a member of the National Committee of the ACLU in the folder.

34. See notes 1,3, and 4, *supra* See also the cases cited and the records and briefs in those cases.

Justice Frankfurter took no part in the *Engel* (State-sanctioned prayer) case.

A series of articles about the ACLU, based on files of the Federal Bureau of Investigation (FBI), appeared in the *National Catholic Register* during September-November, 1977. The two lead articles in that series titled, respectively, "Justices Tied To ACLU Decided Church Lawsuits," and "Possible Court Bias In Church-State Cases," reported on some aspects of the relationship of certain Justices to the Union.

The latter article disclosed that Justice Frankfurter joined his colleagues Justices Tom C. Clark and Douglas as sponsors of a testimonial dinner to honor Roger Baldwin, founder of the Union, on February 22, 1950. That same article cited Canon Number 3 of the American Bar Association's "Canons of Judicial Ethics," which stipulates: "A judge . . . should not suffer his conduct to justify the impression that any person can improperly influence or unduly enjoy his favor, or that he is affected by the kinship, rank, position or influences of any party or other person." See the *National Catholic Register,* Los Angeles, Cal., September 18, 1977, p. 1.

35. "Burton Papers, Box 51. Letter from Davies to Burton, dated February 28, 1947.

36. *The Jefferson Bible With Annotated Commentaries On The Religion Of Thomas Jefferson,* New York, Clarkson N. Potter, Inc., 1964, p. 10. The "bible" basically is a compilation in several languages of the King James version in which all references to Christ as the Son of God and Messiah are omitted, as are all references to His miraculous and supernatural activities.

37. "Burton Papers," box 51.

38. *The Washington Post,* September 15, 1949, p. 2-B.

39. *Everson,* p. 33. The Court handed down its decision on February 10, 1947.

40. *Ibid.,* p. 59.

41. *The New Columbia Encyclopedia,* entry on Michael Servitus, New York, Columbia University Press, 1975, p. 2480.

42. *The Mind And Faith Of A. Powell Davies,* edited by Justice William O. Douglas, Garden City, New York, Doubleday and Co., 1959, pp. 242-243.

43. *Ibid.* pp. 245-246.

44. "Justice Black's Papers," box 25, "General Correspondence, Davies, A. Powell, 1953-1957." The sermon is titled, "When Dreams Dissolve," and is dated, Sunday, April 26, 1953.

45. Hugo L. Black, Jr., *My Father, A Remembrance,* New York, Random House, 1975, p. 204

46. "Justice Black's Papers," box 25, "General Correspondence, Davies . . .," letter to Mrs. Davies, September 27, 1957.

47. *Ibid.,* letter to Adams, June 30, 1959.

48. "Justice Black's Papers," box 53, "General Correspondence, Unitarian Church." The church service was held on May 9, 1963.

49. *Ibid.* Also see box 25, "General Correspondence, Davies . . .," which shows that Black gave a check for $100 to All Souls Church on April 9, 1963, and an identical sum on December 11, 1964. On September 8, 1965, he gave $100, and an additional $25 on March 3, 1959.

50. "Universalist Values Linked To Nonbelievers," Religious News Service dispatch, *The Washington Post,* November 5, 1976,

51. *Ibid.*

52. Davies, A. Powell, *The Faith Of An Unrepentant Liberal,* Boston, Mass., The Beacon Press, 1946, p. 3.

53. *Ibid.,* Davies said the question reflected a perception of Liberalism held by some people, but never denied that it also represented his own views.

54. *Ibid.,* p. 14.

55. *Ibid.,* p. 23.

56. *Ibid.,* pp. 24-25.

57. *The Mind And Faith Of A. Powell Davies,* op. cit., p. 29.

58. *Ibid.,*

59. *Ibid.,* p. 322.

Other books by Davies which express similar sentiments denigrating Christian beliefs are: *American Destiny (A Faith For America),* Boston, The Beacon Press, 1942; *The Temptation To Be Good,* New York, Farrar, Straus and Young, 1952; and *The Urge To Persecute,* Boston, The Beacon Press 1953.

60. "Burton Papers," box 60.

61. Information compiled from a variety of sources, but principally, William R. Denslow's *Ten Thousand Famous Freemasons* [Introduction by Brother Harry S. Truman, Past Grand Master, Missouri], St. Louis, Transactions of the Missouri Lodge, 4 vols.; Ronald E. Heaton's *Justices Of The United States Supreme Court Identified As Masons*, Washington, D. C., Masonic Service Association, 1969; and the *New Age* magazine, Washington, D.C., the official organ of the Supreme Council, 33rd degree, Mother Council of the World of the Ancient and Accepted Scottish Rite of Freemasonry for the Southern Jurisdiction of the United States.

62. Justice Murphy came from an anti-clerical family. "The father, enamored of Jefferson and his teachings, was skeptical about the verities of the priests . . . none of the children attended parochial schools." The family "share a dominant secular ideology which borrowed heavily from the Enlightenment, American nationalism and the Social Gospel . . ." See: J. Woodford Howard's *Mr. Justice Murphy*, Princeton, New Jersey, Princeton University Press, 1968, p. 4.

Justice Murphy was a board member of the ACLU. *Ibid.*, p. 203.

Justice Brennan was a dominant figure on the Warren Court. Chief Justice Earl Warren "had led a judicial revolution that reshaped many social and political relationships in America." His "consensus builder" and "the key strategist among the liberal bloc" was Justice Brennan. Brennan also was a key molder of the *Roe v. Wade* abortion decision in 1973. See: Bob Woodward and Scott Armstrong, *The Brethern*, New York, Simon and Schuster, 1979, pp. 9, 23, 232, 239.

Chief Justice Warren was a 33rd degree Mason.

63. Justice Goldberg was considered a part of the liberal Warren majority, and wrote a concurring opinion in the Schempp decision which struck down prayer and Bible reading in public schools.

Justice Fortas was part of the "working Warren majority." See Woodward and Armstrong, p. 8.

64. Statements by the four future Justices in support of "court packing" may be found in *The New York Times,* February 6, 1937, pp. 1,8; October 13, 1937, p. 6; February 11, 1938, p. 6; and August 22, 1938, p. 11.

65. In *Roth v. United States,* 354 U.S. 476 (1957), Justice Brennan in the majority opinion, while denying that obscenity is protected by the Constitution, posited the unique definition of obscenity as "material which deals with sex in a manner appealing to prurient interests." He then said the test for obscenity is "whether to the average person, applying contemporary community standards, the dominant theme of the material, taken as a whole, appeals to prurient interests." That permitted such publications as *Playboy* and *Penthouse* to display pornographic nudity in their magazines along with articles on politics, the arts, economics, etc. by recognized experts in their respective fields.

Other decisions enhanced the distribution of salacious and depraved material, butressed by such decisions as *Kingsley Books v. Brown,* 354 U.S. 436 (1957); *Butler v. Michigan,* 352 U.S. 380 (1957); *Smith v. California,* 361 U.S. 147 (1959; *Manual Enterprises v. Day,* 370 U.S. 478 (1960; and *John Cleland's Memoirs Of A Woman of Pleasure v. Attorney General* 383 U.S. 413 (1966).

66. In *Dennis v. United States* (1951), the Court upheld the constitutionality of the Smith Act which made it unlawful "to knowingly or willfully advocate . . . or teach the duty, necessity, desirability or propriety of overthrowing or destroying any government in the United States by force or violence.

Six years later, in *Yates v. United States,* the Court ruled that the Smith Act does not prohibit the advocacy or teaching of forcible overthrow as an abstract principle—divorced from any effort to instigate action to that end.

The Court, in *Brandenburg v. Ohio* (1969), found that "mere advocacy" of overthrowing the government, or other crimes, cannot be punished if "incitement to imminent lawless action" is not involved.

And in *Elfbrandt v. Russell,* 384 U.S. 11 (1966), the Court struck down legislation that required dismissal of a government employee who "knowingly and willfully remains" a member of the Communist Party or any other organization "having for one of its purposes" the violent overthrow of government. See also *Keyishian v. Board of Regents,* 385 U.S. 589 (1967).

67. J. Allen, "The New Age Dawns," *New Age,* October, 1959, p. 553

68. *Ibid.,* "Report of the Committee on Publications," January 1980, p. 16.

Notes   Chapter 1

1. Elbert Bede, "What About Today?", *New Age,* November, 1946, p. 667.

2. *New Encyclopedia of Freemasonry,* vol. II, article on the Grand Inspector General (33rd degree), New Hyde Park, N.Y., University Books, 1970, p. 435.

3. Patricia Pullen, "The Politics of Freemasonry," *The Sun,* Baltimore, Maryland, December 15, 1976, p. B-1.

4. Sari Gilbert, "Scandal Erupts Over Italian Masonic Lodge," *The Washington Post,* May 26, 1981, p. A-16; "Italian Banking Rocked By Scandal," *ibid.,* June 22, 1982, p. D-7; and Rupert Cornwell, *God's Banker* Counterpoint, Unwin Paperbacks, London, 1984, pp. 47, 134.

The Vatican Bank's relationship with P-2-related bankers Roberto Calvi and Michele Sindona is set forth by Cornwell on pp. 27-30, 37, 53, 102, ff.

5. Cornwell, p. 45.

6. *Ibid.*

7. *Ibid.,* pp. 47, 134.

8. Charles Grant Hamilton, "Freemasonry, A Prisoner of War," *New Age,* August, 1949, pp. 485-486.

Hamilton acknowledged his "indebtedness" to Justice Jackson, "who revealed to me the possibilities within this subject, [and] who has rendered invaluable assistance and personal encouragement."

Jackson, in his introduction to the series, said: ". . . among the earliest and most savage of the many persecutions undertaken by every modern dictatorship are those directed against the Free Masons." The Supreme Court Justice also declared that Masons "have suffered persecution under dictators more uniformly than any other class of victims."

Hamilton noted that some of the material in the series had been presented in the Nuremberg War Crimes Trials which followed World War II.

Justice Jackson resigned his seat on the high bench to accept the post of Chief Prosecutor at those Trials.

9. "Mussolini Infallible," editorial in the *New Age,* April, 1934, p. 209.

10. Hamilton, *New Age,* August, 1949, pp. 486-487.

11. *Ibid.,* p. 487.

12. *Ibid.,* p. 488.

13. Joseph S. Roucek, "Jan Amos Komensky", *New Age,* July, 1944, pp. 283-285.

See also: William R. Denslow's *Ten Thousand Freemasons* vol. 3, Transactions of the Missouri Lodge of Research, 1957, p. 38. It is of interest to note that the introduction to Denslow's work was written by Brother Harry S. Truman, Past Grand Master of the Grand Lodge of Missouri, and former President of the United States.

14. Hamish Fraser, "Freemasonry and the Vatican," *Approaches,* Ayrshire, Scotland, February, 1977, p. 26.

15. John Robison, *Proofs Of A Conspiracy Against All The Religions And Governments Of Europe Carried On In The Secret Meetings Of Free Masons, Illuminati, And Reading Societies,* 3rd edition, New York, George Foreman, 1798, p. 37.

16. Abbé Augusten de Barruel, *Memoirs Illustrating The History Of Jacobinism,* 4 volumes, volume 3, "The Anti-Social Conspiracy," London, T. Burton, 1798, p. xiv.

17. Barruel, volume 1, pp. xxii-xxiii.

18. *Ibid.*

19. *Ibid.,* p. 4

20. *Ibid.,* P. 27. The letters of Voltaire and his colleagues may be found in the 92-volume work *Ouevres Completes de Voltaire* by Pierre Augustin de Beaumarchais, published by *Societe Litteraire-Typographique,* Paris, 1785-89.

See particularly the following volumes: 29: "The Rights of Man and the Usurpation of the Popes;" "The Tocsin of Kings;" and "The Cry of Nations;" 52-63: "Letters of Voltaire;" 64-66: "Letters of the Prince of Prussia to Voltaire;" 68-69: "Letters Between Voltaire and D'Alembert;" and 70: "Voltaire and Condorcet."

21. Barruel, volume 1, p. 6.

22. *Ibid.,*

23. *New Age,* November, 1934, p. 677; March, 1948, p. 143; March, 1977, pp. 5-6. See also: Charles S. Lobinger, *The Supreme Council,* the "official history of the Supreme Council" of the Southern Jurisdiction , The Standard Printing Company, Louisville, Kentucky, 1931, p. 110.

24. Barruel, volume 2, pp. 282-286, 288-289; and 321-323.

25. *Ibid.,* pp. 294-295.

26. *Ibid.* pp. 409-410.

The wording of some Masonic oaths will be set forth below.

27. *Ibid.,* pp. 282-286; 288-289.

28. *Ibid.,* p. 313-314.

29. *Ibid.,* pp. 311-312.

30. Barruel, volume 3, p. 139.

31. *Ibid.,* pp. 23-24.

Karl Marx, in his "Manifesto of the Communist Party," speaking of rule by the proletariat, said such rule "cannot be effected except by means of despotic inroads on the rights of property and on the conditions of bourgeois production . . ."

He added: "When, in the course of development, class distinctions have disappeared, and all production has been concentrated in the hands of a vast association of the whole nation, the public power will lose its political character."

And, in 1844, Marx wrote: "The criticism of religion is the beginning of all criticism."

Frederich Engels declared: "All religious bodies without exception are to be treated by the state as private associations. They are not to receive support from public funds or exercise any influence over public education."

The program of the Communist International, adopted at the Sixth World Congress in 1928, states: "One of the most important tasks of the cultural revolution affecting the wide masses is the task of systematically and unswervingly combatting religion—the opium of the people. The proletarian government must withdraw all state support from the church, which is the agency of the former ruling class; it must prevent all church interference in state-organized educational affairs, and ruthlessly suppress the counterrevolutionary activity of the ecclesiastical organisations [sic]. At the same time, the proletarian state, while granting liberty of worship and abolishing the privileged position of the formerly dominant religion, carries on antireligious propaganda with all the means at its command and reconstructs the whole of its educational work on the basis of scientific materialism."

The above citations may be found in House Report No. 2241, 84th Congress, Second Session, *The Communist Conspiracy,* Part I, Section A: Marxist Classics, prepared by the *Com*mittee on Un-American Activities, U.S. Government Printing Office, Washington, D.C., 1956, p. 63 (regarding the "Manifesto"); pp. 153-154 (relative to Lenin on *Religion,* from the Little Lenin Library No. 7, vol. I, pp. 3-10, 14-15, 17-18, 47-48); and p. 156 (from The Programme of the Communist International, Workers' Library Publisher, New York, p. 53.).

32. Barruel, vol. 1, pp. 7-8.
33. *Ibid.,* pp. 9-10.
34. Robison, pp. 82-83.
35. *Ibid.,* p. 85
36. *Ibid.,* p. 95
37. *Ibid.,* p. 147.
38. *Ibid.*
39. *Ibid.,* p. 148.
40. *Ibid.*
41. *Ibid.*
42. *Ibid.,* p. 149.
43. Robison, p. 116.

44. *Ibid.*, p. 122.

45. *Ibid.*, p. 140

46. Barruel, vol. 3, p. 147.

47. Robison, p. 146.

48. *Ibid.*, p. 156.

49. *Ibid.*, pp. 343-344.

50. Barruel, vol. 4, p. 232.

51. *Ibid.*, p. 233.

52. *Ibid.*, p. 248

Rupert Cornwell, commenting on those involved with the P-2 in Italy, wrote: "The main appeal to the bulk of the members of [Licio Gelli's] lodge was the apparent short cut it offered to powers, riches and the best jobs; and for such an advantage, surrender of secret information to the grandmaster must have seemed a reasonable price to pay." Cornwell, p. 48.

53. *The Herald,* New York, December 4, 1794, p. 2.

54. *The Writings of George Washington From Original Manuscript Sources,* volume 36, John C. Fitzpatrick, editor, Washington, D.C., U.S. Government Printing Office, 1941, pp. 452-453.

See also Appendix B below.

55. *Ibid.*, pp. 518-519.

About the time of Rev. Snyder's letter, the United States was concerned with "self-created," or so-called "Democratic Societies." In that connection, on November 19, 1794, President Washington had sent a message to Congress in which he said "self-created societies" had led the Whiskey Rebellion in Western Pennsylvania. The insurgents, he stated, had "a spirit inimical to all order," and had disseminated "suspicions, jealousies, and accusations of the whole Government." See: *Annals of Congress* [the title under which the present *Congressional Record* was known], November 19, 1794, p. 787.

See also the *Federal Intelligencer and Boston Daily Gazette,* Baltimore, Maryland, November 23, 1794, p. 2.

Although Congress was expected to concur quickly with the President, it soon became evident that friends of the "self-created societies" were reluctant to support him.

Senator Aaron Burr of New York moved to expunge the following words from the Senate committee's draft response to the Chief Executive: "Our anxiety arises from the licentious and open resistance to the laws . . . and has been increased by the proceedings of certain self-created societies relative to the laws of the administration of Government; proceedings, in our apprehension, founded in political error, calculated, if not intended, to disorganize our Government, and which . . . have been influential in misleading our fellow-citizens in the scene of insurrection."

The motion was defeated and the President was praised by the Senate for his prompt and vigorous action in sending 15,000 militia to put down the insurrection.

During the ensuing debate, Senator Theodore Sedgwick of Massachusetts said Democratic Societies were set up following the arrival at Charleston, South Carolina from France of Citizen [Edmond] Genet, who did the utmost "mischief that was in his power."

Sen. Thomas Scott of Pennsylvania said he knew for a fact that Democratic Societies not only caused insurrection by their propaganda, but that members of those societies led the riots.

The Senate voted on November 28, 1794 to condemn the Democratic Societies. See *Annals,* same date, pp. 912, 922, 937-938.

That is the political environment at the time President Washington wrote to Rev. Snyder to concede that "individuals of" Masonic lodges "may" have propagated "the diabolical tenets" of the Illuminati and the "pernicious principles" of the Jacobins in this country to separate the people from their government.

Sen. Burr was tried for treason in 1807 for conspiring with General James Wilkinson to establish a republic in Spanish territory near New Orleans. He was found not guilty by Chief Justice John Marshall, a finding which the American public failed to support. See *The Trial of Aaron Burr On An Indictment For Treason* before the Circuit Court of the United States, Richmond, Virginia, May Term, 1807, Westcott and Co. Washington, City, 1807.

Justice John Marshall was a Freemason, as was General Wilkinson. The latter was buried from the home of Joel Poinsett, the U.S. Consul in Mexico. Poinsett, after whom the poinsetta flower is named, organized Royal Arch Masonry in Mexico.

Moreover, correspondence in the Burr conspiracy was carried out in "the Royal Arch cypher." See Henry Dana Ward (editor) *The Anti-Masonic Review and Magazine,* Vanderpool and Cole, Printers, New York, 1828, vol. 1, No. 10, p. 297; *New Age,* July 1941, p. 445; and Heaton's *Justices Of The Supreme Court.*

56. *Columbia Encyclopedia,* entry on Freemasonry, p. 1007.

57. Paul Hazard, *The European Mind,* 1680-1715, Meridian Books, The World Publishing Co., Cleveland, Ohio, pp. 254-255.

58. *Ibid.*

59. "Masonry in America," editorial, *New Age,* April, 1940, p. 202.

60. Bernard Fay, *Revolution and Freemasonry—1680-1800,* Little Brown and Co., Boston, 1935, pp. 238-239.

See also *New Age,* June, 1931, p. 326, where it is stated that members of the St. Andrew's Lodge of Freemasons comprised "the Boston Tea Party."

61. Fay, p. 233.

62. *Ibid.,* pp. 254-255.

63. *Ibid.,* p. 256.

Fay, at one time, had been considered by Masons an "unbiased student of the life and times" of Franklin. However, that favorable attitude toward Fay changed when the Craft learned he headed the Secret Societies Bureau of the

Vichy regime in France during World War II. In that position he published the names of Freemasons and maintained duplicates of Grand Orient documents. See: Harry L. Baum, "Democracy and Freemasonry, *New Age,* March, 1935, p. 143; "Paris Editor Defends Craft . . .," unsigned news item, *ibid,* December, 1941, p. 755, where it is noted that Fay charged Masons with responsibility for the fall of the Third Republic; and Reynold E. Blight, "Why Hitler Hates and Fears Masonry," *ibid.,* October, 1942, pp. 539-41, in which Fay's work is mentioned favorably.

Following World War II, Masons severely condemned his work exposing Freemasonry. The Catholic French historian was sentenced to prison for life at hard labor on a charge of intelligence with the enemy. He later escaped to Switzerland. See *New Age* issues: January, 1949, p. 99; March 1956, p. 176; September, 1966, p. 25; and April, 1976, pp. 13-19.

64. *Report Of A Committee To the New York Senate, Together With Extracts From Other Authentic Documents Illustrating The Character And Principles Of Free Masonry,* published by request, and under the direction of several citizens of New Haven, New Haven, printed by Hezekiah Howe, 1829, pp. 13-14.

65. *Ibid.,* p. 15.

66. *Ibid.,* p. 11.

67. *Ibid.,* pp. 7-8.

68. *Ibid.,* p. 11.

69. *Ibid.,* p. 4.

70. *Investigation Into Freemasonry* by a Joint Committee of the Legislature of Massachusetts House of Representatives, March, 1834, pp. 9-10.

71. *Ibid.,* pp. 14-21.

72. *Ibid.,* p. 11.

73. *Testimony Taken by the Committee of the Pennsylvania House of Representatives To Investigate the Evils of Freemasonry,* Read in the House of Representatives June 13, 1836, Theodore Finn, Harrisburg, 1836, p. 15.

74. *Ibid.,* pp. 39-42, 46.

75. Dee A. Strickland, "Masonry In Louisiana," *New Age,* August, 1962, pp. 19.

76. Joseph Schlarman, *Mexico, A Land Of Volcanoes,* Bruce Publishing Co., Milwaukee, Wisconsin, 1950, pp. 224-261.

77. *New Age,* "Library Notes," May, 1941, p. 315.

78. Strickland, *ibid.,* p. 21.

79. Henry Zelchenko, "The Renegade Mason," *ibid.,* March, 1963, p. 46.

Notes   Chapter 2

1. *The Catholic Encyclopedia,* entry on "Freemasonry" by Fr. Hermann Gruber, New York, Encyclopedia Press, 1913, p. 776.

2. *Ibid.,* p. 781.

3. *Ibid.*

4. *Ibid.,* p. 776.

5. *Ibid.,* p. 777.

6. *Ibid.,* p. 775.

7. *Ibid.,* pp. 782-783.

8. *Ibid.,* p. 783.

8-A. Quoted in *Fortnightly Review,* November 15, 1921, p. 412.

9. Albert Pike, *Morals and Dogma of the Ancient and Accepted Rite of Freemasonry,* Charleston, S.C., published by the author, 1871. The purpose of the book is written on its title page.

10. *New Age,* January, 1950, "Report of the Committee on Publications," pp. 27-28.

11. *Ibid.,* December, 1935, "Comment" section, p. 709; *ibid.,* August, 1961, p. 9.

12. *Ibid.,* June, 1948, "Grand Commander's Message," p. 347.

13. Pike, *op. cit.,* Introduction, pp. iii, iv.

14. Lobinger, *op. cit.,* p. 341. See also *New Age,* May, 1928, pp. 270-271.

15. Lobinger, p. 342.

16. *New Age,* April, 1924, editorial comment, p. 197.

17. *Ibid.,* May, 1970, John C. Montgomery, "An Invaluable Working Tool: The Use of Albert Pike's *Morals and Dogma,*" pp. 28-29.

18. Pike, *op. cit.,* p. 1.

19. *Ibid.,* p. 2.

20. *Ibid.,* p. 4.

21. *Ibid.,* pp. 5-6. See also Chapter 1, above, p. 30.

22. *Ibid.,* pp. 9-14. Thus, the lodge rooms throughout the world display the Blazing Star, and Masonic triangle. Inside the latter is the letter "G."

Masonry's dedication to the Ancient Mysteries further emphasizes the pagan orientation of the Craft.

The novice Mason is informed by the second full page of his Entered

Apprentice handbook that many of Freemasonry's symbols and teachings "go back to the very childhood of the race." He is reminded of "the ceremonies of ancient Egypt," and of the mysteries of Eleusis, as well as the rite of Mithras and the Ancient Mysteries. See Carl H. Claudy, *Introduction to Freemasonry, I, Entered Apprentice*, Washington, D.C., The Temple Publishers, 1931, pp. 8, 27, 31, 41.

Masonic literature is replete with references to Isis, Osiris, and their son Horus, who also was the son of Re, the sun-god. In the initiation ceremonies of Egyptian mysteries the candidate knelt blindfolded on his bare knees and, with a sword pointed at his throat, he vowed fidelity to the secrets of the Order. The identical ceremony is enacted in the Apprentice [First] Degree of Masonry. Similarly, in the Egyptian mysteries and in Masonry, the ceremony includes a ladder with seven steps, symbolic language, hieroglyphic writing, passwords, secret handgrips, a cap shaped like a triangle [pyramid] and an apron. See Charles W. Heckthorn *The Secret Societies Of All Ages And Countries* vol 1, p. 51. For Masonic initiation rites, see William Whalen, *Christianity and American Freemasonry*, Milwaukee, Bruce Publishing Co., 1958, pp. 24-47; Barruel, vol 2, pp. 288-89; *ibid.*, vol. 3, p. 87; and Robison, p. 91. See also Appendix C.

23. See footnotes 7 and 19, above, regarding "the great revolution" and commitment to the "universal social republic."

24. Pike, *op. cit.*, pp. 14, 814.

25. *Ibid.*, pp. 23, 161.

26. *Ibid.*, pp. 260, 275.

27. *Ibid.*, p. 275.

28. *Ibid.*, p. 524

29. *Ibid.*, pp. 323, 816.

30. *Ibid.*, p. 817.

31. *Ibid.*

32. *Ibid.*

33. *Ibid.* pp. 817-818.

34. *Ibid.*, p. 818.

Gnosticism is the doctrine of salvation by knowledge, that is, knowledge of the mysteries of the Universe and of magic formulae indicative of that knowledge. It echoes Eden and man's desire to be a god. See Genesis 2:17; 3:4-7. This knowledge involves man's refusal to recognize his status as a created being subject to his Creator.

Gnosticism was an early Church heresy, the most formidable opponent of which was St. Irenaeus (A.D. 140-202). It was ultimately defeated in the second century when the Church asserted episcopal authority and drew the bonds of catholicity closer. Subsequently its principles were incorporated into Manicheaism and Albigensianism which were propagated into the Fourteenth Century before dying out.

35. Malcolm Barber, *The Trial of the Templars*, Cambridge, England,

Cambridge University Press (Paperback), 1980, pp. 1, 45, 48, 63, 178-192.
    36. Pike, p. 818.
    37. *Ibid.*, p. 820.

Historic judgements on the reasons for the dissolution of the Templars by
the Council of Vienne differ, but it is interesting to note that the Council also
condemned the Beghards, a Gnostic and Manichean group that flourished in
Europe at the same time. The Beghards held that "perfect men" could not be
blamed for any act they performed. See the *New Columbia Encyclopedia*,
New York, McGraw Hill, 1975, p. 261; John F. Clarkson, *et. al.*, *The
Church Teaches*, Rockford, Ill., Tan Books and Publishers, 1973, p. 349.

Abbé Barruel observed: "It would be one of the most extraordinary facts
in history to see two hundred Knights accusing themselves of the greatest
abominations. It would be a still greater atrocity to see so many Bishops,
Noblemen, magistrates, Sovereign of different nations, sitting in judgement
on the Templars and publishing to the world, as free and uncontrolled declarations which had only been extorted from them by the fear of torture. Such a
conduct would be still more horrible than that of the Templars themselves."

The Abbé added: "Even if the Templars were entirely innocent of the
crimes imputed to them, what could have been the virtue and courage of an
order, which could demean itself so much as to make such declarations
against itself? How can Freemasonry glory in such an ancestry who, if their
crimes were not monstrous, must themselves have been monsters of the bas-
est cowardice." See Barruel, *op. cit.*, vol. 2. pp. 381-382.

The Abbé also noted that 30,000 to 40,000 Knights survived condemnation of the Order—and Philip the Fair and Pope Clement V. They lived in
different parts of the world, where they had nothing to fear from their perse-
cutors who had died. Yet, not a single one had made a retraction, "not one
leaves such a declaration to be published after his death." *Ibid.*, pp. 386-387.
    38. Pike, *ibid.*, p. 823.
    39. *Ibid.*, p. 23.
    40. *Ibid.*, p. 139.
    41. *Ibid.*, p. 140.
    42. *Ibid.*, p. 231.
    43. *Ibid.*, p. 248.
    44. *Ibid.*, p. 277.
    45. *Ibid.*, p. 294.
    46. *Ibid.*, pp.539-540.
    47. *Ibid.*, pp. 304-305, 744.

The word Kabbalah is spelled in various ways, including Kabala and Cabala. It means "to receive," and refers to the reception of traditional lore
which goes back to pre-Christian times. Unlike the Scriptures, it purportedly
was entrusted only to "the few elect ones." See *The Jewish Encyclopedia*,
vol. 3, entry on "Cabala," New York, Funk and Wagnalls, 1925, pp. 456-
479; *Encyclopedia Judaica*, entry on "Kabbalah," Jerusalem, Israel, Keter

Publishing House, Macmillan Co., N.Y., 1979, vol. 10, p. 653.

According to the apocryphal IV Esdras xiv: 5-6, Moses received instructions from God on Mount Sinai to "hide" certain things that were made known to him during that particular theophany. The secret knowledge reputedly comprised 70 written volumes. See: *Jewish Encyclopedia*, vol. 3, p. 356.

Even more instructive, the *Encyclopedia* says, is "The Book of Jubilees," which refers to the writings of Jared, Cainan and Noah. Abraham is presented as the renewer, and Levi is the permanent guardian of those ancient writings. *Ibid.*, p. 457.

The Cabala essentially is pagan in origin and has its roots in Chaldea and Gnosticism, according to the *Jewish Encyclopedia*, vol. 3, p. 458

48. Pike, p. 148.

49. *Ibid.*, p. 161.

50. *Ibid.*, p. 196.

51. *Ibid.*, p. 213.

52. *Ibid.*, p. 287. See also, *ibid.*, p. 308 where it is again asserted that the Messiah has not necessarily arrived.

53. *Ibid.*, p. 287.

54. *Ibid.*, p. 155.

55. *Ibid.*, p. 843.

56. *Ibid.*, p. 819.

57. *New Age*, January, 1950, "Report of the Committee on Publications, p. 27.

58. Francis St. Clair, *The Katapunan, Or The Rise And Fall Of The Filipino Commune*, Manila, 1902.

59. *New Age*, March, 1923, G. Fernandez, "A Masonic Legend," p. 134.

60. Mildred J. Headings, "French Freemasonry Under The Third Republic," *The Johns Hopkins University Studies In Historical And Political Science*, Baltimore, MD., Johns Hopkins Press, vol. LXVI, p. 34.

Miss Headings work is based "for the most part on the official minutes of the French Masonic councils and general assemblies; on Masonic periodicals; and on histories and monographs written by Masons. *Ibid.*, p. 8

61. *Ibid.*, p. 123.

62. *New Age*, June, 1932, "Allocution By The Grand Commander," p. 348.

63. The facts about Pike's statue are in James M. Goode's "The Outdoor Sculpture of Washington, D.C.", Washington, D.C., Smithsonian Institution Press, 1974, p. 228.

Pike was indicted for treason in the Circuit Court of the United States for the United States for the Eastern District of Arkansas, and an undated brief by Pike, in response to the indictment, is available in the Rare Book Room, Library of Congress.

After the Civil War, Pike was involved in a law suit regarding property of a person who had been involved in treason. See: *Pike v. Wassell*, 94 U.S. 711. Briefs on the case were not available in the Law Library of the Library of Congress.

Pike and a number of other Masons wrote to President Andrew Johnson several times to appeal for the General's pardon. The Presidential pardon was granted April 23, 1866.

Microfilm copies of the correspondence are available at the National Archives, Series M-1003: 10-33-9, reel 14, frames 02226-02266.

On the scalpings, see: *The War of Rebellion, A Compilation of the Official Records of the Union and Confederate Armies*, War Department, U.S. Government Printing Office, Washington, D.C., 1902, Series I, vol. 8, pp. 206-207; 795-97. The series will hereafter be referred to as *Rebellion Records*.

64. *Ibid.*, pp. 206-207. Letter from Major General Samuel R. Curtis, headquarters, Army of the Southwest, May 21, 1862 to Congressman B.F. Wade, chairman of the Committee on Conduct of the Present War.

65. *Ibid.*, p. 236.

66. *Ibid.*, p. 207.

67. *Ibid.*, pp. 795-796.

68. *The New York Times*, March 12, 1862, p. 4.

69. *New Age*, October, 1927, Charles S. Lobinger, "The Master Builder," p. 475.

70. *Rebellion Records*, seres IV, vol. 1, pp. 426-443, 513-527, 542-554, 669-687, 785.

On the Comanchees astonishment, see: Frank Moore, editor, *The Rebellion Record, A Diary of American Events*, New York, G. P. Putnam, vol. 3, 1862, p. 35.

71. *New Age*, January, 1980, Jesse W. Gern, "Albert Pike Memorial," p. 11.

72. *Ibid.*, March, 1980, Grand Commander's Message: "Albert Pike— The Monumental Man," p. 2.

73. C.S. Lippencott and E.R. Johnston, *Masonry Defined*, Memphis, TN., Masonic Supply Co., 1930, p. 233.

74. *Ibid.*, p. 238. That also is the reason Negroes have their own separate rite of Masonry, The Prince Hall Rite.

75. Albert Pike, *Lectures On The Arya*, Louisville, Ky., The Standard Printing Co., 1873, copyright 1930 by the Supreme Council, Washington, D.C., pp. 1, 2.

It is curious that Pike would so severely judge the Semitic race in view of praising Masonry's indebtedness to the Jewish Kabbalah which, although it had Chaldean origins, remained Semitic.

Further, Hiram, King of Tyre, (a Phoenician city) is a key figure in Masonic initiations. The Phoenicians gave the world the alphabet, without which we could not read Pike at all.

76. *Ibid.*, pp. 11-12.

77. *New Age*, February, 1928, pp. 175-176.

78. *Ibid.*, September, 1932, A Special Contributor, "Facts Relative To Masonry In Mexico," p. 540.

79. *Ibid.*, May, 1932, Grand Commander's Allocution, delivered at the 1931 Biennial Session of the Supreme Council, p. 288.

80. *Ibid.*, March, 1947, editorial, "Negroes and Freemasonry," p. 146.

81. *Ibid.*,

82. *Ibid.*

83. *The Washington Post*, November 26, 1976, p. B-15.

84. *The New York Times*, December 14, 1976, p. 39.

85. *The Washington Star*, August 5, 1979, p. A-8.

86. *Ibid.*

87. *The Washington Post*, May 7, 1983, p. A-1

88. *Ibid.*, January 8, 1986, p. A-7

89. *Ibid*, April 10, 1983, p. B-1.

90. *New Age*, January, 1932, G. Kenderdine, "The Idea of God In Masonry," p. 269.

91. Pike, *Morals and Dogma*, p. 644.

92. *Ibid.*

93. Joseph Fort Newton, *The Religion of Masonry, An Interpretation*, Richmond, VA., The McCoy Publishing and Supply Co., 1969, p. 3.

94. *Ibid.*, pp. 48-49.

95. *New Age*, June, 1948, George H. Steinmetz, "Why Do You Go To The Lodge?", p. 335.

96. *Ibid.*, April, 1945, John H. Boyd, "Faith," pp. 159-160.

97. Headings, *op. cit.*, p. 123.

98. *Ibid.*, pp. 125-129.

99. Lobinger, *op. cit.*, p. 776.

100. *Ibid.*, p. 777.

101. *Ibid.*

102. Lobinger, pp. 777, 771-772. Also see: *New England Craftsman*, June, 1921, "Americanism and Americanization" pp. 239, 241; *New Age*, July, 1922, "The Liberal Provision of the Towner-Sterling Bill," p. 411; *ibid.*, August, 1923, p. 487; *ibid.*, January, 1927, pp. 4, 28; *ibid.*, July, 1932, Maurice F. Lyons, "The Fourteenth Amendment To The Constitution, p. 410; *ibid.*, April, 1934, "Comment" section, where the *New Age* advocated the public school as the "only agency" capable of fusing various peoples, tongues and customs; and where it is noted that Masonry was the pioneer in advocating a federal Department of Education, pp. 197-198.

Interestingly, the March 1924 issue of the *New Age*, p. 140, reported that in a general essay competition among pupils of parochial and public schools in New York, students of the former schools received 165 of 277 medals (60 percent) which had been awarded in the competition.

103. Lobinger, p. 778.

104. Richard J. Gabel, *Public Funds For Church And Private Schools*,

doctoral dissertation Washington, D.C., The Catholic University of America, 1937, pp. 266-267.

105. *New Age,* September, 1930, A Special Contributor, "A Divisive Factor In Our National Life," p. 543.

106. *Ibid.,* December, 1934, "Comment Section," p. 710.

107. *Ibid.,* December, 1935, editorial, pp. 711-712.

108. *Ibid.,* November, 1948, Henry Ware Allen, "Religion In The Public Schools," p. 664.

109. *Ibid.,* January, 1949, p. 10.

110. *Ibid.,* September, 1958, editorial, p. 516.

In Genesis 2:16-17, God commanded Adam: "Of the tree of knowledge of good and evil, thou shalt not eat. For in what day soever thou shalt eat of it, thou shalt die the death."

In the following chapter of Genesis we learned that the serpent tempted Eve and said: "No, you will not die the death. For God knows on what day soever you shall eat thereof, your eyes shall be opened: and you shall be as gods, knowing good and evil. . . ."

111. *New Age,* March, 1959, Dr. James D. Carter, "Why Stand Ye Here Idle?", p. 155.

112. *Ibid.*

113. *Ibid.,* January, 1959, William A. Brandenburg, "More Than Ritual," pp. 23,26.

114. *Ibid.,* February, 1968, Leonard A. Wenz, "Masonry And The Bible," p. 17.

115. *Ibid.*

116. *Ibid.,* February, 1959, Frank C. Lorey, Jr., "The Evolution of American Education, pp. 112-113.

117. *Ibid.,* January, 1959, Grand Commander's Message: "Grass Roots Activities," pp. 3-4.

118. *Ibid.,* June, 1959, editorial, "Virginia School Libraries," p. 365.

119. *Ibid.,* February, 1965, Luther A. Smith, Grand Commander, "Encouraging Words," inside back cover page.

120. *Ibid.,* December, 1965, "Current Interest" section., p. 34.

121. *Ibid.,* June, 1966, "Current Interest" section, p. 34.

122. *Ibid.,* May 8, 1968, p. 3.

123. *New Age,* August, 1925, p. 506; *ibid.,* July, 1934, "Comment" section, p. 392; *ibid.,* February, 1956, editorial, "Scholarship Fund For Diplomatic Training," p. 98; *ibid.,* May, 1956, editorial, "Financial Aid For Students," p. 280; *ibid,* October, 1957, Dr. Cloyd H. Marvin, President of George Washington University, and a 33rd Degree Mason, "The Scottish Rite Fellowships and Their Significance," p. 587.

124. *Ibid.,* May, 1966, "Current Interest" section, pp. 36-37.

125. See Albert C. Stevens, *op. cit.,* pp. xv, ff.; *New Age,* November, 1965, pp. 13, 16.

Notes   Chapter 3

1. Anson Phelps Stokes, *Church And State In The United States*, 3 vols., New York, Harper and Bros., 1950, vol. 1, p. 833.

2. Stokes, vol. 1, p. 834.

3. Albert C. Stevens, *The Cyclopedia Of Fraternities*, 2nd ed., New York, E.B. Treat and Co., 1907, p. xv.

4. Stevens, p. xix.

5. *Ibid.*

6. *The Columbia Encyclopedia*, entry: "Quebec Act," p. 2256. The "Declaration" protested King George giving his assent "for abolishing the free system of English laws in a neighboring Province, establishing therein an arbitrary Government, and enlarging its boundaries, so as to render it at once an example and fit instrument for introducing the same absolute rule into these colonies." See: "The Declaration Of Independence and The Constitution Of The United States Of America," 92nd Congress, House Document No. 92-328, 1972 U.S. Government Printing Office, Washington, D.C., p. 3.

7. W. Woodhouse, *The Constitutions Of The United States According To The Latest Amendments: To Which Are Annexed The Declaration of Independence and the Federal Constitution, With Amendments Thereto*, printed by E. Oswald, Philadelphia, 1796.

8. Sister Marie Lenore Fell, *The Foundations Of Nativism In American Textbooks, 1783-1860*, doctorate dissertation, Washington, D.C., The Catholic University of America, 1941, pp. v, vi.

9. Fell, p. 224

10. *Ibid.*, pp. 11, 21, 33, 35, *passim.*

11. *Ibid.*, p. 39.

12. Fell, p. 39, quoting from Whelpy, pp. 72-73.

13. Fell, pp. 102-103, citing Eliza Robbins, *Tales From American History*, 1829, p. 13.

14. Fell, pp. 149-150.

15. Michael Williams, *The Shadow Of The Pope*, New York, Whittlesey House (McGraw-Hill Co.), 1932, p. 64.

16. Sister M. Evangeline Thomas, *Nativism In The Old Northwest*, doc-

torate dissertation, Washington, D.C., The Catholic University of America, 1936, p. 45

17. *Ibid.,* p. 501

18. Williams, p. 65.

19. Rev. Lyman Beecher, *A Plea For The West,* 2nd ed., Cincinnati, Truman and Smith, 1835, p. 12.

20. Beecher, p. 182

21. Quoted in Thomas, p. 53.

22. *Ibid.*

23. Cited in Thomas, p. 106, from the *Presbyterian Of The West,* November 8 and 15, 1838.

24. Carleton Beals, *Brass Knuckle Crusade,* New York, Hastings House, 1960, pp. 45-57.

25. *Ibid.,* p. 63.

26. *Ibid.,* p. 441

27. See; William O. Bourne, *History of the Public School Society of the City of New York,* 1870, pp. 7, 31, 45.

See also: Arthur Jackson Hall, *Religious Education In The Public Schools of the State and City of New York,* doctorate dissertation, Chicago, Ill., University of Chicago Press, 1914, pp. 21, 39.

28. Bourne, p. 45.

29. Hall, pp. 50, 61-62.

30. Ray Allen Billington, *The Protestant Crusade,* New York, Macmillan and Co., 1938, p. 144.

See also: Stokes, vol, 1, p. 827, where almost identical views are expressed.

Neither man was Catholic. Stokes was Canon of the Washington Episcopal Cathedral, Washington, D.C.

31. Billington, p. 147.

32. Billington, pp. 153-155.

33. *Ibid.,* p. 157

34. The Catholic Church has always revered, taught and propagated the Sacred Scriptures. Virtually every Church liturgical ceremony, document, or other pronouncement pertaining to the Faith, is based on the Old and New Testaments.

The Council of Trent (1545-1563) reaffirmed the listing of the canonical books of the Bible given by the Council of Florence (1438-1445)—a listing that agrees exactly with the list given as early as the year 382 in the Council of Rome under St. Damasus I. See: John F. Clakson, S.J., et. al., *The Church Teaches, Documents of the Church in English Translation,* Rockford, Ill., Tan Books and Publishers, Inc., 1973, p. 44.

Vatican Council II (1963-1965) reaffirmed this consistent teaching of the Church in its document *Dei Verbum, Dogmatic Constitution on Divine Revelation.*

Thus, the Catholic Church has adhered to and taught the Scriptures, both Old and New Testament, centuries before Protestant Churches were founded, and nearly 1500 years before America was discovered. Indeed, it was the Catholic Church that determined which books of the Bible are inspired.

35. Billington, p. 156.

36. *Ibid.*, pp. 165-166, 173.

37. *Ibid.*, p. 183.

38. Billington, p. 229; Williams, p. 75. *The New York Times*, June 15, 1894, p. 9.

39. Peter Condon, "Freedom of Religion and the Revival of Religious Tolerance," *History Records and Studies*, Philadelphia, American Catholic Historical Society, vol. 4, October, 1906, p. 214.

40. Stokes, vol. 1, p. 833.

41. Condon, p. 214.

42. Stokes, vol. 1, p. 835; Williams, p. 82.

43. Williams, pp. 84-85.

44. *The New York Daily Times*, July 8, 1854, p. 1

45. *Ibid.*, July 11, 1854, p. 1.

46. *Ibid.*, July 15, 1854, p. 1.

47. Gabel, *op. cit.*, p. 291.

Also, Robert H. Lord, John E. Sexton, and Edward T. Harrington, *History Of The Archdiocese of Boston*, New York, Sheed and Ward, 1944, vol. 2, pp. 592-593.

48. Williams, p. 89.

49. *The New York Daily Times*, November 7, 1854, p. 4; November 10, p. 1.

Barker was founder of the notorious anti-Catholic Know-Nothing organization, the Order of the Star Spangled Banner. See: *Who Was Who In America, 1607-1896*, revised, ed., A.N. Marquis Co., New York, 1967, p. 108.

50. *The New York Daily Times*, editorial, November 9, 1854, p. 4.

51. *Ibid.*

52. *Ibid.*, November 14, p. 1.

53. *Ibid.*, June 9, 1855, p. 3.

54. *Ibid.*, June 18, 1855, p. 1.

55. Charles S. Lobinger, *op. cit.*, pp. 209-210.

Commenting on Pike's concern for the threat of the "foreign" vote, Lobinger said: "Surely in its attitude on this great question, the Supreme Council of today is following in the footsteps of its acknowledged leader."

56. Stokes, vol. 1, p. 823.

57. *The New York Daily Times*, June 14, 1856, p. 3.

58. *Ibid.*, June 16, 1856, p. 3.

59. Charles H. Pullen, *Miss Columbia's Public School*, New York, Francis B. Felt and Co., 1871, pp. 25, 39.

Similar books were: Stephen F. Blackwell's *Garfield Or The Pope* (1880);

Justin D. Fulton's *Washington In The Lap Of Rome* (1888); and also by the latter author: *Why Priests Should Wed; The Way Out, Or The Escape Of A Nun;* and his *Woman In The Toils Of Rome.*

60. Lord, et. al., vol. 3, p. 65.

61. *Ibid.*

62. Stokes, vol. 2, p. 68.

63. *Ibid.*

64. See: Francis Newton Thorpe, *The Federal And State Constitutions . . .* 7 vols., Washington, D.C., 1909, U.S. Government Printing Office.

The 1802 Constitution of Ohio is of particular interest, in view of the fact that the Catholic Church was so bitterly opposed in that State.

Article VIII, Sec. 26 provided that "laws shall be passed by the legislature which shall secure to each and every denomination of religious societies in each surveyed township . . . an equal participation, according to their number of adherents, of the profits arising from the land granted by Congress for the support of religions . . ." Thorpe, vol. 5, p. 2912.

A similar provision was in the Constitution of 1851 (Article I, Sec. 7).

Also, Article VI, Sec. 2 of that same Constitution stipulated that "no religious or other sect, or sects, shall ever have any *exclusive* right to, or control of, any part of the school funds of this state." [Emphasis added]. Thorpe, vol. 5, p. 2913.

Those provisions are of interest because they evidence (a) that after the religion clause of the First Amendment was ratified, early Congresses provided funds for the advancement of the Christian religion; and (b) that the general view at the time was that no single sect or group of sects should have "exclusive" right to or control over religious education funds.

65. *The New York Times,* January 14, 1884, p. 4

66. *Ibid.,* April 19, 1984, p. 1.

67. *The Catholic Citizen,* Milwaukee, Wisconsin, April 26, 1884, p. 1.

68. Encyclical Letter, *Humanum Genus,* by Pope Leo XIII, April 20 1884, published in *The Church Speaks To the Modern World,* Etienne Gilson, editor, Garden City, New York, Image Books, 1954, October, 1961, edition, sections 1 and 2, p. 117.

69. *Ibid.,* secs. 4, 5, p. 118.

70. *Ibid.,* sec. 6, pp. 118-119.

71. *Ibid.,* secs. 6, 7, p. 119.

72. *Ibid.,* sec. 9, p. 121.

73. *Ibid.,* sec. 10, p. 122.

74. *Ibid.,* sec. 12, p. 123.

75. *Ibid.,* sec. 13, p. 123.

76. *Ibid.,* sec. 21, p. 128

77. *Ibid.,* sec. 27, p. 131.

78. *Ibid.,* sec. 28, p. 131.

79. Donald L. Kinzer, *An Episode In Anti-Catholicism*, Seattle, University of Washington Press, 1964, pp. 35, 40-41.

80. *Ibid.*, p. 54.

81. *Ibid.*, p. 45, APA Principles numbers 3 and 4.

82. See notes 75, 76, above.

83. Kinzer, p. 49.

84. Washington Gladden, "The Anti-Catholic Crusade," *Century Magazine*, March, 1894, p. 792.

85. *Ibid.*, p. 791.

86. *Ibid.*

87. *Ibid.*

88. *The New York Times*, June 21, 1894, p. 9.

89. *Ibid.*

90. *Ibid.*, June 22, 1894, p. 9.

91. Kinzer, p. 56.

92. *The New York Times* June 9, 1894, p. 8.

On June 11, 1894, the League was viewed with favor by the *Times*, p. 5.

93. Kinzer, pp. 74, 75.

94. The *Congressional Record* (House), June 14, 1894, pp. 6311, 6312.

95. Gabel, p. 525.

96. The *Tribune* commentary appeared on December 25 and 20, respectively, and can be found in the *Congressional Record*, January 16, 1889, p. 871.

97. See: *Reuben Quick Bear v. Leupp*, 210 U.S. 50 at 78.

Kinzer, p. 78.

Gabel, p. 508, cites a circular published by the U.S. Office of Indian Affairs, titled "Indian Schools and Education," which observed that Indian eduction was under religious auspices from 1568 until 1880.

Sen Richard F. Pettigrew noted that the federal government invited religious organizations to build schools for Indian children beginning in 1870. *Congressional Record*, April 21, 1896, p. 4208.

98. Gabel, p. 526.

99. Kinzer, pp. 47-79.

See also: *Congressional Record* (House), June 14, 1894, p. 6311 where the League's petition appears, stating that its efforts to prohibit such appropriations began with the first session of the 51st Congress (which convened March 4, 1889).

100. Kinzer, p. 92.

101. APA membership in various States is set forth in Kinzer, Table 1, p. 178.

Von Fossen's Masonic background is listed in *ibid.*, p. 109.

102. *The New York Times* June 7, 1894, p. 8.

103. *Congressional Record*, June 7, 1894, pp. 5928, 5932.

Rep. Linton's Masonic membership is cited in Kinzer, p. 60.

104. *Congressional Record,* June 8, 1894, pp. 5997, 60095.

105. *Ibid.,* June 14, 1894, pp. 6310-6311.

106. James M. King, *Facing The Twentieth Century,* New York, American Union League Society, 1899, pp. 224-225.

107. *Ibid.,* p. 580.

108. *Ibid.,* p. 583.

109. *Ibid.,* p. 588.

110. *Congressional Record* (House) February 4, 1896, pp. 1308-1309.

111. *Ibid.,* p. 1309.

112. *Ibid.,* pp. 1340-1341.

Subsequently, the entire bill was defeated by a vote of 134-144. *Ibid.,* pp. 1341-1342.

113. *Congressional Record* (Senate), April 21, 1896, p. 21.

114. *Ibid.* (House), March 15, 1895, p. 2080.

115. Kinzer, pp. 202-203.

116. *Ibid.,*

117. See, for example, the Act Making Appropriations for the Indian Department, and for Fulfilling Treaty Stipulations, June 7, 1897, 30 Statutes-At-Large 62.

See also, entry on "Sectarian" and "Sectarian Institutions" in the legal reference, *Words and Phrases,* Permanent Edition, 1658 to Date, vol. 38-A, St. Paul, Minn., The West Publishing Co, 1967, pp. 109-110, 111.

118. John Tracy Ellis, *The Life of James Cardinal Gibbons* (People's Edition), edited by Francis L. Broderick, Milwaukee, The Bruce Publishing Co., 1963, pp. 133-134.

119. *Ibid.*

120. Leo XIII, Letter to Cardinal Gibbons, *Testem Benevolentiae,* January 31, 1899, in *The Catholic World,* New York, April, 1899, p. 133-134, 135.

The "Americanism" which concerned Leo at the beginning of 20th Century blossomed into fullness in the States following Vatican Council II in the 1960s.

Notes   Chapter 4

1. *The New York Times*, June 1, 1909,p. 9.
2. *Ibid.*, October 13, 1911, p. 8; February 7, 1912, p. 6.
3. *Ibid.*, April 8, 1916, p. 11; November 30, 1916, p. 6.
4. *Ibid.*
5. *Ibid.*, March 1, 1920, p. 9; March 2, 1920, p. 10.
6. *Ibid.*, January 20, 1919, p. 8; February 6, 1919, p. 24. See also Kahn's reiteration of his views in his article, "Why Most American Jews Do Not Favor Zionism," *ibid.*, February 16, 1919 Sec. 7, *The New York Times Magazine*, p. 7.
7. *The New York Times*, February 13, 1919, p. 1.
8. *Ibid.*, February 15, 1919, p. 16.
9. *Ibid.*, September 25, 1919, p. 10.
10. *Ibid.*, September 26, 1919, p. 12.
11. *Ibid.*, November 20, 1920, p. 16.
12. See *ibid.*, October 11, 1920, p. 16; October 13, p. 2; November 3, p. 11; November 12, p. 5; December 1, p. 14; and December 14, p. 6.
13. *The New York Times*, editorial, "The Assailants of the Jews," December 1, 1920, p. 14.
14. *Ibid.*
15. *Ibid.*, December 1, 1920, p. 19.
16. *Ibid.*, February 25, 1921, p. 11, quoting from an article by Isaac Landman in *The American Hebrew*, February 25, 1921.
17. *The Times* (London), May 8, 1920, p. 8.
18. *Ibid.*, "Jewish World Plot. An Exposure. the Source Of The Protocols. Truth At Last," August 16, 1921, p. 9.
19. *Ibid.*, August 17, 1921, p. 9.
20. *The World* (New York), September 16, 1921, p. 2, quoting from *The Searchlight*, July 30, 1921.
21. *The World*, September 6, 1921, p. 1.
22. *Ibid.*, September 14, 1921, pp. 1, 2.
23. *Ibid.*, p. 2
24. *Ibid.*
25. *Ibid.*, September 18, 1921, p. 2.
26. *Ibid.*, September 15, 1921, p. 1.

27. *Ibid.*, September 17, 1921, pp. 1-2.

28. U.S. Congress, House of Representatives, Committee on Rules, 67th Congress, *Hearings on the Ku Klux Klan,* October 12, 1921, published as *Mass Violence In America,* New York, The Arno Press and The New York Times, 1969, pp. 37, 23.

The quotation concerning Evans' Masonic activity appears in The *Fortnightly Review,* October 1, 1925, p. 401.

Israel Zangwell's statement is attributed to Rev. Ed. Albrecht of Milwaukee, Wisconsin, and appears in Theodore C. Graebner's *A Handbook Of Organizations,* St. Louis, Missouri, Concordia Publishing House, 1924, p. 192.

29. U.S. House Rules *Hearings,* pp. 19, 72.

30. Charles P. Sweeney, "The Great Bigotry Merger," *The Nation,* July 5, 1923, p. 10.

31. *Ibid.*

32. U.S House Rules *Hearings,* p. 75.

33. David M. Chalmers, *Hooded Americanism, The First Century of the Ku Klux Klan,* Garden City, New York, Doubleday and Co., 1965, p. 149 (on Minneapolis); p. 191 (on Wisconsin); and p. 254 (on New York).

34. Lem A. Dever, *Masks Off!—Confession of An Imperial Klansman,* 2nd revised ed., published by author, 1925, pp. 39, 51.

35. *New Age,* January 4, 1924, p. 43.

36. *Ibid.*, John Jay Chapman, "Strike At The Source," p. 214.

37. *New Age,* May, 1926, p. 306.

38. *The New York Times,* February 21, 1926, "The Klan's Invisible Empire Fading," section 8, p. 1.

39. The five incident cited are found in Sweeney, *op. cit.*, pp. 8, 9.

40. House Rules Committee *Hearings,* p. 73.

41. See *The New York Times,* October 8, 1921, p. 4; and *ibid.*, October 18, 1921, p. 6.

42. *Ibid.*, May 16, 1922, p. 14; May 21, 1922, p. 14.

43. Lowell Mellett, "Klan And Church," *Atlantic Monthly,* November, 1923, p. 586.

44. *Ibid.*, p. 588.

45. *Ibid.*, pp. 589, 588.

46. *Ibid.*, p. 588.

47. *Ibid.*, p. 591.

48. *Ibid.*

49. *Ibid.*, pp. 591-592.

50. "A Citizen From Oklahoma," (letter), *Atlantic Monthly,* November, 1923, p. 720.

51. *The Nation,* untitled editorial, August 19, 1925, p. 199.

52. *The Sunday Star* (Washington, D.C.), August 9, 1925, p. 1.

53. *Ibid.*, p. 2

54. *Ibid.*

55. *The Evening Star* (Washington, D.C.), August 10, p. 6.

56. William R. Pattangall, "Is the Ku Klux Klan Un-American, *Forum,* September, 1925,p. 321.

57. *Ibid.,* p. 325.

58. *Ibid.,* p. 327.

59. Hiram W. Evans, "the Klan: Defender Of Americanism," *Forum,* November, 1925, pp. 799, 811.

60. "The Klan's Invisible Empire Is Fading," no author cited, *The New York Times,* February 21, 1926, Sec. 8, p. 1.

61. *Ibid.*

62. *Ibid.*

63. *The New York Times* November 20, 1928. See also: *New York, ex rel., Bryant v. Zimmerman,* 278 U.S. 63 (1928).

Notes   Chapter 5

1. *The New York Times,* September 17, 1937, p. 12.

It is of interest to note that, in 1917, Tate had objected to Black serving as Chief Prosecuting Attorney for the Circuit Court in Birmingham, Alabama. See the *Birmingham Age-Herald,* January 23, 1917, p. 10. Subsequently, the Alabama Supreme Court ruled that both Black and Tate were co-Prosecuting Attorneys. *Ibid.,* February 16, 1917, p. 10.

2. *Birmingham Age-Herald,* December 12, 1916, p. 10. The date Black embarked upon his legal career in Birmingham may be found in the *Micropedia,* Chicago, Encyclopedia Britannica, Inc., 1981, vol. 2, p. 251, entry on Black.

3. Charles P. Sweeney, "Bigotry In The South," *The Nation,* November 24, 1920, p. 585.

4. *Ibid.*

5. *Ibid.*

6. *Birmingham Age-Herald,* August 11, 1921, p. 1.

7. *Ibid.,* August 12, 1921, p. 1.

8. *Ibid.*

9. *Ibid.*

10. *Ibid.*

11. *Ibid.,* August 13, 1921, p. 5; August 14, p. 5.

12. *Ibid.,* August 14, p. 5.

13. *Ibid.*

14. *Ibid.,* p. 1.

15. *Age-Herald,* August 17, 1921, p. 5.

16. *The Papers of Justice Hugo L. Black,* Box 511, "Miscellany," Legal Papers, Alabama v. Stephenson." *Transcript of Trial, Official Report,* August 23, 1921, p. 8.

17. *Ibid.,* pp. 30-31.

18. *Ibid.,* pp. 136-137.

19. *Ibid.,* pp. 37, 34-35, 49.

20. *Ibid.,* pp. 49, 3.

21. *Ibid.,* pp. 145-146. Also see *Birmingham Age-Herald,* August 25, 1921, p. 1.

22. *Age-Herald,* August 28, 1921, p. 4.

23. *Ibid.*, October 18, 1921, p. 1.

24. *Pittsburgh Post-Gazette*, September 29, 1937, p. 1.

25. *Ibid.*

26. *Ibid.*

27. *Age-Herald*, October 22, 1921, p. 2.

28. *Pittsburgh Post-Gazette*, September 29, 1937, p. 1.

29. *Birmingham Age-Herald*, October 22, 1921, p. 6.

30. *Ibid.*, p. 5.

31. Virginia Van Der Veer Hamilton, *Hugo Black, The Alabama Years*, Baton Rouge, Louisiana, Louisiana State Press, 1972, pp. 92-93.

32. *Ibid.*, p. 93.

33. *Ibid.*, pp. 112-113.

34. Black's *Papers*, Box 28, "General Correspondence," Letter by Black addressed "To Whom It May Concern," recommending William E. Fort, Jr., who was seeking a fellowship. The letter noted that Fort's father had resigned his judgship to become Black's law partner.

Ibid., letter from Fort, Sr. to Black, May 21, 1933.

35. *The New York Times*, September 22, 1937, p. 1.

The *Times* article also mentioned Black's law partnership with Fort, and the fact that Fort was a special assistant to the Attorney General of the United States in 1937.

36. *Pittsburgh Post Gazette*, September 29, 1937, p. 1.

37. *The New York Times*, September 13, 1937, p. 3.

38. *Ibid.*

39. *Ibid.*, August 9, 1926, pp. 2,4.

40. *Ibid.*, January 20, 1928, p. 1.

41. Black's *Papers*, Box 72, Senatorial File, Campaign Materials, Presidential Campaign, 1928-Correspondence.

42. *Ibid.*

43. *Ibid.* Senator Swanson's letter is dated September 15, 1928.

44. *The New York Times*, October 7, 1928, Section III, p. 2.

45. Virginia Van Der Veer Hamilton, p. 157.

46. *The New York Times*, September 14, 1937, p. 18.

47. *Congressional Record*, 70th Congress, 2nd Session, Senate Proceedings, February 5, 1929, pp. 2848-2853.

48. *The New York Times*, December 28, 1929, p. 9.

49. *Ibid.*, March 7, 1936, p. 1. The word "subterfuge" is in the *Times* article.

50. The words "vague" and "a dragnet" were attributed to unidentified Senators by the *Times*.

51. *Ibid.*, March 12, 1936, p. 6.

52. *Ibid.*, March 12, 1936, p. 1.

53. *Ibid.*, March 28, 1936, p. 1.

54. *Ibid.*, April 7, 1936, pp. 1, 16-17.

55. *Ibid.*, February 24, 1937, p. 2.

56. *Ibid.*, September 27, 1937, p. 5, where the McReynolds statement is noted. The reference to Roosevelt's "unusual secrecy" may be found in *The Evening Star* (Washington, D.C.), August 12, 1937, p. 1.

57. *The Evening Star*, August 12, 1937, p. 1.

58. *The New York Times*, August 13, 1937, p. 4.

59. See *The Evening Star*, August 12, 1937, p. 1 on the views of Senators Borah and Austin. The same periodical carried an editorial on August 14, 1937, p. A-6, regarding the issue of Black's constitutional ineligibility to sit on the high bench.

Black's Constitutional infirmity to succeed to the high bench under similar circumstances was not unprecedented. However, in earlier instances of such conflict the Constitutional proscription was legally resolved.

For example, in 1889, the Attorney General at the time ruled that a Senator appointed Minister to Mexico could not serve in that post because the emoluments of the Minister had been increased after the Senator's term in Congress began.

Also, President-elect William Howard Taft selected Senator Philander Knox of Pennsylvania to be Secretary of State. But it was discovered that the emoluments of the Secretary's position had been increased when Knox was a Senator. The Senator was qualified when Congress reduced the emoluments to what they previously had been. See: Thomas J. Norton, *The Constitution of the United States—Its Sources And Its Applications*, New York, Committee for Constitutional Government, Inc., 1971, pp. 32-33.

60. The fact that Cummings never investigated Black's background was noted in the *Pittsburgh Post-Gazette*, September 13, 1937, p. 2.

It also is of interest that a man named Walter S. Brower was a special assistant to Cummings. Brower's name appeared on a list of members of the Ku Klux Klan, which included the name of Hugo L. Black. See: *The New York Times*, October 2, 1937.

See also note 35, *supra*, where it is noted that the judge who presided at the 1921 Birmingham trial when Black successfully defended the murderer of Fr. James E. Coyle, and who later became Black's law partner, served in the Attorney General's office when the decision was made not to investigate Black's background as a prelude to the Alabama Senator's nomination to the Supreme Court.

61. *The Evening Star*, August 16, 1937, p. 1; *ibid.*, August 7, 1937, p. 1.

62. *Ibid.*, August 18, 1937, p. 1.

63. *The Evening Star*, August 20, 1937, p. 1.

64. *The New York Times*, September 13, 1937, p. 3.

65. *Ibid.*

66. *Pittsburgh Post-Gazette*, article by Ray Sprigle, September 13, 1937, p. 1.

67. Virginia Van Der Veer Hamilton, *op. cit.*, pp. 136-137.

68. *Post-Gazette,* September 14, 1937, p. 1.

69. *Ibid.,* September 16, 1937, p. 2; September 18, 1937, p. 2.

70. *The New York Times,* September 13, 1937, p. 3.

71. *The Nation,* October 2, 1937, editorial: "The Education of Hugo Black," p. 337.

See also: *ibid,* October 9, 1937, Max Lerner's article, "Hugo Black—A Personal History," for a similar encomium of the new Supreme Court Justice, pp. 367-369.

72. *The New York Times,* September 25, 1937, p. 16.

73. *Ibid.,* October 1, 1937, p. 20. The identical editorial appeared in the *Times* two days later. See *ibid.,* October 3, Sec. IV, p. 8.

74. *Ibid.,* October 2, 1937, p. 1.

75. *Ibid.*

76. Quoted in *ibid,* October 2, 1937, p. 7.

77. *Ibid.*

78. *Ibid.*

79. *Ibid.,* October 3, 1937, p. 2.

80. *Ibid.*

Other editorials negative toward Black's broadcast appeared in the *Chicago Tribune, Boston Transcript,* and the *St. Louis Post Dispatch.*

81. *The New York Times,* October 23, 1937, p. 16.

82. Hugo L. Black, Jr., *My Father, A Remembrance,* New York, Random House, 1975, p. 13.

83. *Ibid.,* p. 104.

Paul Blanshard was a notorious anti-Catholic writer whose screeds were particularly popular in the years immediately following World War II.

84. *Ibid.,* p. 176.

85. *Ibid.,* p. 182.

86. *Ibid.,* p. 172.

87. Black's *Papers,* Box 63, "General Correspondence. Letter from Law Professor Julius Paul of the State University of Fredonia, New York, dated January 10, 1972, to John F. Davies, clerk of the U.S. Supreme Court. Professor Paul noted in the press that 600 volumes of Justice Black's notes had been destroyed, and he inquired whether it was a tradition of the Court to destroy bench notes and other material that might contain comments of judicial conferences.

There was no indication in Black's *Papers* that a reply was made to the professor.

88. Hugo L. Black, Jr., *op. cit.,* p. 255; 250-251.

89. Black's *Papers,* Box 63.

No record was located which showed the papers had been destroyed, nor was there any record which indicated which specific papers were to be burned.

90. *In re Murchison,* 346 U.S. 136, 138 (1954).

Notes   Chapter 6

1. See p. 121, *supra*.
2. *Bradfield v. Roberts,* 175 U.S. 291 (1899), at p. 269.
3. *Meyer v. Nebraska,* 262 U.S. 410 (1923).
4. *Pierce v. Society of Sisters,* 268 U.S. 510 (1925).
5. *Cochran v. Louisiana Board of Education* 281 U.S. 370 (1930).
6. *Church of the Holy Trinity v. U.S.,* 143 U.S. 457 (1892) at pp 465-466.
7. *Ibid.,* p. 466-467.
8. Francis N. Thorpe, *The Federal and State Constitutions . . . ,* Washington, D.C., U.S. Government Printing Office, 1909, vol. 4, p. 2471.
9. *Ibid.,* vol. 3, pp. 1889, 1908-1909.
10. *Ibid.,* vol. 5, p. 2597; vol 1, p. 568; vol. 3, pp. 1689-1690; and vol. 5, p. 2793.
11. *Ibid.,* vol. 5, p. 3100.
12. Jonathan Elliott, *The Debates In The Several State Conventions On The Adoption Of The Federal Constitution,* 5 vols., Philadelphia, J.B. Lippencott, Co., 1896, vol. 3, p. 659.
13. *Ibid.,* vol. 1, p. 328.
14. *Ibid.,* vol. 1, p. 326.
15. *Ibid.,* vol. 1, p. 334; vol. 4, p. 244.
16. *Ibid.,* vol. 2, p. 353.
17. *The Debates And Proceedings In The Congress Of The United States,* Washington, D.C., Gales and Seton, Publishers, vol. 1, pp. 433-434. Hereafter this work will be cited as *Annals of Congress, or Annals.*
18. *Annals,* p. 729.
19. *Ibid.,* pp. 729-730.
20. *Annals,* p. 730.
21. *Ibid.,* p. 730-731.
22. *Ibid.,*   p. 756.
23. *Ibid.,* p. 766.
24. Chester J. Antieu, Arthur T. Downey and Edward C. Roberts, *Freedom From Federal Establishment,* Milwaukee, The Bruce Publishing Co., 1964, p. 130.
25. *Ibid.,* pp. 130-131.

26. *The Declaration Of Independence And The Constitution Of The United States Of America,* 92nd Congress, 2d Session, House Document No. 92-328, Washington, D.C., U.S. Government Printing Office, 1972, p. 22.

27. Charles C. Tansill, editor, *Documents Illustrative Of The Formation Of The Union Of The American States,* Washington, D.C., U.S. Government Printing Office, House Document No. 398, 1965, p. 52.

28. Rep. William McCullough, *Congressional Record,* House, April 1, 1968, p. 2372.

29. *Annals,* House, May 12, 1796, p. 1349.

30. *Ibid.,* May 17, 1796, p. 1385. See also Senate Proceedings in *Ibid,* p. 113.

31. *Ibid.,* April 7, 1798,

32. See *Congressional Record,* House, April 1, 1968, pp. H-2372-2373. *Ibid.,* Senate, April 30, 19687, p. S-4676. Also see Public Law 90-304, 1968.

33. Gabel, *op. cit.,* p. 302.

34. *Quick Bear v. Leupp,* 210 U.S. 50 (1908), at p. 78. The sentence with the word "for" appearing three times is recorded as it appears in the citation.

35. *Report* of the Committee of the Senate, 32nd Congress, 2nd Session, 1852-1853; Senate Report No. 376, January 19, 1853, p. 1. The *Report* is cited in Franklin, *et. al.,* "Appellee Brief," *McCollum* case, pp., 63-64.

36. Gabel, p. 532.

37. U.S. Congress, Senate, 79th Congress, 1st Session, *Hearings on Federal Aid To Education, S. 181 and S. 717,* testimony of Selma M. Borchard, Vice President, American Federation of Teachers, A.F.L., April 25, 1945, pp. 735, 737.

38. Each year, on or near Washington's Birthday, the First President's Farewell Address is read on the floor of Congress. See, for example, *Congressional Record,* February 20, 1984, pp. S1353-1358.

39. See *Inaugural Addresses Of The Presidents Of The United States,* Washington, D.C., U.S. G.P.O., 1961, pp. 11, 84, 116, and 126.

40. Memorandum to author (as Legislative Assistant to the late Congressman James J. Delaney (D., N.Y.), from the Congressional Research Service, February 14, 1968.

41. *A Compilation Of The Messages And Papers Of The Presidents, 1789-1897,* Washington, D.C. U.S. G.P.O., 1896, vol. 1, p. 504.

42. *Ibid.* Note his reference to what often is called the "Golden Rule" [Matthew 7:12], and to his use of "our holy religion."

43. *Terret v. Taylor,* 9 Cranch 43 (1815) at p. 49.

44. Joseph Story, *Commentaries On The Constitution Of The United States,* Boston, Little Brown and Co., vol. 2, 1865, section 1871, p. 722. The first edition of the *Commentaries* was written in 1833 while Justice Story was a member of the U.S. Supreme Court.

45. *Ibid.*, Sections. 1865, 1868, 1871, pp. 726-728.

46. *Vidal v. Girard's Executors,* 2 Howard, 127, at pp. 198, 200, 201.

47. *Mormon Church v. United States,* 136 U.S. (1889), at p. 49.

48. *United States v. Macintosh,* 283 U.S. 605 (1931), at p. 625

49. *New Age,* October, 1933, Harry E. Grant, "Law," p. 619.

50. Robert H. Jackson, *The Struggle For Judicial Supremacy,"* New York, Alfred A. Knopf, 1941, p. 178.

51. *Ibid.,* p. 180.

52. *Ibid.,* p. xiv.

53. Statements of Scottish Rite opposition to public transportation of children to parochial schools (and other government aid to children attending such institutions), appeared in the *New Age* May, 1935, p. 255; November, 1935, p. 647; March, 1939, p. 133; November, 1939, pp. 655-656; April, 1940, pp. 196, 200; June, 1941, p. 330; October, 1941, pp. 581-582; January, 1942, pp. 15-16; January, 1943, pp. 5, 14; February, 1943, pp. 69-70; April, 1945, p. 146 November, 1946, p. 647; and December, 1946, pp. 710-711.

54. *New Age* commentary opposing religion in school, including prayer and Bible reading, appeared in April, 1940, pp. 225-226; November, 1942, pp. 655-656; November, 1943, pp. 655-656; December, 1943, pp. 593-594; November, 1944, pp. 457, 459-460, 467-468; January, 1945, pp. 5-7; January, 1946, p. 27; May, 1946, p. 262; and January, 1948, p. 8.

Opposition to released time religious instruction of children in public schools, appeared in the same publication in February, 1941, p. 71; June, 1941, pp. 328, 331; July, 1941, p. 390; October, 1941, p. 584; February, 1942, pp. 70-71; September, 1942, p. 526; October, 1942, p. 533; July, 1943, p. 332; December, 1943, pp. 593-594; May, 1944, pp. 198-199; October, 1944, pp. 390-391, 393-394; November, 1944, pp. 456-457; January, 1945, pp. 10-11; October, 1945, p. 389; January, 1946, pp. 256-267; August, 1946, p. 457; and December, 1946, p. 716.

55. See *New Age,* November, 1935, "Comment" section, p. 647. *Ibid.,* editorial comment, "Worth Remembering," pp. 648-649.

56. U.S. Congress, House of Representatives, Committee on Education, *Hearings,* April 6, 1937, Washington, D.C. U.S. G.P.O., pp. 267-269.

57. *Ibid.*

58. *New Age,* April, 1940, editorial, "Strange Times Have Come," p. 200.

59. See p. 128, *supra.*

60. Journal of the Virginia Senate, 1789, pp. 61-64. See also *The Daily Advertiser,* New York, N.Y., June 26, 1790.

The quotation and references are listed in "Appellees Brief" by John L. Franklin, *et. al.,* counsel for the Board of Education and Mr and Mrs. Basch, in the case of *McCollum v. Board of Education,* p. 50, filed in the U.S. Supreme Court, November 17, 1947.

61. In his Inaugural Address on March 4, 1881, President Garfield said:

"The Mormon Church not only offends the moral sense of mankind by sanctioning polygamy, but prevents the administration of justice through ordinary instrumentalities of law.

"In my judgment it is the duty of Congress, while respecting to the uttermost the conscientious convictions and religious scruples of every citizen, to prohibit within its jurisdiction all criminal practices, especially of that class which destroy the family relations and endanger social order. Nor can any ecclesiastical organization be safely permitted to usurp in the smallest degree the functions and powers of the National Government." See: *Inaugural Addresses,* p. 146.

On March 4, 1885, President Grover Cleveland, in his Inaugural Address, said: "The conscience of the people demands . . . that polygamy in the Territories destructive of the family relation and offensive to the moral sense of the civilized world, shall be repressed." *Ibid.,* p. 152.

62. *Reynolds v. United States,* 98 U.S. 145 (1878), at pp. 163, 164.

63. *Ibid.,* pp. 164, 165.

64. *Davis v. Beason,* 133 U.S. 333 (1890), at p. 341.

65. *Ibid.,* pp. 342-343.

66. *Watson v. Jones,* 13 Wall. 679 (1871) at 729.

67. *Ibid.,* p. 728.

68. See *supra,* pp. 133, 124-5, 132-3.

Notes Chapter 7

1. *New Age,* March, 1939, editorial, "New Education Bill," p. 133. See also: *ibid.,* November, 1939, a Scottish Rite policy statement views aid to parochial schools as "menacing", p. 656; and *ibid,* April, 1940, an editorial, "Aid For Parochial Schools," against aid to church schools, p. 196.

2. *Ibid.,* April, 1940, editorial, "Strange Times Have Come," p. 200.

3. See: *U.S. Statutes At Large,* 78th Congress, 2nd Session, volume 58 [1944], Part 1, Sec. 301(4), "List of approved institutions," which authorized the Administrator of Veterans Affairs to recognize and approve educational institutions not approved by the various States, p. 289

4. See: U.S. Congress, Senate, 78th Congress, 1st Session, Committee on Education and Labor, *Hearings on S.1295, S.1509, The Servicemen's Education and Training Act of 1944,* December 13-15, 1943. See also: U.S. Congress, House, 78th Congress, 2nd Session, Committee on World War Veterans, *Hearings on H.R. 3917 and S. 1767,* Jan. 11-13, 17-18; February 24; March 9-10, 27-31, 1944.

5. See *Congressional Record,* 78th Congress, 2nd Session, March 13-May 17, 1944, pp. 2490-2493; 3075-3087; 4320-4367; 4434-4461; 4502-4523; 4607-4628; 4635-4678.

6. *Ibid.,* May 12, 1944, p. 4517.

7. *Ibid.,* March 13, 1944, p. 3087.

8. *Ibid.,* May 11, 1944, p. 4342.

9. *Ibid.,* pp. 4434-4435.

10. *Ibid.,* May 12, p. 4441.

11. *Ibid.,* May 12, p. 4446.

12. *Ibid.,* May 15, pp. 4504-4505

13. *Ibid.,* March 13, 1944, p. 2491; March 24, 1944, p. 3081.

14. *Ibid.,* May 17, 1944, pp. 4677-4678.

15. The Catholic population of the United States in relation to the general population, as of December 31, 1944, may be found in *The Official Catholic Directory,* P. J. Kennedy and Sons, pubiishers, New York, "General Summary", p. 2, which is an insert following p. 1277.

Also see: *The National Catholic Almanac For 1953,* published by St. Anthony's Guild, Paterson, N.J., 1953, "United States Catholic War Records," under section headed: "World War II," p. 195.

16. See: *New Age,* September, 1957, Dr. Cloyd H. Marvin, 33rd Degree, President of George Washington University, "Education For Government Service," Part II, pp. 525-533.

Also see *ibid.,* July, 1956, an advertisement soliciting applications from college graduates "with Masonic parentage or relationship" to apply for scholarships at GWU.

17. *Ibid.,* October, 1957, Dr. Cloyd H. Marvin, "The Scottish Rite Fellowships And Their Significance," pp. 587, 588.

See also *ibid,* August, 1925, p. 506; and July, 1934, p. 392, relative to the $1,000,000 endowment by the Scottish Rite for GWU

18. *Ibid.,* p. 588.

19. *America,* December 16, 1944, "Federal Aid Issues," p. 211.

20. *Congressional Digest,* February, 1946, "The Question Of Federal Funds For Public Schools," p. 41.

Sen. Hill's 32nd degree membership in Masonry is noted in the *Congressional Directory,* 79th Congress, 1st Session, published by the U.S. Government Printing Office, Washington, D.C., August, 1945,p. 18.

Also see Denslow's *Ten Thousand Famous Freemasons, op. cit.,* vol. 2, p. 230.

21. *New York Times,* January 28, 1945, Sec. 4, p. 9.

22. U.S. Congress, Senate, 79th Congress, 1st Session, Committee on Education and Labor, *Hearings, Part 1, on S. 181, Federal Aid To Education,* pp. 1262-1263 .

23. *Ibid.,* p. 264.

24. *Ibid.,* pp. 265, 266. See also *supra,* this book, Chapter 3, pp. 74-76.

25. *Ibid.,* pp. 267-269. Also see *supra,* Chapter 6, pp. 135-6.

26. *Ibid.,* p. 377.

27. *Ibid.,* p. 381.

28. *Congressional Digest,* February, 1946, p. 64.

29. See *supra,* Chapter 5, p. 121.

30. *Black Papers,* Box 34, General Correspondence, Hill, Senator and Mrs. Lister.

31. *Scottish Rite News Bulletin,* No. 61, April 5, 1945, p. 7.

32. Sen. Hill letter, *Black Papers,* Box 34.

33. *Sen. Hill's Papers* are stored at the University of Alabama Library in the Special Collections Office. Researchers are required to seek permission from Mrs. Hubbard to review the files.

The author dispatched a letter to Mrs. Hubbard by Express Mail on January 27, 1987, requesting permission to review her father's files, specifying exactly which letter was needed. There was no reply.

The Post Office Department advised that the letter was received at Mrs. Hubbard's home on January 29.

During a follow-up telephone call on March 11, 1987 to Mrs. Hubbard's residence, the woman who answered said Mrs. Hubbard was not home, but that she would be informed of the author's effort to get in touch with her. There was no further reply.

34. *Black's Papers,* Box 28, "General Correspondence, Fraternal Organizations" communication.

35. *Ibid.*

36. *Ibid.*

37. *Ibid.* Black's letter to Andrews, dated April 5, 1945.

Justice Black told Andrews: "In my present position, I do not desire to become involved in any controversy over pending legislation,."

That statement is somewhat confusing because Black's inquiry to Andrews focused on efforts to "defeat" aid to public schools. He did not inquire what the Fraternity's position was broadly on the school issue, pro and con.

Moreover, Black had initiated a letter to Sen. Hill 25 days earlier, to express his support for the Senator's aid to education bill, and to express his pique because leaders of Scottish Rite Masonry of the Southern Jurisdiction were ostensibly opposing the Senator's legislation to aid public schools.

Justice Black also said he needed a response from Andrews "before I make a final decision as to my future course in relation to membership [in the Birmingham Lodge?]. That comment emitted the savor of a veiled hint that if the Craft was in fact working to "defeat" aid to public schools, it could be embarrassed by the loss of membership of a Justice of the United States Supreme Court.

38. *Scottish Rite News Bulletin,* No. 61, April 5, 1945, p. 1.

39. Senate Education and Labor Committee *Hearings,* Part 2, April 13, 1945, p. 440.

40. *Ibid.,* p. 452.

For Senator Donnell's Masonic affiliations see Denslow., *op. cit.*

41. Senate *Hearings,* Part 2, p. 452.

42. *Ibid.,* pp. 490-491.

43. *Ibid.,* pp. 494, 495, 496, 497.

44. *Ibid.,* April 26, 1945, pp. 766-767.

Sen. Donnell dominated the examination of witnesses supporting federal assistance to parochial schools. Such a high profile for a freshman Senator, who had only been sworn into office a few weeks prior to commencement of the Committee hearings, was unusual in a body that takes the matter of seniority very seriously indeed.

45. *Ibid.,* May 4, 1945, p. 916.

46. *Ibid.*

47. *Ibid.,* p. 918.

48. *Ibid.,* pp. 918-919.

49. *Ibid.,* p. 920.

50. *Ibid.* pp. 920-921.

In Black's own "Remonstrance" against those outraged by his membership in the Ku Klux Klan, the then neophyte Justice, in his 1937 nationwide radio address, said the First Amendment safeguarded "complete liberty of religious belief." Any program, he continued, "which tends to breed or revive religious discord or antagonism can and may spread with such rapidity as to imperil" freedom of religious belief.

Such a situation, he warned, would fan the flames of prejudice and project "religious beliefs into a position of prime importance in political campaigns." It would "reinject our social and business life with the passion of religious bigotry." Moreover, he cautioned, it would "bring the political religionist back into undeserved and perilous influence in the affairs of government." [See *supra*, p. 118.]

51. Senate *Hearings*, Part 2, pp. 925-927.

52. *Ibid.* Letter to Sen. Murray from Dr. Walsh, dated June 4, 1945. Included with the letter is Dr. Walsh's report, titled, "A Novel Theory Of Crime," pp. 927-931. See particularly, pp. 928, 930.

53. *Ibid.*, pp. 930-931.

54. *Congressional Digest*, February, 1946, p. 41.

55. See: *Biographical Directory Of The American Congress, 1774-1971*, Washington, D.C. U.S. Government Printing Office, 1971, entries on the Committee members: James E. Murray, p. 1457; David I. Walsh, p. 1874; Elbert D. Thomas, p. 1805; Claude Pepper, p. 1528; Allen J. Ellender, p. 906; Lister Hill, p. 1118; Dennis Chavez, p. 729; James M. Tunnel, p. 1835; Joseph F. Guffey, p. 1041; Olin D. Johnston, p. 1200; J. William Fulbright, p. 974; Robert M. La Follette, Jr. p. 1255; Robert Taft, Jr., p. 1786; George D. Aiken, p. 497; Joseph H. Ball, p. 5467; II. Alexander Smith, p. 1714; Wayne Morse, p. 1445; and Forrest C. Donnell, p. 871.

56. *America*, July 28, 1945, editorial, "Church And Federal Aid," p. 335.

57. The editorials in the *New Age* in July, 1945 were titled, respectively: "Foreseeable," p. 261; Changing Of The United States Culture," p. 264; and "Ideal Church," p. 265.

58. *America*, June 29, 1946, editorial, "Amend Federal Aid Bill," p. 274.

59. *Everson v. Board of Education*, 132 N.J.L. 98; 330 U.S. 1 (1947), p. 3; *New Age*, November 1944, p. 456.

60. New Jersey Court of Errors and Appeals, volume 1785 (1945), *Transcript of Record, Everson v. Board of Education*, Brief of Prosecutor-Respodent, pp. 59-61.

Rogers statements are in the *New Age*, November, 1935, p. 647; April, 1940, p. 200; and U.S. Congress, House of Representatives, Committee on Education, *Hearings*, April 6, 1937, pp. 267-269.

61. N.J. Court of Errors and Appeals, vol. 1785, transcript, pp. 7-8.

62. 133 N.J.L. 350.

63. See: Philip B. Kurland and Gerhard Casper (eds.), *Landmark Briefs And Arguments Of The Supreme Court Of The United States*, vol. 44, *Ever-*

son v. Board of Education, Arlington, Va. University Publications of America, p. 691.

Transcript of Record, Supreme Court of the United States, October Term, 1946, No. 52, *Everson v. Board of Education,* Washington, D.C., Archives of the United States, pp. 128, 130.

64. Kurland and Casper, pp. 853, 855-858.

Notes   Chapter 8

1. *Everson v. Board of Education,* 330 U.S. 1, at p. 7.
For Justice Black's personal views see *supra,* Chapter 5 pp. 121-122.

2. *Everson.,* pp. 7-8.

3. *Ibid.,* p. 10.

4. *Ibid.,* p. 13.

5. *Ibid.,* pp. 13, 14, 15.

6. *Ibid.,* p. 12

Note the majority opinion equates "non-believers" in God and His Son with believers. Madison's "Memorial" never mentions non-believers. Actually, Madison's document says the the bill he was opposing in the "Memorial" was worthy of defeat because it was "adverse to the diffusion of the light of Christianity." *Ibid.,* p. 70.

The specific opponents of the legislation mentioned in the "Memorial" were Quakers and Menonists (*Id.* p. 66); although Madison, who was a Deist, a precursor of modern day Unitarian-Universalism, obviously had his own sect in mind as well.

7. *Everson,* p. 16.

8. *Ibid.,* pp. 15-16.

See also, *supra,* pp. 146-150 relative to Justice Black sending Sen. Hill the five principles on education advocated by Scottish Rite Freemasonry.

9. *Ibid.,* p. 19.

10. *Ibid.,* pp. 22-23.

11. *Ibid.,* p. 23.

12. *Ibid.,* pp. 23-24.

13. "Memorial," sec. 8, in *Everson* at p. 68.

14. *Everson,* p. 25.

15. *University of Chicago Law Review,* vol. xx, No. 3, spring, 1953, p. 248.

16. "Memorial," sec. 9, in *Everson* at p. 69

17. Justice Rutledge said: "In the documents of the times, particularly Madison, . . . but also in the writings of Jefferson . . . is to be found irrefutable confirmation of the [First] Amendment's sweeping content." *Everson,* p. 34.

Rutledge added: ". . . the Remonstrance is at once the most concise and the most accurate statement of the views of the First Amendment's author concerning what is 'an establishment of religion.' " *Ibid.*, 37. Also see the text of the "Memorial," *ibid.*, pp. 63-72.

18. *Ibid.*, pp. 45-47, 59.

19. *Ibid.*, p. 59.

20. "Memorial," sec. 4, in *Everson* at p. 66.

21. *Everson*, pp. 41, 42-43. *Annals*, vol. 1, p. 730.

22. *Everson*, p. 43, footnote 34.

23. *Annals*, p. 731.

24. *Ibid.*

25. *Everson*, pp. 40-43, footnote 35.

26. *Reuben Quick Bear v. Leupp*, 210 U.S. 50, at pp. 81-82.

27. *Ibid.*, p. 79.

28. *Ibid.*, pp. 53-54.

29. *Supra*, p. 153 and footnote no. 50 Ch. 7.

30. *Supra*, pp. 117-118.

31. *Supra.*, pp. 137-138, 140; "Memorial," section 1, in *Everson* at p. 64; and *supra*, p. 309.

32. See *Reynolds v. U.S.*, 98 U.S. 145 at 164 (1870);. *Beason*, 133 U.S. 333, at p. 342 (1890); and *U.S. v. Macintosh*, 283 U.S. 605, at p. 633 (1931).

33. *Supra*, pp. 127-129; 133-34; and 132-33.

34. Madison's "Memorial," sec. 1, in *Everson* at p. 64.

35. *Black's Papers*, Box 285, Public Correspondence on *Everson*, Folder I, Letter from Prof. Dunne, dated September 25, 1947.

36. *Ibid.* It has been shown that Black was a reader of Scottish Rite publications. The arguments supporting both the majority and minority opinions in *Everson* largely paralleled arguments which had earlier appeared in the *New Age*, the *Scottish Rite News Bulletin*, and in testimony by Elmer Rogers of the Scottish Rite.

37. *New York Times*, May 8, 1947, p. 26.

38. *Ibid.*, May 9, 1947, p. 18.

39. *Black's Papers*, Box 286, Public Correspondence on *Everson*, Folder I. Mr. Crossland's letter is dated February 21, 1947.

40. *New York Times*, May 15, 1947, p. 20.

41. *McCollum v. Board of Education*, 333 U.S. 203, at p. 212.

Twenty-four articles opposing released time for religious education appeared in the *New Age* between February, 1941 and January, 1948.

42. *McCollum*, p. 210.

Either full or abbreviated versions of that same paragraph appeared in the following decisions: *Torcaso v. Watkins*, 367 U.S. 488 (1961), at pp. 488-489; *Abington School District v. Schempp*, 374 U.S. 203 (1963), at p. 219; *Board of Education v. Allen*, 392 U.S. 236 (1967), at p. 239; *Lemon v.*

Kurtzman, 403 U.S. 602 (1971), at p. 640; *Committee For Public Education v. Nyquist,* 413 U.S. 756 (1973), at p. 767; *Meek v. Pittenger,* 421 U.S. 341 (1975), at p. 358; and *Grand Rapids v. Ball,* No. 83-990 (1985), at p. 8.

43. *New York Times,* November 21, 1948, p. 63.

44. See particularly the *Appellees' Brief* in the *McCollum* case filed by Attorneys John L. Franklin, *et. al.,* which provides a superb analysis of the true meaning and intent of the religion clause. It is a devastating indictment of the Court's total disregard for the relevant history of that fundamental charter of religious freedom in the context it was was formulated by Congress, and as it was understood by the American people during the ratification process.

Among other things, Mr. Franklin and his colleagues said: "Persons having no religion have no constitutional right to prohibit exercise of religion by those who have." *Id.,* p. 23.

The brief invited attention to the following statement set forth by a respected source of jurisprudence: ". . . a Constitution derives its validity not from the act of the convention in framing it, but from that of the people in ratifying it, so that the intent of the latter is the real question in arriving at its proper construction. [70 ALR 26] Franklin Brief, p. 40.

And further: "The plain fact is that whatever Mr. Madison's personal political or philosophical views were about the undesirability of conferring the benefits and aid of government upon religion or religious education, he did not, as a legislator, attempt to write into the amendment any prohibition against equal government aid to all religions." Id., p. 43.

The Franklin Brief did not persuade Brother Black and his colleagues. The arguments set forth therein were brushed away with the curt remark: ". . . we are unable to accept . . . these contentions." *McCollum* at p. 211.

(That remark is particularly worrisome in view of the hand-written note on Professor Dunne's letter in Justice Black's files which indicates the Alabama Jurist had never read the Congressional debates that provide documentation on how the religion clause was crafted. See: *supra,* p. 171.

The Court's imperious dismissal without comment of an awesomely detailed account of the legislative history of the religion clause is nothing less than frightening.

To his great credit, Justice Stanley Reed (who also was a Mason) tacitly acknowledged, in his *McCollum* dissent the validity of many arguments made by Attorney Franklin and his colleagues.

Reed himself catalogued a long history of government accommodation of religion; and with reference to Jefferson's "wall," said: "A rule of law should not be drawn from a figure of speech."

Four years later, in the *Zorach* case, Justice Douglas in an oblique reference to a truncated version of the Court's earlier ruling in *Girard,* said: "We are a religious people whose institutions presuppose a Supreme Being . . ." [343 U.S. 306, 313-314].

Justice Byron White made favorable reference to that statement in his partial dissent in *Lemon,* (1971) and Justices Burger, Rhenquist and White became increasingly uneasy with the Court's quarantine of religion in society, as their dissents made clear in the 1973 *Nyquist* decision, the 1975 *Meek* case, and their opinions in subsequent cases.

However, it was Judge W. Brevard Hand of the U.S. District Court at Mobile, Ala., who made a laser-like strike on the *Everson* thesis. He documented the paucity of reality surrounding the high bench's putative history of the religion clause, and faulted its reasoning which elevated non-religion as the Established national philosophy.

Judge Hand's 66-page opinion in *Jaffree v. Board of School Commissioners,* issued on January 14, 1983, stated, in part: "It should be clear that the traditional interpretation of Madison and Jefferson is historically faulty if not virtually unfounded . . ."

He said a careful review of the religion clause makes it "abundantly clear" that "the founding fathers of this country and the framers of what became the First Amendment never intended the establishment clause to erect an absolute wall of separation between the federal government and religion." Judge Hand referred to Justice Black's citation of Jefferson's "wall" as a "revisionary literary flourish."

The Alabama jurist acknowledged his indebtedness to Dr. James McClellan, former professor of Constitutional Law at the Universities of Emory and Alabama, and later chief counsel of the Senate Subcommittee on Separation of Powers. [See: *The Wanderer,* February 10, 1983, Paul A. Fisher, "Court Decision On Religion Gets Congressional Notice," p. 1. See also: James McClellan, "The Making And The Unmaking Of The Establishment Clause," in *A Blueprint for Judicial Reform,* edited by Patrick B. McGuigan and Randall R. Rader, Washington, D.C., Free Congress Research and Education Foundation, Inc., pp. 295-325.

Judge Hand was overruled, in part, by the Supreme Court in *Wallace v. Jaffree,* No. 83-812 (1985).

45. *Torcaso v. Watkins,* 367 U.S. 488 (1961).

46. *Engel v. Vitale,* 370 U.S. 421 (1962); and *Abington School District v. Schempp,* 374 U.S. 203 (1963).

47. *Board of Public Works v. Horace Mann League* (385 U.S. 97 (1966).

48. *Lemon v. Kurtzman,* 403 U.S. 602 (1971).

49. *Committee for Public Education v. Nyquist,* 413 U.S. 756 (1973).

50. *Meek v. Pittenger,* 421 U.S. 349 (1975)

51. *Stone v. Graham,* No. 80-321 (1980)

52. *Grand Rapids v. Ball,* No. 83-990 (1985); and *Aguilar v. Felton,* No. 84-287 (1985).

53. *Wallace v. Jaffree,* No. 83-812 (1985).

54. *Vidal v. Girard's Executors,* 2 How. 127 (1844), concerned the will

of Steven Girard, a Mason and founder of Girard College in Philadelphia. He decreed that, following his demise, no clergy could enter the precincts of the College to teach.

The Court, contrary to the impression given by Justice Frankfurter, said discussion of the public policies of a State "scarcely come within the range of judicial duty and functions, and . . . men may and will complexionally differ; above all, when that topic is connected with religious polity, in a country composed of such a variety of religious sects as our country, it is impossible not to feel that it would be attended with almost insuperable difficulties, and involve differences of opinion almost endless in their variety. We disclaim any right to enter upon such examinations, beyond what the state constitutions, and laws, and decisions necessarily bring before us." *Girard* at pp. 197-198.

55. See: *Schempp* at p. 307, and *Allen* at p. 249.

56. *Harvard Law Review,* vol. 82, p. 1680 (1969).

57. See *Walz v. Tax Commissioners,* 397 U.S. 664 (1970) at p. 695; *Lemon,* at p. 623; *Nyquist,* at p. 790; and *Meek,* at pp. 371, 373-374.

58. *Girard,* at p. 198.

59. *New Age,* January, 1959, William A. Brandenburg, "More Than Ritual," p. 25. *Ibid.,* March, 1959, "Freemasons and Politics," p. 156.

60. *Ibid.,* August, 1966, Grand Commander's Message: "A Major Victory For Separation Of Church And State," pp. 3-11, p. 7.

61. *Horace Mann League v. Board of Public Works of Maryland,* 242 Md. 645; 387 U.S. 97 (1966).

62. *New Age,* August, 1966, p. 8.

63. POAU was organized in Chicago, Illinois on November 20, 1947. Included on its executive committee was Elmer Rogers, long-time top aide to the Grand Commander of the Scottish Rite, and Charles Williams of the National Education Association (NEA). The executive director of POAU was Glenn L. Archer, former legislative director of the NEA. See: Lawrence P. Creedon and Welton D. Falcon, *United For Separation,* Milwaukee, Bruce Publishing Co., 1959, pp. 13-15. Archer also was a 33rd Degree Mason.

Reportedly, 50 to 75 percent of POAU's first year budget came from the Scottish Rite Masons of the Southern Jurisdiction. See Luke E. Ebersole, *Church Lobbying In The Nation's Capital,* New York, The Macmillan Co., 1951, p. 71.

POAU regularly has been mentioned favorably in the New Age since its founding in the mid-1940s. Moreover, the Form 990-A on file with the U.S. Internal Revenue Service (IRS) shows the Scottish Rite Foundation, 1735 Fifteenth Street, N.W., Washington, D.C., donated $105,000 to POAU between 1959-1964. Further, the Grand Commander noted that the Scottish Rite gave POAU $40,000 to purchase an office building. See: *New Age,* July, 1965, "Grand Commander's Visitations", pp. 55-56.

Those random statistics are replicated, more or less, in later reports made to the (IRS) by the Supreme Council and by POAU (under that name and under its changed name, Americans United).

No effort was made to find the tax reports filed by other entities integral to Scottish Rite Masonry, primarily because the names of those groups could not be identified.

As for the Horace Mann League, Luther Smith, Grand Commander of the Scottish Rite, received a certificate of life membership from the League "for the fine service and support he and the Scottish Rite gave to the organization." See: *New Age,* August, 1967, pp. 34-35.

64. *Ibid.,* October, 1955, Henry C. Clausen, "Report of Conference of Grand Masters In North America," p. 589.

Chief Justice Warren's support for public schools was again noted four years later in another article by Clausen. See: *New Age,* May, 1959, Henry C. Clausen, "Ban Masonic Cornerstones?", pp. 280-281.

65. *Ibid.,* September, 1968, p. 34. See: *Flast v. Cohen,* 392 U.S. 83 (1967).

66. *Ibid. Flast* effectively permitted PEARL to bring the *Nyquist* case to Court in 1973, a decision which culminated in the anti-parochial school *Aguilar* decision in 1985.

67. *New Age,* September, 1968, p. 34.

Included among PEARL's members are: Americans United (formerly POAU); American Civil Liberties Union; National Education Association; American Humanist Association; American Jewish Congress; Baptist Joint Committee on Public Affairs; Board of Church and Society of the United Methodist Church; Central Conference of American Rabbis; National Council of Jewish Women; National Women's Conference, American Ethical Union; Union of American Hebrew Congregations; and Unitarian-Universalist Association. See: "Who's Who in PEARL v. Mathews," *Church & State,* March, 1976, p. 6. *Church and State* is a publication of Americans United.

One or another of those groups (frequently several at the same time) have been involved in virtually every religion clause case which has come before the Supreme Court from *Everson* onward.

68. *Flast,* p. 84.

Sen. Ervin, who often has been hailed as an outstanding Constitutional lawyer, consistently opposed aid to church schools, and authenticated his views on the subject by regularly citing judicial opinions in the *Everson* case.

He received the Scottish Rite's "Individual Rights Support" award in 1972 for "his efforts to articulate the true meaning and significance of the U.S. Constitution, especially first amendment rights for the American people. See: *New Age,* July, 1972, Current Interest section, pp. 33-34.

On May 24, 1972, the Senator held a luncheon at the U.S. Senate in honor of Sovereign Grand Commander Clausen; and on October 16, 1973, he delivered an address at the Banquet given by the Grand Commander. His address centered on Justice Black's majority opinion in *Everson*. See: *New Age,* September, 1972, Current Interest section, "Sen. Ervin Honors Grand Commander Clausen," p. 42; *ibid.,* January, 1974, Hon. Sam J. Ervin, Jr., "Church, State and Freemasonry," pp. 7-11.

69. *New Age,* January, 1974, "Report of the Committee on Education and Americanism," p. 44.

70. *Ibid.*

71. *Ibid.,* January, 1976, "Report of the Committee on Education and Americanism, pp. 19-22.

72. *Lemon,* Brief by United Americans For Public Schools, p. 6.

73. *Lemon,* at pp. 613, 614.

74. *New Age,* October, 1971, Grand Commander's Message: "A Tremendous Triumph," pp. 2-3.

75. *Horace Mann League v. Board of Public Works of Maryland,* 242 Md. 645 at 679.

76. *Ibid.,* p. 680.

77. *Ibid.,*

78. *Roemer v. Board of Public Works of Maryland,* 426 U.S. 736 (1976) at p. 755.

79. *Ibid.,* p. 756.

80. *Ibid.,* p. 778.

81. *McCollum,* Appellees Brief by John R. Franklin, *et. al.,* November 17, 1947, p. 24.

82. *In Re: Murchison,* 349 U.S. 133 at p. 136.

Notes   Chapter 9

1. *New Age,* March, 1922, Alfred H. Henry, "The Kingdom of Heaven—Contrasting Views," pp. 131-132.

2. See: *Triumph* magazine, June, 1974, Paul A. Fisher, "The 'Catholic Vote' . . . A Sleeping Giant," p. 12.

3. *New Age,* May, 1945, Grand Commander's Message, p. 195.

4. *Ibid.,* November, 1950, E.P. White, Knight Templar, "New World Evangelism," p. 662.

5. *Ibid.,* August, 1952, editorial, "Bill Would Open Floodgates For 300,000 More Refugees," p. 457.

6. *Ibid.,* March, 1954, Grand Commander's Message, p. 130.

7. *Ibid.,* January, 1956, Dr. Ellis H. Dana, Executive Vice President, Wisconsin Council of Churches, the National Council of Churches, and a Trustee of Protestants And Other Americans United for Separation of Church and State (POAU), "The National Council And Rome," pp. 20-22, pp. 21-22.

Dr. Dana noted that he helped organize POAU, p. 20.

8. *Ibid.,* September, 1954, book review of Geddes MacGregor's *The Vatican Revolution,* published by Beacon Press, Boston, pp. 559-560. The Beacon Press is operated by the Unitarian Church.

9. *New Age,* July, 1958, Leonard A Wenz, "A Growing Mistrust," p. 429.

10. *Ibid.*

11. *Ibid,* January, 1926, W.B. Zimmerman, "Let There Be Light," p. 28.

12. *Ibid.,* May, 1949, editorial, "State-Church Issue," pp. 198-199.

13. *Ibid.,* July, 1951, editorial, "U.S. Attorney General Hits Supreme Court Decision," pp. 390-391.

A similar theme was echoed in the same publication a year earlier by Glenn H. Ruth in "Is Democracy Threatened," *New Age,* August, 1950, pp. 481-482.

See also: *ibid.,* May, June, July, 1951, Emilio Gouchan, "The Historic Truth On The Objects And Action Of Masonry," a three-part series in which the Buenos Aires Mason emphasized in his concluding segment that help "will come from lay Roman Catholics and many priests,." *ibid.,* p. 359.

14. *Ibid.,* April, 1955, Harold Rafton, "The Roman Catholic Church and Democracy," pp. 217-218.

15. *Ibid.*, p. 372.

16. *Ibid.*

17. *Ibid.*, p. 373.

18. *Ibid.*

19. *Ibid.*, pp. 373-374.

20. *Ibid.*, March, 1959, Grand Commander's Message, "An Autocracy Within Our Republic," pp. 135-136.

21. *Ibid.*, November, 1961, Willard Givens and Belmont A. Farley, "Our U.S.A.," p. 16.

22. *Ibid.*, December, 1967, "Report of the Supreme Council's Commission On Education And Americanism," pp. 135-136.

23. *Ibid.*, p. 136.

24. *Ibid.*, January, 1971, Grand Commander's Message, "An Arrogant Assault On Church-State Security," p. 4.

25. For a brief overview on the similarities between the new Catholicism and the Reformation, see: *The New Columbia Encyclopedia, op. cit.*, entries on "Protestantism," and "Reformation," pp. 2229; 22291-2292.

For a more comprehensive treatment of this phenomenon, see: Msgr. George A. Kelly, *The Battle For The American Church*, Garden City, N.Y., Doubleday and Co., 1979; also, Joseph A. Varacalli, *Toward The Establishment of Liberal Catholicism In America*, Lanham, MD., University Press of America, 1983.

26. *New Age*, February, 1950, editorial, "When Pius IX Was Ignominously Expelled From Masonry," pp. 71-72.

27. *Ibid.*, p. 72.

Other articles tying priests to membership in the Masonic Fraternity included the following: *ibid.*, October, 1931, Emerson Easterling, "The Strange Case of the Abbe Turmel," p. 535; *ibid.*, June, 1935, "Comment" section, article titled, "Surprising," p. 326; *ibid.*, July, 1939, Frederic B. Acosta, "A Great Mason Of His Day," p. 418; and *ibid.*, May, 1959, Aemil Pouler, "Freemasonry In Hungary," p. 286, coupled with *The New York Times*, November 3, 1932, p. 2, in which the priest spoken of, Fr. Janos Hock, is tied to Communism.

28. The other Encyclicals by Pius IX against Freemasonry are: *Quibus Quantisque*, April 20, 1849; *Multiplices Inter*, September 25, 1865; *Apostolicae*, October 12, 1869; and *Esti Multa*, November 21, 1873.

The fact that the Masons themselves say the Pope had been a Mason at one time, coupled with the fact that he vehemently condemned the Craft, evidences that Freemasonry is a moral evil which even some of its own members (or former members) provide testimony.

29. *Extension* magazine, July, 1934, "The Question Box," Question No. 4023, p. 27.

30. *America*, April 30, 1938, "Comment" section, p. 74.

31. *Extension*, November, 1949, William J. Whalen, "Why The Church Condemns Freemasonry, pp. 13, 51.

32. *New Age,* July, 1950, editorial, "Emphasizing An Old Attitude," p. 392.

33. *Ibid.*

34. *Ibid.*

35. *Ibid.*

36. *America,* July 7, 1951, editorial: "Masonry and 'Americanism'," pp. 345-346.

37. *Ibid.*

38. *Ibid.*

39. *The New York Times,* August 17, 1932, p. 38; *ibid.,* October 11, 1932, p. 20.

40. *Ibid.,* December 3, 1934, p. 11; *ibid.,* January 12, 1935, pp. 3, 34; *ibid.,* January, 22, 1935, p. 5; and *ibid.,* February 11, 1935, p. 8.

41. *Ibid.,* December 18, 1935, p. 4

42. *Ibid.,* February 18, 1933, p. 4

43. *Ibid.*

44. *America,* January 14, 1956, Father Robert A. Graham, S.J., "Apostle To The Freemasons," p. 243.

45. *New Age,* November, 1957, "Grand Commander's Visitation," p. 685.

46. *America,* November 29, 1958, p. 273.

47. *Ibid.,* p. 274.

48. *Ibid.,* pp. 274-275.

49. *Ibid.,* p. 275.

50. *Ibid.,* April 22, 1961, "Comment" section, "Priest And Freemason," p. 168.

51. *U.S. Catholic,* March, 1968, Father John A. O'Brien, "Our Friends, The Masons," pp. 25-26.

52. *Ibid.,* p. 26.

53. *Ibid.,* April, 1966, "The Church And The World" section, headlined: "The Masons Invite A Bishop To Speak, p. 59.

54. *Ibid.,* March, 1968, O'Brien, *op. cit.,* p. 27.

55. *New Age,* June, 1966, Alphonse Cerza, "The Vatican Council And Religious Liberty," p. 12.

56. *U.S. Catholic,* September, 1966, "Catholic Membership In The Masons, Why Not?", p. 44.

57. *America,* March 11, 1967, "Milestones In Ecumenism," p. 335.

58. *Ibid.,* April 15, 1967, "Letters" section, p. 544.

59. *Approaches,* February, 1977, pp. 12-13.

60. *New Age,* March, 1925, Frank C. Higgins, "Beneath The Ninth Arch," p. 220.

61. *Ibid.,* June, 1924, editor's response to a question regarding exoteric and esoteric aspects of Masonry, p. 371.

62. See: *Catholic Encyclopedia, op. cit.,* p. 780.

63. *New Age,* November, 1922, John Van Niece Bandy, "The Great Light," p. 517.

64. *The New York Times,* March 29, 1976, p. 31.

65. *Ibid.*

66. *N.C. News* wire service dispatch No. 24, August 4, 1976, "Church Suspension Of Archbishop Defended." The dispatch did not cite specific quotations from Conciliar documents which would authenticate that the three-word slogan of the French Revolution, which also is a slogan of International Freemasonry, had been embraced by the Roman Catholic Church.

67. *Catholic Standard,* Archdiocese of Washington, June 1, 1978, p. 1.

68. *Pittsburgh Catholic,* Diocese of Pittsburgh, March 13, 1981, p. 6.

69. *Religious News Service (RNS)* dispatch, March 13, 1984.

70. The Old Canon 2335, which dictated excommunication for membership in Masonry is set forth in its Latin and English versions in *Approaches,* February, 1977, pp. 24-25.

The New Canon 1374, concerning "an association which plots against the Church," may be found in *The Code Of Canon Law* (English translation), prepared by the Canon Law Society of Great Britain and Ireland, London, Collins Liturgical Publications, 1983, p. 244. The book is distributed in the United States by William B. Eerdmans Publishing Company, Grand Rapids, MI.

71. *The Wanderer,* St. Paul, MN., December 15, 1983, Paul A. Fisher, "Vatican Reaffirms Church's Opposition To Freemasonry," pp. 1, 9.

72. The English language version of the editorial appeared in *The Wanderer,* March 28, 1985, p. 3.

73. *Ibid.*

74. *Catholic Standard,* June 13, 1985, p. 8.

Notes   Chapter 10

1. Sarah Gertrude Millan, *Cecil Rhodes*, New York, Harper & Bros., 1933, pp. 36-37.

2. *Ibid.*, p. 195. See also: *New Age*, September, 1972, Art Brown, "Cecil Rhodes, A Mason Whose Influence For Good Still Lives Through His Scholarships." p. 28.

3. *The Washington Post*, "Potomac" section, March 23, 1975, Rudy Maxa, "The Professor Who Knew Too Much," p. 17.

The subject of the *Post* piece, the late Professor Carroll Quigley in his book, *Tragedy And Hope*, demonstrated that an intimate link exists between international bankers and the British and American organizations which flowed from Rhodes' secret society. Such a link would naturally follow since Rhodes wished to control the world by "gradually absorbing" all its wealth.

4. *New Age*, May, 1955, Dr. Berthold Altmann, "Freemasonry And Political Parties In Germany," p. 278.

5. Pike, *Morals and Dogma, op. cit.*, p. 109.

6. C.S. Lipencott and E.R. Johnston, *Masonry Defined*, "compiled from the writings of Albert G. Mackey, 33rd Degree, and many other Eminent Authorities," Memphis, Tenn., Masonic Supply Co., 1930, pp. 233-240.

7. *Ibid.*, p. 240.

8. See: *supra*, 74.

9. *Origins*, NC Documentary Service, a publication of the National Catholic News Service of the U.S. Catholic Conference of Bishops, Washington, D.C., June 27, 1985, p. 83.

The *Osservatore Romano* article appeared in Italian on February 23, 1985. The English language version appeared March 11, 1985.

10. *New Age*, April, 1935, Walter F. Meier, 33rd Degree, "Mason To Mason," p. 210.

11. *Ibid.*, May, 1955, Dr. Berthold Altmann, "Freemasonry And Political Parties In Germany, p. 278.

12. *New Age*, March, 1977, Grand Commander's Message, "Freedom And Freemasonry,", p. 6.

13. *Ibid.*, July, 1935, p. 438. Other articles affirming the Masonic origins of the Great Seal appeared in *ibid*, July, 1948, p. 409; August, 1948, p.

498; February, 1978, pp. 51-55; and September, 1976, pp. 44-49.

Although a pamphlet published by the U.S. Department of State in July, 1980, titled, "The Great Seal of the United States," makes no reference to any Masonic symbolism in the Great Seal, the publication fails to reflect the complete background of the Seal, as evidenced by former Vice President Henry A. Wallace, also a Mason.

Wallace disclosed that when the new design for the U.S. dollar bill was shown to President Franklin D. Roosevelt in 1935, the latter "at first worried that using the Eye of Providence (the Masonic emblem atop the 13-step pyramid on the reverse of the Seal) would offend Catholics. After being assured by Post Master General James A. Farley [a Catholic] that it would not, Roosevelt gave the go-ahead." See: *The Washington Post,* November 9, 1982, p. D-7.

14. *New Age,* February, 1980, Grand Commander's Message, "The Masonic Seal Of The California Supreme Court," pp. 2-5.

15. Quoted in Allen E. Roberts' *A House Undivided,* The Story Of Freemasonry And The Civil War, St. Louis, Missouri Lodge of Research, 1961, pp. 33-35.

16. *Ibid.,* p. 75.

17. *The War Of The Rebellion, A Compilation Of The Official Records Of The Union And Confederate Armies, As Corrected,* U.S. War Department, Washington, D.C., Government Printing Office, 1902, Series II, Volume VII, p. 932.

The Grand Commander of the *Corps De Belgique,* one of the secret societies operating in the State of Missouri, was Charles L. Hunt, who served as the Belgian Consul in the United States. *Ibid.,* p. 236.

18. *Ibid.,* p. 231. Letter from Colonel J.P. Sanderson, Provost Marshal General, Department of the Missouri, to Major General W.S. Rosecrans, Commander of the same Department, June 12, 1864.

Referring to the Order of American Knights (OAK), Sanderson said the Order "is rigidly secret," and its objective and aim is "the overthrow of the Federal Government, and the creation of a North West Confederacy," *ibid.*

19. Sanderson to Rosecrans, *ibid.,* p. 234.

20. *Ibid.,* p. 233.

Albert Pike said the initiate into the Blue Degrees (the first, second and third degrees of Freemasonry) "is intentionally misled by false interpretations" of Masonic symbolism. "It is not intended that he shall understand them; but is is intended that he shall imagine he understands them. Their true explanation is reserved for the Adepts, the Princes of Masonry." *Morals and Dogma,* pp. 818-819.

21. *Rebellion Records,* Series II, Volume VII, Sanderson to Rosecrans, p. 233.

See also: Report by Colonel J. Holt, Judge Advocate General to Secretary of War Edwin M. Stanton, October 8, 1864. Violation of the oath of obligation to one of the secret subversive organizations can result in "a shameful death," in which the body of the guilty person shall be "divided into four parts and cast out of the four 'gates' of the temple." *Ibid.,* p. 938.

22. The penalty for violating an oath of the Peace Society, one of the secret organizations operating in the South, required the initiate to swear to the following: "I bind myself under no less penalty than that of having my head cut open, my brains taken from thence and strewn over the ground, my body cast to the beasts of the field or to the vultures of the air should I be so vile as to reveal any of the secrets of this order." *Rebellion Records,* Series IV, Volume III, p. 395.

Compare the above with Masonic penalties set forth *supra,* p. 35.

23. *Ibid.,* Series II, Volume VII, pp. 234, 238.

24. "Report On The Order Of American Knights," Sanderson Reports, 1864, Second Report, August 20, 1864, Copy 2, Records of the Office of the Judge Advocate General (Army), R.G., 153, Entry 33, Box No. 4, p. 22, Washington, U.S. U.S. Archives.

25. Albert Pike, *Morals and Dogma,* p. 155.

26. Sanderson, Second Report, pp. 89-90. The company was to "oppose the central government" by means of "insurrection" and a "grand revolutionary movement."

27. Sanderson Reports, *op. cit.,* Third Report, September 3, 1864, pp.116, 118.

28. *Ibid.,* Second Report, pp. 43, 47.

29. *Rebellion Records,* Series II, Volume VII, Judge Advocate Holt report to Secretary of War Stanton, pp. 931, 932.

30. *New York Times,* June 19, 1871, p. 1.

31. *Rebellion Records,* Series II, Volume VII, Holt report to Secretary Stanton, pp. 943-944, 949-950.

32. Lobinger, *op. cit.,* p. 224. See also: Adjutant General's Records, Series M-1003: 10-33-9, Reel 14, frames 0226-0266, Washington, U.S. Archives.

33. Lobinger, p. 226.

34. *Ibid.*

35. *New York Times,* January 10, 1867, p. 1.

36. *Ibid.,* March 4, 1864, p. 5; March 15, 1867, p. 4; November 26, 1867, p. 1.

37. Lobinger, p. 226. Lobinger cites Pike's "Reminisces" as the source for Granger's remarks before the Judiciary Committee.

38. Lobinger, p. 273.

39. *New York Times,* June 23, 1867, p. 1; June 24, 1867, p. 8.

40. *Ibid.,* June 25, 1867, p. 1.

41. *Ibid.,* p. 8.

42. *The New Columbia Encyclopedia, op. cit.,* article on the Republic of the Philippines, p. 2131.

43. *Ibid*

44. See: John T. Farrell, "An Abandoned Approach to Philippine History: John R.M. Taylor And The Philippine Insurgent Records," *The Catholic Historical Review*, vol. 39, January, 1954, pp. 385-407.

See also: "History of the Philippine Insurrection Against the United States, 1899-1903, and Documents Relating to the War Department Project for Publishing the History," National Archives Microfilm Publications Pamphlet Describing M719, Washington, U.S. Archives and Records Service, 1973.

45. *Ibid.*, pp. 9-10.

46. John R.M. Taylor, *The Philippine Insurrection Against The United States: A Compilation Of Documents With Notes And Introduction*, Galley Proofs, U.S. War Department, Washington, D.C., 1909, U.S. Archives, Microfilm M719, 10-29-8, Roll No. 9 p. 27.

In the Introduction, Taylor says (p. 2): ". . . it may be considered that in this introduction I have done more than justice to the work of Spanish missionaries in the Philippines. I am not a Catholic, and have said only what my investigations of the subject have led me to believe was the truth in the matter."

47. Taylor, p. 27.

48. *Ibid.*, p. 67, Exhibit 7.

49. *Ibid.*, p. 80, Exhibit 9.

50. *Ibid.*

51. *Ibid.*

52. *Ibid.*, p. 82.

53. *Ibid.*, p. 83.

54. *Ibid.*, p. 91, Exhibit 11-C

55. *Ibid.*, pp. 91-92.

56. *Ibid.*, pp. 85-86.

57. *Ibid.*, p. 98.

58. *Ibid.*, pp. 27-28.

59. *Philippine Insurgent Records*, 1896-1901, Micro Copy No. 254, Roll 9, frames 306-309, U.S. Archives.

60. *Ibid.*, frames 322-323.

61. *Ibid.*, frame 323. the letter from Tolentino is dated October 10, 1899, and written on *La Patria* stationery.

62. *Ibid.*

63. *New York Times*, July 30, 1899, p. 3; August 5, 1899, p. 6; August 7, p. 6.

64. *Los Angeles Times*, July 31, 1917, Part II, p. 1.

65. *Ten Thousand Freemasons*, *op. cit.*, volume 1, pp. 7-8.

66. *New Age*, April, 1955, Mauro Barad, "Emilio Aguinaldo, Mason," p. 232.

67. *Ibid.*, p. 234.

68. *Ibid.*, June 1947, pp. 397-398.

69. *Ibid.*, June, 1947, pp. 334, 398.

70. *Ibid.*, May, 1955, editorial, "War Damage Claim Disallowed," p. 268.

71. *Ibid.*, June, 1932, Allocution Of The Grand Commander, delivered at the 1931 Biennial Session of the Supreme Council, p. 348.

72. *Ibid.*, September, 1952, editorial, "Abuse Of The Public Press," p. 519.

73. An Explanation of the Black Hand's Masonic link is set forth in James A. Billington, *Fire In The Minds Of Men,* pp. 110-111 and footnotes 159-161.

74. See: Mary Edith Durham, *The Serajevo Crime,* London, George Allyn and Unwin, Ltd., 1925, p. 85.

75. *Ibid.*, p. 86.

76. Billington, p. 92.

Billington also substantially confirms what the Abbé Barruel and Professor Robison had disclosed in the late 18th Century about the Order of Illuminati.

77. Billington, p. 91.

78. *New Age,* February, 1945, Frederick C. Loofbourow, citing a Russian exile and Mason, Dr. M.J. Imchanitzky, an "active member of the Masonic Club 'Rossia' in New York City," p. 82.

79. *Ibid.*

80. Lobinger, p. 831.

81. *New Age,* September, 1931, p. 527.

82. *Ibid.* January, 1939, editorial, "More Help Needed For Spain," p. 15; February, 1939, "Comment" section, pp. 69-70; March, 1939, "Comment" section, pp. 138-139.

83. *Ibid.*, February, 1939, editorial, "For And Against The Embargo," p. 79.

84. *Ibid.*,

85. *Ibid.*, May, 1951, pp. 283-284.

86. *Ibid.*, November, 1964, Robert Maxwell Walker, "Masonry And The Spanish Revolution," p. 41.

87. *Ibid.*, pp. 43-44.

88. *Ibid.*, October, 1925, p. 602. The information was attributed to Dr. H.E. Stafford, Past Grand Master of the Philippines.

89. *Ibid.*, November, 1968, Morris B. DePass, "The Hoon Bong or Red Society Of China," p. 51.

90. *Ibid.*, March, 1939, a Special Correspondent, "The Sian Agreement." p. 106.

91. *Ibid.*, July, 1948. Service established the Lodge on March 27, 1943, p. 403.

92. M. Stanton Evans, *The Liberal Establishment,* New York, The

Devin-Adair Company, 1965, p. 226.

93. *Ibid.*, pp. 228-229, 231.

Service also signed an ad sponsored by the National Association of Chinese Americans which appeared in *The Washington Post* in April, 1977 opposing continued U.S. support for Free China, or Taiwan.

The address of the headquarters of the National Association of Chinese Americans was given as 3524 Connecticut Avenue, N.W., Washington, D.C. The address is the same as that of the Yenching Palace, a Chinese restaurant owned by Van S. Lung, president of the Sino-American Export Company.

According to the late Congressman Lawrence McDonald, the Sino-American Export Company "imports propaganda films from Red China." See: *Congressional Record,* 95th Congress, Extension of Remarks, "Red Chinese Propaganda," April 27, 1977, p. E-2538

94. *New Age,* Comment by the Grand Commander, June, 1948, p. 323.

95. *Ibid.*, January, 1950, editorial, "The Protestant Revival," p. 9

96. *Ibid.*, November, 1950, E.P. White, "New World Evangelism," p. 662.

97. *Ibid.*, April, 1951, editorial, "Catholic Action And The Three Exhibits Of Its Dangers," p. 198.

98. *Ibid.*, March, 1954, editorial, "The Paralysis Of Hysteria," p. 180; January, 1955, Wallace Ruff, "Always Pushing," pp. 43-44; and February, 1955, Claud F. Young, "Our Problem," pp. 79-80.

99. *Ibid.*, May, 1931, Frederick J. Juchoff, "World Politics," p. 221

100. *Ibid.* Also see *ibid.*, p. 264.

101. *Ibid.*, Jan., 1939, p. 31.

102. *Ibid.*, April, 1932. The commentary was in a letter from which the author's name was withheld. It appeared in a section of the magazine titled, "Important News From Other Countries," p. 209.

103. *Ibid.*, May, 1933, "Comment" section, pp. 327-328.

104. The item about the lodges changing their names appeared in the *Times* on April 10, 1933, p. 1. The related editorial appeared April 22, 1933, p. 12.

105. *New York Times,* April 24, 1933, p. 4.

106. *Ibid.*

107. *New Age,* April,1934, Arduino Melaragno, "Mussolini the Infallible," p. 209.

108. *Ibid.*, February, 1934, "Masonry Overseas," p. 14.

109. *Ibid.*, April, 1939, news item: "England's New Grand Master, pp. 298-99.

Identification of Masonry with the Royal Family of England goes back as far as 1737 when two sons of King George II, Frederick, Prince of Wales, joined in 1737; and Augustus, Duke of Cumberland, was initiated in 1743. See: *ibid.*, June, 1928, which traces an unbroken line of English royalty as members of the Masonic Fraternity from 1743 through George VI, father of the presently reigning Queen Elizabeth.

In 1977, a book by Stephen Knight was published by George G. Harrap and Co., Ltd., titled, *Jack The Ripper, The Final Solution*. The volume provided interesting details linking the famous "Jack-the Ripper" murders to Lord Salisbury, then Prime Minister of England and Sir William Gull, Physician Ordinary to Queen Victoria.

The murders were precipitated, so the book reports, because Queen Victoria's grandson, Prince Eddy, sired a child out of wedlock by a liaison with a poor commoner who was a model. The Prince and the model, Anne Elizabeth Cook, were married in a Catholic ceremony, and the child, a girl, was baptized Catholic.

Salisbury was one of the country's most influential Freemasons, as was Gull and the Assistant Commissioner of Metropolitan Police, Sir Robert Anderson. All were involved in the plot; and it was the secret brotherhood, said Knight, which carried out the murders in an effort to silence the witnesses to the marriage and baptism. Meanwhile, the mother, Anne Elizabeth Cook was placed in a mental institution on orders of the Prime Minister.

The child of the union, Alice Margaret, was the mother of the man who told the intriguing story to the author of the book, the late Stephen Knight.

110. *New Age*, August, 1940, editorial, "May Prove Disastrous," p. 455; ibid., Joseph P. Marcombe, "But One Answer Possible," p. 464.

111. *Ibid.*, September, 1940, editorial, "Masonry And The Dictators," pp. 520-521.

112. *Ibid.*, March, 1949, Hamilton, *op. cit.*, p. 151.

113. Schick letter, October 1, 1945, to Commander, U.S. Forces Europe, paragraph II. Modern Military Records, Headquarters, U.S. Forces European Theatre, G-5 (Civil Affairs), File: 080, "Agencies—From 1945," Washington, D.C., U.S. Archives.

Schick's letter is in German, but an English translation accompanies it. The citations are from the English translation.

114. *Ibid.*, paragraphs, V, VI.

115. *Ibid.*, paragraph XI.

116. *Ibid.*, paragraph XIII.

117. *Ibid.*,

Weishaupt said: "The great strength of our Order lies in its concealment; let it never appear in any place in its own name, but always covered by another name, and another occupation. None is fitter than the three lower degrees of Freemasonry . . . Next to this, the form of a learned or literary society is best suited to our purpose . . . By establishing reading societies, and subscription libraries, and taking these under our direction, and supplying them through our labors we may turn the public mind which way we will." See: Robison, *op. cit.*, p. 148.

See also Pope Leo XIII's comments, *supra,* p. 74 which made the same point.

118. Schick letter, paragraph XIV.

119. *Ibid.*, paragraph XV.

120. *Ibid.*, paragraph XVI.

121. Letter, dated December 10, 1945, to Schick from Headquarters, U.S. Forces European Theatre (G-5), File: 080, reference as in footnote 113.

122. Cablegram, March 28, 1946, from USFET (Main), File: 1945-46, AG080, Societies and Associations (German Social And Fraternal Groups, American German Clubs), Office of Military Government For Germany, OMGUS Headquarters, Modern Military Records, Washington, U.S. Archives.

123. Memorandum, 1 April 1946, Subject: Freemason Lodges in Germany, same reference as in footnote 122.

124. Memo to AGWAR, from OMGUS, signed CLAY, 271835B June, 46, *ibid*, Modern Military Records.

125. *Ibid.*, Letter from Gen. Bull to Gen. Clay.

126. *Ibid.*

127. *Ibid.*, Letter from Potter to OMG, Germany, October 8, 1947.

128. Headings, *op. cit.*, pp. 52-53.

129. *New Age*, July, 1941, Charles H. Tingley, "Masonry And the Impending New Era," p. 124.

130. *Ibid.*, April, 1943, Karel Hundee, "The Turning Point Of History," pp. 211-212.

131. *New Age*, November, 1976, Robert E Sconce, "A Soldier's Faith In Masonry," pp. 10-11.

132. *Ibid.*, January, 1942, editorial, "Masonry In Far East," p. 8.

133. *Ibid.*, February, 1942, "A Japanese Opinion Of Freemasonry," translation of an article titled, "Temple of Mystery On Road to Destruction," published in the Osaka *Mainichi* on October 4, 1941. The translation was made by the American Vice Counsel of Kobe, Japan, Otis W. Rhodes, 32nd Degree, p. 92.

134. *Ibid.*

135. *Ibid.*, October, 1942, "Japan Strikes At Freemasonry." The Author is listed as "A Mason On The Gripsholm," pp. 603-604.

136. *Ibid.*, Sconce, *op. cit.*, p. 11.

137. *Ibid.*, p. 12.

138. *Ibid.*

139. *Ibid.*, p. 13.

140. *Ibid.*, April, 1954, Benton Weaver Deckey, "Masonry In Japan," p. 215

141. *Ibid.*, September, 1958, article by Grand Commander titled "Far East Itinerary," pp. 529, 537.

Notes   Chapter 11

1. *The New York Times,* July 6, 1977, "The Shriners Came To Town," p. 21.

In 1928, the U.S. Supreme Court said the order known as Nobles of the Mystic Shrine was founded "by and their membership is restricted to masons . . . who have become Knights Templar or have received the 32nd degree in a Scottish Rite consistory. See: *Ancient Egyptian Order vs. Michaux,* 279 U.S. 737 (1928) at p. 739.

2. Robison, *op. cit.,* p. 147.

3. *New Age,* October, 1945, John C. Parsons, "What Do Masons Do?", pp. 403-404.

4. *Ibid.,* October, 1968, Grand Commander's Message: "How To Create A Favorable Opinion Of Freemasonry In The World Of The Profane," pp. 2-3.

5. *Ibid.,* p. 3.

6. Quoted by Lobinger, *op. cit.,* p. 244.

7. Barruel, *op. cit.,* vol. 4, p. 232.

8. *Ibid.,* p. 233.

Common to Masonry and the Illuminati are:

- References to mankind as a "rough, split and polished ashlar. Robison, p. 122; Pike in *Morals and Dogma,* pp. .5-6.
- Atheism. The Illuminati were instructed that "the Grand Secret is no Superintending Deity." Robison, p. 156. Pike said Nature is "self-originated, or always was and had been the cause of its own existence." *Morals and Dogma,* p. 644. Another Mason said: "When we talk to God we are talking to ourselves, for God and Man are one and the same through the ties of Love . . ." See: *New Age,* April, 1945, John H. Boyd, "Faith," p. 159.
- "Examine, Read, Think," was a command of the Illuminati, Robison, p. 140. The *New Age* used a very similar admonition: "Read, Mark, Learn." See *ibid.,* July, 1924, p. 439; November, 1924, p. 690; April, 1926, p. 238; and March, 1934, p. 149. In 1945, the words were altered to say: "Read, Think, Study." See: *ibid,* April, 1945, p 133; July, 1945, p. 261; August, 1945, p. 327; and October, 1945, p. 389. Also see *ibid,* July, 1948, p. 454.
- Gnosticism. The Scotch Knight of the Illuminati is "particularly recommended to study the doctrines of the ancient Gnostics and Mani-

chaens. See: Barruel, vol. 3, p. 147. And Pike wrote: "The real mysteries of knowledge handed down from generation to generation by superior minds were the teachings of the Gnostics . . . and in them [we find] some of the ideas that form part of Masonry." *Morals and Dogma*, p. 248.

9. *New Age*, February, 1947, George Steinmetz, "The Worthy And Well-Qualified," p. 79.

10. *Ibid.*, p. 80.

11. *Ibid.*, July, 1950, editorial: "Why Men Become Freemasons," pp. 393-394.

12. *Ibid.*, p. 394.

13. *Ibid.*, May, 1940, editorial: "Investigation of Candidates," pp. 262-263.

14. *Ibid.*, April, 1969, Richard B. Rule, "Freemasonry In The Home," p. 28.

15. *Ibid.*, October, 1965, Homer C. Bryant, Jr., "Who? What? Why?, pp. 53-54.

16. *Ibid.*, July, 1948, "Read, Think, Study," pp. 454-455.

17. Whalen, *op. cit.*, pp. 28-29.

See also: *Report of New York State Senate Committee, op. cit.*, p. 4; and Theodore Graebner, *Is Masonry A Religion*, Concordia Publishing House, 1947, St. Louis, Mo., pp. 27-28. Both publications report the contents of the oath substantially as does Whalen.

18. Letter of John Quincy Adams to William L. Stone, August 29, 1832, *Adams Letters*, Providence, printed by E. and J.W. Cory, 1833, p. 8.

19. Carl H. Claudy, *Introduction To Freemasonry, I, Entered Apprentice*, Washington, D.C., The Temple Printers, 1946, pp. v, 8.

20. *Ibid.*, pp. 30, 31, 38-39.

21. *Ibid.*, p. 60.

22. *Ibid.*, pp. 26-27.

23. *Ibid.*, p. 28.

24. *Ibid.*, pp. 50, 51.

25. Whalen, p. 36.

26. *Ibid.*, p. 42.

See also Chapter 1, p. 35.

27. Whalen, p. 59.

28. Whalen, pp. 61-64.

29. *Ibid.*, p. 65.

30. *Ibid.*, p. 65.

31. *New Age*, January, 1945, W.O. Bissonett, "The Philosophy Of Scottish Rite Masonry," p. 27.

32. *Ibid.*, May, 1940, Rabbi H. Geffen, "The Antiquity Of Symbolism," p. 290.

33. *Ibid.*, September, 1968, Joseph H. Schwartz, " Together, But Differently," p. 52.

34. Gruber in the *Catholic Encyclopedia, op. cit.,* p. 779.

35. *Ibid.,* p. 775.

36. Preuss, *A Study In American Freemasonry, op. cit.,* pp. 38-39.

37. *New Age,* December, 1952, Archie M. Rankin, "Masonry Means Opportunity," p. 743.

See also: *Ibid.,* February, 1954, editorial on the Philippines, p. 108; November, 1957, William E. Hammond, "Mouth to Ear," pp. 677-679; and Lobinger, p. 315.

38. Headings, *op. cit.,* pp. 92-95.

39. Lobinger, p. 777.

40. *New Age,* October, 1924, Grand Commander's "Allocution" at the Supreme Council's Session at Charleston, S.C., September 24, 1924, pp. 594-595.

41. *Ibid.,* January, 1926, editorial, "Friendly Press," p. 138.

42. *Ibid.,* July, 1928, p. 394.

43. *Ibid.,* July, 1938, p. 436.

44. *Ibid.,* February, 1939, p. 115.

45. *Ibid.,* August, 1946, p. 656.

46. *Ibid.,* February, 1947, p. 123.

47. *Ibid.,* December, 1965, p.,11.

48. *Ibid.,* p. 10; and September, 1970, p. 37.

49. *The Wall Street Journal,* April 15, 1987, editorial, "Senate Mud Balls," p. 5.

50. Letter from author to Mr. George Melloan, Deputy Editor, *The Wall Street Journal,* April 16, 1987.

51. *The Washington Times,* Blair Dorminey, "Iced because he's a Mason?" [*sic*] p. 2, "Commentary" section.

52. Letter to the editor, *The Washington Times,* June 8, 1987.

53. *Minneapolis Star,* May 21, 1980, pp. 13A, 14A

54. *Ibid.,* p. 14A.

55. *Ibid.*

56. *Ibid.*

57. *Ibid.*

58. Headings, *op. cit.,* p. 110.

59. *Ibid,* p. 111.

60. For early Masonic influence in public life in America through Nativist, Know-Nothing, APA, and Ku Klux Klan movements, see: *supra,* chs. 3-4.

For Masons in Congress in 1923, see: Chalmers, *Hooded Americanism, op. cit.,* pp. 282-283.

61. *America,* December 29, 1929, p. 290.

62. *New Age,* May, 1941, p. 309; *ibid.,* February, 1957, p. 68.

63. *Congressional Directory,* 95th Congress, Joint Committee on Printing, Washington, D.C., U.S. Government Printing Office, 1977, pp. 4 through 196; *ibid.,* 98th Congress, 1983-1984, pp. 4 through 209.

64. *Ibid.*, p. 140. *Buffalo News*, October 16, 1986, p.

See also: *New Age*, July, 1956, Dudley Bunn, "Freemasonry And Politics," where it is stated that it is ethical for a politician to publicize the fact he is a Mason. However, it is not ethical to list "all his Masonic affiliations and honors," p. 421.

65. *Empire State Mason*, February, 1953, p. 19.

66. *Ibid.*

67. *New Age*, March, 1973, p., 15, Grand Commander's "Tribute."

68. The Masonic identification of the various Cabinet members were listed as brief "filler" items in various issues of the *New Age*. See, for example, the issues dated January, 1942, pp. 20, 53; February, 1942, p. 119; July, 1945, p. 294; April, 1949, p. 178; June, 1959, p. 265; and May, 1961, p. 38.

69. *Ibid.*, August, 1962, editorial, "An Anniversary", pp. 12-13.

See also: Headings, *op. cit.*, p. 79, where it is noted that it was sometimes of advantage in France "to conceal the masonic connections of those in high political office." The same point is made in *ibid.*, at p. 101.

70. *New Age*, August, 1962, p. 13.

The editorial followed immediately after another editorial expressing concern about President John F. Kennedy's alleged effort to amass more power in the Executive Branch. See: *ibid.*, "The Thrust Of Power." pp. 9-10.

71. *Ibid.*, May, 1972, Stuart Parker, PGM Manitoba, Canada, "The Heart Of The Fraternity," p. 24. Although Brother Parker did not name those organizations which required Masonic initiation, one such group is the Philalethes Society, "an international association of Freemasons who seek more light." See: *ibid.*, January, 1956, p. 18.

72. *New Age*, September, 1948, p. 535.

73. *Ibid.*, July, 1950, Harry L. Baum, 33rd Degree, "Masonic Responsibility," pp. 419, 420.

74. *Ibid.*, October, 1955, editorial: "Hearings On The Bill Of Rights," p. 602; and *ibid.*, November, 1955, editorial: "Hearings Cancelled," p. 645.

75. *Ibid.*, September, 1960, Grand Commander's commentary, "Mission to Italy, pp. 20, 21, 49-50. Although the Grand Commander's report was made in 1960, the incident referred to was resolved in 1959, but no specific date is shown in the article, except that there was a deadline set for February 18, 1960.

76. Mr. Herter's high rank in Masonry is noted in *ibid.*, June, 1959, p. 265. His award from the Craft is noted in *ibid.*, December, 1959, p. 719.

77. *Ibid.*, September, 1976, "Grand Commanders Honored By Congress," pp. 33-34.

78. *The Washington Times*, "Alice In Potomac Land," April 5, 1983, p. 2; *ibid.* December 13, 1983, p. 2.

79. *New Age*, July, 1924, under headline: "Read, Mark, Learn," p. 442.

80. *Ibid.*, April, 1944, Clarence R. Martin, 33rd Degree, "Travelling Military Lodges," p. 165.

Military Lodges," p. 165.

81. *Ibid.*, p. 166. 86.

82. *Ibid.*, February, 1945, editorial, "California College In China," p. 86.

83. *Ibid.*, August, 1968, p. 33. In 1965, General Nickerson had distributed Scottish Rite publications on "Americanism" in all schools under his command.

Notes   Afterword

1. Christopher Dawson, "Religion and the Life of Civilisation, in *Enquiries into Religion and Culture*, New York, Sheed and Ward, 1933, p. 15, quoted by Jeremy White, "Christopher Dawson (1889-1970) Historian of Christendom and Europe," *The Dawson Newsletter*, Fayetteville, Ark., Spring, 1987, p. 6.

2. See *supra*, pp. 11, 121.

3. *The World* (New York), September 17, 1921, pp. 1-2.

4. Article V-A Civil Rights Law, c.664, Laws 1923, 1110, Secs. 53, 56. Cited in *New York ex rel. Bryant v. Zimmerman*, 278 U.S. 63 (1928), p. 66.

5. *Ibid.*, pp. 72, 73

6. *Ibid.*, p. 73.

7. *Ibid.*, pp. 73, 75.

8. *Ibid.*, *Records and Briefs*, volume 278, p. 65.

9. Pike, *Morals and Dogma*, pp. 138, 140, 144.

10. Hermann Rauschning, *Hitler Speaks*, London, Thornton, Butterworth, Ltd., 1939, p. 57.

Notes   Appendix C

1. S. Angus, *The Mystery Religions*, New York, Dover Publications, 1975, pp. vii, 1.

The Dover edition is a re-publication of the second (1928) edition of Dr. Angus's work, which originally was published by John Murray, London, 1925, under the title *The Mystery Religions And Christianity*.

2. Jules Lebreton and Jacques Zeiler, *The History Of The Primitive Church*, New York, Macmillan Co. (2 vols.), translated by Ernest C. Messenger, vol. 1, pp. 355, 356.

3. See: 1 Timothy 1: 4-5; 1 Timothy 4: 7-8; 1 Timothy 6: 20-21; Titus: 10-11; Colossians 2: 16 ff; 2 Peter 1-22 (in the latter paragraph he refers to a return to the mysteries as: "The dog is returned to his vomit."); Revelations 2:6; 2:15; and 2:20-25.

4. Charles W. Heckethorn, *The Secret Societies Of All Ages And Countries*, New Hyde Park, N.Y., University Books, 1965, (2 vols.), vol. 1, p. 7.

The work originally was published in 1875 and re-written and re-published in 1897.

5. *Ibid.*, p. 9

6. *Ibid.*, p. 12.

7. *Ibid.*, p. 14.

8. *Ibid.*, pp. 14-15.

9. W.O. E. Oesterley, *The Evolution Of The Messianic Idea*, London, Sir Isaac Pitman and Sons, Ltd., 1908.

Oesterley said: "In these myths elements which were infinitely more significant than earlier ages could ever have conceived them to be; for they contained the germs of eternal truths which could only be realized by men in whom the faculty for apprehending spiritual truth was more fully developed," p. 270.

He added: "In these myths some of the central truths of Christianity were potentially in existence at the time when men first began to be thinking beings." Ibid., p. 272.

See also Frederick Nolan, *The Expectations Formed By The Assyrians That A Great Deliverer Would Appear About The Time Of Our Lord's Advent*, London, published by Bagster and T. and W. Boone, 1826.

In his Encyclical Letter, *Divini Redemptoris* (concerning atheistic Communism), Pope Pius XI opened with these words: "The promise of a Redeemer brightens the first page of the history of mankind, and the confident hope aroused by this promise softened the keen regret for a paradise which had been lost."

10. Heckethorn, p. 15. For Masonic initiation rites see Whalen's *Christianity And American Freemasonry,* pp. 27-47; Barruel, vol. 2, pp. 288-9; ibid., vol. 3, p. 87.

11. *New Age,* June, 1934, G.A. Browne, "A Masonic Pilgrimage To The East," p. 349

12. *Ibid.,* July 1953, editorial, "Civilization and Masonry," quoting from a lecture by Dr. B.G. Wade before the Sydney Lodge of Research, p. 417.

13. *Ibid.*

14. Franz Cumont, *The Oriental Religious In Roman Paganism,* New York, Dover Publications, 1956, pp. 46, 48, 50.

The Dover edition is a republication of the first English translation of Mr. Cumont's *Les religions orientales dans le paganisme romain,* (no translator listed) published by G. Routledge and Sons, London, 1911.

15. St. Augustine, *The City of God,* New York, The Modern Library (Random House), 1950, translated by Marcus Dods, Book II, section 4, p. 43.

16. *Ibid.,* pp. 226, 232.

17. Cumont, pp. 66, 71.

18. *Ibid.,* pp. 90, 91.

19. *Ibid.,* pp. 81-82.

20. *Ibid.,* pp. 97-98.

21. *Ibid.,* pp. 125, 126; 251-255.

22. *Ibid.,* pp. 152, 155, 156.

23. *Ibid.,* pp. 157-158.

24. *Ibid.,* p. 191.

25. Angus, pp. 309-312.

Select Bibliography

Books

Angus, S., *The Mystery Religions*, New York, Dover Publications, 1975.

Antieu, Chester J., Downey, Arthur T., and Roberts, Edward C., *Freedom From Federal Establishment*, Milwaukee, The Bruce Publishing Co., 1964.

Augustine, St., *The City of God*, translated by Marcus Dodd, New York, The Modern Library (Random House) New York, 1950.

Barber, Malcolm, *The Trial of the Templars*, Cambridge, England, Cambridge University Press, (Paperback), 1980.

Barruel, Augusten de, *Memoirs Illustrating The History of Jacobinism*, 4 vols., London, T. Burton, 1798.

Beals, Carleton, *Brass Knuckle Crusade*, New York, Hastings House, 1960.

Beaumarchais, Pierre Augustin de, *Ouevres Completes de Voltaire*, 92 vols., Paris, Societe Litteraire-Typographique, 1785-1789.

Beecher, Lyman, Rev., *A Plea For The West*, 2d ed., Cincinnati, Truman and Smith, 1835.

Billington, James A., *Fire In The Minds Of Men*, New York, Basic Books, 1980.

Billington, Ray Allen, *The Protestant Crusade*, New York, Macmillan and Co., 1938.

Black, Hugo L., Jr., *My Father, A Remembrance*, New York, Random House, 1975.

Bourne, William O., *History of the Public School Society of the City of New York*, N.Y., 1870.

Canon Law Society of Great Britain and Ireland, *The Code of Canon Law* (English Translation), London, Collins Liturgical Publications, 1983.

Chalmers, David M., *Hooded Americanism, The First Century of the Ku Klux Klan,* Garden City, N.Y., Doubleday and Co., 1965.

Clarkson, John F., S.J., et. al., *The Church Teaches, Documents of the Church in English Translation,* Rockford, Ill., Tan Books and Publishers, Inc., 1973.

Claudy, Carl H., *Introduction to Freemasonry: I, Entered Apprentice,* Washington, D.C., The Temple Publishers, 1931.

Cornwell, Rupert, *God's Banker,* London, Counterpoint, Unwin Paperback, 1984.

Creedon, Lawrence P. and Falcon, Welton D., *United For Separation,* Milwaukee, Bruce Publishing Co., 1959.

Cumont, Franz, *The Oriental Religions In Roman Paganism,* New York, 1956.

Davies, A. Powell, *American Destiny (A Faith For America),* Boston, The Beacon Press, 1942.

―――, *The Faith Of An Unrepentant Liberal,* Boston, The Beacon Press, 1946.

―――, *The Mind And Faith Of A. Powell Davies,* edited by Justice William O. Douglas, Garden City, N.Y., Doubleday and Co., 1959.

―――, *The Temptation To Be Good,* New York, Farrar, Staus and Young, 1952.

―――, *The Urge to Persecute,* Boston, The Beacon Press, 1953.

Denslow, William R., *Ten Thousand Famous Freemasons,* (Introduction by Brother Harry S. Truman, Past Grand Master of the Grand Lodge of Missouri), St. Louis, Transactions of the Missouri Lodge of Research, 4 vols., 1961.

Dever, Lem A., *Masks Off!—Confession Of An Imperial Klansman,* Portland, Oregon, Lem A. Dever publisher, 2nd Revised ed., 1925.

Durham, Mary Edith, *The Serajevo Crime,* London, George Allyn and Unwin, Ltd., 1925.

Ebersole, Luke E., *Church Lobbying In The Nation's Capital,* New York, The Macmillan Co., 1951.

Elliott, Jonathan, *The Debates In The Several Conventions On The Adoption Of The Federal Constitution,* 5 vols., Philadelphia, J.B. Lippencott Co., 1896.

Ellis, John Tracy, *The Life of James Cardinal Gibbons,* (People's Edition), Francis L. Broderick, editor, Milwaukee, The Bruce Publishing Co., 1963.

Evans, M. Stanton, *The Liberal Establishment*, New York, the Devin-Adair Co., 1965.

Fay, Bernard, *Revolution and Freemasonry—1680-1800*, Boston, Little Brown and Co., 1935.

Fell, Marie Lenore, Sister, *The Foundations Of Nativism In American Textbooks, 1783-1860*, Washington, D.C., The Catholic University of America, 1941.

Gabel, Richard J., Rev., *Public Funds For Church And Private Schools*, Washington, D.C., The Catholic University Press, 1937.

Leo XIII, Pope, *The Church Speaks*, Etienne Gilson, editor, Garden City, N.Y., Image Books, 1954.

Graebner, Theodore C., *A Handbook of Organizations*, St. Louis, Concordia Publishing House, 1924.

————, Theodore C., *Is Masonry A Religion*, St. Louis, Concordia Publishing House, 1947.

Hall, Arthur Jackson, *Religious Education In the Public Schools of the State and City of New York*, Chicago, University of Chicago Press, 1914.

Hamilton, Virginia Van Der Veer, *Hugo Black, The Alabama Years*, Baton Rouge, La., Louisiana State Press, 1972.

Hazard, Paul, *The European Mind, 1680-1715*, Cleveland, Meridian Books, World Publishing Co., 1967.

Heaton, Ronald E., *Justices Of The United States Supreme Court Identified As Masons*, Washington, Masonic Service Association, 1969.

Heckethorn, Charles W., *The Secret Societies of All Ages and Countries*, 2 vols., New Hyde Park, N.Y., University Books, 1975.

Jackson, Robert H., *The Struggle For Judicial Supremacy*, New York, Alfred A. Knopf, 1941.

Holmes-Laski Letters, The Correspondence of Mr. Justice Holmes and Harold J. Laski, 1916-1935, Mark De Wolfe Howe, ed., Cambridge, Mass., Harvard University Press, 1953.

Howard, J. Woodford, *Mr. Justice Murphy*, Princeton, N.J., Princeton University Press, 1968.

Kelly, George A., Msgr., *The Battle For The American Church*, Garden City, New York, Doubleday and Co., 1979.

King, James M., Rev., *Facing The Twentieth Century*, New York, American Union League Society, 1899.

Kinzer, Donald L., *An Episode In Anti-Catholicism*, Seattle, University of Washington Press, 1964.

Knight, Stephen, *Jack The Ripper, The Final Solution,* London, George G. Harrap and Co., 1977.

Kurland, Philip B. and Casper, Gerhard, editors, *Landmark Briefs And Arguments Of The Supreme Court of the United States,* Arlington, Va., University Publications of America, 1976.

Lash, Joseph P., *From The Dairies Of Felix Frankfurter,* New York, W.W. Nolrton and Co., 1975.

Laski, Harold J., *Reason and Civilization,* London, Victor Gollancz, Ltd., 1944

———, *Studies in Law and Politics,* New Haven, Conn., Yale University Press, 1932.

Lebreton, Jules and Zeiler, Jacques, *The History of the Primitive Church,* 2 vols., translated by Ernest C. Messenger, New York, Macmillan Co., 1946-1947.

Lippencott, C.S. and Johnston, E.R., *Masonry Defined,* Memphis, Tenn., Masonic Supply Co., 1930.

Lobinger, Charles S., *The Supreme Council,* Louisville, The Standard Printing Co., 1931.

Lord, Robert H., Sexton, John E., and Herrington, Edward T., *History Of The Archdiocese of Boston,* New York, Sheed and Ward, 1944.

McGuigan, Patrick B. and Rader, Randall R., editors, *A Blueprint For Judicial Reform,* Washington, D.C., Free Congress Research and Educational Foundation, 1981.

Millan, Sarah, *Cecil Rhodes,* New York, Harper and Bros., 1933.

Newton, Joseph Fort, *The Religion of Masonry, An Interpretation,* Richmond, Va., The McCoy Publishing and Supply Co., 1969.

Norton, Thomas J., *The Constitution of the United States—Its Sources And Its Applications,* New York, Committee for Constitutional Government, Inc., 1971.

Oesterley, W.O.E., *The Evolution of the Messianic Idea,* London, Sir Isaac Pitman and Sons, Ltd., 1908.

Phillips, Harlan, *Felix Frankfurter Reminisces,* New York, Reynal and Co., 1960.

Pike, Albert, *Morals and Dogma of the Ancient and Accepted Rite of Freemasonry,* Charleston, S.C., published by the author, 1871.

Pullen, Charles H., *Miss Columbia's Public School,* New York, Francis B. Felt and Co., 1871.

Roberts, Allen E., *A House Undivided, The Story of Freemasonry and the Civil War,* St. Louis, Missouri Lodge of Research, 1961.

Robison, John, *Proofs Of A Conspiracy Against All The Religions And*

Governments Of Europe Carried On In The Secret Meetings Of Free Masons, Illuminati, And Reading Societies, 3d ed., New York, George Foreman, 1798.

Schlarman, Joseph, *Mexico, A Land Of Volcanoes,* Milwaukee, Bruce Publishing Co., 1950.

Stevens, Albert C., *The Cyclopedia of Fraternities,* New York, E.B. Treat and Co., 1907.

Stokes, Anson Pehlps, *Church And State In The United States,* 3 vols., New York, Harper and Bros., 1950.

Story, Joseph, *Commentaries On The Constitution Of The United States,* Boston, Little Brown and Co., 1833.

Tansill, Charles C., editor, *Documents Illustrative Of The Formation Of The Union Of The American States,* Washington, D.C., U.S. Government Printing Office, 1965.

Thomas, M. Evangeline, Sister, *Nativism In The Old Northwest,* Washington, D.C., The Catholic University of America, 1936.

Thorpe, Francis Newton, *The Federal And State Constitutions . . . ,* 7 vols., Washington, D.C., U.S. Government Printing Office, 1909.

Varacalli, Joseph A., *Toward The Establishment of Liberal Catholicism In America,* Lanham, Md., University Press of America, 1983.

Whalen, William J., *Christianity and American Freemasonry,* Milwaukee, Bruce Publishing Co., 1958.

Williams, Michael, *The Shadow of the Pope,* New York, Whittlesey House (McGraw-Hill), 1932.

Woodhouse, W., *The Constitution Of The United States According To The Latest Amendments,* Philadelphia, E. Oswald, 1796.

Periodicals

America, New York, N.Y.

Approaches, Ayrshire, Scotland. (No longer printed)

Anti-Masonic Review and Magazine, New York, N.Y. (No longer printed)

Extension Magazine, Chicago, Ill.

New Age Magazine, the official organ of the Supreme Council, 33rd Degree, Scottish Rite Freemasonry of the Southern Jurisdiction, Washington, D.C.

Scottish Rite News Bulletin, Washington, D.C.

U.S. Catholic, Chicago, Ill.
Wanderer, St. Paul, Minn.

Newspapers

Birmingham Age-Herald, Birmingham, Ala.
Chicago Tribune, Chicago, Ill.
Evening Star, Washington, D.C. (No longer published)
National Catholic Register, Los Angeles, Ca.
New York Times, The, New York, N.Y.
Pittsburgh Post-Gazette, Pittsburgh, Pa.
Sun, The, Baltimore, Md.
Sunday Star, Washington, D.C. (No longer published)
Times, The, London.
Washington Post, The, Washington, D.C.
World, The, New York, N.Y. (No longer published)

Articles

Condon, Peter, "Freedom of Religion and the Revival of Religious Tolerance," Philadelphia, *History, Records and Studies,* American Catholic Historical Society, October 1906.

Farrell, John T., "An Abandoned Approach to Philippine History: John R.M. Taylor And The Philippine Insurgent Records," *Catholic Historical Review,* January, 1954.

Gladden, Washington, "The Anti-Catholic Crusade," *Century Magazine,* Boston, March, 1894.

Headings, Mildred J., "French Freemasonry Under The Third Republic," *The Johns Hopkins University Studies In Historical And Political Science,* Baltimore, Md., The Johns Hopkins Press, vol. LXVI, 1947.

Mellett, Lowell, "Klan and Church," *Atlantic Monthly,* New York, November, 1923.

Pattangall, William R., "Is The Ku Klux Klan Un-American," *Forum,* New York, September, 1925.

Sweeny, Charles P., "The Great Bigotry Merger," *The Nation,* New York, July 5, 1923.

Government Publication

Biographical Directory Of The American Congress, 1774-1971, Washington, D.C., U.S. Government Printing Office, 1971.

Congressional Directory, Washington, D.C., U.S. Government Printing Office, 1945.

Congressional Record, Washington, D.C., U.S. Government Printing Office, various years.

Debates and Proceedings in the Congress of the United States, Annals of the Congress of the United States, 1789-1824, 42 vols., Washington, D.C., Gales and Seton publishers, 1834-1856.

Inaugural Addresses of the Presidents of the United States, Washington, D.C., U.S. Government Printing Office, 1961.

Investigation Into Freemasonry by Joint Committee of the Legislature of Massachusetts House of Representatives, Boston, Mary, 1834.

Report of a Committee To The New York Senate, . . . , New Haven, Conn., printed by Hezekiah Howe, 1829.

Testimony Taken by the Committee of the Pennsylvania House of Representatives To Investigate the Evils of Freemasonry, Theodore Finn, printer, Harrisburg, Pa., 1836.

Trial of Aaron Burr On An Indictment For Treason, Washington, D.C., Westcott and Co., 1807.

U.S. Congress, House of Representatives, Committee on Rules, *Hearings on the Ku Klux Klan,* New York, The Arno Press and The New York Times under title *Mass Violence In America,* 1969.

U.S. Congress, House of Representatives, Committee on Un-American Activities, The Communist Conspiracy, Part I, Sec. A, Washington, D.C., U.S. Government Printing Office, 1956.

U.S. Congress, House of Representatives, 78th Congress, Committee on World War Veterans, *Hearings on H.R. 3917 and S. 1767,* Servicemen's Readjustment Act.

U.S. Congress, Joint Committee on Printing, *Congressional Directory,* Washington, D.C., U.S. Government Printing Office, various years.

U.S. Congress, Senate, 78th Congress, 1st Session, Committee on Education and Labor, *Hearings on 1295, S.1590, The Servicemen's Education and Training Act of 1944,* Washington, D.C., U.S. Government Printing Office.

U.S. Congress, Senate, Committee on Education, 79th Congress, 1st Session, *Hearings On Federal Aid To Education, S.181 and S.717,* Washington, D.C., U.S. Government Printing Office, 1945.

War of Rebellion, The, *A Compilation of the Official Records of the Union and Confederate Armies,* War Department, Washington, D.C., U.S. Government Printing Office, 1902.

Writings of George Washington From Original Manuscript Sources, 40 vols., John C. Fitzgerald, ed., Washington, D.C., U.S. Government Printing Office, 1941.

Manuscript Sources

Manuscript Division, Library of Congress:
The Papers of Justice Hugo Black.
The Papers of Justice Harold O. Burton.
The Papers of Felix Frankfurter.

Archives of the United States:
Taylor, John R.M., *The Philippine Insurrection Against the United States* (Galley Proofs), U.S. War Department, Washington, D.C., 1909.

Encyclopedias

Catholic Encyclopedia, The, New York, Encyclopedia Press, 1913.
Jewish Encyclopedia, New York, Funk and Wagnalls, 1925.
New Columbia Encyclopedia, New York, Columbia University Press, 1975.
New Encyclopedia of Freemasonry, New Hyde Park, N.Y., 1970.

Supreme Court Decisions

Abington School District v. Schempp, 374 U.S. 203
Bd. of Ed. v. Allen, 392 U.S. 306
Bradfield v. Roberts, 175 U.S. 291
Church of Holy Trinity v. U.S., 143 U.S. 457
Cochran v. Louisiana Bd. of Ed., 281 U.S. 370
Committee for Public Ed. v. Nyquist, 413 U.S. 756

Davis v. Beason, 133 U.S. 333
Engel v. Vitale, 370 U.S. 421
Everson v. Bd. of Ed., 330 U.S. 1
Flast v. Cohen, 392 U.S. 83
Horace Mann League v. Bd. of Pub. Wks., 387 U.S. 97
In Re: Murchison, 349 U.S. 133
Lemon v. Kurtzman, 403 U.S. 602
McCollum v. Bd. of Ed., 333 U.S. 203
Meek v. Pittinger, 421 U.S. 341
Meyer v. Nebraska, 262 U.S. 410
Mormon Church v. U.S., 136 U.S. 1
Pierce v. Society of Sisters, 268 U.S. 510
Reuben Quick Bear v. Leupp, 210 U.S. 50
Reynolds v. U.S., 98 U.S. 145
Roe v. Wade, 410 U.S. 113
Roemer v. Bd. of Pub. Wks., 426 U.S. 736
Roth v. U.S., 354 U.S. 476
Terret v. Taylor, 9 Cranch 43
Torcaso v. Watkins, 367 U.S. 488
U.S. v. MacIntosh, 283 U.S. 605
Vidal v. Girard's Executors, 2 How. 127
Walz v. Tax Commissioners, 397 U.S. 664
Watson v. Jones, 13 Wall 679

INDEX

If you have enjoyed this book, consider making your next selection from among the following . . .

The Facts About Luther. Msgr. Patrick O'Hare.................13.50
Little Catechism of the Curé of Ars. St. John Vianney............ 5.50
The Curé of Ars—Patron Saint of Parish Priests. Fr. B. O'Brien...... 4.50
Saint Teresa of Ávila. William Thomas Walsh................18.00
Isabella of Spain: The Last Crusader. William Thomas Walsh........16.50
Characters of the Inquisition. William Thomas Walsh..............12.00
Blood-Drenched Altars—Cath. Comment. on Hist. Mexico. Kelley....16.50
The Four Last Things—Death, Judgment, Hell, Heaven. Fr. von Cochem 5.00
Confession of a Roman Catholic. Paul Whitcomb................ 1.25
The Catholic Church Has the Answer. Paul Whitcomb............ 1.25
The Sinner's Guide. Ven. Louis of Granada....................11.00
True Devotion to Mary. St. Louis De Montfort................. 6.00
Life of St. Anthony Mary Claret. Fanchón Royer.................12.00
Autobiography of St. Anthony Mary Claret....................10.00
I Wait for You. Sr. Josefa Menendez........................ .75
Words of Love. Menendez, Betrone, Mary of the Trinity............ 4.50
Little Lives of the Great Saints. John O'Kane Murray.............16.00
Prayer—The Key to Salvation. Fr. Michael Müller................ 7.00
Sermons on Prayer. St. Francis de Sales...................... 3.50
Sermons on Our Lady. St. Francis de Sales.................... 3.50
Sermons for Lent. St. Francis de Sales...................... 9.00
Passion of Jesus and Its Hidden Meaning. Fr. Groenings, S.J........10.00
The Victories of the Martyrs. St. Alphonsus Liguori.............. 7.50
Canons and Decrees of the Council of Trent. Transl. Schroeder......12.00
Sermons of St. Alphonsus Liguori for Every Sunday..............13.50
A Catechism of Modernism. Fr. J. B. Lemius.................. 4.00
Alexandrina—The Agony and the Glory. Johnston................ 3.50
Blessed Margaret of Castello. Fr. William Bonniwell............. 5.00
The Ways of Mental Prayer. Dom Vitalis Lehodey...............11.00
Fr. Paul of Moll. van Speybrouck.......................... 9.00
St. Francis of Paola. Simi and Segreti...................... 6.00
Communion Under Both Kinds. Michael Davies................. 1.50
Abortion: Yes or No? Dr. John L. Grady, M.D................. 1.50
The Story of the Church. Johnson, Hannan, Dominica............16.50
Religious Liberty. Michael Davies.......................... 1.50
Hell Quizzes. Radio Replies Press.......................... 1.00
Indulgence Quizzes. Radio Replies Press..................... 1.00
Purgatory Quizzes. Radio Replies Press...................... 1.00
Virgin and Statue Worship Quizzes. Radio Replies Press........... 1.00
The Holy Eucharist. St. Alphonsus......................... 7.50
Meditation Prayer on Mary Immaculate. Padre Pio............... 1.00
Little Book of the Work of Infinite Love. de la Touche............ 1.50
Textual Concordance of The Holy Scriptures. Williams............35.00
Douay-Rheims Bible. Leatherbound.........................35.00
The Way of Divine Love. Sister Josefa Menendez................16.50
The Way of Divine Love. (pocket, unabr.). Menendez............. 7.50
Mystical City of God—Abridged. Ven. Mary of Agreda............18.50

Prices guaranteed through December 31, 1992.

Raised from the Dead. Fr. Hebert............................13.50
Love and Service of God, Infinite Love. Mother Louise Margaret. 10.00
Life and Work of Mother Louise Margaret. Fr. O'Connell........10.00
Autobiography of St. Margaret Mary...........................4.00
Thoughts and Sayings of St. Margaret Mary....................3.00
The Voice of the Saints. Comp. by Francis Johnston............5.00
The 12 Steps to Holiness and Salvation. St. Alphonsus..........6.00
The Rosary and the Crisis of Faith. Cirrincione & Nelson.......1.25
Sin and Its Consequences. Cardinal Manning...................5.00
Fourfold Sovereignty of God. Cardinal Manning................5.00
Catholic Apologetics Today. Fr. Most.........................8.00
Dialogue of St. Catherine of Siena. Transl. Algar Thorold.......9.00
Catholic Answer to Jehovah's Witnesses. D'Angelo.............8.00
Twelve Promises of the Sacred Heart. (100 cards)..............5.00
St. Aloysius Gonzaga. Fr. Meschler..........................10.00
The Love of Mary. D. Roberto................................7.00
Begone Satan. Fr. Vogl......................................2.00
The Prophets and Our Times. Fr. R. G. Culleton...............10.00
St. Therese, The Little Flower. John Beevers..................4.50
St. Joseph of Copertino. Fr. Angelo Pastrovicchi..............4.50
Mary, The Second Eve. Cardinal Newman......................2.50
Devotion to Infant Jesus of Prague. Booklet...................75
The Faith of Our Fathers. Cardinal Gibbons..................13.00
The Wonder of Guadalupe. Francis Johnston...................6.00
Apologetics. Msgr. Paul Glenn...............................9.00
Baltimore Catechism No. 1...................................3.00
Baltimore Catechism No. 2...................................4.00
Baltimore Catechism No. 3...................................7.00
An Explanation of the Baltimore Catechism. Fr. Kinkead.......13.00
Bethlehem. Fr. Faber.......................................13.50
Bible History. Schuster.....................................10.00
Blessed Eucharist. Fr. Mueller..............................13.00
Catholic Catechism. Fr. Faerber.............................5.00
The Devil. Fr. Delaporte....................................5.00
Dogmatic Theology for the Laity. Fr. Premm.................15.00
Evidence of Satan in the Modern World. Cristiani.............8.50
Fifteen Promises of Mary. (100 cards).......................5.00
Life of Anne Catherine Emmerich. 2 vols. Schmoger..........37.50
Life of the Blessed Virgin Mary. Emmerich..................13.50
Manual of Practical Devotion to St. Joseph. Patrignani.......12.50
Prayer to St. Michael. (100 leaflets).......................5.00
Prayerbook of Favorite Litanies. Fr. Hebert..................8.50
Preparation for Death. (Abridged). St. Alphonsus.............7.00
Purgatory Explained. Schouppe.............................12.50
Purgatory Explained. (pocket, unabr.). Schouppe.............5.00
Fundamentals of Catholic Dogma. Ludwig Ott...............16.50
Spiritual Conferences. Tauler..............................10.00
Trustful Surrender to Divine Providence. Bl. Claude..........4.00
Wife, Mother and Mystic. Bessieres.........................7.00
The Agony of Jesus. Padre Pio.............................1.00

Prices guaranteed through December 31, 1992.

Is It a Saint's Name? Fr. William Dunne.................... 1.50
St. Pius V—His Life, Times, Miracles. Anderson.............. 4.00
Who Is Teresa Neumann? Fr. Charles Carty.................. 1.25
Martyrs of the Coliseum. Fr. O'Reilly......................15.00
Way of the Cross. St. Alphonsus Liguori.................... .75
Way of the Cross. Franciscan version...................... .75
How Christ Said the First Mass. Fr. Meagher................15.00
Too Busy for God? Think Again! D'Angelo.................. 4.00
St. Bernadette Soubirous. Trochu..........................15.00
Passion and Death of Jesus Christ. Liguori................. 7.50
Treatise on the Love of God. 2 Vols. St. Francis de Sales.......16.50
Confession Quizzes. Radio Replies Press.................... 1.00
St. Philip Neri. Fr. V. J. Matthews........................ 4.50
St. Louise de Marillac. Sr. Vincent Regnault................ 4.50
The Old World and America. Rev. Philip Furlong............13.50
Prophecy for Today. Edward Connor........................ 4.50
The Book of Infinite Love. Mother de la Touche.............. 4.50
Chats with Converts. Fr. M. D. Forrest.................... 8.00
The Church Teaches. Church Documents....................13.50
Conversation with Christ. Peter T. Rohrbach............... 8.00
Purgatory and Heaven. J. P. Arendzen..................... 3.50
What Is Liberalism? Sarda y Salvany....................... 5.00
Spiritual Legacy of Sr. Mary of the Trinity. van den Broek...... 9.00
The Creator and the Creature. Fr. Frederick Faber............13.00
Radio Replies. 3 Vols. Frs. Rumble and Carty..............36.00
Convert's Catechism of Catholic Doctrine. Fr. Geiermann....... 3.00
Incarnation, Birth, Infancy of Jesus Christ. St. Alphonsus....... 7.50
Light and Peace. Fr. R. P. Quadrupani..................... 5.00
Dogmatic Canons & Decrees of Trent, Vat. I. Documents....... 8.00
The Evolution Hoax Exposed. A. N. Field.................. 5.00
The Primitive Church. Fr. D. I. Lanslots.................. 8.50
The Priesthood. Bishop Stockums..........................10.00
The Priest, the Man of God. St. Joseph Cafasso................10.00
Blessed Sacrament. Fr. Frederick Faber.....................15.00
Christ Denied. Fr. Paul Wickens.......................... 2.00
New Regulations on Indulgences. Fr. Winfrid Herbst........... 2.50
A Tour of the Summa. Msgr. Paul Glenn.....................15.00
Spiritual Conferences. Fr. Frederick Faber..................12.50
Latin Grammar. Scanlon and Scanlon......................12.50
A Brief Life of Christ. Fr. Rumble........................ 1.50
Marriage Quizzes. Radio Replies Press..................... 1.00
True Church Quizzes. Radio Replies Press.................. 1.00
St. Lydwine of Schiedam. J. K. Huysmans.................. 7.00
Mary, Mother of the Church. Church Documents.............. 3.00
The Sacred Heart and the Priesthood. de la Touche............ 7.00
Revelations of St. Bridget. St. Bridget of Sweden.............. 2.50
Magnificent Prayers. St. Bridget of Sweden.................. 1.50
The Happiness of Heaven. Fr. J. Boudreau.................. 7.00
St. Catherine Labouré of the Miraculous Medal. Dirvin.........11.00
The Glories of Mary. (pocket, unabr.). St. Alphonsus Liguori.... 8.00

Prices guaranteed through December 31, 1992.

At your bookdealer or direct from the publisher.

Prices guaranteed through December 31, 1992.

NOTES

NOTES

NOTES